TWENTIETH-CENTURY CHINA

Twentieth-Century China: New Approaches is an important revisionist study of China's recent past. The chapters throw light on a variety of subjects within the field which has recently undergone considerable change. The four major parts of this Reader take into account the historical shape of the century, local perspectives on national history, political language, and the upheavals that punctuated the last dozen years of China's turbulent twentieth century.

The chapters reflect a move away from a Western-centered analysis of Chinese history and draw on the wealth of archival material made accessible over the last decade. They highlight in new and challenging ways important topics that have generated considerable excitement among historians. Subjects discussed include the watershed year of 1949, feminism, the revolutions, the discourse of the Communist Party, and patterns of popular protest in modern China.

This Reader will be indispensable to anyone interested in new approaches to the field of contemporary Chinese history.

Jeffrey N. Wasserstrom is Associate Professor of History at Indiana University and Director of the East Asian Studies Center. He has published widely on contemporary Chinese history, including *Student Protests in Twentieth-Century China: The View from Shanghai* (Stanford, 1991).

Series editor **Jack R. Censer** is Professor of History at George Mason University.

REWRITING HISTORIES
Series editor: Jack R. Censer

TWENTIETH-CENTURY CHINA

New Approaches

Edited by
Jeffrey N. Wasserstrom

London and New York

First published 2003
by Routledge
2 Park Square, Milton Park, Abingdon, Oxon, OX14 4RN

Simultaneously published in the USA and Canada
by Routledge
270 Madison Ave, New York NY 10016

Routledge is an imprint of the Taylor & Francis Group

Transferred to Digital Printing 2005

Typeset in Palatino by
Keystroke, Jacaranda Lodge, Wolverhampton

British Library Cataloguing in Publication Data
A catalogue record for this book is available from the British Library

Library of Congress Cataloging in Publication Data
A catalog record for this book has been applied for

ISBN 0–415–19503–9 (hbk)
ISBN 0–415–19504–7 (pbk)

CONTENTS

SERIES EDITOR'S PREFACE

Rewriting history, or revisionism, has always followed closely in the wake of history writing. In their efforts to re-evaluate the past, professional as well as amateur scholars have followed many approaches, most commonly as empiricists, uncovering new information to challenge earlier accounts. Historians have also revised previous versions by adopting new perspectives, usually fortified by new research, which overturn received views.

Even though rewriting is constantly taking place, historians' attitudes towards using new interpretations have been anything but settled. For most, the validity of revisionism lies in providing a stronger, more convincing account that better captures the objective truth of the matter. Although such historians might agree that we never finally arrive at the "truth," they believe it exists and over time may be better approximated. At the other extreme stand scholars who believe that each generation or even each cultural group or subgroup necessarily regards the past differently, each creating for itself a more usable history. Although these latter scholars do not reject the possibility of demonstrating empirically that some contentions are better than others, they focus upon generating new views based upon different life experiences. Different truths exist for different groups. Surely such an understanding, by emphasizing subjectivity, further encourages rewriting history. Between these two groups are those historians who wish to borrow from both sides. This third group, while accepting that every congeries of individuals sees matters differently, still wishes somewhat contradictorily to fashion a broader history that incorporates both of these particular visions. Revisionists who stress empiricism fall into the first of the three camps, while others spread out across the board.

Today the rewriting of history seems to have accelerated to a blinding speed as a consequence of the evolution of revisionism. A variety of approaches has emerged. A major factor in this process has been the enormous increase in the number of researchers. This explosion has reinforced and enabled the retesting of many assertions. Significant ideological shifts have also played a major part in the growth of revisionism. First, the crisis of Marxism, culminating in the events in Eastern Europe in

1989, has given rise to doubts about explicitly Marxist accounts. Such doubts have spilled over into the entire field of social history which has been a dominant subfield of the discipline for several decades. Focusing on society and its class divisions implied that these are the most important elements in historical analysis. Because Marxism was built on the same claim, the whole basis of social history has been questioned, despite the very many studies that directly had little to do with Marxism. Disillusionment with social history, simultaneously opened the door to cultural and linguistic approaches largely developed in anthropology and literature. Multiculturalism and feminism further generated revisionism. By claiming that scholars had, wittingly or not, operated from a white European/American male point of view, newer researchers argued that other approaches had been neglected or misunderstood. Not surprisingly, these last historians are the most likely to envision each subgroup rewriting its own usable history, while other scholars incline towards revisionism as part of the search for some stable truth.

Rewriting Histories will make these new approaches available to the student population. Often new scholarly debates take place in the scattered issues of journals which are sometimes difficult to find. Furthermore, in these first interactions, historians tend to address one another, leaving out the evidence that would make their arguments more accessible to the uninitiated. This series of books will collect in one place a strong group of the major articles in selected fields, adding notes and introductions conducive to improved understanding. Editors will select articles containing substantial historical data, so that students – at least those who approach the subject as an objective phenomenon – can advance not only their comprehension of debated points but also their grasp of substantive aspects of the subject.

Few fields have been more in flux than that of twentieth-century China. Political developments have had their effect. Changes in the regime have allowed significant use of the archives for the last generation of scholars. Furthermore, the blending of political control with the embrace of capitalism has made the Communists look more like their predecessors. Consequently, continuity, as well as revolution, appears as an important variable. These shifts, along with other more international influences, have led to a rise in the consideration of gender, local variations, and linguistic changes and stasis. Most provocatively, this volume changes the chronology from the Communist revolution in 1949 as the central point to embrace the entire century as one of a long upheaval that currently seems to be giving way to some spectacular shifts. Readers will be engaged by the rich documentation in the studies included here. Overall, this version of events seeks to impose some order and stimulate further debate in the rich field of modern Chinese history.

ACKNOWLEDGEMENTS

The editor would like to express his gratitude to many colleagues who gave him advice on this volume as it evolved over the course of several years, as well as to the anonymous readers from whom Routledge solicited critical comments on the proposed table of contents. I am particularly grateful to suggestions offered by Steve Averill, Prasenjit Duara, and Lynn Struve, though none of these three scholars nor the others with whom I discussed the project should be held accountable in any way for the idiosyncratic final form it has taken. I also want to thank Heather McCallum (formerly of Routledge) for encouraging me to take on this volume; Victoria Peters (of Routledge) for her excellent work guiding the book through its final stages; and Jack Censer for being a model of what a series editor should be throughout the process.

All essays (except Chapters 1 and 2) have already been published. We should like to thank the following copyright holders and authors for permission to reproduce their work.

Chapter 1   Written for this volume by Jeffrey N. Wasserstrom.

Chapter 2   A previously unpublished essay by Paul A. Cohen, revised specially for inclusion in this volume; permission for inclusion kindly granted by the author.

Chapter 3   Reprinted from *Modern China*, vol. 21, no. 1 (January 1995), pp. 44–76; permission for inclusion kindly granted by Sage Publications.

Chapter 4   Reprinted from *Dissent* (Fall 1995), pp. 477–485; permission for inclusion kindly granted by *Dissent* (and by the author of the essay).

Chapter 5   Reprinted from *Past & Present*, vol. 166 (February 2000), pp. 181–204; permission for inclusion kindly granted by Oxford University Press (and by the author of the essay).

ACKNOWLEDGEMENTS

Chapter 6   Reprinted from the *Journal of Asian Studies*, vol. 51, no. 4 (November 1992), pp. 770–796; permission for inclusion kindly granted by the Association for Asian Studies.

Chapter 7   Reprinted from Kathleen Hartford and Steven M. Goldstein, eds, *Single Sparks: China's Rural Revolutions* (Armonk, NY: M.E. Sharpe Inc., 1989), pp. 3–33; permission for inclusion kindly granted by M.E. Sharpe Inc.

Chapter 8   Reprinted from Gail Hershatter *et al.*, eds, *Remapping China: Fissures in Historical Terrain* (Stanford: Stanford University Press, 1996), pp. 242–257; permission for inclusion kindly granted by Stanford University Press.

Chapter 9   Reprinted from the inaugural issue (September 1998) of *Intersections: Gender, History and Culture in the Asian Context* (an online journal located at: http://wwwsshe.murdoch. edu.au/intersections/); permission for inclusion kindly granted by the editors of that publication, Anne-Marie Medcalf and Carolyn Brewer (and by the author of the essay).

Chapter 10   Reprinted from the *Indiana East Asian Working Paper Series on Language and Politics in Modern China*, vol. 2 (July 1993), pp. 1–18; permission for inclusion kindly granted by the editors of that series, Sue M. C. Tuohy and Jeffrey N. Wasserstrom (and by the authors of the essay).

Chapter 11   Reprinted from Marta Dassù and Tony Saich, eds, *The Reform Decade in China: From Hope to Dismay* (London: Kegan Paul, 1992), pp. 132–150; permission for inclusion kindly granted by Marie-Claire Bergère.

Chapter 12   Reprinted from *Dissent* (Spring 2000), pp. 17–22; permission for inclusion kindly granted by that publication.

NOTES ON CONTRIBUTORS

Marie-Claire Bergère was, until her recent retirement, Professor of Chinese Civilization at the Institut National des Languages et Civilisations Orientales in Paris. She has contributed essays to numerous conference volumes and journals, including the *China Quarterly* and *Annales*, and her books include *Sun Yat-sen*, which appeared in French in 1994 and was subsequently translated into English (Stanford University Press, 1998)

Chen Yung-fa is Research Fellow at the Institute of Modern History, Academia Sinica, Taibei, and Professor of History, National Taiwan University. He has published widely, in both Chinese and English, on the upheavals that took place in China in the 1940s. His books include *Making Revolution: The Communist Movement in Eastern and Central China, 1937–45* (University of California Press, 1986).

Paul A. Cohen was, until his recent retirement, the Edith Stix Wasserman Professor of History at Wellesley College and remains an associate of Harvard's Fairbank Center for East Asian Research. His books include *Discovering History in China* (Columbia University Press, 1984) and *History in Three Keys: The Boxers as Event, Experience, and Myth* (Columbia University Press, 1997).

Joseph W. Esherick is Professor of History and Hsiu Professor of Chinese Studies at the University of California at San Diego. His books include *Reform and Revolution in China* (University of California Press, 1976), *The Origins of the Boxer Uprising* (University of California Press, 1987), and, as editor, *Remaking the Chinese City* (University of Hawaii Press).

Harriet Evans is a senior lecturer and Coordinator of the Program in Contemporary Chinese Cultural Studies at the University of Westminster's Centre for the Study of Democracy. She is the author of *Women and Sexuality in China* (Continuum, 1997), and co-editor (with Stephanie Donald) of *Picturing Power in the People's Republic of China: Posters of the Cultural Revolution* (Rowman and Littlefield, 1999).

Steven M. Goldstein is the Sophia Smith Professor of Government at Smith College. He has written, co-authored or edited eight books and has contributed essays to various journals, including *China Quarterly* and the *Journal of Contemporary China*. He also served as a writer and on-screen commentator for the documentary series "The Chinese," a PBS production.

Henrietta Harrison teaches in the East Asian Studies Department at the University of Leeds and in 2001/2 was a visiting fellow at Princeton's Institute for Advanced Study. Her publications include two recent Oxford University Press books: *The Making of the Republican Citizen: Political Ceremonies and Symbols in China, 1911–29* (2000) and the *China* volume in its "Inventing the Nation" series (2001).

Kathleen Hartford is a professor in the Political Science Department at the University of Massachusetts-Boston. She has contributed essays to numerous conference volumes, as well as to periodicals such as the *World Policy Journal* and *Socialist Review*. Her books include *China's Search for Democracy: The Student and Mass Movement of 1989* (M.E. Sharpe Publishers, 1992), for which she was one of four co-editors.

Li Xun is currently an independent scholar based in Northern California and a former visiting fellow at Berkeley's Institute of East Asian Studies. She is the author of a monograph on Shanghai workers that was published in Taiwan in 1996 and a co-author of *Proletarian Power: Shanghai in the Cultural Revolution* (Westview Press, 1997).

Lin Chun teaches in the Government Department of the London School of Economics. Her major research areas include China and the New Left in Europe. Her major publications include, as editor, a three-volume series of readers all published by Ashgate in 2000: *China: Modernizing Chinese Polity* (Vol. I); *The Contradictions and Transformation of Chinese Socialism* (Vol. II); and *Defining a Changing China in Global Politics* (Vol. III).

Elizabeth J. Perry is the Henry Rosovsky Professor of Government. Her most recent books are *Challenging the Mandate of Heaven: Social Protest and State Power in China* (M.E. Sharpe, 2001) and *Changing Meanings of Citizenship in Modern China* (Harvard University Press, 2002), which she co-edited with Merle Goldman.

R. Keith Schoppa holds the Edward and Catherine Doehler Chair in Asian History at Loyola College in Maryland. His books include *Blood Road: The Mystery of Shen Dingyi in Revolutionary China* (University of California Press, 1995) and *Revolution and Its Past: Identities and Change in Modern Chinese History* (Prentice Hall, 2002).

Jeffrey N. Wasserstrom (editor and contributor) is Associate Professor of History at Indiana University where he is also Director of the East Asian Studies Center. He is the author of *Student Protests in Twentieth-century China* (Stanford University Press, 1991) and articles that have appeared in scholarly journals and general interest publications such as the *Nation* and the *Times Literary Supplement* (London). His most recent book (co-edited with Susan Brownell) is *Chinese Femininities/Chinese Masculinities* (University of California Press, 2002).

BRIEF CHRONOLOGY

1900:	Boxer siege of Beijing; lifted by eight allied armies. Campaigns of reprisal begin
1901:	Boxer Protocol signed
1901–1910:	Qing reforms, including abolition of Confucian examinations, instituted
1905:	Sun Yat-sen founds Revolutionary Alliance (Tongmenghui), precursor to GMD (Nationalist Party)
1911:	Republican revolution, fall of the Manchu Qing Dynasty (founded 1644)
1912:	Sun inaugurated as first president of Republic of China (ROC). He abdicates. Warlord era begins
1915:	Yuan Shikai (Sun's successor as President) accepts Japan's Twenty-one Demands
1915:	*New Youth* magazine launched, New Culture movement begins (ends early 1920s)
1919:	May 4th Movement (student-led anti-Japanese, anti-warlord multi-class movement)
1921:	Formal establishment of the Chinese Communist Party (CCP).
1924–1927:	First United Front alliance between GMD and CCP
1925:	Sun Yat-sen dies; May 30th Movement (multi-class anti-imperialist struggle)
1926:	Northern Expedition (anti-warlord military campaign) begins
1927:	GMD launches anti-Communist purge. Nanjing Decade (GMD rule) begins
1928:	CCP establishes Jiangxi Soviet
1931:	Japanese invade Manchuria (Mukden Incident)
1934:	CCP Long March begins (Yan'an base area established at its end a year later)
1935:	December 9th Movement (student struggle, anti-imperialist)
1936:	Xian Incident (Chiang Kai-shek kidnapped until he agrees to ally with CCP)

1937–1945:	Second United Front between GMD and CCP to fight Japanese invaders
1937:	Marco Polo Bridge Incident (escalation of war with Japan)
1938:	Rape of Nanjing (massive atrocities against Chinese civilians by Japanese soldiers)
1945:	Japanese surrender
1945–1949:	Civil War between GMD and CCP
1949:	GMD retreats to Taiwan. People's Republic of China established
1950:	New marriage law enacted by CCP. Korean War begins
1950–1959:	CCP seeks to impose rule on Tibet; Tibetan resistance
1958–1962:	Great Leap Forward and massive famine; afterwards Mao less powerful
1966:	Red Guards (youth groups intensely loyal to Mao) formed. Mao resurgent
1966–1969:	Most intense period of the Great Proletarian Cultural Revolution (GPCR)
1966–1976:	GPCR "Ten Years of Turmoil" (official designation of decade in PRC today)
1975:	Chiang Kai-shek dies (succeeded by his son Jiang Jingguo)
1976:	April 5th Movement. Mao dies (succeeded by Hua Guofeng). Fall of "Gang of Four"
1978:	Reform era begins (Deng Xiaoping rises). Democracy Wall Movement
1985–1988:	Scattered student protests (varied causes and aims)
1989:	Tiananmen student-led, multi-class protests; Massacres in Beijing and Chengdu
1997:	Deng dies (succeeded by Jiang Zemin). Hong Kong becomes part of the PRC
1999:	Anti-NATO protests (after embassy in Belgrade hit). Falun Gong sit-in
2000:	GMD loses national elections in Taiwan

1

INTRODUCTION

Jeffrey N. Wasserstrom

The twentieth century was a traumatic and transformational one for China – as indeed it was for many countries. One major reason for this, which is far from unique to this context, is the prevalence of warfare in China throughout the 1900s. Most notable, in terms of the human costs on the battlefront, were the 1930s and first half of the 1940s which saw a bloody protracted struggle against Japanese military aggression. Japan's surrender was, in turn, followed immediately by a civil war (1945–1949) that pitted the Guomindang (GMD) or Nationalist Party, which was founded early in the century by Sun Yat-sen (1866–1925) and later led by Chiang Kai-shek (1887–1975), against the Chinese Communist Party (CCP) of Mao Zedong (1893–1976).[1] The second half of the century, though less marked by military conflagrations, began with Chinese involvement in the Korean War. Before the century ended, moreover, the People's Liberation Army of the CCP would have used its weapons many more times. Sometimes, their targets were foreign foes, as in the Sino-Vietnamese battles of the 1970s. Often, though, the enemies were groups located within CCP-ruled territory, such as participants in the Tibetan uprisings of the 1950s and the protesters slain in Beijing and Chengdu in 1989.

In addition to warfare, China's twentieth century was marked by dramatic peacetime social and economic shifts. These were frequently the result of official policies, as was the case with the redistribution of property that occurred during the land reform and collectivization experiments of the Maoist era (1949–1976), and the moves back toward privatization instigated by Deng Xiaoping (1904–1997) at the start of the Reform period (1978–). Sometimes, though, they were harder to link to any single official directive. For example, due to multiple reasons, over the course of the century China became a much less overwhelmingly rural country than it had been in the past. More than half of the populace still lived in villages when the twentieth century ended. Nevertheless, at least according to some estimates, the percentage of Chinese residing inside of or very near to cities (including ones such as Shanghai and Chongqing that are now among the biggest in the world) rose from less than a quarter to close to half during the century.

1

On top of all this, in ways that are harder to quantify, the century was a time of profound cultural changes that radically reshaped both ways of thought and public and private modes of behavior. Some of the most important of the cultural changes came midway through the century when, for example, the CCP introduced a new marriage law that stipulated equal rights (including that of divorce) for husbands and wives. Many other cultural shifts, though, can be linked back to the century's opening decades. For example, many of these were set in motion by the challenges to conventional beliefs and behaviors made during the New Cultural Movement (1915–1923). This was a struggle in which intellectuals called into question everything from canonical literary and philosophical texts to familial practices that perpetuated inequalities not just between men and women but between members of older and younger generations.

Perhaps the easiest way to give a sense of just how much China was transformed during the century, however, is to focus not on war, social, and economic shifts or cultural transformation but rather on the realm of high politics. China in the late nineteenth century was still an empire ruled by a dynasty. This was the Qing (1644–1911), a royal family that traced its roots back to Manchuria. And the Emperor at that point still controlled the country with the help of a large civil service, most of the members of which had gained their positions in a time-honored fashion: by passing examinations that required those being tested to demonstrate a thorough knowledge of Confucian texts.

By the early 1920s, by contrast, the last Emperor had abdicated and the country had a new name. It was now the "Republic of China" (ROC), thanks to a rechristening that took place in 1912 when Sun (the hero of the 1911 revolution that had toppled the Qing) was inaugurated as the new country's first president. Sun and his comrades in arms were no longer, however, the most powerful people in the land by the early 1920s. This distinction went to a group of regional militarists – often referred to now as "warlords" – who varied widely when it came to personal style and ideology (some modeled themselves on Confucian gentlemen, one of the most powerful had converted to Christianity, and so forth). What they had in common were large armies, the troops in which owed to them high degrees of personal loyalty. Aside from foreign-run enclaves within Shanghai and other treaty ports (which the militarists left alone for the most part) and the Canton area (which became the main focus of Sun's activities), they divided the country among themselves.

Political shifts continued through the rest of the first half of the century. First, the militarists were unseated by the Northern Expedition of the late 1920s, which was carried out by forces linked to both the GMD and the CCP. This struggle brought to power Chiang Kai-shek – who immediately turned against his erstwhile Communist allies in a dramatic about-face. For the next two decades, he and other leaders of the GMD ran the country. Or, rather, the Nationalists ran those parts of China that were not foreign-run enclaves, did not come under the sway of Communist insurgents (who established a base in the northern mountain stronghold of Yan'an, as well as in other remote regions), and did not fall prey to Japanese invaders. Then, in 1949, Mao's armies defeated Chiang Kai-shek's and the Nationalists retreated to the island of Taiwan.

This 1949 event established a basic political configuration that remained in place throughout the rest of the twentieth century. The Nationalists took the name "Republic of China" with them and the CCP, with whom the GMD had briefly allied a second time to fight Japan between 1937 and 1945, renamed the mainland the "People's Republic of China" (PRC), by which it continues to be known. The fifty years from 1949 until 1999 saw CCP rule continue in the PRC and Nationalist rule continue on Taiwan.

This said, the second half of the century continued to be one of political turmoil (even before the GMD lost its grip on Taiwan in 2000 due to an unexpected election victory by a rival party). In the late 1960s, for example, the PRC was shaken by the anarchic events of the Cultural Revolution. In the late 1970s it was rocked again by Deng's rise and his announcement of policies that challenged many tenets of Maoism. Then, in 1989, the Tiananmen uprising precipitated a legitimacy crisis, in part because the protests demonstrated how widespread had become the belief that the CCP was riddled with corruption. As a new century began – even though the main features of the Reform era set in place by Deng remained in operation, and even though the CCP continued to hold a monopoly on state power – it was still an open question as to whether that crisis had been fully resolved. High economic growth rates and other factors (such as resurgent nationalism) kept the CCP from going the way of its counterparts in Eastern Europe. Nevertheless, many people continued to feel at century's end that these leaders cared less about any ideology than about maintaining their own positions of power. In addition, new challenges to the regime had appeared on the horizon. To cite just one example, there were tax and labor strikes throughout the 1990s by villagers and workers in various regions who felt they were being left behind by the economic reforms.

Given the volatility of the century that has just concluded, it is hardly surprising that its history has undergone and continues to undergo a continual process of rewriting – some of it, predictably, inspired by regime shifts. If we leave aside that sort of revisionism (which has periodically led to "heroes" being redefined as "villains" and vice versa), it seems fair to say that some of the most dramatic shifts in understanding China's recent past have come in the last dozen years.

This has been due to several overlapping developments, some generic, others distinctive to Chinese studies. A case in point, in the distinctive category, is provocative new work fueled by a desire to break away from conventional modes of analysis that overstated the role of the West in determining the course of China's history after the Opium Wars (1839–1842).[2] An example of a development that is somewhat distinctive yet parallels moves in specific other fields with which Chinese studies has much in common relates to archives. Much recent work has taken advantage of increased access to document collections that were formerly off-limits to foreign scholars (and many of our Chinese counterparts as well). The parallel here is with Eastern Europe.[3] Then, finally, some recent developments in Chinese studies have been very similar to those that have occurred in many fields. The influence of interdisciplinary approaches associated with first the "New Social History" and then the "New Cultural History" is one example.[4] The rise of the internet and other new technologies that make it easier for scholars in disparate parts of the world to exchange opinions and collaborate is another.

Due to these varied factors, so much has changed in Chinese studies since the mid-1980s that no single volume could hope to give a comprehensive view of all the transformations that have occurred. My strategy in organizing this book, therefore, has been to be very selective thematically, while working with a canvas that is relatively capacious when it comes to chronology and geography. More specifically, I have chosen eleven works published between 1989 and 2000 that highlight in interesting ways four general topics that have generated considerable excitement among historians with revisionist inclinations, broadly defined, and among some scholars in related discipline.[5]

The first theme examined, in a section called "The shape of a century," is a temporal one, as each chapter in this part explores the nature of 1949 as a year of transition. This year has long been seen as constituting a political and intellectual midway point. It was thought to separate the Republican era (1912–1949) and a distinctively different Communist period (1949–) and was often thought of as also separating the domain of the historian from the domain of the social scientist. Now, however, many have raised doubts about the solidity of this dividing line.[6]

The second part, "Going local," focuses on spatial as opposed to temporal boundaries. The main question asked is what local perspectives reveal that remains obscured when history is written solely in terms of the nation-state.

The final two sections are shorter, each containing just a pair of chapters apiece. In the first of these, "Symbolic turns," the essays call attention to the tension between modes of analysis that stress non-material as well as or in contrast to material factors.[7] In the final part, "Political legitimacy at century's end," two chapters examine recent challenges to CCP rule and efforts by the regime to reposition itself to stay in power at a time when many one-party states were collapsing.

Many other themes could have been flagged for attention, since revisionist energy has fueled important work on other subjects – ranging from ethnicity to legal practices, business history to the vexed question of

Taiwan's status within "Chinese" history – that are not treated directly in the pages to come.[8] Nevertheless, when taken together, this volume's ten reprinted essays and one newly published work (Paul A. Cohen's chapter) will give the reader a sense of some of the main contours of the landscape of Chinese studies at the turn of the millennium. Moreover, in choosing essays, I have looked for those that are not only insightful contributions to the themes singled out for attention in the part titles but shed light on debates associated with other topics.

One result of this is that many subjects other than the 1949 divide, regional variation, symbolism, and political legitimacy are given a good deal of coverage below *en passant*. For example, while there is no section devoted to "Gender," readers will gain an appreciation for several of the important ways that feminist analytical tools have been used to challenge conventional wisdom in Chinese studies in recent years. An early chapter ("Toward a Chinese feminism") takes for granted, as Joan Scott famously put it, that gender is a "category of historical significance," and sexual politics is also of central concern in a later chapter ("The language of liberation").[9] Similarly, there is no "Nationalism" section yet this topic is hardly given short shrift. Nearly every chapter pays some attention to nationalist struggles, nationalist ideologies, competing visions of the Chinese nation, or all of these. And, in some of these chapters, including an early one ("Ten theses on the Chinese Revolution") and the last one ("The year of living anxiously"), the theme of nationalism looms very large indeed.[10]

A quick tour through the volume

Taking each section in turn, what exactly will the reader find? "The shape of a century" opens with Cohen commenting on the links as well as ruptures between the Communist and pre-Communist eras. This is followed by a chapter by Joseph W. Esherick that raises a series of questions about the nature of 1949 as a boundary marker and birth year of "New" China. Cohen and Esherick are unusual in that, well before it was fashionable to do so, each was already routinely publishing works that looked at more than one period or drew links between eras usually treated separately. Thus both wrote early books based on archival research that focused on the decades leading up to the fall of the Qing Dynasty, then went on to contribute to debates on the Republican and Communist eras.

This makes them well qualified to reflect on the meaning of the 1949 divide and to look for connections between late twentieth-century events and processes that began as far back as 1900 or earlier still. Neither Cohen nor Esherick denies that the founding of the PRC and the retreat to Taiwan of the Nationalist Party were of great importance. Each insists, though, that it is now possible to ask, and it behooves us to question just how dramatically the rise of Mao and the CCP changed China's social, economic, political, and cultural trajectory. It is time, they suggest, for a new agenda defined by a new set of questions.

Did the rise to power of the Communist Party (an organization founded at the start of the 1920s) really alter virtually everything, either for good (as the official CCP historical line has always claimed) or for ill (as GMD official histories have just as fervently insisted)? Or are there continuities as well as discontinuities that need to be underscored? For example, while the GMD was certainly anti-Marxist under Chiang Kai-shek, it was heavily influenced by Soviet organizational models and Lenin's critique of imperialism. Should we therefore think of a Chinese Leninist era that began not in 1949 but in the late 1920s when the Nationalists gained power at the end of the Northern Expedition (1926–1928)?[11] And how important are the continuities that can be teased out between the reformist policies and repressive actions of the CCP in the 1980s and those that the Qing turned to in the first decade of the twentieth century?

In posing and answering questions of this sort, Cohen and Esherick introduce readers to a host of major issues in Chinese history and direct their attention to a wide range of works by historians and social scientists based in varied parts of the world who have grappled with these topics. Their approaches to the theme of 1949's significance push them in different directions, but they share a common conviction that we are best off if we acknowledge the significance of ongoing processes as well as points of rupture as we move forward from the late Qing, Warlord (1912–1927), and Nationalist (1927–1949) eras up to the Maoist and Reform periods of PRC history.[12]

Following these essays by prominent North American historians of China, and serving as a powerful counterpoint to them, is a much more personal chapter by Lin Chun, who was born and raised in China but now teaches politics at the London School of Economics. Her essay, "Toward a Chinese feminism," does not directly address chronological questions. Nevertheless, through its discussion of the author's life history and engagement with feminist issues, it reminds us of some of the specific ways that the world was turned upside down in 1949, at least for some people. The author shows, in particular, how dramatic the difference between the Communist era and the periods that came before it was for some Chinese women. Her vivid description of the distinctive social and cultural milieu in which she came of age in the 1960s and 1970s brings this point home in a poignant and effective manner.[13]

"Going local" shifts gears by focusing almost exclusively on the first half of the century and highlighting issues of regional variation. To appreciate the revisionist nature of the four local studies it contains, it is important for the reader to understand that official histories produced in the PRC and the Republic of China (ROC) on Taiwan alike have tended to frame the story of the recent past in national terms. Moreover, China specialists in other lands have often fallen into the trap, until recently, of taking for granted that a national perspective is best, at least when trying to capture the meaning and explain the causes of major turning-point events such as the rise to power of the CCP.

Works that stress regional variation thus need to be seen as contributing to general efforts to "rescue" China's history – to borrow a phrase from a justly acclaimed book by Prasenjit Duara – from the straitjacket of officially endorsed patriotic mythologies.[14] They also challenge narratives less overtly tied to formal political agendas that assume that, in the modern age, the main job of historians is to treat nation-states, conceived of as clearly defined and relatively stable entities, as the key subjects of history.

Some of the first important efforts to "rescue" Chinese history from national frameworks and foreground local variation were made between the late 1960s and the 1980s by social historians focusing on popular unrest. These scholars argued that, when trying to understand rebellious acts of various sorts, it was crucial to concentrate on specific locales and view phenomena from the ground up.[15]

Beginning in the 1970s, some cultural historians joined this call for emphasizing the significance of variation from place to place within China, as well as from group to group within any given locale.[16] A sense of the directions in which this new concern with regional differences has led is provided in the "Going local" part by chapters that draw attention to everything from ecological variation between provinces to distinctions from village to village associated with ritual practices. As these chapters show, it is possible that all of these differences not only alter the experiences of individuals and collectivities but, in the end, change the course of large-scale transformations of the political order.

Part II opens with a pair of essays that illuminate the locally varied meanings of Chinese nationalism. In the first, Henrietta Harrison focuses on rural North China in the first decades of the 1900s and uses as her main source of information and perspective an unusual diary kept by a member of the local elite. In the second, R. Keith Schoppa looks at how successive revolutionary tides of the first half of the century were shaped by and changed social patterns within a single county just south of the Yangzi River.

The next two chapters complete the section by directing our attention to the value of adopting local history techniques when analyzing the rise of the CCP in the years immediately preceding 1949. In the first of these, which was written as the introduction to an important conference volume, *Single Sparks: China's Rural Revolutions*, Kathleen Hartford and Steven M. Goldstein bring together the findings of several studies of Communist efforts to gain a foothold in different kinds of rural settings. One of their main arguments is that we need to stop thinking of a single upper-case Chinese Communist Revolution and think instead of a set of overlapping lower-case revolutions that took varied forms even while leading up to a single national outcome. Following their chapter is one by Chen Yung-fa on events in Yan'an, the base area where Mao lived and worked. Chen argues that to understand fully the things that Mao and his allies did nationally after 1949, we need to look very closely at what they did locally before that time. Many experiments carried out in Yan'an, he argues, laid the foundation for the policies and mass campaigns of the 1950s and the Cultural Revolution era (1966–1976).[17]

The third part, "Symbolic turns," contains two of the many recent essays on China to be influenced by the increased concern with discursive issues that has reshaped many fields since work by François Furet and others began to alter conventional views of the French Revolution in the late 1970s.[18] Here, again, one specific impulse, in the case of Chinese studies, has been to break free of the constraints imposed by official narratives. These tend to emphasize the special qualities of individual leaders (Sun, for example, in the case of the 1911 Revolution) or material factors (such as class struggle, in the case of orthodox Marxist readings of 1949). The two chapters in this section, like other recent studies that take a linguistic or symbolic turn in interpreting China's recent past, argue that we need to combine analysis of personalities and material forces with close attention to issues such as rhetoric and representation.[19]

The pay-off of a sophisticated understanding of a semiotic issue is made clear in "The language of liberation," in which Harriet Evans looks at official CCP understandings of and references to *funü jiefang* (women's liberation). The same can be said for the essay co-authored by Elizabeth J. Perry, an American political scientist, and Li Xun, a Chinese researcher (now an independent scholar based in California) who lived through the Cultural Revolution. Their essay is the result of a collaboration that would have been impossible to imagine let alone carry out prior to the late 1980s, since it deals with a politically charged period and began while Li was still based in the PRC. It is also robustly comparative in approach, using as it does insights by scholars of European history such as William H. Sewell, Jr. to illuminate the rhetorical battles that accompanied the physical ones that took place in the late 1960s in China.[20]

The last part of the book, "Political legitimacy at the century's end," contains two chapters tied together by concern with the dynamics of popular unrest and the CCP's continued monopoly of state power at the close of the 1990s. It opens with an essay on Tiananmen by one of France's most distinguished (and most versatile) China specialists, Marie-Claire Bergère, who has published works on topics ranging from the history of banking in China to the life and thought of Sun Yat-sen. In her piece, which was written soon after the dramatic protests and brutal June 4 massacre of 1989 had captured the attention of the world, she takes issue with various overly simplistic readings of those events. To make sense of Tiananmen, she insists, we need to break free of the erroneous assumption that, except for the differing endings, it was just like the upheavals that took place virtually simultaneously in the Soviet Empire. And we need to take into account a range of factors, some economic, some political, some cultural.

This chapter is followed by one that I wrote for *Dissent* magazine, which moves us forward to the very end of the twentieth century, to another pivotal year when unexpected events took place on China's streets. In "The year of living anxiously: China's 1999" I look at continuities and discontinuities between recent expressions of popular sentiment (agitation by the Falun Gong sect, nationalistic demonstrations such as that triggered by NATO's destruction of the Chinese Embassy in Belgrade) and those of earlier periods. I also argue that there are common threads that connect the government's responses to mass action in different stages of the Reform era – up to and including the late 1990s.

Both of the chapters in this final part underscore the extent to which, when trying to make sense of contemporary events, knowledge of the acts of protest and repression that helped define China throughout the 1900s is crucial. They also draw attention to the value of placing the CCP's resilience as a ruling force into a broad historical as well as comparative perspective.

A quick tour through a century

Having introduced briefly the contents of this volume, some further general comments on twentieth-century China as a subject of analysis are in order. It is worth asking, first of all, when exactly this "century" began and ended. This may seem a strange question to anyone unfamiliar with debates among historians, yet it is one that needs to be posed and answered. Much has been made lately of the notion that Europe had a "long nineteenth century" (lasting from 1789 to 1914) and that the world had a "short twentieth century" (which began when World War One broke out and ended with the collapse of the Soviet Empire). In addition, some historians have claimed that Britain had an "eighteenth-century" that was a decade or two less than one hundred years, while others have insisted that it had one that was more than twice as long as that.

All of these claims for short and long centuries notwithstanding, with the case at hand we have one of the relatively rare instances where a very good argument can be made for a century that lasted just about a hundred years.[21] And, moreover, for one that began and ended virtually when it should have. This in any case is how things look from the admittedly close-up perspective of the last days of 2001.

What I mean is that the period lasting from the Boxer Crisis (1899–1901) to the present moment seems to me to constitute a definite arc, at least where some key issues are concerned. And this same sense is conveyed by Graham Hutchings in the introduction to his new book, *Modern China: A Guide to a*

Century of Change. In this opening section of one of the first general looks at recent Chinese history to appear in the twenty-first century, Hutchings, the long-time Beijing correspondent for the *Daily Telegraph*, writes as follows:

> China entered the twentieth century in decline. Its territorial fringes – and, thanks to the Boxer Rebellion, its capital – were occupied by the powers, its sovereignty impaired by Unequal Treaties. The country's ideology and institutions . . . were in crisis, its Manchu, Qing Dynasty rulers unable or unwilling to reform. Dissent stalked the capital; regional governors resisted re-centralization. Hardly a province was untouched by rebellion. Outside half a dozen major urban centres, the economy remained stubbornly, overwhelmingly, agrarian . . . In almost every respect, China was ill prepared for the struggle between industrialized nations destined to shape the new century. In 1900, China's very existence seemed under threat.
>
> China enters the twenty-first century in stronger shape. It has regained much of its lost territory and is determined to recover more. Beijing cannot always get its way in adjacent provinces let alone distant frontiers. But neither rich nor remote regions dare defy the central government when the national interest is at stake. China's nuclear weapons, military modernization and above all its recent rapid economic growth have assured it a seat at the world's top table.[22]

The arc I have in mind is clearest, as this passage implies, where diplomacy is concerned. Let us linger on this topic for a moment, then, before moving on.

When the Boxers laid siege to the foreign legation quarter of Beijing in June 1900, after killing a small number of Westerners and a much larger number of Chinese converts to Christianity, the foreign view of China reached depths that it had never plumbed before. And it is fair to say that, in the century since that point, the international status of China has never sunk any lower. This is because the violence of the Boxers (a group discussed in more detail in Chapter 5) led many of the most powerful countries of the day to view China as having placed itself beyond the pale of the "civilized" world.[23]

The international press excoriated China and its people that June, claiming that, despite the long history of its civilization, the country had become a barbarous place inhabited by savages. And foreign outrage increased as the siege wore on and two rumors spread. The first of these (which proved ungrounded) was that all Westerners in Beijing had been killed, including the wives and children of foreign diplomats and missionaries. The second rumor (which proved true) held that the Qing, whose armies had been defeated by Japan in the 1890s and by the West in the 1840s and 1860s, had switched from treating the Boxers as bandits to be suppressed to embracing them as loyalists to be praised and supported.

When the Boxer Rising was finally crushed in August 1900, the job was done by a multinational force made up of soldiers representing the United States, six European powers and Japan. And what followed made China's already dismal predicament even worse. Foreign troops quickly moved from freeing the legations to engaging in an orgy of looting, which deprived China of many of its national treasures. Then, some of these same soldiers (as well as reinforcements sent from several of the foreign countries involved) took part in brutal campaigns of reprisal. These were ostensibly aimed at putting an end to all Boxer groups, but they resulted in the deaths of many Chinese men who had never been Boxers and were accompanied by the raping of Chinese women.[24]

Finally, in September 1901, the crisis concluded with a humiliating treaty known as the Boxer Protocol. This accord placed the blame for all of the violence that had racked North China during the preceding three years squarely on the side of the Chinese. It also placed the Qing Emperor, who had gone into hiding when the foreign troops arrived, back on the Dragon Throne. But it did so by insisting on several things. One was that all parties accept the fictional tale that the Boxers had from start to last been "rebels" (whom the Qing had failed to control) as opposed to renegade loyalists (whom the Qing had actively supported during their fifty-five-day siege). Another was that the regime would pay an enormous indemnity to compensate the West and Japan for Boxer damage to foreign property and the loss of foreign lives.

The foreign military actions of 1900 are often viewed within China as one of the darkest passages in the nation's history, while the Protocol is often seen as having dramatically exacerbated a diplomatic predicament that had gone steadily from bad to worse since the Opium Wars. In addition, the "Invasion of the Eight Allied Armies" (the term PRC schoolbooks use for events of August 1900 and the months that followed) and the Boxer Protocol are said to have laid the foundation for almost half a century of further diplomatic and military defeats at the hands of foreign powers. The most notable of these defeats were the traumatic Japanese invasions of the 1930s and 1940s, which are discussed below in Chapter 7, as well as elsewhere.

It is not surprising, in light of all this, that the CCP and GMD would both stake their claims to legitimacy on the same idea: that only their party could create a nation strong enough to ensure all Chinese a future free of further incursions by foreign powers. This focus on strengthening the nation at all costs would be used to justify many brutal campaigns against internal dissent during the course of the century. These included the White Terror that Chiang Kai-shek launched against the Communists in 1927 and the Red Terrors of later decades. Two other acts of repression defended in the same terms were the massacres of 1989 – plural because, even though the Beijing killings are much better known, some protesters and onlookers were definitely slain in the Sichuan Province city of Chengdu that June.

The country's position in the international order rose and fell at various points of the century, but a steady upward trajectory only began in the years immediately following 1949. This is because Mao, for all of his many faults, proved better than his predecessors at creating a regime that could protect China from threats to its national sovereignty. But though China's international stature rose in the 1950s, it was only around the turn of the millennium that the apotheosis of China as a great power was complete.

The sense of a long arc reaching completion as one century gave way to the next was clear to Hutchings when he wrote his introduction in the year 2000. He cited as evidence of the change then very recent events such as China's moves toward full acceptance into the World Trade Organization (WTO) less than one hundred years after the end of the Boxer catastrophe. Had Hutchings completed his book a year later, however, he would have been able to point to two additional striking examples that tell us much about just how changed is China's position in the world now as opposed to in 1901. First, immediately before the arrival of the centenary of the humiliating Boxer Protocol, the International Olympic Committee decreed that Beijing would serve as the site for the 2008 Summer Games. Then, a few days after the centenary passed, in the wake of the horrific terror attacks of September 11, an international coalition was formed to combat terrorism and "save civilization" from a threat emanating from Asia. This time around, though, in sharp contrast to what had happened in 1900, China was invited to be part of the multinational force.

A different but in some ways complementary arc to the diplomatic one described above relates to the coining and refashioning of the meanings of centrally important political terms. I am thinking here of many of the words used to describe and justify the revolution of 1911, the anti-warlord Northern Expedition, and later upheavals. Many of these terms first entered the mainstream of Chinese political discourse around 1900 and either began to disappear or had their meanings radically altered as the century ended.

Two good examples of terms that began to circulate widely in China near the start of the twentieth century and were clearly undergoing dramatic shifts in meaning as the century ended are *renquan* (human rights) and *minzhu* (democracy). But there is a third centrally important political term whose discursive history is even more useful to trace, if one's goal is to argue for a twentieth-century of approximately one hundred years. That term, on which we will focus for a time here, which is typically translated as "revolution," is made up of two characters: *ge* (which literally means "strip" or "skin") and *ming* (which means "mandate," as in right to rule).

What makes the linguistic arc of this term so important is that it was used for decades by both CCP and GMD leaders, as well as other political actors, to refer to the sacred mission of saving the nation via a course of dramatic action. It is, however, tricky to analyze. It is often difficult to tell whether it should be translated as "Revolution" or "revolutions," since there is frequently no way to tell in Chinese, except from context, whether terms such as this are meant to be understood as singular or plural, upper or lower case. Also, *geming* is both a recent term and one with links to the distant past. Its two component parts have been used in Chinese texts from ancient times, and for more than two millennia they have sometimes been paired to refer to a change of regime. Still, as a compound referring to an uprising that seeks to establish a new political order, and more specifically to create a republic, it is of much more recent vintage and came to China from Japan.[25]

Leaving aside the question of breaks between earlier and twentieth-century definitions, but keeping in mind the ambiguity of *geming* as a term for both a singular event and a series of interrelated struggles, what can we say about its place within twentieth-century Chinese discourses? One thing to note is that it first gained currency, in its modern sense, in Japan in the late nineteenth century and then started being used in select Chinese political circles a few years before the Boxer Crisis. According to legend, this originally Chinese and then Japanese compound made its way back across the China Sea when it caught the fancy of a young Sun Yat-sen. This frustrated reformer turned partisan of republicanism apparently saw a story in a Japanese newspaper that described his efforts to overthrow the Qing as an attempt to foster *geming*. He liked the way it looked, and soon the term began gaining currency, since more and more radicals started to think that the Qing and the imperial system in general were irredeemable. It was not merely reform that was needed, they concluded, but something more comprehensive. *Geming* seemed an apt term for it.[26]

Indications of the term's rising importance early in the new century included its appearance in the title of a major radical tract published in 1903, Zou Rong's *The Revolutionary Army (Gemingjun)*.[27] Even more significant was its frequent use by leaders of the Tengmenghui (Revolutionary Alliance), the precursor to the GMD that Sun founded in Tokyo in 1905. By this point, whether or not one supported *geming* was seen as the key distinction between those agitating merely for an updating of the imperial system and those demanding the creation of a republic. Thus, when the Qing was overthrown in 1911, due to the combined effects of a series of regional mutinies and isolated uprisings, and a Republic of China (ROC) was established, it was natural to refer to the event as constituting the *Zhonghua Geming* (Chinese Revolution).

For decades to follow, political struggles were generally defined in terms of disagreements not over whether *geming* was a good thing (the word itself was quickly invested with not just positive but sacred connotations) but over who had the right to speak in its holy name. To wrap one's cause in the aura of revolution was to legitimize it, and all kinds of political stances were celebrated as "revolutionary," even if they seem in retrospect to have been conservative or even reactionary. This pattern was in place before the Nationalists came to power at the close of the Northern Expedition but grew more entrenched after that. So entrenched, in fact, that when Chiang Kai-shek launched his periodic campaigns against the CCP, he did not accuse his radical rivals of being too revolutionary but rather of being counter-revolutionary.

It was after 1949, however, that the sacred nature of the term *geming* reached its apogee. And, in particular, it was during the intense linguistic battles of the Cultural Revolution era, which are so effectively discussed in Chapter 10 that people grew most worried that something they did or said would be seen as insufficiently revolutionary. This was not a mere semantic matter: once deemed counter-revolutionary in thought or deed, one became potentially and often actually a target for arrest or physical attack. The sacrality of *geming* as a term was challenged when Mao died, Deng Xiaoping came to power and the Cultural Revolution was officially repudiated. Even Deng, though, insisted when pushing for reform (*gaige*) that he was doing so primarily to save, not challenge the cause of *geming*.

The arc that began with Sun Yat-sen and Zou Rong and continued up through Chiang Kai-shek, Mao and Deng has now finally reached a completion of sorts, albeit one that is not as clearly associated with a particular point in time as that described for international relations. As recently as the protests of 1989, dissidents and officials all still tended to frame their goal as that of protecting the *geming* or getting it back on course.[28] But exhaustion with "revolutionary" projects and language began to set in during the 1990s, as important works by Chinese dissidents (such as Liu Xiaobo) and leading analysts of Chinese cultural history (such as Geremie Barmé) have shown.[29]

Geming, in its legitimating sense, does certainly continue to be invoked at times. When NATO bombs mistakenly hit the Chinese Embassy in 1999, for example, the CCP leaders in Beijing immediately consecrated the three people who died "revolutionary martyrs" as well as patriots.[30] And officials still periodically make the claim, which has always sounded strange when translated into other languages, that the economic *gaige*, pushing China toward capitalism, and the great Socialist *geming* go together naturally.[31] Nevertheless, the salience of such rhetoric has diminished in the PRC and there is much less reliance on "counter-revolutionary" as a term of denigration, both within the legal system and in other realms. Moreover, as alluded to above, 2000 saw the leadership of the ROC on Taiwan pass for the first time to a party other than the GMD. Thus the ROC is now officially ruled, as was never the case from the late 1920s onwards, by an organization that is not directly and tightly tied symbolically to Sun and to the events of 1911.

The sense of China's twentieth century as constituting a clearly demar-cated period is the main reason I have chosen to organize this volume in the

Rewriting Histories series in terms of this time period rather than, say, the Chinese Revolution as an event or the "modern" period. However, there is also the desire alluded to above to break free of the constraints imposed by official narratives. Among the most interesting general revisionist moves in Chinese studies of late have been efforts to move away from narrative frameworks that focus on a sacred revolutionary struggle for national renewal that began in 1911 or 1949. A first step toward "rescuing" Chinese history from the hold of CCP and GMD nationalist mythologies has been to pursue chronologies that question traditional ones, and not just where the 1949 divide is concerned. There has been no revisionist rush to organize tales of the past around the twentieth century as a unit, though some people besides Hutchings have done just that, but doing so here seems a sensibly agnostic approach. Moving from 1900 to 2000 allows us to defer rather than try to settle definitively questions for which CCP and GMD official narratives demand clear-cut answers, such as when exactly the Revolution really began. We can dodge or at least place on the back-burner for a time the debate over whether 1911 was merely a prelude to 1949 or the main event.

In addition, focusing on a century as a unit allows us to defer or skirt around the vexed issue of when China began its "modern" period. Here, I definitely part company with Hutchings, who suggests in the title of his book that China's modern period and the twentieth century are coeval. I prefer to leave open the dating of modernity. I say this knowing full well that there has been a vibrant debate within Chinese studies for some time now over how far back it makes most sense to trace the roots of modernity. Back to 1900, 1911, or merely to the 1930s? Back to the Opium Wars? To the moves toward urbanization and commercialization that preceded the coming of the West? To the early Qing or to the days of an earlier dynasty, an idea first promoted by leading Japanese Sinologists?[32] Many different starting points have been proposed over dating the modern, and the accompanying debate has raised and shed new light on a host of important issues, including the risk of applying concepts derived from the Western experience to the pattern of Chinese history.[33]

Nevertheless, for the purposes of this book, I want to place the issue on hold. I do this to encourage readers to begin their consideration of twentieth-century developments in China with open minds about the modern age and modernity in general. My working assumption is that we may have reached a moment in Chinese studies when it is worth trying to rescue the lived experience of twentieth-century historical actors not only from nationalist narratives but from narratives that center on the theme of the coming of the modern age. If nothing else, bracketing off the debate on modernity from other questions for a time may help those who care about the topic to return to it at a later point and see it in a fresh way.

A brief note on contributors

A few final comments are in order here about the authors of the chapters to come. They comprise a very diverse group. This is true when we consider the range of academic generations represented. Most of the contributors finished graduate school in the 1970s or 1980s and took up academic positions soon afterwards. But Cohen published his first essay on China in the 1950s and has recently retired (as has Bergère), while Harrison did not receive her doctorate until late in the 1990s and had her first book published in 2000. The contributors also comprise a diverse group when it comes to disciplines and areas of specialization. Most of them teach in history departments, but the list also includes four political scientists (Hartford, Goldstein, Lin, and Perry) and two scholars who were trained in history but are primarily based in interdisciplinary units (Harrison and Evans). Among the historians are those whose work draws most heavily on anthropology and those who gravitate more toward sociological or literary modes of analysis; while among the political scientists there are specialists in the study of social movements and specialists in the study of political philosophy. Finally, there is geographic diversity represented in the list of contributors. It is true that a majority of the authors were trained and now work in the United States. There are, however, three chapters by scholars who teach at British universities (Harrison, Evans, and Lin), one by a China specialist based in Paris (Bergère), and one by a scholar who is originally from and currently works in Taiwan (Chen).

This said, it is important to note that, due in part to the types of themes singled out for special attention and a desire to find articles that worked well together, some kinds of authors may appropriately be described as under-represented. China specialists who encounter this book may wonder, for example, about the absence of chapters by Japanese and Canadian Sinologists and scholars based in other parts of Europe (Germany, for example), since academics in all of these locales have contributed much to recent debates in the field. The same goes for scholars based in Australia (a particularly vibrant hub of exciting intellectual activity relating to twentieth-century China at the moment) as well as Singapore and elsewhere. Similarly, in terms of disciplinary variation, these same specialists may wonder why there are essays by historians and political scientists only, when historically minded scholars in other areas have produced important work as well.

It is certainly worth letting non-specialists know how very different this book could easily have been, in terms of the geographic and disciplinary mix of authors. And yet, the lacunae just described do not ultimately seem problematic. One reason for this is simply that a book of this size can only do so much. Beyond this, though, it is worth pointing out that, via the footnotes to this Introduction, much has already been done to alert readers to the role that scholarship produced in disciplines and locales not represented in the list of contributors has played in shaping understanding of China's twentieth century.[34] In addition, though the robustly international and interdisciplinary nature of Chinese studies today may be most clearly evidenced in Perry and Li's chapter, which as noted above was the product of a very special type of collaboration, one can find it in many other chapters. As careful readers will see, especially if they follow the trails laid down by footnotes, many kinds of cross-fertilization have shaped nearly all of the essays to come, just as they have the opening pages by the editor.[35]

NOTES

1 Throughout this Introduction, the pinyin style of romanization now used in the People's Republic of China will be used for all but a few Chinese terms. The exceptions are two individuals (Chiang Kai-shek and Sun Yat-sen) and one placename (Canton). These continue to be much more familiar to non-specialists in the alternate romanization just provided. When in doubt – as in the case of the once more common Kuomintang (KMT) and the now increasingly common Guomindang (GMD) for the party Sun and then Chiang led – I have gone with pinyin. The same pattern holds constant through the chapters to come, though sometimes pinyin is even used for Chiang (Jiang Jieshi), Sun (Sun Zhongshan), and Canton (Guangzhou).
2 For an overview of debates on Western influence, an excellent starting point remains Paul A. Cohen, *Discovering History in China: American Historical Writings on the Recent Chinese Past* (New York: Columbia University Press, 1984). Cohen distinguishes between four general approaches to the subject. Two of these (the "Impact Response" and "Modernization" paradigms) treat the West as a relatively benign or positive centrally important factor in China's modern history. A third (the "Imperialism" paradigm) interprets it much more negatively but still grants it centrality. And the last (the "China-Centered" paradigm) moves away from emphasizing the centrality of Western influences in shaping the course of Chinese history since 1839. For a sense of how China specialists have been grappling with the issue since 1984, see Cohen's Preface to the second edition of *Discovering History in China* (New York: Columbia University Press, 1997); Tani Barlow, "Colonialism's Career in Postwar China Studies," *positions: east asian cultures critique*, vol. 1, no. 1 (1993): 224–67; James L. Hevia, *Cherishing Men from Afar: Qing Guest Ritual and the Macartney Embassy of 1793* (Durham, NC.: Duke University Press, 1985); Robert Bickers, *Britain in China: Community, Culture and Colonialism 1900–1949* (Manchester: University of Manchester Press, 1999), pp. 6–10 and *passim*; and Hamashita Takeshi, "The Intra-regional System in East Asia in Modern Times," in Peter J. Katzenstein, ed., *Network Power, Japan and Asia* (Ithaca and London: Cornell University Press, 1997), pp. 113–135.
3 For interesting comments on the impact that the opening of new archives has made on studies of Russia's recent past, see an earlier work in this *Rewriting Histories* series, Sheila Fitzpatrick, ed., *Stalinism: New Directions* (London: Routledge, 2000).
4 For general overviews of these genres, see Olivier Zunz, ed., *Reliving the Past: The Worlds of Social History* (Chapel Hill: University of North Carolina Press,

1985); and Lynn Hunt, ed., *The New Cultural History* (Berkeley: University of California Press, 1989). The New Social History's impact on the China field is discussed well in William A. Rowe, "Approaches to Modern Chinese Social History," in Zunz, *Reliving the Past*, pp. 136–296; and *idem.*, "Modern Chinese Social History in Comparative Perspective," in Paul S. Ropp, ed., *Heritage of China: Contemporary Perspectives on Chinese Civilization* (Berkeley: University of California Press, 1990). See also Philip C. C. Huang, "The Paradigmatic Crisis in Chinese Studies: Paradoxes in Social and Economic History," *Modern China*, vol. 17, no. 3 (1991), pp. 299–341; and Jeffrey N. Wasserstrom, "Towards a Social History of the Chinese Revolution: A Review" (in two parts), *Social History*, vol. 17, nos. 1 and 2 (January and May, 1992), pp. 1–21 and 289–317. On the New Cultural History's impact on Chinese studies, see Elizabeth J. Perry, "Introduction: Chinese Political Culture Revisited," in Jeffrey N. Wasserstrom and Elizabeth J. Perry, eds, *Popular Protest and Political Culture in Modern China*, second edition (Boulder, Col.: Westview Press, 1994), pp. 1–14; and various contributions to Frederic Wakeman, Jr. and Richard Louis Edmonds, eds, *Reappraising Republican China* (Oxford: Oxford University Press, 2000).

5 The preceding overview of developments in Chinese studies is one that will strike some specialists as idiosyncratic. It may be useful, therefore, to point the reader to significant alternative views of the situation, beginning with a pair of stimulating essays by two prominent historians of twentieth-century China: Arif Dirlik, "Reversals, Ironies, Hegemonies: Notes on the Contemporary Historiography of Modern China," *Modern China*, vol. 22 (July 1996), pp. 243–284; and John Fitzgerald, "In the Scales of History: Politics and Culture in Twentieth Century China," *Twentieth-Century China*, vol. 24, no. 2 (April 1999), pp. 1–28. Another significant alternative account, co-written by a leading anthropologist and a leading specialist in the history of imperialism, is Judith Farquhar and James L. Hevia, "Culture and Post-war American Historiography of China," *positions: east asian cultures critique*, vol. 1, no. 2 (1993), pp. 486–525.

6 One sign of this interest is that in October 2000, the Historical Society for 20th Century China, an international organization of scholars, held a conference in Canada devoted exclusively to the theme of "Bridging 1949: Historical Continuity in 20th Century China." For details on the conference and the organization, see http://www.lcsc.edu/hstc

7 My selection of topics is inspired in part by comments made by Fitzgerald in his "In the Scales of History" and the symposium organized around that essay. In addition to his piece, see the responses to it by Prasenjit Duara, William Kirby and others published in the same April 1999 issue of *Twentieth-Century China*.

8 Exemplary recent works on ethnicity, legal history and business history, the footnotes from which will easily lead readers to other relevant works, are: Emily Honig, *Creating Chinese Ethnicity* (New Haven: Yale University Press, 1992); Louisa Schein, *Minority Rules: The Miao and the Feminine in China's Cultural Politics* (Durham, NC.: Duke University Press, 2000); Kathryn Bernhardt and Philip C. C. Huang, eds, *Civil Law in Qing and Republican China* (Stanford: Stanford University Press, 1994); and Sherman Cochran, ed., *Inventing Nanjing Road: Commercial Culture in Shanghai, 1900–1945* (Ithaca, N.Y.: Cornell East Asia Series, 1999). For a sense of how moves to rethink Taiwan's place within "Chinese history" may come to reshape discussion of major twentieth-century events in the ROC on Taiwan, see http://www.sinica.edu.tw/as/intro/ith.html. This website describes the development of

an Institute on Taiwan History at the prestigious Academia Sinica. I am grateful to my colleague Lynn Struve for drawing my attention to the growing importance of this subject, which has been given a dramatic push by political changes in Taiwan.

9 Joan W. Scott's "Gender: A Category of Historical Significance" first appeared in the *American Historical Review*, vol. 91, no. 5 (December 1986), and has been reprinted in several places, including in Scott's own *Gender and the Politics of History* (New York: Columbia University Press, 1988), pp. 28–50. Two very recent works that address the impact of feminism on Chinese studies are Xueping Zhong, Wang Zheng, and Bai Di, eds, *Some of Us: Chinese Women Growing up in the Mao Era* (London: Rutgers University Press, 2001); and Susan Brownell and Jeffrey N. Wasserstrom, eds, *Chinese Femininities/Chinese Masculinities: A Reader* (Berkeley: University of California Press, 2002). See also important earlier collections such as Christina Gilmartin *et al.*, eds, *Engendering China: Women, Culture and the State* (Cambridge: Harvard University Press, 1994), Tani Barlow, ed., *Gender Politics in Modern China: Writing and Feminism* (Durham, N.C.: Duke University Press, 1993), and Marilyn B. Young, ed., *Women in China* (Ann Arbor: University of Michigan Center for Chinese Studies, 1973). For valuable narrative overviews of broad sweeps of Chinese history that place feminist concerns at the center, see Ono Kazuko, *Chinese Women in a Century of Revolution, 1850–1950* (Stanford: Stanford University Press, 1989), English-language edition edited by Joshua A. Fogel, and Elizabeth Croll, *Socialism and Feminism in China* (London: Routledge, 1978). And for an excellent review of debates in the 1980s over the Chinese Communist Party's policies toward women – debates to which anthropologists (Margery Wolf) and sociologists (Judith Stacey) as well as historians (Patricia Stranahan, among others) contributed, see Emily Honig, "Socialist Revolution and Women's Liberation in China – A Review Article," *Journal of Asian Studies*, vol. 44, no. 2 (1985), pp. 329–336.

10 An important work that brings together essays on nationalism written from different disciplinary and topical perspectives is Jon Unger, ed., *Chinese Nationalism* (Armonk, N.Y.: M. E. Sharpe, 1996). Major recent single-author books on the subject include John Fitzgerald, *Awakening China: Politics, Culture, and Class in the Chinese Revolution* (Stanford: Stanford University Press, 1996); Prasenjit Duara, *Rescuing History from the Nation: Questioning Narratives of Modern China* (Chicago: University of Chicago Press, 1995); Henrietta Harrison, *The Making of the Republican Citizen: Political Ceremonies and Symbols in China, 1911–29* (Oxford: Oxford University Press, 2000); Dru Gladney, *Muslim Chinese: Ethnic Nationalism in the People's Republic* (Cambridge, Mass.: Harvard University Press, 1996); Rebecca Karl, *Staging the World: Chinese Nationalism at the Turn of the Twentieth Century* (Durham, N.C.: Duke University Press, 2002); and S. A. Smith, *Like Cattle and Horses: Nationalism and Labor in Shanghai, 1895–1927* (Durham, N.C.: Duke University Press, 2002).

11 See, for a somewhat differently framed presentation of this point, William C. Kirby, "The Nationalist Regime and the Chinese Party-State, 1928–1958," in Merle Goldman and Andrew Gordon, eds, *Historical Perspectives on Contemporary East Asia* (Cambridge, Mass.: Harvard University Press, 2000), pp. 211–237.

12 Two of the best general introductions to the events of China's recent past are Jonathan D. Spence, *The Search for Modern China*, second edition (New York: Norton, 1999) and R. Keith Schoppa, *Revolution and Its Past: Identities and Change in Modern Chinese History* (Upper Saddle River, N.J.: Prentice Hall, 2002). For overviews of specific blocks of time, see the chapters by Mary B.

Rankin, Ernest P. Young and others in Goldman and Gordon, *Historical Perspectives on Contemporary East Asia*.

13 Zhong *et al.*, *Some of Us*, contains a series of autobiographically driven essays that make related points clearly and well.

14 Duara, *Rescuing History from the Nation*.

15 A masterful introduction to this literature is Frederic E. Wakeman, Jr., "Rebellion and Revolution: The Study of Popular Movements in Chinese History," *Journal of Asian Studies*, vol. 36, no. 2 (1977), pp. 301–327. See also such landmark works of the time as Jean Chesneaux, ed., *Popular Movements and Secret Societies in China, 1840–1950* (Stanford: Stanford University Press, 1972); Philip A. Kuhn, *Rebellion and Its Enemies in Late Imperial China: Militarization and Social Structure, 1796–1864* (Cambridge, Mass.: Harvard University Press, 1970); and Elizabeth J. Perry, *Rebels and Revolutionaries in North China, 1845–1949* (Stanford: Stanford University Press, 1980). An important review of the literature that picks up where Wakeman left off is Stephen C. Averill, "The Chinese Revolution Reevaluated," *Problems of Communism* (January–February 1989), pp. 76–84. It should be noted that there were also important early works on social history that focused on patterns of ordinary daily life as opposed to rebellion; for example, Jonathan D. Spence, *The Death of Woman Wang* (New York: Viking, 1978). And there were works that looked at elites as opposed to disadvantaged groups, for example, Joseph W. Esherick and Mary B. Rankin, eds, *Chinese Local Elites and Patterns of Dominance* (Berkeley: University of California Press, 1990), Parks Coble, *The Shanghai Capitalists and the Nationalist Government 1927–1937* (Cambridge, Mass.: Harvard University Press, 1980), and Christian Henriot, *Shanghai, 1927–1937: Municipal Power, Locality, and Modernization* (Berkeley: University of California Press, 1993).

16 See, for example, David Johnson *et al.*, eds, *Popular Culture in Late Imperial China* (Berkeley: University of California Press, 1985); and Perry Link *et al.*, eds, *Unofficial China: Popular Culture and Thought in the People's Republic* (Boulder, Col.: Westview Press, 1989). The line between the New Social History and the New Cultural History has never been a clear one, in part because they share some of the same foundational texts. E. P. Thompson's *The Making of the English Working Class* (London: Gollancz, 1963) and Natalie Davis's *Society and Culture in Early Modern France* (Stanford: Stanford University Press, 1975) are among the most important examples. In Chinese studies, the line has often been blurred most when it comes to local histories that focus on individual villages (or sets of villages in a particular part of the country) and individual cities. Some examples of blurred genre works in urban studies are David Strand, *Rickshaw Beijing* (Berkeley: University of California Press, 1989) and Gail Hershatter, *The Workers of Tianjin, 1900–1949* (Stanford: Stanford University Press, 1986), each of which may be mainly social historical in approach but is by an author concerned with issues of representation and ritual. See also various contributions to Frederic E. Wakeman, Jr. and Yeh Wen-hsin, eds, *Shanghai Sojourners* (Berkeley: Institute of East Asian Studies, 1992) and Joseph W. Esherick, ed., *Remaking the Chinese City: Modernity and National Identity, 1900–1950* (Honolulu: University of Hawaii Press, 1999). Important works on the countryside that show the influence of trends in both social and cultural history include Prasenjit Duara, *Culture, Power, and the State: Rural North China, 1900–1942* (Stanford: Stanford University Press, 1988) and Edward Friedman, Paul G. Pickowicz, and Mark Selden, with Kay Ann Johnson, *Chinese Village, Socialist State* (New Haven: Yale University Press, 1991).

17 An excellent introduction to the complexities of the Cultural Revolution decade, which focuses on its first years (1966–1969), is Michael Schoenhals, ed., *China's Cultural Revolution: Not a Dinner Party* (Armonk, N.Y.: M. E. Sharpe, 1996). Nearly everything about the Cultural Revolution remains under dispute among scholars, including even the question of whether it lasted three or ten years.

18 On Furet's influence and related matters, see an earlier contribution to the *Rewriting Histories* series, Gary Kates, ed., *The French Revolution: Recent Debates and New Controversies* (London: Routledge, 1997).

19 Many China specialists other than those represented in this volume have turned their attention to discursive issues in recent years. See, for example, David Apter and Tony Saich, *Revolutionary Discourse in Mao's Republic* (Cambridge, Mass.: Harvard University Press, 1994); Rudolf Wagner, "Political Institutions, Discourse, and Imagination in China at Tiananmen," in Jon Manor, ed., *Rethinking Third World Politics* (London: Longman, 1991), pp. 121–144; Michael Schoenhals, *Doing Things with Words in Chinese Politics* (Berkeley: Institute of East Asian Studies, 1992); and Frank Dikötter, *The Discourse of Race in Modern China* (Stanford: Stanford University Press, 1992).

20 Early works on Tiananmen are cited in that chapter, but readers should be alerted to two important works that appeared several years after its publication: Timothy Brook, *Quelling the People: The Military Suppression of the Beijing Democracy Movement* (Stanford: Stanford University Press, 1998), and Craig Calhoun, *Neither Gods nor Emperors: Students and the Struggle for Democracy in China* (Berkeley: University of California Press, 1997).

21 Though I argue here for a Chinese twentieth century of roughly one hundred years, I have contributed to a world history textbook that posits a global twentieth century that was several decades longer. See Choi Chatterjee, Jeffrey L. Gould, Phyllis M. Martin, James C. Riley, and Jeffrey N. Wasserstrom, *The 20th Century: A Retrospective* (Boulder, Col.: Westview Press, 2002).

22 Graham Hutchings, *Modern China: A Guide to a Century of Change* (Cambridge, Mass.: Harvard University Press, 2001), p. 1.

23 The two most important books on the Boxers are Paul A. Cohen, *History in Three Keys: The Boxers as Event, Experience, and Myth* (New York: Columbia University Press, 1997); and Joseph W. Esherick, *The Origins of the Boxer Uprising* (Berkeley: University of California Press, 1987). See also Mark Elvin, "Mandarins and Millenarians: Reflections on the Boxer Uprising of 1899–1900," which is reprinted in Elvin's stimulating and wide-ranging collection, *Another History: Essays on China from a European Perspective* (Sydney: Wild Peony, 1996), pp. 197–226.

24 On the suppression of the Boxers, see James L. Hevia, "Leaving a Brand on China: Missionary Discourse in the Wake of the Boxer Movement," *Modern China*, vol. 18, no. 3 (1992), pp. 304–332; Robert Bickers, "Chinese Burns: Britain in China, 1842–1900," *History Today* (August 2000); and Henrietta Harrison, "Justice on Behalf of Heaven," *History Today* (September 2000). My understanding of the Boxers was greatly enriched by the papers I heard presented, by scholars from many different parts of the world, at the conference on "1900: The Boxers, China, and the World," which was held at the School for Oriental and African Studies in London, June 22–24, 2001.

25 On the flow of terms between China and Japan, see Lydia Liu, *Translingual Practice: Literature, Culture, and Translated Modernity China, 1900–1937* (Stanford: Stanford University Press, 1995).

26 On Sun Yat-sen's career and political views, see Marie-Claire Bergère's superb recent biography (translated by Janet Lloyd), *Sun Yat-sen* (Stanford: Stanford

University Press, 1998). On the reformer/revolutionary distinction (and instances in which it blurred early in the century), see Joan Judge, *Print and Politics: "Shibao" and the Culture of Reform in Late Qing China* (Stanford: Stanford University Press, 1996). And for the 1911 Revolution in general, the best starting point remains Mary C. Wright, ed., *China in Revolution: The First Phase* (New Haven: Yale University Press, 1968), but see also Eto Shinkichi and Harold Z. Schiffrin, eds, *The 1911 Revolution in China* (Tokyo: University of Tokyo Press, 1984). For the legend of Sun seeing the Japanese report on his activities as constituting a struggle for *geming*, see Don C. Price, *Russia and the Roots of the Chinese Revolution, 1896–1911* (Cambridge, Mass.: Harvard University Press, 1974), p. 91. I am grateful to Katherine Edgerton for research assistance on the history of the term *geming*, as well as for allowing me to incorporate findings here from an unpublished conference paper that we co-authored.

27 A carefully edited English-language rendition of this important text, which works very well in the classroom, is Tsou Jung [Zou Rong], *The Revolutionary Army: A Chinese Nationalist Tract of 1903*, translated by John Lust (The Hague: Mouton, 1968).

28 On this point and other related ones, see Liu Xiaobo, "That Holy Word, 'Revolution,'" in Wasserstrom and Perry, *Popular Protest and Political Culture*, pp. 309–324.

29 Liu, "That Holy Word, 'Revolution,'" and Li Zehou and Liu Zaifu, *Gaobie Geming [Farewell to Revolution]* (Hong Kong: Tiandi Tushu Ltd, 1995). See also, to place works such as these into historical and cultural context, various works by Geremie Barmé. Of particular value are his wide-ranging collection of essays, *In the Red: On Contemporary Chinese Culture* (New York: Columbia University Press, 1999) and "The Revolution of Resistance," in Elizabeth J. Perry and Mark Selden, *Chinese Society: Change, Conflict, and Resistance* (London: Routledge, 1999), pp. 198–220. For more on Li and Liu's book, see Liu Qingfeng, "The Topography of Intellectual Culture in 1990s Mainland China: A Survey," in Gloria Davies, ed., *Voicing Concerns: Contemporary Chinese Critical Inquiry* (Lanham, Md.: Rowman and Littlefield, 2001), pp. 47–70. For a fascinating look at the transformations that another key term underwent over the course of the century, see the documents on *renquan* compiled (and well introduced and translated) in Stephen C. Angle and Marina Svensson, eds, *The Chinese Human Rights Reader* (Armonk, N.Y.: M. E. Sharpe, 2001).

30 On the anti-NATO protests, see Susan Brownell, "Gender and Nationalism," in Tyrene White, ed., *China Briefing 2000: The Continuing Transformation* (Armonk, N.Y.: M. E. Sharpe, 2000).

31 For a sense of the strange shifting in the discursive and actual ground of Chinese "Marxism" in the post-Mao era, a good place to start is Arif Dirlik and Maurice Meisner, eds, *Marxism and the Chinese Experience* (Armonk, N.Y.: M. E. Sharpe, 1989).

32 See, for efforts to push modernity back the furthest, Joshua A. Fogel, *Politics and Sinology: The Case of Naito Konan (1866–1934)* (Cambridge, Mass.: Harvard University Press, 1984), and Naito Torajiro, and Joshua A. Fogel, eds, *Naito Konan and the Development of the Conception of Modernity in Chinese History* (Armonk, N.Y.: M. E. Sharpe, 1984). An important recent work that argues for the idea that many aspects of modernity only made their mark on China much later is Leo Ou-fan Lee, *Shanghai Modern: The Flowering of a New Urban Culture in China, 1930–1945* (Cambridge, Mass.: Harvard University Press, 1999). Debates on modernity are touched on in a great many of the works cited in previous notes.

33 On the general issue of the distorting influence that Western categories can have on the study of countries outside of Europe and North America, see Dipesh Chakrabarty, *Provincializing Europe: Postcolonial Thought and Historical Difference* (Princeton: Princeton University Press, 2000). Important discussions of the topic that focus on China include R. Bin Wong, *China Transformed: Historical Change and the Limits of European Experience* (Ithaca, N.Y.: Cornell University Press, 1997); and Kenneth Pomeranz, *The Great Divergence: China, Europe, and the Making of the Modern World Economy* (Princeton: Princeton University Press, 2000).

34 In some cases, this will be obvious to those who read the notes carefully. One point worth stressing is that most of the edited volumes cited above contain chapters by scholars who are based in different parts of the world and/or were trained in different disciplines. For example, Wright, *China in Revolution*, has chapters by historians from Japan and Europe as well as the United States. Ito and Schiffrin, *The 1911 Revolution*, was an editorial collaboration between a scholar based in Japan and a scholar based in Israel, and had a contribution by Min Tu-ki, a leading Korean Sinologist. And Unger, *Chinese Nationalism*, was edited by a sociologist who is from the United States but is now based in Australia and, along with chapters by historians and political scientists from various places, has a piece by a scholar affiliated with the Institute of Ethnology in Taiwan (Allen Chun). Two countries where good work has been done on China, but you would not necessarily know it from the notes so far, are Denmark and Canada. Sample impressive works from these two countries, respectively, are: Soren Clausen and Stig Thogersen, eds, *The Making of a Chinese City: History and Historiography in Harbin* (Armonk, N.Y.: M. E. Sharpe, 1995), which explores to good effect the way that officially endorsed scholarship in the PRC can skew visions of a city; and Alexander Woodside, "Emperors and the Chinese Political System," in Kenneth Lieberthal *et al.*, eds, *Perspectives on Modern China: Four Anniversaries* (Armonk, N.Y.. M. E. Sharpe, 1991), pp. 5–30, an excellent introduction to patterns of dynastic rule up to and including the late Qing.

35 Consider, for example, "The Language of Liberation," which was written by a British China specialist (Evans) who refers to the impact that ongoing conversations with PRC colleagues had on her thinking. That essay was first presented at a Swedish workshop linked to an interdisciplinary project on "Keywords of the Chinese Revolution" that was funded primarily by the National Endowment for the Humanities (based in Washington), with additional support from the Pacific Cultural Foundation (of Taibei). That project produced a working paper series that included essays by Sinologists based in Sweden (Michael Schoenhals) and Germany (Barbara Mittler), a linguist based in Taiwan (Jennifer Wei), a literary critic originally from the PRC (Wang Youqin), an American sociologist (Carolyn Hsu), and so on. I should mention, in the spirit of disclosure, that I was the director of the project and one of two co-editors, the other being folklorist Sue M. C. Tuohy, of the working papers. Full-text versions of many of those working papers can be found at http://www.indiana.edu/~easc/pages/easc/working_papers/default.htm.

Part I

THE SHAPE OF A CENTURY

2

REFLECTIONS ON A
WATERSHED DATE

The 1949 divide in Chinese history

Paul A. Cohen

In 1949, after a protracted civil war (1945–1949) with its Nationalist rivals, the CCP took control of the country. Mao Zedong announced the founding of a new nation, a People's Republic of China, and declared that the Revolution begun in 1911 had entered a completely new phase. Until that point, he claimed, vestiges of the old order, indeed of "feudalism," had managed to survive and lead the revolutionary cause astray; now they would not. His rhetoric, and that of other CCP leaders, was filled with images of rupture, and references to a "New China" being born in 1949 saturated the mass media, showing up in the names of magazines, the headlines of newspaper stories, the slogans on political posters, and so on. This sense of 1949 as a year of transformation was buttressed by developments outside of the Chinese mainland. After all, the Nationalists also insisted that it was a moment of total change – but change for the worse. And Western and Soviet Cold War visions of the world, as Paul A. Cohen points out below, reinforced still further the notion that 1949 was not just a watershed like many others. By the 1970s, it was habitual for textbooks either to stop at 1949, treating all that came later as a kind of postscript, or to begin there, with just a brief look backward to provide the necessary foundation. And historians rarely ventured across the 1949 divide, except in settings (France and Germany, for example) where there were so few China specialists that they were expected to write about many periods.

This situation began to change in the 1990s as many historians started to rethink the notion that 1949 was a year when Old China died and New China was born. One of many reasons for this was simply that in suppressing the popular protests that rocked scores of Chinese cities in 1989, the now forty-year-old CCP regime behaved in ways that resembled closely those of earlier power-holders threatened by mass unrest. Another was that, in moving away from a command economy, the Communist regime no longer seemed so radically different from its predecessors in terms of economic policies. This chapter began as a comment presented during a 1994 conference on "China's Mid-Century Transitions: Continuity and Change on the Mainland and on Taiwan, 1946–1955" that was held at Harvard. (That gathering was co-organized by one of the aforementioned French Sinologists who had long been accustomed to traversing the 1949 divide: Marie-Claire Bergère.) For Cohen, however, the idea that there were linkages as well as ruptures to keep in mind as one moved forward through China's twentieth century was hardly a new one when he spoke at Harvard. His interest in the subject predated by at least six years that gathering and by at least one year the upheavals associated with the term "Tiananmen." In 1988, as he notes at the beginning of this essay (which he updated in 1998 with inclusion in this volume in mind), he had published an important article that highlighted various parallels between reforms instituted in the 1980s and in several pre-Communist periods. This chapter extends substantially the scope of that 1988 effort to rethink the 1949 barrier.

* * *

Ten years ago I published an article entitled "The Post-Mao Reforms in Historical Perspective," one purpose of which was, as I framed it at the time, "to break through the '1949' barrier"[1] in recent Chinese history. This barrier had a sociological dimension as well as a temporal one. Different people, for the most part, studied the pre- and post-1949 periods. They asked different questions, relied on different kinds of source materials, read different books, and as often as not attended different conferences. Temporally, the 1949 barrier was reflected in the general tendency of social scientists to view developments in post-1949 China from a systemic perspective rather than a historical one. Their preference was to understand the reform process of the Deng years, for example, as unfolding within a particular kind of social, economic, and political system and to infer from other reform attempts in comparable systems something about the course the Chinese reforms were likely to take. What had happened in Chinese history prior to 1949 was not relevant.

In my article I attempted to look at the Deng-era reforms from a historical rather than a systemic perspective. Although not discounting the important changes that had taken place in China with the advent of Communist rule, I put a good deal of emphasis on certain broad patterns that could be discerned in the reform process from the late nineteenth century on into the period of Deng Xiaoping's ascendancy. The year 1949, from this perspective, certainly did not disappear. But its meaning shifted perceptibly, becoming increasingly complicated and ambiguous.

In the present essay I want to take another look at 1949, this time from a somewhat broader perspective. I will start out by touching on certain aspects of the issue of continuity versus discontinuity, as it bears on the 1949 divide; then I will explore some of the factors that I believe contributed to the original construction of this divide in our minds; finally, I will suggest that it has been the weakening of these very factors in recent years that, more than anything else, has resulted in the more complex understanding of 1949 that we have today.[2]

1949: Continuity versus discontinuity

One tangled aspect of the continuity–discontinuity issue, as it surfaces in 1949, is the whole question of how it relates to the revolution that was supposed to have taken place in that year. If there was indeed a revolution – the ultimate discontinuity – how do we square this with the very substantial continuities growing numbers of scholars have discerned between pre- and post-1949 China? If, on the other hand, there wasn't a revolution, what did happen in 1949? How do we identify and label the very great changes that unquestionably occurred as a direct or indirect result of the Communists' coming to power?

One way of cutting through this tangle is to reframe the problem. Instead of asking *whether* a revolution took place in (and after) 1949, it may make more sense to ask what *kind* of revolution – or revolutions – occurred. Certainly, if we look at some of the more radical social changes that accompanied the Communist rise to power – the physical elimination of the landlord and rich peasant classes in the countryside or, in urban China, the severe reduction in the freedom of intellectuals, and of professional and managerial elements, to operate and express themselves socially and culturally[3] – or the transformative experiences of the period from the late 1950s until the mid-1970s – above all, the Great Leap Forward and the Cultural Revolution – we can talk of a specifically *Communist* or *Marxist-Leninist* or *Maoist* revolution. But many of the most dramatic and far-reaching changes that occurred in the first years of Communist rule represented the realization of what I would call a consensual Chinese agenda. That is, they were changes that would have been supported by the Guomindang – and even in some instances the rulers of the late Qing – as well as the Communists.

Among the changes I have in mind are the following: the complete elimination of the last remnants of foreign imperialism and the reestablishment of full central government control over Chinese territory after over a hundred years of partially curtailed sovereignty; the greatly enhanced capacity of the central government to gain control (through the elimination of middlemen) of revenues extracted from the farming sector;[4] the reestablishment of domestic peace after decades of civil and foreign warfare; the more than doubling of the size of the work force; the rapid extension of education and consequently of literacy at all levels; the dramatic improvement in public health; and, partly owing to this last change, a rapid growth in population.

These were changes of major import. In their impact on the lives of hundreds of millions of Chinese people, they were without question revolutionary. But, although brought about by the Communists and certainly viewed by Mao and his colleagues as part of their revolutionary program, they did not really constitute a "Communist" revolution in any substantive sense. Add to the revolutionary changes of the early 1950s the enormous forces of change unleashed in the post-Mao era, starting in the late 1970s – changes that overturned some of the most striking innovations of the Mao years – and arguably we are presented with yet another revolution – this one in certain respects more a continuation of developments that had their beginnings *prior* to 1949 than of developments that came out of the 1949–1976 period (the years of Mao's rule). So, one point I would make, although it is somewhat awkward-sounding, is that in the years after 1949 China experienced not just one revolution but a number of different revolutions, partly overlapping and partly in conflict with one another.

Let me return to the notion of a "consensual Chinese agenda." I take this phrase to embrace, in its broadest sense, not only a set of *goals* that most Chinese, regardless of political affiliation, would support (such as the elimination of imperialism or the establishment of domestic peace and stability), but also certain *means, methods,* or *instrumental strategies* that Chinese of differing political commitments would agree were natural and appropriate for the realization of specified goals. So far so good. The trouble is that the consensus that exists with respect to such goals on a fairly high level of abstraction or generality often breaks down when the focus shifts to the specific content of the goals to be realized. *Formal continuity*, in such situations, may well coexist with *substantive discontinuity*.

David Wang, for example, says that "For all the ideological antagonism between the two regimes, one finds striking similarities in Nationalist and Communist ways of administering literary activities." Among both Nationalists and Communists there was substantial consensus that it was right and proper for the state to exercise control in the realm of literary production and distribution. But there was a complete lack of consensus after 1949 concerning the *contents* of the literature to be permitted: Communist writers celebrating the Communist victory in the Civil War and the huge changes that had taken place in China in the aftermath of that victory, Guomindang writers embracing one or another form of anti-Communist stance, including the notion that 1949 signaled the loss of the Chinese mainland to foreign – that is, Soviet – control.[5]

Essentially the same point has been made with respect to the film industry. On the level of specific content, important shifts took place from the late 1940s to the early 1950s. But on a more formal level, we can identify a continuity of some importance, namely, the state's assumption that the film industry needed to be placed under a greater or lesser degree of control – greater in the case of the Communists, lesser in that of the Guomindang – to ensure, at the very least, that films would not contain content that opposed or undermined government policy.[6]

Another factor complicating our efforts to plumb the meaning of 1949 is that, as suggested earlier, some fairly sharp discontinuities characterizing the periods immediately prior to and after this year were substantially moderated, if not completely reversed, in the post-Mao era, so that by the late 1980s one can point to important continuities – or at least resonances – with the period of Guomindang rule, in particular the 1930s. One clear example of this is the relationship between foreign influences and freedom, on one hand, and foreign influences and control, on the other, as it affected scientific and technical personnel, artists, students, and other social groups. In the case of the student community, for example, foreign influences were a source of liberation and empowerment in both the 1930s and the 1980s, insofar as they opened the minds of young Chinese to new worlds of experience. But in both decades they also created a line of tension and potential conflict between students and the government, exposing the former to frequently shrill, uncomprehending criticism from the latter. The government's periodic lashing out against such expressions of "spiritual pollution" as rock and roll in the 1980s was a clear echo of criticisms of Western popular culture leveled in the 1930s, when Minister of Education Chen Lifu warned sinisterly that "Hollywood films lay traps of decadence" and the head of the Board of Education of Shanghai stigmatized imported movies as "propaganda pieces of American commercial culture!"[7]

In both the 1930s and the 1980s there was also competition between officials and students over who had the greater standing to speak on behalf of nation and society. And there were tensions between a *modernization* that was collective in orientation and focused above all on the achievement of greater wealth and power for the nation – something both a Chiang Kai-shek and a Deng Xiaoping could support – and a *modernism* centered on individual liberation and creative freedom, which both Chiang and Deng felt distinctly uncomfortable about and periodically lashed out against. In the broadest sense all of these resonances had to do with conflictual interaction between the state and one or another sector of society, thus pointing to larger issues of state–society relations that plagued China in the 1930s and continued to plague it in the 1980s and on into the 1990s.

Apart from such resonances between decades separated by a half-century, the 1980s also witnessed the *reappearance* of a variety of phenomena that had existed in one form or another up to 1949 and then been eradicated in the immediate post-1949 era: rich peasants, entrepreneurs, prostitution, links between home places within China (*guxiang*) and regional associations (*tongxianghui*) overseas, American influence on Chinese higher education, and so on. We have to be careful, however, not to think of such phenomena as continuities or even, strictly speaking, revivals. Labels can be highly misleading. To understand any social class – or for that matter any historical phenomenon – in any period, we need to look at it in the context of the reality in which it is embedded in that time period. When the multifaceted ties between overseas Chinese and their native places, which had been sundered by the Communists after 1949, were revived in the 1980s, the terminology describing these ties remained the same. But there were significant substantive differences from the pre-1949 period, the most conspicuous being the unprecedented efforts of mainland authorities at all levels in the 1980s to put overseas Chinese talent and wealth to work in support of China's new development plans.[8] Similarly, my guess is that if we were to conduct a serious study of rich peasants, prostitutes, or entrepreneurs in the 1940s and the 1980s, we would find that there were enormous differences between the two periods, masked to some extent by the shared vocabulary with which we refer to them.

Historical sources of the 1949 divide

If there have in fact been significant continuities, resonances, and points of correspondence between aspects of Chinese life that predated and postdated 1949, how did the sense of 1949 as a total break, a complete rupture in historical time, come into existence in the first place? Among Western academics, this sense of stark discontinuity was a consequence of several factors. One – and this was perhaps the most important factor – was the master narrative the Chinese Communists themselves constructed to define the meaning of 1949. This master narrative was superimposed on the changes that had actually taken place as a result of the Communist victory in the Civil War; and, increasingly, as memories dimmed, it shaped and simplified (if it did not entirely displace) these real changes in people's minds. As everyone who went to China in the 1970s and asked people to tell their life stories will recall, the 1949 break (framed as "before liberation" and "after liberation") was, in popular rhetoric, absolutely fundamental.[9] It established the line between darkness and light, between suffering and joy, between oppression and empowerment, the transition from the first to the second term in each case being framed as a precious gift from "our beloved savior Chairman Mao" and the Communist Party that embodied his will and every wish. This master narrative, highlighting the profound dichotomy between the pre-1949 and post-1949 Chinese worlds, was arguably the principal foundation-stone on which the legitimacy of the Chinese party-state existed after 1949. The Chinese leadership therefore had a powerful vested interest in its perpetuation, regardless of the changes that did or did not occur in fact. In time, the notion of 1949 as a profound divide in historical time became an important component of Chinese consciousness and, as such, a very real factor influencing Chinese thinking and behavior, with little or no concern evinced for the degree to which its content was mythic.[10]

Western academics, especially perhaps American social scientists, also developed a strong vested interest in 1949 as a major historical divide. The reasons, however, were quite different from those governing Chinese Communist thinking. Initially, it is well to keep in mind, there wasn't much post-1949 China to deal with in any case; also, as of mid-century, the number of social scientists specializing in China was extremely small. Moreover, even when such persons began to emerge as a significant academic force in the 1960s, we find that for some time they paid little attention to developments prior to 1949; indeed, precious few of them were equipped by training to do research of any sort on the Republican era. Another way of putting this, to elaborate on a point made earlier, is that the initial crop of social scientists was taught to approach societies as systems. Inasmuch as Communist societies were a particular variety of system, their natural tendency was to study them comparatively, looking at the features any given

Communist society shared with other such societies. Since 1949 was the inaugural year of the Communist system in China, the idea of this year as a decisive break, a new beginning, was greatly reinforced. It was further magnified, as we have seen, by the fact that the post-1949 period tended, until fairly recently, to be almost exclusively the preserve of social scientists, while historians concentrated their labors on the period prior to this date.

The Cold War, by greatly inflating the importance of communism and by crudely mythologizing the distinction between the "communist" and the "free" worlds, created yet another vested interest in the concept of 1949 as radical break. The one change that took place in 1949 that no one seriously contests – that the Communists came to power on the Chinese mainland and the Guomindang retreated to Taiwan – was defined by Cold Warriors as the most significant event by far of all the events that may or may not have taken place in that year. To suggest anything else was to imply that communism was not the evil monster Cold Warriors said it was, thereby laying oneself open to the charge of being soft on it, which in the United States and Taiwan in the Cold War years was a dangerous thing to be accused of. Since neither the Chinese world nor the Western academic world existed in isolation from the Cold War environment, this environment had the effect of reinforcing the importance already attached for other reasons to the 1949 divide in these worlds.

Conclusion

In recent years all of these sources of a powerful and historically decisive 1949 divide have undergone significant change. The Chinese Communist master narrative focusing on the profound contrast between the bad old society that existed before 1949 and the good new society that came into being after this date has by no means disappeared. It may still be found in official and officially inspired rhetoric. But its influence on Chinese consciousness has weakened palpably since the late 1970s, partly owing to the emergence in intellectual circles of a more affirmative stance toward aspects of the pre-1949 past and the dramatic resurgence at the popular level of a whole range of older beliefs and practices that an earlier generation of Communists had attempted to stamp out, and partly resulting from the open criticism of major phases of the Maoist era that, beginning in the late 1970s, it became possible to articulate.

The sociology of Western scholarship has also undergone major changes during the past decade or two. As the period or post-1949 Chinese history has expanded (it is now a full half-century long), social scientists, even those with minimal training in pre-1949 China, have been forced to think in more historical terms. Meanwhile, newer generations of social scientists have emerged that include individuals with a significantly stronger historical foundation and the ability to carry on research in pre-1949 materials. For their part, historians of twentieth-century China have, with the augmented heft of the post-1949 era, become increasingly unwilling to allow social scientists to exercise monopolistic rights over it. These changes together have resulted in growing intellectual cross-fertilization between historians and social scientists, one consequence of which has been an increased disposition on the part of the latter to see 1949 in less starkly dichotomous terms.

Finally, the break-up of the Soviet Union and the collapse of East European communism, by bringing an abrupt end to the Cold War, removed the most powerful ideological support of the notion of 1949 as simple discontinuity – a shift that has, if anything, been reinforced by the increasingly "uncommunist" look of many aspects of Chinese life during the Deng and post-Deng years.

This retreat or eclipsing of forces that in an earlier time magnified the salience of 1949 has clearly encouraged the tendency of recent years to reduce its importance as a historical breach. There is a temptation, in these circumstances, to turn complete discontinuity into complete continuity, or to substitute for the concept of a revolution that changed everything the equally unpersuasive concept of a revolution that changed nothing, that, indeed, wasn't a revolution at all. This would be bad history. The challenge, instead, is to develop a picture of 1949 that is adequately complex, certainly more complex than the one we had in the 1950s and 1960s. This picture should acknowledge and probe the ways in which 1949 did indeed signal abrupt and important change, as well as the ways in which it did not. It should analyze (as I attempted briefly in the first portion of this essay) the variety of ways in which historical processes can be continuous and discontinuous, sometimes at the same time. And it should also be sensitive to the degree to which the past is ever hostage to an unforeseen and unforeseeable future, with the consequence that events and dates that have a certain meaning or cluster of meanings at one moment in time at subsequent moments shed some of their earlier meanings and acquire new ones, their importance in the larger sweep of history undergoing a process of continual renegotiation, with results that are unpredictable and can sometimes be quite startling.

NOTES

1 *Journal of Asian Studies* 47.3 (August 1988): 519.
2 The ensuing reflections are loosely based on oral comments I made following a talk by Benjamin Schwartz at a conference, "China's Mid-Century Transitions: Continuity and Change on the Mainland and on Taiwan, 1946–1955," held at Harvard University, September 9–10, 1994.
3 On the situation of Chinese intellectuals in the 1950s and 1960s, see the work of Merle Goldman, especially her *Literary Dissent in Communist China* (Cambridge, Mass.: Harvard University Press, 1967), and her *China's Intellectuals: Advise*

and Dissent (Cambridge, Mass.: Harvard University Press, 1981). The plight of professional and managerial elements after 1949 is dealt with in Deborah S. Davis, "Social Class Transformation: Training, Hiring, and Promoting Urban Professionals and Managers after 1949," in Marie-Claire Bergère and William Kirby, eds, *China's Mid-Century Transitions: Continuity and Change on the Mainland and on Taiwan, 1945–1955* (Cambridge, Mass.: Harvard University Press, forthcoming).

4 This point is emphasized in Philip A. Kuhn, "Maoist Agriculture and the Old Regime," in ibid.

5 David Der-wei Wang, "Reinventing National History: Communist and Anti-Communist Fiction from 1946 to 1955," in ibid. Some would argue that, even at the instrumental level, although there were similarities, the literary policies of the Communists and the Guomindang after 1949 were hardly identical, much more creative freedom being permitted to writers on Taiwan than to those on the mainland.

6 See the unpublished paper of Corinne Cabusset, "Film Industry and Artists in the Process of Transition to Communism, 1948–1953," presented at the conference on "China's Mid-Century Transitions."

7 Wen-hsin Yeh, *The Alienated Academy: Culture and Politics in Republican China, 1919–1937* (Cambridge, Mass.: Harvard Council on East Asian Studies, Harvard University, 1990), p. 192.

8 Elizabeth Sinn makes this point with specific reference to links with overseas Chinese in Hong Kong. See her "Xin Xi Guxiang: A Study of Regional Associations as a Bonding Mechanism in the Chinese Diaspora. The Hong Kong Experience," *Modern Asian Studies* 31.2 (1997): 375–397, especially 394–397.

9 For further discussion, along with specific examples, see Paul A. Cohen, *Report on the Visit of the Young Political Leaders Delegation to the People's Republic of China* (New York: National Committee on United States–China Relations, 1978), pp. 11–13.

10 For an analogous discussion of the meaning of the Opium Wars in Chinese consciousness, see Paul A. Cohen, *Discovering History in China: American Historical Writing on the Recent Chinese Past*, 2nd edn (New York: Columbia University Press, 1997), p. xiii.

3

TEN THESES ON THE CHINESE REVOLUTION[1]

Joseph W. Esherick

*The journal **Modern China**, which was founded in the 1970s, has long served as both a vehicle for the publication of new research, often by junior scholars who are still in graduate school or have just completed dissertations in fields ranging from sociology to literature, and a place for debate. Its founding and current editor (as I write this in early 2002) is Philip C. C. Huang, who has made important contributions as a writer to fields ranging from economic history to legal studies. In recent years, as an editor, he has been particularly active in putting together (and contributing to) symposia that take on big themes. Thus, for example, in 1993 **Modern China** published an oft-cited series of exchanges in which leading scholars in different fields argued with one another over whether concepts such as "Civil Society" and "Public Sphere" were helpful for making sense of or merely served to distort our understanding of China's past. Two years later, it published another important symposium that grew out of a U.C.L.A. workshop on "Rethinking the Chinese Revolution," in which Joseph W. Esherick was one of the participants. The chapter reprinted here was part of that January 1995 **Modern China** symposium that included other essays on China (such as a piece by Mark Selden on the role social policies played in attracting rural support for the CCP in the 1940s) and an article by French historian Edward Berenson. Berenson's essay, to which Esherick refers below, was intended to introduce China specialists to relevant trends in the study of 1789.*

*The place in which "Ten Theses on the Chinese Revolution" appeared is important to underscore, since it helps give non-specialists a better sense of its revisionist thrust. **Modern China** was, from its inception, thought of as a journal that was more readily disposed than were many other periodicals published in the Cold War-era West to focus on positive (as well as negative) aspects of the rise to power of the CCP. And, it should be noted, though **Modern China** sometimes published articles that were harshly critical of the CCP, even in the 1970s, Esherick's early works for that publication and others had not fallen into that category. Rather, near the very start of his career he had co-written a textbook (with Orville Schell) that presented the Revolution in a positive light overall. And he had written a much-*

discussed polemic that attacked mainstream American Sinologists for downplaying, as he saw it, the negative effects on China of Western imperialism. It would thus have been a jolt for someone who had only read **Modern China** *or the* **Bulletin** of **Concerned Asian Scholars** *(in which Esherick's polemic appeared) in the 1970s to come across his 1995 essay. After all, its Thesis II reads: "The Revolution was not a Liberation but (for most) was the replacement of one form of domination with another." Esherick's "Ten Theses" is not a complete reversal of his earlier positions but reflects the fact that, over time, he had certainly reconsidered many things. The Chinese Revolution simply no longer looked quite the same to him as it had in the 1960s and 1970s. One thing that had not changed, though, as readers will see below, was his readiness to state his opinions in a forceful and provocative way.*

* * *

The function of the historian is neither to love the past nor to emancipate himself from the past, but to master and understand it as the key to the understanding of the present.

E. H. Carr [1961: 29]

The twentieth century has been the century of revolution. Although the revolutionary model began with the eighteenth-century revolutions of North America and France, the nineteenth century was an era of failed revolution, and it was only in the current century that revolution swept the world – most notably in the revolutions of Mexico, Russia, Yugoslavia, China, Korea, Vietnam, and Cuba, but also in the national revolutions of Algeria, the Middle East, Indonesia, and much of Africa. Some would even subsume the radical changes brought by the Nazi and Fascist movements of Germany and Italy within the definition of "revolution" (Schoenbaum, 1966). Revolutions have reshaped the global environment and reordered the structures of daily life in this century (Arendt, 1963).

An enormous, useful, and insightful literature analyzes both the general phenomenon of revolution and the variety of specific national revolutionary movements. That literature provides an essential foundation for understanding the world in which we live. But as we approach the twenty-first century, we face a world in which, one after the other, revolutionary regimes are falling and revolutionary changes are being reversed. Gone are the revolutionary regimes of Russia, Yugoslavia, and Eastern Europe. Mexico is slowly dismantling the structures created by its revolution. Cuba waits only for Castro's death. China struggles to replace state socialism with a market economy while maintaining Communist Party dictatorship and the transparent fiction of revolutionary ideology. To all present appearances, the revolutionary era as we know it will end with the twentieth century. In this context, the narrative of revolutionary progress (and of progress through revolution) is no longer compelling. The revolutionized populations no longer accept its legitimacy. It is time to rethink revolution.

As Berenson's essay in this issue indicates, revolutions elsewhere – even the French Revolution, which inspired so many of our revolutionary models – are also undergoing radical reevaluation. My task in this essay is to suggest and provoke a rethinking of the Chinese Revolution, of the historical process that brought to power a revolutionary party that radically reshaped the Chinese polity, economy, and society. In the Chinese case, a rethinking is not only called for by world historical events, it is also facilitated by a wealth of new scholarship, an explosion of new materials on party history and the beginnings of access to archives and field work in the People's Republic of China (PRC). The ideas that follow have been inspired by this new scholarship and by my own archival and oral history research on the revolution in the Shaan-Gan-Ning border region. Although much of the argument here is derivative and even commonplace, the form I have chosen – ten theses – is designed to provoke debate. I subscribe to these theses with varying degrees of conviction. Some are old friends with whom I would be reluctant to part. Others are newer formulations, designed to fill out the logical structure and decimal integrity of this essay. All can be read as an autocritique of my own past thinking and writing on modern China. As a whole, I am striving for a reassessment of the revolution that acknowledges both the failings and the contingency of the revolution without reverting to the shibboleths of anti-Communist scholarship whose purpose is to deny all legitimacy to revolutionary change, and for an interpretation that recognizes the revolution's importance, but not necessarily its centrality, in China's modern history.

I. Guomindang rule was as much the precursor of the Chinese Revolution as its political enemy

Journalistic writing on China during the 1930s and 1940s by authors such as Edgar Snow (1961), Theodore White and Annalee Jacoby (1946), or Jack Belden (1949) and much of the scholarship of the 1950s and 1960s were shaped by the political context of life-and-death struggle between the Guomindang and the Chinese Communist Party (CCP). In that competition, each of the actors tended to paint its rival as a dialectical opposite. Much of the picture of the Guomindang era, even by judicious liberal scholars such as John Fairbank (1983 and earlier editions) and Lloyd Eastman (1974, 1984) is colored by the persuasive discourse of the Guomindang's leftist and progressive critics. The Guomindang is seen to be trapped in a conservative political culture, defending the forces of tradition, suppressing progressive intellectuals, and abandoning workers and peasants to their miserable fates. Its leaders were inspired by both fascism and Confucianism and opposed the democratic forces in China.

The problem with this picture is not that it is hostile to the Guomingdang; the historian is not obliged to sympathize with the object of his or her scholarship. The problem is its failure to take due account of important continuities between the Guomindang and the CCP. William Kirby's work on the National Resources Commission is an important example of continuity in economic planning in the pre- and post-1949 period (Kirby, 1984: chap. 4). One aspect of Prasenjit Duara's work is its focus on state building under the Guomindang and the unprecedented attacks on the "cultural nexus" of traditional values and religion (Duara, 1988). But there are many more examples that could be raised: the structures of Leninism in the Nationalist Party, the attempts at mass organization especially among youth (Wasserstrom, 1991), the establishment of a party-army, the use of censorship to control culture and the press, the establishment of a national system of education and significant advances (especially during the war) in using this system to mold a modern citizenry, and the appeal to science against "superstition" and to "Chinese national characteristics" against foreign efforts to impose Western standards on Chinese politics and society.

The CCP did not only rise to power as the dialectical opposite of the Guomindang. There were important points of unity in the dialectic – areas where the Guomindang paved the way for the Communists, where the latter built on the foundations laid by the former. Many activists joined both parties during the 1920s. Memories and friendships from that first Guomindang–CCP collaboration were never erased at the local level. Millions of Chinese rallied to the CCP during the war against Japan in part because the Communists seemed the proper heirs of the revolutionary anti-imperialism of Sun Zhongshan's (Sun Yat-sen) party during the 1920s – seemed better to embody the nationalist rhetoric of Guomindang propaganda and public school textbooks than did the Guomindang itself.

Corollary: 1949 was a watershed, not an unbridgeable chasm

A corollary to Thesis I is the need to break the 1949 barrier. Already the best scholars of modern China are doing this: Philip Huang (1985, 1990) on rural China, Elizabeth Perry (1993) on Shanghai strikes, Jeffrey Wasserstrom (1991) on student protests, Friedman, Pickowicz, and Selden (1991) in their *Chinese Village, Socialist State*. Fortunately, the time is past when historians worked on China before 1949 and political scientists and sociologists worked on the period since, neither attending the others' conferences or reading enough of the others' books. But we need to go further.

If we are really to understand the ways in which the PRC built on Guomindang foundations, we need to study specific continuities in models, discourse, and personnel. We need to understand both the magnitude of the social changes attempted in the PRC and the limits of the achievements in creating a wholly new socialist China. Topics in economics, popular culture, demography, gender relations, and political culture need to be studied across the 1949 barrier. The example of French historiography is instructive. When one turns to these areas of French history, the French Revolution looms a good deal less large; amid the significant political changes, there were important continuities in the daily lives of individual Frenchmen.

II. The revolution was not a Liberation but (for most) was the replacement of one form of domination with another

In rethinking the Chinese Revolution, we must rethink the analytical baggage that comes with the term *revolution*. As a historical metaphor, the term revolution has, since the French Revolution, been associated with *liberty* (Arendt, 1963: 25). Most Marxist historiography (which has been so important in shaping our understanding of revolutionary processes) has taken France as the original model for revolution (Furet, 1981: 81–9) and seen revolution as bringing *liberation* from the oppressive constraints of the old regime. The Chinese Communists themselves build on this implied meaning by calling their revolution a Liberation. Much of our own scholarship has accepted this conceptualization, as we have studied Chinese struggles for liberation from imperialist domination, peasants' and workers' struggles for freedom from landlords' exactions or employers' exploitation, and women's struggles to escape the bondage of patriarchy.

Whereas we should not deny that the revolution was fueled by the efforts of millions of Chinese actors to escape some form of oppression, we should also realize that there was probably an even greater number of Chinese who experienced the revolution as the replacement of one form of domination with another. Most Chinese did not experience the success of the revolution and the coming to power of the CCP as some form of personal liberation. It was a new world, in many respects, and for most it was a better world. But the PRC ushered in a better world in part because the CCP brought order and discipline to their environment, and this was probably as important to many as was any sense of liberation.

In the countryside, peasants demanded above all that the new regime be fair (*gongdao*), and the party made tremendous efforts in rectification campaigns to ensure that cadres not be guilty of favoritism, that they take the lead in making sacrifices, that they lead simple lives free of corruption, and that they ensure that the burdens of revolutionary struggle were borne equitably (Selden, 1971: chaps. 5–6; Chen Yung-fa, 1986: chap. 6; Madsen, 1984: chap. 3; Esherick, forthcoming). Thus peasants were highly approving of party efforts to force idlers and paupers (*erliuzi*) into productive work (Forman, 1945: 70; Keating, 1989: 188–9). When we consider that there was little to distinguish the Communist pauper policy from the poor houses of eighteenth-century England, it is difficult to see this as any sort of liberation of the poor. But the measures were welcomed because they were perceived as a discipline that was fair – idlers would have to work for an honest living like everyone else.

The importance of this principle is self-evident. Given the tight PRC controls over employment, residence, education, culture, political activity, and even biological reproduction, if one views the revolution as liberation, then one must view the postrevolutionary regime as a betrayal. Yet few Chinese saw it that way, and I would suggest that such a "betrayal" theory is ill-founded. It makes far more sense to recognize that the revolution was not so much a process of liberation as a process wherein a new structure of domination was created to do battle with, to defeat, and to replace another structure of domination. In this process, the Communists certainly empowered new actors and mobilized new social constituencies. They also broke down old structures of domination – eliminating, expelling, humiliating, and intimidating old elites. But those who escaped the domination of these old elites were not just liberated; they were also implicated in a revolutionary process, indebted to a revolutionary party, and subordinated to a new revolutionary regime.

III. Despite Mao's "Sinification of Marxism," the Soviet model of Lenin and Stalin exerted a powerful influence on the Chinese Revolution

Since the 1950s, it has been a staple of anti-Communist propaganda to portray the Chinese Revolution as the product of a Moscow-directed conspiracy (Chiang Kai-shek, 1957). In reaction to such propaganda and right-wing scholarship, the liberal and progressive conventional wisdom has been to stress the nationalism of the revolution and Mao Zedong's "Sinification of Marxism" (Schram, 1969; Schwartz, 1960). There is no questioning Mao's creative adaptations of Marxist thought, the original development of rural revolutionary model, the struggles of Mao and his cohorts against the "28 Bolsheviks" who adhered more closely to the Comintern's line, the importance of nationalism in the revolutionary movement, or the political independence of the CCP – an independence that ultimately produced the Sino-Soviet split of the 1960s. These aspects of the conventional wisdom are beyond dispute.

Nonetheless, recent scholarship suggests that Soviet influence on the CCP was greater than once thought. The role of Comintern agents in founding the party and guiding its early members out of their intellectual study societies and into revolutionary work in combination with the reorganized Guomindang is now well known and non-controversial. I would only revise the conventional wisdom by suggesting that, despite Stalin's mistakes in 1927, the net effect of Comintern advice was positive. Only the prodding of Comintern agents forced Chinese Communist intellectuals out of their Marxist study groups and into the work of organizing workers and peasants. Only the protective wing of its Guomindang ally allowed the CCP to grow from 100–250 members in June 1923 to more than 57,000 in April 1927 (van de Ven, 1991: 194). Especially in the interior, many Communists made important personal and political connections to local Guomindang leaders – contacts that would be revived to excellent effect during the war against Japan (Wou, 1994: 209, 289, 337). Whereas the White Terror of 1927 decimated the Communist Party, it also stained forever the Guomindang's reputation in progressive intellectual circles. The CCP's dramatic wartime revival would not have been possible without the stature it had acquired during the National Revolution of the 1920s.

Less well appreciated than the Comintern's role during the 1920s – and certainly obscured in official party histories – is Soviet influence during the

War of Resistance. The conventional history of this period stresses Mao's struggle with Wang Ming as the triumph of the Chinese Communist over the Soviet stooge. Little mentioned are the important roles of others who returned on the same plane with Wang Ming: Chen Yun and Kang Sheng. Kang Sheng's role in the rectification movement of the 1940s suggests that, as security chief, although he may have substituted Mao's injunction to "cure the sickness and save the patient" for a bloody Soviet-style purge, he was nonetheless quite adept at Stalinist political struggle. Later, Ren Bishi brought the Soviet system of ranks and privilege to the supply system that supported cadres in Yan'an (Chen Yung-fa, 1990, 1993).

My point is not to suggest that Yan'an became a little Moscow. It is merely to urge a reassessment of the Soviet influence on Chinese Communist practice during this period. We must not forget that Mao's first act on assuming leadership of the Long March at Zunyi was to dispatch Pan Hannian and Chen Yun to report to Moscow (Salisbury, 1985: 134–5), that Mao's key contribution to the first session of the critical Senior Cadres' Meetings of 1942–1943 was to rehearse (in a three-day speech) Stalin's twelve conditions for achieving Bolshevism (Seybolt, 1986: 53), that many of the key documents for study in the rectification movement were Stalinist tracts (Compton, 1966: x–xi, xxxix–xlvi), and that China is one of the few Communist states that defended Stalin's legacy after Khrushchev's secret speech of 1956. If we achieve a better appreciation of Soviet and Stalinist influences on CCP revolutionary practice, the systematic importation of the Soviet model during the 1950s looks much more logical. The degree to which so much of China's political, military, scientific, educational, and cultural apparatus continues to this day to follow the Soviet model becomes a good deal more understandable.

It should be possible to acknowledge Soviet influence without succumbing to silly cold war arguments that the CCP was a tool of Moscow. There is no questioning the fact that Mao, reacting against leftist mistakes made by Moscow-trained leaders in the Jiangxi Soviet, fought, in Yan'an, against the Internationalists' uncritical importation of "foreign models" from the Soviet Union. The evidence would seem to support Mao's claim that, during the civil war period, the CCP led the revolution to victory by acting contrary to Stalin's will. *Politically*, the CCP has certainly been an autonomous actor at least since 1935. But that political independence is not inconsistent with the notion that Mao and other CCP leaders would find the experience of the Soviet Union highly instructive, even essential, in their own search for a Chinese road to socialism (Goncharov, Lewis, and Xue Litai, 1993).

For the critical Yan'an period, I would suggest two important sources of Soviet influence. First, following the return of Wang Ming in 1937, Mao Zedong prepared himself for theoretical struggle with the Internationalists by engaging in the most intensive period of Marxist study in his life, and the texts studied were largely translations of standard Stalinist tracts on philosophy, political economy, and Bolshevik history (Fogel, 1987: 61–71; Schram, 1989: 61–5). Mao certainly did not absorb these texts uncritically, and the writings that emerged from this period of study managed to imbue Soviet Marxism with a distinct Chinese style. But there were certain products of this experience – a phrasing of problems in terms of "two-line struggle," an almost paranoid attitude toward the threat of Trotskyism, a concern for the leading role of cadres and the related commitment to seeing that cadres' thought and behavior be correct – that become enduring features of party life.

Second, there is the role, mentioned earlier, of key returnees from the Soviet Union who rather quickly signaled their adherence to Mao in his struggles with Wang Ming. Kang Sheng in the security apparatus, Ren Bishi in organizational matters, and Chen Yun in party rectification and economic policy were all returned students from Stalin's Russia, and all played critical roles during the 1940s and after. They were most important in the areas of economic policy, party organization, and rectification, and it is here that Soviet models were most important.

IV. The triumph of the CCP was the product of a series of contingent events

In the summer of 1989, a retired cadre – aging, blind, and bitterly critical of recent corruption in the party – sat on a *kang* in his cave in Yan'an and talked about his experiences in the Chinese Revolution. At one point, he stated flatly, "Without the Xi'an Incident, the Shaanbei revolution could not have survived to the War of Resistance" (Shaanbei interview, No. 19, June 1989). The comment struck me because my own research was also suggesting that before the war, the Communist foothold in northern Shaanxi was very fragile indeed. In 1936, the Red Army totaled some 20,000 men and controlled only a few county seats. They were surrounded in a desolate corner of Northwest China by more than 300,000 Guomindang and Northeast Army forces (Braun, 1982: 149). It seemed reasonable to accept this participant's judgment that, without the Communists' spring 1936 truce with the Northeast Army and that army's December kidnapping of Jiang Jieshi (Chiang Kai-shek), the Guomindang might have tightened the noose and eliminated the Red Army.

The Xi'an Incident may indeed have saved the Red Army and been one of those critical turning points in Chinese history (Wu Tien-wei, 1976, 1984). But it was only the most striking of many points where the contingency of history was demonstrated. Obviously, the Long March is replete with instances in which the party and the Red Army were almost eliminated, saved only by a combination of extraordinary determination, incompetent adversaries, and plain old luck. In 1947, Hu Zongnan's pincer movement to trap Mao and the party center in northern Shaanxi between forces advancing from north and south failed when the southern force was delayed one day. In this case, even had Hu Zongnan's trap succeeded in catching Mao, the party had ample forces elsewhere to survive for some time; but it is abundantly clear that without Mao, the Chinese Revolution would have taken a very different course. (Indeed, Mao came so close to embodying the revolution that one could argue that his death marked the end of the revolutionary era.)

If the contingency of the revolution is evident in these turning points of the national struggle, it is also evident in a vast number of smaller events and struggles chronicled in local studies of the revolutionary process. My research on the revolution in northern Shaanxi shows how local defections in reaction to the ultra-left *sufan* campaign of 1935 virtually wiped out the Soviet base on the Shaanxi–Gansu border until the arrival of the Central Red Army overturned the verdicts and reversed the process (Esherick, 1980). Similarly, essays by Gregor Benton, David Paulson, Kathleen Hartford, and Steven Levine in the volume *Single Sparks* stress the precarious nature of the revolutionary struggle in Jiangxi, Shandong, Hebei, and the Northeast, respectively – and how close the party came to failure in each of these cases (Hartford and Goldstein, 1989: 28–31, 124, 155).

My point is not to reduce the revolution to a series of historical accidents. It is simply to counsel against excessive determinism. We should be suspicious of suggestions that China's economic, political, or agrarian crisis predetermined China's revolutionary history. I suspect that, to some degree, broad theoretical approaches to the Chinese Revolution commit what David Hackett Fischer has called "the *fallacy of identity*" – the "assumption that a cause must somehow resemble its effect" and, in particular, that "big effects [such as a revolution] must have big causes" (Fischer, 1970: 177). It is intellectually unsatisfying to conclude that a momentous social and political transformation like the Chinese Revolution was simply the product of a series of contingent events – that, indeed, if things had happened just a little bit differently, it might not have occurred at all. This is the fundamental attraction of the grand theories of Barrington Moore or Theda Skocpol. I would not advocate the abandonment of these powerful and thought-provoking models, but we should not give them an overly deterministic reading. Our search for the causes of the Chinese Revolution must acknowledge that however much socioeconomic structures formed the preconditions for revolution, the revolution itself was an extended historical process in which a series of contingent events interacted over time and space to constrain and ultimately determine the revolutionary outcome.

V. The revolution was produced by a conjuncture of domestic and global historical processes among which the worldwide depression and Japanese imperialism were particularly important

Returning to the Xi'an Incident, I would argue that although we should recognize it as an important demonstration of the contingency of China's revolutionary history, we should not follow Guomindang apologists such as Ramon Myers and Thomas Metzger to suggest that the incident, and the war and revolution that they see deriving from it, were only accidents of history (Myers and Metzger, 1980: 26).[2] While recognizing the pivotal role of the Xi'an Incident, we should understand it as the product of a rising tide of anti-Japanese agitation among students and military men throughout the 1930s. Zhang Xueliang did not just act because the Japanese had invaded his Manchurian homeland. He was moved to action by public (and especially student) resistance to continued concessions to Japan's creeping imperialism in North China, including critical student demonstration in Xi'an on the eve of the kidnapping (Wu Tien-wei, 1976, 1984).

Parkes Coble's (1991) fine book on the politics of the 1930s focuses on the Japanese challenge as Jiang Jieshi's Achilles' heel. From the time of the Manchurian Incident, Jiang's halfhearted and ineffective efforts to forestall Japanese aggression left the Nanjing government open to constant criticism from the Reorganizationists in Guangzhou, the Guangxi Clique in the Southwest, and students and intellectuals everywhere. Despite Guomindang censorship, a public opinion calling for an end to civil war and unified resistance to Japan slowly gathered force. When that public opinion began to infect the Northeast and Northwest Army troops sent to suppress the Communists in northern Shaanxi, their officers entered into a series of contacts with the Communists resulting in local and regional accommodations between the two sides. With this, the groundwork was laid for the Xi'an Incident and subsequent moves toward a United Front against Japan.

Should we then proceed along a reductionist course and say that Japanese militarism caused the Chinese Revolution by its insatiable demands for power and resources in North China? That is obviously a question for Japanese historians to answer, but my own view is that Japanese imperialism during the 1930s cannot be understood apart from the Great Depression and the worldwide crisis of capitalism. The closing of Western markets to Japanese goods made Japan all the more intent on pressing a colonialist policy in its East Asian sphere of influence. Depression-caused distress in the Japanese countryside gave both cause and pretext for the military to seek new areas to colonize and develop as a Japanese-dominated East Asian co-prosperity sphere.

This was the global political-economic context for the Chinese Revolution, and it interacted with national and local politics in China to produce the revolutionary conjuncture. At a minimum, a satisfactory explanation of the

Chinese Revolution will have to include (a) the Chinese state's military weakness in peripheral areas that gave the Communists their initial room to maneuver, (b) an agrarian regime that allowed the party to gain a measure of popular acquiescence and support on the basis of class (antilandlord) and tax-resistance (antistate) appeals, (c) rising nationalist sentiment (especially in urban areas) to which the Communists successfully appealed in United Front declarations and which the Nationalists antagonized by pursuing the civil war, and (d) a world economic crisis that both weakened the Chinese state and economy and helped impel Japanese imperialism in Northeast and Northern China.

VI. The larger structures of China's state and society did not make revolution inevitable, but they imposed significant constraints on the agents of revolution and counterrevolution

Recognizing the contingency of the Chinese Revolution does not require us to ignore the larger socioeconomic structures that constrained the agents of revolution and counterrevolution. These structures have formed the focus of some of the most fruitful comparative scholarship on revolution, especially the work of Barrington Moore (1966) but including that of Theda Skocpol (1979), Eric Wolf (1969), Joel Migdal (1974), and Jeffrey Paige (1975). Comparative analysis certainly suggests that China's largely agrarian but highly commercialized economy, its relatively weak a dependent bourgeoisie, and its centralized bureaucratic political system were related to its modern revolutionary experience. But how are we to describe that relationship without violating our thesis on the contingency of the revolution?

The problem is both enormous and highly contentious, but I would venture the following. The apparent strength of the late imperial state (prior to the nineteenth century) lay in the absence of powerful rivals, either domestic or foreign. The Chinese landed elite, lacking judicial or military functions and weakened economically by the practice of partible inheritance, was a much smaller threat to central authority than were any of the European aristocracies or the daimyo of Japan. Internationally, the late imperial state was not seriously threatened prior to the arrival of the West. Precisely because it had no rivals, the Chinese imperial state was quite weak by world standards. It commanded an extraordinarily small portion of national revenues: the land tax, which was the basis of state finances, took only 5 percent to 6 percent of the harvest (Wang Yeh-chien, 1973: 131) against some 30 percent to 40 percent in Japan.

Low tax rates meant that, in comparative terms, the state's burden on the peasantry was quite light. In addition, the practice of partible inheritance restrained land concentration so that most peasants were guaranteed access to at least a small plot of land. These barriers to complete pauperization, plus the access to wage or petty trade incomes afforded by China's highly commercialized rural economy and the efficient safety net provided by the centralized Qing state's famine relief measures (Will, 1990), lay behind China's enormous population increase during the late imperial period.

These characteristics of China's political economy meant that during the modern era, China confronted the West and Japan with a weak state and an enormous population. The modern Chinese state was never able to control anything like the Meiji state's hefty proportion of the agricultural product, in part because population had now grown to an extent that even marginal tax increases were seen by peasants as subsistence threats and provoked violent resistance. In consequence, the weak and impoverished Chinese state was humiliated repeatedly by the foreign powers, and the massive indemnities of the Sino-Japanese War and the Boxer Protocol meant that just as China roused itself to a major state-building effort with the late Qing reforms, it was further drained of potential revenues.

During the twentieth century, the Chinese economy showed significant signs of real growth. Although one might quarrel with some details, Thomas Rawski's argument for an extremely respectable 8.1 percent growth rate in industrial production seems entirely plausible. His arguments for 1.4 percent to 1.7 percent annual growth in the agricultural sector are far more controversial (Huang, 1990: 137–9; Wong, 1992; Republican China, November 1992), but there is no denying that some growth in per capita earnings was taking place (Rawski, 1989: 275, 329). But there are two problems.

First, as Rawski acknowledges, virtually all of the recorded growth was taking place along the coast and in core areas. There is little evidence that real economic growth was occurring in the peripheries, and Kenneth Pomeranz (1993) has argued that the modernization process actually hurt the neglected hinterland. This meant that the peripheries still harbored a depressed peasantry left out of the modernization process. It was, of course, precisely in these peripheries that the Chinese Revolution took root.

Second, even in the coastal and core areas, the modernization process was not taking place fast enough to allow Chinese state making and military self-strengthening to keep pace with Japan. The modern sector of the economy furnished new sources of revenue for the republican state, but China was always playing catch-up to its primary rival and threat. In all its modern interactions with Japan, China came out on the losing end. In 1915, in part because many of its modern enterprises had gone heavily into debt to Japanese banks, China was forced to agree to Japan's 21 Demands. In 1917, warlord governments turned to Japan for the Nishihara Loans and, in exchange, acquiesced to Japan taking over Germany's sphere of influence in Shandong. Finally, during the 1930s, as Japan's designs on China became openly imperialist, Jiang Jieshi was compelled to retreat, trading space for time, hoping in vain that political unification and defense-related economic construction could be completed before Japan launched a full-scale invasion.

In short, the key byproduct of China's social structure and political economy was a weak Chinese state. Unable to protect the Chinese nation during an age of imperialism, the late Qing and republican states were constantly criticized and challenged by nationalist rivals in the urban classes and civil and military elites. Unable to penetrate or bring the benefits of modernization to peripheral and "backward" areas of the country, the state left a vast hinterland where the Communists were able to organize those left out of the fragile modernization process.

VII. The determination, sacrifice, and commitment of individual Communist revolutionaries – the subjective element of the revolutionary dialectic – were both essential to the revolution's success and critical in shaping its nature

The revolution was not easily made. One of the greatest weaknesses of determinist theories of revolution is their underestimation of the effort made by revolutionaries. The success of the revolution required dedicated revolutionaries and much sacrifice. Time and again, the Communist Party suffered catastrophic defeats: in Jiang Jieshi's White Terror of 1927; after the suicidal attacks on urban centers under the Li Lisan line in 1930; during 1933–1934 when, one after the other, the Red Soviets fell to Guomindang extermination campaigns; during 1941–1942 when Japanese counterattacks following the Hundred Regiments offensive reduced Communist forces and territory by roughly one half. Yet, brought to the brink of disaster, the Communists regrouped, retreated to safer havens, revised their strategies, and fought on. Any satisfactory interpretation of the revolution must acknowledge and explain the personal commitment and determination that led thousands of young men and women, often scattered in small groups across the map of China, to fight on against overwhelming odds.

The Long March is a tale filled with close calls and remarkable sacrifice. In the end, less than 4,000 of the 86,000 who started out arrived in Shaanxi with Mao (Salisbury, 1985: 2). Every river crossing was a potential disaster, and some – like the famous crossing of the Luding Bridge over the Dadu River – have been mythologized as acts of supreme revolutionary courage. China's revolutionary history is replete with such tales of heroism, large and small, and every local struggle saw comparable evidence of revolutionary commitment. Gregor Benton's (1992) rich study of those left behind when the Long Marchers departed the South is filled with examples of incredible determination and faith in the revolutionary cause, even as every rearguard unit was suffering losses of about 90 percent of its forces.

The period from 1927 to 1937 is critical in this regard because these years of civil war were certainly the most trying for the party. In North China on the eve of the war, there remained at best a few thousand Communist Party members – scattered in isolated party cells and many in jail. These men (and a few women) had survived years of political persecution as underground party members, and many of their comrades had been arrested and executed or had died in prison. Those who lacked the commitment to carry on – and there were many – dropped out or defected to the Guomindang. But a dedicated few struggled on. Then, with rising anti-Japanese nationalism in 1936, and especially after the Xi'an Incident, Communists were quietly released from jail and returned to their homes where they formed the core of the Communist resistance during the war (Van Slyke, 1986: 631). The rapid growth of the North China base areas during the early years of the war relied on the critical role of these local cadres. Their survival to play this role is testimony to a remarkable revolutionary dedication.

This revolutionary commitment helps to explain more than the success of the revolution; it also helps explain the *nature* of the revolution. The Long March did more than preserve the Red Army; it also changed forever the lives of the survivors. Remembering the lives lost, they fought on to ensure that their comrades had not died in vain. As the march itself (or other great watersheds of party history) passed from history to legend, the survivors became ever more committed to protecting that myth and their part in it – to ensuring that their contribution would be one chapter in a glorious tale of revolutionary triumph. They knew that should their revolution fail, should the Japanese or the Guomindang succeed in reversing the tide of history (and, struggling against great odds, *they* understood the contingency of revolution), they would lose not only their lives but everything that gave their lives meaning.[3]

At the same time, we must recognize that no one began with an intense commitment to Communist revolution. Even the senior party leaders were only slowly transformed from radical friends to Communist Party cadres (van de Ven, 1991). Among ordinary peasants, the initial commitment to revolutionary struggle was quite tentative. One peasant informant told me that he joined the Red Army in 1935 because it was the fad (*shimao*). Others joined because they were hungry and the army fed them (Esherick, 1989). But once in the ranks, the very process of revolutionary participation increased commitment. Meetings and propaganda taught party discipline and party spirit; struggle sessions and rectification movements rooted out personal weaknesses and competing loyalties. The longer one survived, the higher one rose in the party and the greater one's commitment grew. In time, a fad became a cause, and the revolution became a way of life.

Those who made the revolution a way of life naturally sought comrades with a like-minded faith in the justice and certain victory of their cause. They were suspicious of those who wavered or showed signs of skepticism,

51

cynicism, or doubt because these people might give up the struggle, defect to the enemy, or break under torture, revealing the identity and location of their comrades and endangering an entire local revolutionary base. This dynamic of revolutionary struggle helps to explain why Communist revolutionaries so frequently – even while fighting for their lives as small guerrilla bands in isolated mountain bases – turned on their comrades in bloody and destructive purges (Benton, 1992: 172, 198–9, 237–9, 283, 354–6). The revolutionary survivors were the winners of these inner-party struggles and, as their revolution became increasingly successful during the 1940s, they became convinced of the correctness of their methods. So purging the hesitant and cautious became integral to party life. The inevitable result was a pattern of party conflict that automatically favored the left – with well-known and often disastrous consequences in the PRC (Li Rui, [1988] 1994, provides a vivid example).

VIII. The CCP was a social construct of considerable internal complexity, not an organizational weapon of obedient apparatchiks commanded by the Party Center

Few questions have provoked more contentious debate than the role of Communist Party organization in the revolutionary dynamic. Those stressing the role of organization have usually discounted social factors as a basis for revolution (Hofheinz, 1977; Levine, 1987). The organizational strengths of the party are deemed sufficient to explain Communist victory even in the absence of popular support. Drawing on early cold war scholarship such as Philip Selznick's (1952) *The Organizational Weapon*, organizational interpretations have often been associated with a conservative anticommunist political stance that challenges the legitimacy of Communist rule (Hartford and Goldstein, 1989: 9–18).

Despite this political stance, some of the best scholarship on the revolution has demonstrated the essential role of the Communist Party and its military forces in mobilizing the peasantry for revolution and resistance to Japan (Chen Yung-fa, 1986; Kataoka, 1974). Virtually all close studies of the revolution have come to the conclusion that popular support for the revolution was always the product of painstaking efforts by party members to demonstrate the benefits of tax relief, rent reduction, defense against the Japanese, political participation in elections, land reform, production campaigns, mutual aid, cooperatives, and so forth. The party's own attention to party building and organizational questions is obvious in internal documents from this period. (Indeed, recent scholarship's stress on organizational factors in part reflects the concerns of the inner-party documents on which much of this research is based.) A recognition of the key role of party organization need not be read as either hostility to the revolution or an alternative to popular support but as evidence that support for the revolution depended on the new party-state's ability to penetrate village society and mobilize the populace for its program.

There are, however, two analytical traps waiting to snare those who rely too much on organizational explanations. First is the danger of fetishizing organization. My own research on the northern Shaanxi revolution during the 1930s suggests that significant success came only when the CCP's Shaanxi provincial organization was destroyed following the arrest and defection of its party secretary in 1933. The destruction of the provincial party apparatus freed the guerrilla forces under Liu Zhidan from higher party directives that they avoid "flightism" and "opportunism" and engage in suicidal attacks on major urban centers. Released from the discipline of a party organization following an adventurist line, Liu Zhidan built a significant guerrilla base on the Shaanxi-Gansu border. Then, in 1935, new representatives from the center arrived, arrested Liu and his officers, executed a number of his followers, and nearly destroyed the base until stopped by the arrival of Mao and the Central Army. As this case illustrates, disciplined party organization could be a recipe for disaster, not a guarantee of victory (Esherick, 1989).

Second, there is the danger of reifying the party. Because reference to "the Party" is a convenient stylistic shorthand and because party documents constantly stress the role of the party in the revolution, we stand in constant danger of writing and thinking about the party acting as some unified, disciplined historical agent. But we know that, in fact, this was not the case. Recent work on the origins of the CCP by Hans van de Ven has demonstrated that the party did not come into being full-blown with the First Congress in 1921. A gradual process turned local cells of friends into a national organization of comrades. Patterns of association among intellectuals, schoolmates, and fellow provincials were slowly transformed through experience and struggle into the new habitus of a Leninist party. According to van de Ven, a true Communist Party worthy of the name did not come into being until 1927.

If we turn from the founding of the CCP to the collapse of communist parties in the former Soviet Union and Eastern Europe, we see that in every case but that of Romania, communist party leaders made key decisions not to resist with force the dismantling of the party-state. Thus, at the end of their historical paths as well, communist parties prove to be anything but monolithic machines. They are composed of a variety of historical actors with important identities beside their roles as party members. These people are not all mindless apparatchiks in a communist machine. They are also members of society – with families and social connections, personal lives and aspirations, and national, regional, and ethnic identities.

Party discipline at the height of communist power was no doubt more effective than it was at a party's founding or during its last days.

Nonetheless, that discipline was never perfect. Even in the most secure bases such as Shaan-Gan-Ning, the rural party included an enormous number of peasants with marginal literacy, little education, and no knowledge whatsoever of Marxist-Leninist theory. These peasant communists' consciousness and behavior had little in common with the thinking and activities of the urban intellectuals of the Party Center who wrote the key documents that inform our thinking of what "the Party" represented. Rural cadres were deeply enmeshed in a variety of local networks from which they could never be completely separated. Between rural cadres and the Party Center were county party members who partook imperfectly of both worlds – but whom the Party Center periodically recalled to work conferences in efforts to bind them ever more closely to the Party Center's way of thinking.

The CCP, at all its levels, was a historical product, a cultural construction, an association of human beings. Its successes were not just the successes of organization and discipline. They were also the successes of a complex interaction among central and base area strategists, county executives and enforcers, and village activists. Out of that interaction, new social roles were constructed. Rural cadres began as young village activists who placed a value on work and struggle over face and harmony. And then gradually, as their own actions tied their interests and identities ever more closely to the new regime, they were themselves transformed into leaders "not afraid to offend" their fellow villagers and eager to complete the tasks assigned by their party-state superiors. This certainly made them effective agents of state-directed social change. But the party-state of which they were agents was itself a multilayered social construct – full of new public rituals and confidential bureaucratic routines. To understand the workings of that party-state, we must deconstruct it, not reify it. We need a historical anthropology of the Chinese party-state that can chart the evolution of its customs and habits, its discourse and rhetoric, its methods of cooptation and patterns of domination (Esherick, forthcoming).

IX. Revolution is a process

Between the extremes of a deterministic view of the revolution as the inevitable product of the political-economic structures of Chinese society and the analytically defeatist view of the revolution as a historical accident, we need to conceive of the revolution as an evolving historical process in which each stage built on the political consequences, the institutional creations, the evolving habits, and the collective memories of what went before. We need a processual model of the Chinese Revolution, similar to George Lefebvre's ([1939] 1957) conception of the French Revolution as a series of revolutions that followed from and built on one another. I would tentatively propose the following sketch of such a processual model.

When the 1911 Revolution left China without a strong central government or any elite consensus about what a legitimate government might look like, the way was left open for the Guomindang to reorganize and revitalize itself as a claimant to national leadership. During the 1920s, with the advice and assistance of the Soviet Union, the reorganized Guomindang established some of the fundamental contours of twentieth-century Chinese politics: Leninist party organization, a party-army with political officers binding the military to the party's political agenda; party-directed mass organizations of students, workers, and peasants with nationalist and social reformist agendas; political rituals involving public celebrations of obedience to the national leader and the creation of a new citizenry (Wasserstrom, 1991); and a revolutionary discourse that stigmatized opponents as counterrevolutionary agents of imperialism and feudal reaction (Tsin, 1990).

Among students and intellectuals, the Guomingdang's nationalist and social reformist agenda attracted growing support, especially after the May 30th Movement of 1925. But in part because the foreign and conservative Chinese press stressed the role of Russian aid and Bolshevik advisers in the movement, the Guomindang's Chinese Communist allies shared in the support garnered by the National Revolution. In consequence, when Jiang Jieshi purged the Communists in 1927, although his short-term success was complete, he created the impression among many that he had betrayed the revolutionary legacy of Sun Zhongshan. The Communists were able to claim that they were the true heirs to the revolutionary tradition of the 1920s.

Driven from the cities and forced into the hinterland in 1927, the revolution first required military forces. These were usually, in the first instance, defectors from the Guomindang armies – or, more accurately, men who saw the Guomindang betraying the revolution in 1927 (or, later, in their failure to resist to Japan) – who resumed some prior contact or affiliation with leftist forces. Second, civil adherents to the revolution worked through established elite networks to establish the basis for revolutionary action. Third, bandits, secret society members, and a variety of discontented individuals were recruited to join the initial Red Army units and form small but powerful guerrilla bands in isolated peripheral areas (Averill, 1987, 1990).

These initial guerrilla bands represented a minuscule portion of the rural population. At this stage, there was nothing resembling mass mobilization. However, by selective and "just" violence against hated state agents and cruel landlord and militia elites, they managed to eliminate or neutralize their political opponents. Once this was done, they could spread propaganda, recruit more broadly into the party, organize mass organizations, and eventually abolish the old tax regime and carry out land reform or (during the War of Resistance) rent and interest reduction and progressive tax reform.

As successful as these efforts were, they could not have succeeded without the war with Japan. Economic development and Guomindang state-building efforts were proceeding well enough along the coast and in economic core areas so that the Nationalists were able to contain the Communist appeal to peripheral zones. As Japanese aggression intensified following their 1931 occupation of the Northeast, Jiang Jieshi and the Nanjing government lost political support in urban areas, but there was no urban opposition strong or cohesive enough to pose an alternative. Once full-scale war with Japan broke out in 1937, however, the rapid retreat of Guomindang officials and regular army units from North China left rural elites and former warlord forces to contend with the Communists (and Japanese) on their own.

In this situation, a number of factors favored the Communists. Many local Communists had contacts going back to the 1920s to establish their local credibility. Most of these had superior nationalist credentials to Guomindang rivals who had defended Jiang's attempts to appease the Japanese aggressors. Years in the political wilderness made these Communist leaders more capable of accepting the hardships of partisan warfare, and both their egalitarian ideology and their years of struggle led them to enforce a severely spartan lifestyle on all full-time political cadres and military officers. In the context of war with Japan, the new Communist party-state built support for a program of shared sacrifice in which the burden of progressive taxation and rent and interest reduction fell heavily on the elite. But in large measure because the regime's leaders could demonstrate that they were not benefiting materially from these new burdens, their demands were regarded as fair (*gongdao*) by the rural population – and fairness was all that was required.

These factors allowed the CCP to establish a number of reasonably stable bases in north and central China. But midway through the war, their victory was by no means assured. The New Fourth Army Incident of January 1941 effectively brought the United Front with the Guomindang to an end. The economic blockade of Shaan-Gan-Ning was resumed, and the Guomindang subsidy for the Communist armies ended. At roughly the same time, Japanese mopping-up campaigns severely tested the other Communist bases. Faced with these challenges, the party-state was forced to increase significantly its demands on the rural population, but it also undertook a serious rectification of its own work (Selden, 1971; Schran, 1976).

The rectification campaign of 1942–1944 was one of the most important turning points in China's revolutionary history. To the extent that the party was transformed into an effective organizational weapon, this is when it was done. Three aspects of this movement strike me as essential. First, the initial campaign in Yan'an unified the revolutionary leadership around Mao. The Internationalist group around Wang Ming was finally eliminated as a force in the party. Equally as important, dissenting voices among the intellectuals were both cowed into submission by the vehemence of the attack on Wang Shiwei and won over to a new and deeper commitment by a process of criticism and self-criticism that ended by excusing their sins and welcoming them into the beleaguered revolutionary community.

With the revolutionary leadership in Yan'an thus solidified, the campaign was spread to other areas of Shaan-Gan-Ning and to other base areas. In the Shaan-Gan-Ning hinterland, antitraitor work took center stage. Intellectuals and the wealthier elements in rural society were subjected to intense examination. Large numbers were accused of traitorous activities – often for having voiced some discontent with the new regime. These people were treated harshly, although not executed, as Mao's injunction to "cure the illness and save the patient" was followed – in deliberate contrast to Stalinist purge practices. Nonetheless, the party made its power and will clear enough so that discordant voices were silenced.

The third and final stage of rectification was to raise political consciousness and improve discipline among rural cadres. Most of these had been hurriedly recruited during times of mass mobilization – often in the more leftist phases of the revolution. Largely poor and middle peasants of marginal literacy, their knowledge of either Marxist theory or Leninist discipline was minimal. Once the party apparatus had been unified and disciplined down to the county level, that apparatus could be brought to bear on the rural party. Petty corruption was rooted out, and less competent or activist cadres were reformed or replaced. The end result was a party organization reaching right down to the village level that could effectively carry out a series of important mobilization campaigns during the late war years: for increased agricultural and handicraft production, cooperatives, mutual aid teams, elections, and conscription. The foundations of the new party-state had been laid.

The final test was to come during the civil war years, 1947–1948. Here, military advantage lay with the Guomindang, and the Communists no longer had the advantage of fighting a national enemy. By this time, the party leadership had been effectively unified and rank-and-file cadres had committed themselves to the revolutionary regime. Their past victimization of class and political enemies meant that any return of the old regime would leave them in great personal danger. Faced with an enemy that often had the option of fleeing to the cities or deserting, these communist cadres had a clear edge in political dedication. As for the ordinary peasantry, the poorest certainly benefited from the land reform carried out at this time. Middle peasants benefited politically from the new regime, with a larger voice in village affairs. Convinced in sufficient numbers that a return of the Guomindang would bring back the bad old days of arbitrary taxes and abusive officials, they too tended to side with the revolution.

The basic features of this processual overview of the revolution are not so different from the conventional wisdom. But the emphases and formulations support certain essential points. First, initial support for the Communist Party came from a small group of intellectuals and rural revolutionaries whose commitment to the revolutionary cause was steeled in years of bitter combat. Second, the experience of the wartime base areas allowed these Communist cadres to create a party-state whose influence permeated village life as never before. Third, the wartime and civil war demands of the new party-state were unprecedented in their extent, but they were tolerated because progressive taxes targeted those with the ability to pay and state cadres were able to demonstrate that they were not using their authority for personal enrichment. Fourth, land reform policies established guarantees that each peasant family would have sufficient land to guarantee a basic subsistence whereas the encouragement of handicrafts, cooperatives, and market exchange promised the revival of commercial activity.

The advantage of this formulation is, first, that it highlights the state-building activities of the Chinese Revolution. When we observe that, including officials, clerks, and runners, the Qing state probably had about 750,000 functionaries, or one for every 600 people, whereas the PRC had 5.3 million cadres in 1952 and 29 million cadres in 1988, or one for every 35 citizens (Lee, 1991: 207–9), it is clear that state-building was a central facet of the Chinese Revolution. Second, a critical appeal of the new party-state was the selfless dedication of its cadres. Clearly, once the party's monopoly of power (together with the spread of a market economy) made corruption and abuse of privilege commonplace during the 1980s, the revolutionary era was over and the revolution's own legitimacy was called into question. Finally, nothing in the revolutionary process suggested popular support for an economic program that went beyond small peasant farming, private and (voluntary) cooperative ownership, and free market activity.

Seen in this way, it becomes easier to understand both the pervasive influence of the Chinese state and the current enthusiasm for market reforms. And if we understand the political demands behind the Chinese Revolution to be for fairness and order (far more than democracy or liberation), it becomes easier to understand both the crisis of 1989 and the current resilience of the authoritarian state in China.

X. The history of modern China is not a teleology of revolution

Having devoted nine theses to analyzing the origins and nature of the Chinese Revolution, it is necessary to conclude by observing that one of the most pernicious characteristics of the historiography of modern China is an excessive focus on revolution. Modern Chinese history has been dominated and distorted by a teleology of revolution.[4] All history is seen as leading up to 1949 (or, for a time, to a broader revolutionary process culminating in the Cultural Revolution). The central problem of intellectual history was the rise of Marxism (Levenson, 1958–1965; Schwartz, 1951; Meisner, 1967). Economic history analyzed the weakness of Chinese capitalism (Feuerwerker, 1958). Rural society and peasant uprisings were studied to understand the roots of peasant revolution (Huang, 1985; Perry, 1980; Esherick, 1987). The 1911 Revolution was seen as the "first phase" of a revolutionary process leading up to 1949 (Wright, 1968; Esherick, 1976). The May Fourth Movement was the start of a process leading to the founding of the CCP (Chow Tse-tsung, 1960).

The historiographic tradition is perfectly understandable. The history of the past is written in the present (Carr, 1961: 29). We seek answers about the past to questions formed in the present. For some time, that present has been one in which the CCP sat securely in control of a Leninist party-state and a fundamentally Stalinist economy. In ideology and organization, in political economy and cultural norms, the new revolutionary China was a radical break with the past. This was one of the great revolutions of world history (Moore, 1966; Skocpol, 1979; Goldstone, 1991), and the task of the historian was to explain the historical foundations of the remarkable political and social transformation wrought by the PRC.

During the 1990s, this sort of history is clearly outdated. The year 1949 was not the end of history. Indeed, within a few years, the era of revolutionary socialism may appear as much a transitional period as the republican era. Our study of the revolution must pay as much attention to the antecedents of China's postsocialist present as to those contradictions that produced the revolution itself.[5]

In the realm of politics, scholars have been impressed by the Chinese Communists' success in political mobilization. Supported by substantial contemporary evidence of popular support for the Communists during the 1940s, historians have seen that mass base as a key factor in the CCP's triumph over the Guomindang (Johnson, 1962; Selden, 1971). It would be excessively presentist to abandon inquiry into popular support for the CCP. On the other hand, it would be excessively naive to deny that much popular mobilization in contemporary China has been distinctly coercive. Amid its appeals to "new democracy," the party was building a structure that concentrated power (and increasing degrees of privilege) in the Party Center. The critical political process in modern China was state building. Founded on popular support gained through the revolutionary process, consolidated by the organizational efficacy of the Leninist party-state, inspired by nationalist pride in a new China, and supported by new technologies of violence, communications, surveillance, and medicine (especially birth control), the contemporary Chinese state has brought unprecedented discipline and control over the lives of Chinese people.

In economic history, it will not do to see China's prerevolutionary economy as hopelessly trapped in a process of agricultural involution broken only by socialism and collective agriculture (Huang, 1985: 179–84).

Although the recent boom in China's economy is more industrial than agricultural, and although agricultural advances under the new quasi-private farming have been made on a foundation in infrastructure and modern inputs built under socialism, the fact remains that small peasant farming has been quite successful during recent years and that, in the larger economy, foreign investments and private and small collective enterprises have been spectacularly successful. In this context, it is clearly dated for historians to focus on China's economic failures or the retarded development of capitalism. We need to recognize the substantial vitality of China's prerevolutionary economic structures – a vitality that is now able to flourish under a regime that provides national sovereignty, peace, a degree of political stability, basic technical education, and broad tolerance for market activity.

At the same time, we need to recognize an enduring contradiction between a dynamic coastal economy and a disadvantaged interior. It is no accident that China's current economic boom is concentrated in the coastal provinces of the south and east – long the most commercialized parts of China and the most tied to foreign trade – or that overseas Chinese are integral to the growing economic integration of "Greater China" and all of East Asia (Hamashita, 1988). The Guomindang–Communist conflict was in part the struggle between the modernized, overseas-connected coastal zones and the depressed and forgotten rural interior. The gap between coastal prosperity and interior poverty helped feed the revolution, was checked by the planned economy of the early PRC (Lardy, 1978), and is now regaining salience with the return of the market economy.

In the past, it has always been the powerful unifying forces of state power and official culture that have held such regional disparities and tensions in check. The state is now surely stronger than any prerevolutionary government. In the realm of culture, however, the penetration of the market economy is weakening the state's ability to subordinate cultural practices to its centralizing purposes. The cultural history of urban China is increasingly characterized by a merging of styles and combining of resources of Greater China. In film, music, and dance, in clothing and material culture, Hong Kong, Taiwan, and coastal China are increasingly drawing together – a cultural blending tied to their economic integration. But the relevance and appeal of these cultural products to the rural interior is questionable.

Finally, it is likely that historians looking back from the next century will be impressed by the alteration and degradation of China's physical environment brought about by the twentieth century's tripling of China's already huge population combined with the prolonged and now very rapid growth of industrial production. Vaclav Smil (1984, 1993) has detailed the serious problems of air and water pollution, soil erosion, water depletion, and deforestation in contemporary China. China's cities become increasingly crowded, plagued by congestion and air pollution, and burdened by an unchecked influx of "mobile population."

In all of these changes – political, economic, cultural, demographic, and environmental – the Chinese Revolution has played a crucial role in the transformative process. But in the end, these historical processes are larger than the revolution, and it will be necessary to subordinate the history of the revolution to these larger patterns of change. Only then can we escape the teleology of revolution and gain an understanding of China's past that provides a better key to understanding its present.

NOTES

1   In addition to the participants in the UCLA Symposium on "Rethinking the Chinese Revolution," I thank the many friends and colleagues who offered suggestions and criticisms on earlier drafts of this essay. I am especially indebted to my colleagues at UCSD – Chalmers Johnson, Dorothy Ko, Barry Naughton, and Paul Pickowicz. Steven Averill, Elizabeth Perry, Mark Selden, Lyman Van Slyke, Alexander Woodside, and Ernest Young also offered telling and useful critiques. This revised essay will not fully satisfy any of these critics, and the author remains fully responsible for the shortcomings that remain.

2   Recall E. H. Carr's observation that it is history's losers who stress the role of accident in history: "It is amusing to note that the Greeks, after their conquest by the Romans, also indulged in the game of historical 'might-have-beens' – the favorite consolation of the defeated" (Carr, 1961: 130).

3   The commitment of party survivors to the revolutionary myth has filled the speeches of elders such as Wang Zhen: "The leadership of the Communist Party is not granted by heaven, but by the countless revolutionary martyrs who, wave after wave, shed blood and sacrificed themselves for half a century" (quoted in Schell, 1988: 235). It was certainly no accident that when the fate of the revolution was called into question during the spring of 1989, it was to elders like Wang Zhen that Deng Xiaoping first appealed for guidance and support.

4   For an extended critique of the "revolution paradigm" in modern Chinese history, see Myers and Metzger (1980). Needless to say, I do not agree with much of this article, which is a defense of Taiwan as the truly worthy product of modern Chinese history and an appeal for support from the new Reagan administration. But we should not allow the political bias of the authors to blind us to an important argument they are making.

5   The following sections are inspired by the comments of Alexander Woodside on an earlier draft of this essay.

REFERENCES

Arendt, Hannah (1963) On Revolution. New York: Viking.

Averill, Stephen C. (1987) "Party, society and local elite in the Jiangxi communist movement." J. of Asian Studies 46, 2: 279–303.

Averill, Stephen C. (1990) "Social elites and communist revolution in the Jiangxi hill country," pp. 283–284 in Joseph W. Esherick and Mary Backus Rankin (eds), Chinese Local Elites and Patterns of Dominance. Berkeley: Univ. of California Press.

Belden, Jack (1949) China Shakes the World. New York: Harper.

Benton, Gregor (1992) Mountain Fires: The Red Army's Three-Year War in South China, 1934–1938. Berkeley: Univ. of California Press.

Braun, Otto (1982) A Comintern Agent in China, 1932–1939 [trans. Jeanne Moore]. Stanford, CA: Stanford Univ. Press.

Carr, Edward Hallett (1961) What Is History? New York: Vintage.

Chen Yung-fa (1986) Making Revolution: The Communist Movement in Eastern and Central China, 1937–1945. Berkeley: Univ. of California Press.

—— (1990) Yan'an de yinying (Yan'an's Shadow). Taipei: Academia Sinica, Institute of Modern History.

—— (1993) "The Yenan Way reconsidered." Paper presented to the 1993 annual meeting of the Association for Asian Studies, March, Los Angeles.

Chiang Kai-shek (1957) Soviet Russia in China: A Summing-up at Seventy [trans. Wang Chung-hui]. New York: Farrar, Straus & Cudahy.

Chow Tse-tsung (1960) The May Fourth Movement: Intellectual Revolution in Modern China. Cambridge, MA: Harvard Univ. Press.

Coble, Parkes (1991) Facing Japan: Chinese Politics and Japanese Imperialism, 1931–1937. Cambridge, MA: Harvard Univ. Press.

Compton, Boyd (1966) Mao's China: Party Reform Documents, 1942–44. Seattle: Univ. of Washington Press.

Duara, Prasenjit (1988) Culture, Power, and the State: Rural North China, 1900–1942. Stanford, CA: Stanford Univ. Press.

Eastman, Lloyd (1974) The Abortive Revolution: China under Nationalist Rule, 1927–1937. Cambridge, MA: Harvard Univ. Press.

—— (1984) Seeds of Destruction: Nationalist China in War and Revolution, 1937–1949. Stanford, CA: Stanford Univ. Press.

Esherick, Joseph W. (1976) Reform and Revolution in China: The 1911 Revolution in Hunan and Hubei. Berkeley: Univ. of California Press.

—— (1987) The Origins of the Boxer Uprising. Berkeley: Univ. of California Press.

—— (1989) "The Chinese communist revolution from the bottom up: Shaan-Gan-Ning." Paper presented at the annual meeting of the American Historical Association, December, San Francisco.

—— (forthcoming) "Deconstructing the construction of the party-state: Gulin county in the Shaan-Gan-Ning border region." China Q. 140.

Fairbank, John King (1983) The United States and China, 4th ed. Cambridge, MA: Harvard Univ. Press.

Feuerwerker, Albert (1958) China's Early Industrialization: Sheng Hsuan-huai (1844–1916) and Mandarin Enterprise. Cambridge, MA: Harvard Univ. Press.

Fischer, David Hacket (1970) Historians' Fallacies: Toward a Logic of Historical Thought, New York: Harper.

Fogel, Joshua A. (1987) Ai Ssi-ch'i's Contribution to the Development of Chinese Marxism. Cambridge, MA: Harvard Univ. Council on East Asian Studies.

Forman, Harrison (1945) Report from Red China. New York: Wittlesey House.

Friedman, Edward, Paul G. Pickowicz and Mark Selden, with Kay Ann Johnson (1991) Chinese Village, Socialist State. New Haven, CT: Yale Univ. Press.

Furet, François (1981) Interpreting the French Revolution [trans. Elborg Forster]. Cambridge: Cambridge Univ. Press.

Goldstone, Jack A. (1991) Revolution and Rebellion in the Early Modern World. Berkeley: Univ. of California Press.

Goncharov, Sergei N., John W. Lewis and Xue Litai (1993) Uncertain Partners: Stalin, Mao and the Korean War. Stanford, CA: Stanford Univ. Press.

Hamashita, Takeshi (1988) "The tribute trade system and modern Asia," Memoirs of Toyo Bunko 46: 7–25.

Hartford, Kathleen and Steven M. Goldstein [eds] (1989) Single Sparks: China's Rural Revolutions. Armonk, NY: M. E. Sharpe.

Hofheinz, Roy, Jr. (1977) The Broken Wave: The Chinese Communist Peasant Movement, 1922–1928. Cambridge, MA: Harvard Univ. Press.

Huang, Philip C. C. (1985) The Peasant Economy and Social Change in North China. Stanford, CA: Stanford Univ. Press.

—— (1990) The Peasant Family and Rural Development in the Yangzi Delta, 1350–1988. Stanford, CA: Stanford Univ. Press.

Johnson, Chalmers (1962) Peasant Nationalism and Communist Power: The Emergence of Revolutionary China. Stanford, CA: Stanford Univ. Press.

Kataoka, Tetsuya (1974) Resistance and Revolution in China: The Communists and the Second United Front. Berkeley: Univ. of California Press.

Keating, Pauline (1989) "Two revolutions: Village reconstruction and cooperativization in North Shaanxi, 1934–1945." Ph.D. dissertation, Australian National University.

Kirby, William C. (1984) Germany and Republican China. Stanford, CA: Stanford Univ. Press.

Lardy, Nicholas (1978) Economic Growth and Distribution in China. Cambridge: Cambridge Univ. Press.

Lee, Hong Yung (1991) From Revolutionary Cadres to Party Technocrats in Socialist China. Berkeley: Univ. of California Press.

Lefebvre, George (1957) The Coming of the French Revolution [trans. R. R. Palmer]. New York: Vintage [orig. French ed. 1939].

Levenson, Joseph R. (1958–1965) Confucian China and Its Modern Fate. 3 vols. Berkeley: Univ. of California Press.

Levine, Steven I. (1987) The Anvil of Victory: The Communist Revolution in Manchuria 1945–1948. New York: Columbia Univ. Press.

Li Rui (1994) Lushan huiyi shilu (True Record of the Lushan Plenum). Taibei: Xinrui [mainland ed. 1988].

Madsen, Richard (1984) Morality and Power in a Chinese Village. Berkeley: Univ. of California Press.

Meisner, Maurice (1967) Li Ta-chao and the Origins of Chinese Marxism. Cambridge, MA: Harvard University Press.

Migdal, Joel S. (1974) Peasants, Politics and Revolution: Pressures toward Political and Social Change in the Third World. Princeton, NJ: Princeton Univ. Press.

Moore, Barrington, Jr. (1966) Social Origins of Dictatorship and Democracy: Lord and Peasant in the Making of the Modern World. Boston: Beacon.

Myers, R. H. and T. A. Metzger (1980) "Sinological shadows: The state of modern China studies in the U.S." Australian J. of Chinese Affairs 4: 1–34.

Paige, Jeffery M. (1975) Agrarian Revolution: Social Movements and Export Agriculture in the Underdeveloped World. New York: Free Press.

Perry, Elizabeth J. (1980) Rebels and Revolutionaries in North China, 1845–1949. Stanford, CA: Stanford Univ. Press.

—— (1993) Shanghai on Strike: The Politics of Chinese Labor. Stanford, CA: Stanford Univ. Press.

Pomeranz, Kenneth (1993) The Making of a Hinterland: State, Society and Economy in Inland North China, 1853–1937. Berkeley: Univ. of California Press.

Rawski, Thomas (1989) Economic Growth in Prewar China. Berkeley: Univ. of California Press.

Salisbury, Harrison E. (1985) The Long March: The Untold Story. New York: McGraw-Hill.

Schell, Orville (1988) Discos and Democracy: China in the Throes of Reform. New York: Pantheon.

Schoenbaum, David (1966) Hitler's Social Revolution: Class and Status in Nazi Germany, 1933–1939. Garden City, NY: Doubleday.

Schram, Stuart (1969) The Political Thought of Mao Tse-tung. New York: Praeger.

—— (1989) The Thought of Mao Tse-tung. Cambridge: Cambridge Univ. Press.

Schran, Peter (1976) Guerrilla Economy: The Development of the Shensi-Kansu-Ninghsia Border Region, 1937–1945. Albany: SUNY Press.

Schwartz, Benjamin I. (1951) Chinese Communism and the Rise of Mao. Cambridge, MA: Harvard Univ. Press.

—— (1960) "The legend of the 'legend of Maoism,'" China Q 2 (April–June): 35–42.

Selden, Mark (1971) The Yenan Way in Revolutionary China. Cambridge, MA: Harvard Univ. Press.

Selznick, Philip (1952) The Organizational Weapon: A Study of Bolshevik Strategy and Tactics. New York: McGraw-Hill.

Seybolt, P. J. (1986) "Terror and conformity: Counterespionage campaigns, rectification and mass movements, 1942–1943." Modern China 12, 1: 39–73.

Skocpol, Theda (1979) States and Social Revolutions: A Comparative Analysis of France, Russia, and China. Cambridge, MA: Harvard Univ. Press.

Smil, Vaclav (1984) The Bad Earth: Environmental Degradation in China. Armonk, NY: M. E. Sharpe.

—— (1993) China's Environmental Crisis: An Inquiry into the Limits of National Development. Armonk, NY: M. E. Sharpe.

Snow, Edgar (1961) Red Star over China. New York: Grove.

Tsin, Michael Tsang-Woon (1990) "The cradle of revolution: Politics and society in Canton, 1900–1927." Ph.D. dissertation, Princeton University.

Van de Ven, Hans J. (1991) From Friend to Comrade: The Founding of the CCP, 1920–1927. Berkeley: Univ. of California Press.

Van Slyke, L. (1986) "The Chinese Communist movement during the Sino-Japanese War, 1937–1945," pp. 609–722 in John K. Fairbank and Albert Feuerwerker (eds), The Cambridge History of China, Vol. 13: Republican China 1912–1949, Part 2. Cambridge: Cambridge Univ. Press.

Wang Yeh-Chien (1973) Land Taxation in Imperial China, 1750–1911. Cambridge, MA: Harvard Univ. Press.

Wasserstrom, Jeffrey N. (1991) Student Protest in Twentieth-Century China: The View from Shanghai. Stanford, CA: Stanford Univ. Press.

White, Theodore and Annalee Jacoby (1946) Thunder out of China. New York: William Sloane Associates.

Will, Pierre-Etienne (1990) Bureaucracy and Famine in Eighteenth-Century China [trans. Elborg Forster]. Stanford, CA: Stanford Univ. Press.

Wolf, Eric R. (1969) Peasant Wars of the Twentieth Century. New York: Harper & Row.

Wong, R. Bin (1992) "Chinese economic history and development: A note on the Myers–Huang exchange." J of Asian Studies 51, 3: 600–612.

Wou, Odoric Y. K. (1994) Mobilizing the Masses: Building Revolution in Henan. Stanford, CA: Stanford Univ. Press.

Wu, Tien-Wei (1976) The Sian Incident: A Pivotal Point in Modern Chinese History. Ann Arbor: Univ. of Michigan Center for Chinese Studies.

—— (1984) "New materials on the Sian Incident: A bibliographic essay." Modern China 10, 1: 115–41.

Wright, Mary C. [ed.] (1968) China in Revolution: The First Phase, 1900–1913. New Haven, CT: Yale Univ. Press.

4

TOWARD A CHINESE FEMINISM[1]

A personal story

Lin Chun

Neither Chapter 2 nor Chapter 3 focused on what is sometimes known inelegantly as the "Woman Question," but many interesting issues that could be raised and have at times been raised about the 1949 watershed concern gender equality within the nation and within families. A lively debate broke out in the 1970s and took new turns in the 1980s concerning the tension between the Chinese Communist Party's pronouncements about and policies relating to female equality. On the one hand, some claimed that the famous slogan "women hold up half the sky" (and hence deserve to be accorded a fair share of the benefits of the new society) was much more than mere window-dressing. Women really were treated more fairly by the CCP than by any previous regime. On the other hand, though, there were those who argued that 1949 saw not the demolishing but simply the refashioning of patriarchal patterns, especially in China's countryside. In trying to maintain the support of male villagers, it was claimed, the CCP had been consistently willing to treat women's liberation as something to be achieved later, after class inequalities had been taken care of. When female infanticide resurfaced in the 1980s, as a response to the government's call for "one-child families," the debate took on new meaning. Some argued that the continuing preference for boys showed the persistence of "feudal" ideas despite decades of efforts to uproot them, while others insisted that the CCP had inadvertently at least helped to keep alive practices that made daughters less attractive than sons to rural families.

This debate, which is far subtler and more multifaceted than this brief sketch suggests and has obvious implications for the general arguments made by Cohen and Esherick, is one about which much more is said later in Chapter 9. The present chapter, which first appeared in **Dissent***, a progressive magazine intended for general as opposed to purely academic audiences, does not directly address this particular scholarly debate but rather presents a frank account of one Chinese intellectual's struggle to make sense of her own life history. In doing so, she adds a personal and human dimension to the ongoing arguments over whether 1949 should* *be seen as a year when a genuinely "New China" was born. Lin Chun, who has worked both on Chinese politics and on the history of the European Left, also introduces us to the general tensions that often emerge when the feminist ideas that flow across cultural borders have played out in China. The ongoing effort to conceptualize a "Chinese feminism," which has taken on new dimensions in recent years as the first PRC programs in women's studies have been founded, is a fascinating one. It is also one that resonates historically with many earlier struggles to figure out how to find accord between imported and domestic beliefs relating to politics. This is because, throughout the twentieth century, an enduring concern among Chinese intellectuals and political activists was finding the most appropriate way possible to adapt aspects of attractive foreign ideologies (from Marxism to liberalism) so as better to suit the realities and solve the problems they saw around them.*

* * *

I was born a few years after the founding of the People's Republic of China (1949) in Beijing and grew up an equal of everybody else – judged, at least, by one important criterion, gender equality. My sisters and many friends shared with me their sense of seldom experiencing discrimination for being female in those years, however partial or even, sometimes, false that sense might be.

I have two sisters and no brother. My parents (who are largely self-educated intellectuals among the Communist rank and file) were evidently not unhappy that they did not meet the traditional Chinese ideal of having a son; indeed, they were very proud of each of us. While we were Young Pioneers, whenever we sat at the dining table with them, we used to call our father, the sole man in the family, the "party representative." In one of the most popular movies of the time (later made into a ballet and modern opera as well), based on a true story called "The Red Detachment of Women," the party representative among women soldiers in Hainan in the 1930s was a man, a hero. With the female company commander, he helped to raise class consciousness and to win battles against the White army and the local despotic landlords (both were, so to speak, all male). The theme song of the movie remains today a favorite of mine: "Advance, advance! We bear heavy duties as soldiers; we fight deep injustice as women. . . ."

The fact that the women revolutionaries would have needed a male leader or, to use today's faddish phrase, that there existed a "gender hierarchy" in the Communist forces, did not bother us. What was most fundamental about the revolution seemed so obvious: it was made by and for the exploited and oppressed, including the special underclass of women; if one of its goals was precisely women's liberation, if its moral principles were unity and equal relationships between men and women (and between officers and soldiers, the army and the people, and so on), what else should matter? It was hardly noticed that the first Communist group convened in Shanghai in 1921 formally to set up the party consisted of men only. The general organizational pattern of the Chinese Revolution has ever since been men-a-step-before-women in becoming politically conscious and mobilized, hence promoted. But so what?

Our parents told us very little about their personal stories in relation to the revolution. What impressed me the most from those rare occasions when they talked about themselves turned out to be almost irrelevant. My mother had to cross over a mountain on foot to attend a local school in a southern province where the mountains, she said, were covered with red bayberries throughout the year – this cheered her up from the exhausting daily treks. The picture of a pathway stretched through bayberries was so sweet in my imagination that I completely neglected the bitterness of the conditions of rural education. I did not realize that she, as the only child in her family, was exceptionally lucky among the girls in her home town (probably the poor boys too) to be able to go to school. Later, for some reason, she was taken to Indonesia where my grandmother (who was educated, also unusual then) worked, and they settled down to live a relatively comfortable life.

After the war against the Japanese invasion began (1937), my mother could not help wanting to join her compatriots in the national liberation movement. So, at the age of fourteen or fifteen, she managed to leave her beloved mother and, with a friend two years older, to return to China. She never said much about that extraordinary adventure. I did not and still cannot imagine the immense difficulties the two young women must have encountered on that journey, by sea and land, with little money and nothing else but courage and determination, in the turmoil and chaos of war. They finally lost each other at some point in China proper (I remember seeing their joyful meetings after their reunion sometime in the 1950s). Her friend eventually made her way to Yanan, the central base of the Communists, while my mother got involved in resistance activities in the South. She met my father, survived many more hardships including imprisonment and torture, and at long last found herself in the crowds in Tiananmen Square celebrating the birth of the new China in October 1949.

We heard high praise for our mother from those who had known and admired her since her early years. In our eyes she was no doubt an independent and liberated woman. Yet she was also ordinary, along with millions of others – women peasants, workers, and intellectuals – who believed and participated in the revolution. Did they see their specific "female subjectivities" being in any way sacrificed for the universal cause of liberation? Had she and her fellow female participants ever experienced any "systematic" discrimination in the revolutionary camp? Were they aware of any "male dominance" existing within the Communist power structure? Have they, in fact, ever had a pondering moment or sufficient interest to look at their place in relation to men within and without the family during the revolutionary struggles? Was it possible for them to think of "gender identity" not in the normative context of women's liberation but in terms of the defects of the revolution itself?[2] Moreover, how would my father and his male comrades view the matter? Have they ever thought of or been bothered by it?

I do not know how my parents and friends of the older generation would respond to questions like these. (Perhaps they would simply brush them away?) To my regret, I never asked. I could not ask what did not occur to me. And I still cannot ask without explaining why these are, now for me, valid and necessary questions. Only recently I began my own attempt to approach the gulf between the fundamentals of the revolution and its actual theories and politics by thinking about the intrinsically contradictory character of a communist feminism. Yet how could we, Chinese living and thinking and striving for the decent ideals of equality, have missed the kind of questions that since the late 1970s have stimulated notable contributions by Euro-American feminist critics to China scholarship? I am not concerned here with the qualities of their various analyses, but only with the contrast in our perspectives. What prevented us from seeing things in a critical manner comparable to that of our Western feminist counterparts?

I myself was much confined to a personal experience, above all a home environment (and similar environments extended from it), in which the issue of gender appeared not to exist. But how did it come to be so? Was gender difference and equality really not an issue, or were we simply blind to it? Was my father, for example, the center of attention and care because of his chronic illness or would he have been superior anyway? More generally, is it true that family relations in China were so much penetrated by the social power relations of the party-state hierarchy that a distinguishable private sphere did not survive? What is, at bottom, the nature of the Communist family, in which the wife's rank (and hence grade on the wage scale) is usually lower than the husband's? Moreover, how should we evaluate the relationship between the Communist "masters" and their female domestic helpers, notwithstanding varieties of individual cases? Has the celebrated principle of equality – "whatever the division of labor may be, all are servants of the people," ever been a reality? Or is that articulation itself flawed and hypocritical? Unfortunately, these questions were beyond my range of concern until quite recently.

My own parents had respected, cared for, and helped each other through thick and thin, though they never showed any intimacy in front of us. The worst argument they ever had, as far as I can remember, was over my grandmother, who returned from Indonesia to join us around 1960 (I do not know how and when my mother resumed contact with her). She liked to dress in a silk sari, cook her favorite Nanyang (southern Asian) meals, and make us children luxury snacks such as fried bananas. I say "luxury" because this was during the "three difficult years" following the failed Great Leap Forward (1958–1959), when people were hungry, everything was rationed even in Beijing, even for senior cadres and high intellectuals. My grand-mother, as a privileged "returned overseas Chinese," had some extra supplies of foodstuffs as well as money to spend (probably in the black market), and appeared to be unconcerned with the gap between her life and that of others. My father could no longer tolerate this and demanded that she move out of our place (which was in the housing compound of his work unit). He must have been ashamed, as I understood later, of having such an openly "bourgeois" lady in a "proletarian" family, especially if he knew (did he?) how bad the rural famine of the time was. My mother argued, cried, and in the end gave up; she rented a private studio nearby for her mother whom she really wanted to live with after so many years of separation.

Should the result of that month-long bitter argument affect my view of the equality between my parents – which we all took for granted? (The essence of their relationship is, after all, not for me to judge.) Probably not. For it was not my father, but his principles, which were actually shared by my mother, that won out. I use the word "proletarian" literally to refer to something very characteristic about my own home and the homes of common Communists like us. No wonder Grandma was out of tune with it. Nothing there was private property, for example, including the apartment and the furniture. Everything belonged to "the state," as we said in everyday Chinese. The single non-public piece conspicuously standing in our living room was my father's old grand gramophone, with lots of records (which were all smashed at the beginning of the cultural revolution). He, however anti-bourgeois, was a Western/Russian classical music lover. There were his many precious books, of course, the sole material that could possibly make up "property" of one's own (most of which were also lost during the cultural revolution). As small children, we hardly had a sense of possessing even personal belongings. Money and the notion of "owning" were deemed poisonous, and I was once punished by my father – seriously enough for me to learn the lesson forever – for using two cents to trade with my younger sister. (The enjoyment of public wealth and service by individuals and families to various degrees according to their stratified status in a state-controlled economy and redistributive system needs to be examined separately.)

Beyond the lack both of private property and the sense of privacy, personal and family life itself was "socialized" or "depersonalized" in many "proletarian" families. When we were little, our parents were often absent from home, either away on a working trip or staying in the countryside as members of a work team sent by the central organs during the successive campaigns of economic or political mobilization. Our childhood was spent mostly in a (residential) nursery, a school, or in the care of an "auntie" (nurse). I do not recall whether I ever felt miserable, missing my parents; maybe I did. But I do remember great times with them at dinners, in a park, on a holiday, whenever they were available. They were no doubt among the most loving and responsible parents; but they also, though maybe sometimes reluctantly, trusted public institutions to ensure our well-being.

On the whole, my childhood (and that of my sisters and many friends) was very happy, enriched by what we call "collective life" outside the home. Having followed debates in the West since the 1980s about the overburdened and disrupted motherhood of working women and about related problems such as the financing of daycare facilities, I still think of my own experience with appreciation. After all, this kind of family situation was not unusual in the 1950s and early 1960s, which were the heroic and difficult years of a new country striving for survival, dignity, and prosperity against long odds.

Then there came the nationwide "socialist education movement" which mainly aimed at the rural cadres, while in the urban centers junior high school students like myself and my elder sisters studied Mao's work and engaged in self-criticism. This was the prelude to the now notoriously destructive cultural revolution. (The cultural revolution, however, somewhat like "1968" in the West, in many aspects remains a historical mystery that still needs to be reexamined and understood. I will attempt elsewhere an analysis of the rationality and irrationality of that enormous mass movement, and of the different motives behind it, which reflected the accumulated social conflicts of the previous period. I will also confront the pro-cultural-revolution arguments – advanced even among those who were themselves gravely victimized, yet still engaged in the search for personal and social liberation. The validity of this search and the price paid for it were not fully revealed to me until the huge rehabilitation campaigns following the Mao era. Only then did I meet someone who had lived in a world completely different from my own in its relationship with communism, a world of discrimination, oppression, and independent thinking, and through him I came to know many different life experiences.)

What preoccupied me above all was the peculiar experience of young women in those years. There were confusions, doubts, and pains, but there was also at times a genuine feeling of freedom and self-determination. It was indeed an age more than ever before in China of female participation in politics, management, and all kinds of social and cultural activities; and consequently, so to speak, of empowerment of women within the family as well, especially in the sweeping "modernized" rural areas. On the other hand, acts of humiliation and violence against men and women on the "wrong" side were committed by people of both sexes at every level – a historical page still too heavy to be turned. I myself, always a favored student, without having sensed the slightest oppression, was nonetheless among a group of four to put up the first rebellious "big character poster" among the juniors in our school (which was all-female). As one of those students who quickly organized themselves to exercise their "right to rebel," I participated enthusiastically in the "mass criticism" of the "revisionist educational line" and of the authorities and teachers whom we deemed to have carried it out. Although I happened not to have physically attacked any person, what I was involved in was no doubt part of that massive and blind process of persecution. In fact, the first wave of severe violence in which more than one principal was beaten to death by students or driven to suicide occurred in the best all-girls schools in Beijing.

When the time came years later to think over these events, I simply wanted to know why, and why teenage girls? Working from a preliminary analysis elsewhere,[3] I want now to stress the hidden crisis of ideology and politics, which would not have revealed itself had there not been such large-scale chaos and casualties. Apparently the often arbitrary boundaries dividing perceptions of good and evil, given systematic manipulation by the authorities and a lack of a legal system, misled the post-revolution generation. And the female part of that generation was also trapped in the gender-laden conflicts between the required "class standing" and their natural human compassion, simultaneously viewed as "feminine" and politically unacceptable. In the end, the anti-humanist spirit of Maoism (and struggles over its interpretation in the wake of the paralysis of the "ideological state apparatus") turned out to be profoundly damaging to the very foundation of Chinese socialism, as ideology and social experiment.

Concerning generational relations, one of the exciting scenes of the cultural revolution involved millions of young people travelling the length and breadth of the country to "propagate and establish revolutionary ties." It is extraordinary, looking back, that parents so easily let their children (self-organized in peer groups) make distant journeys, often without a plan, even without a minimum of packing or definite destinations. (The students, in the absence of teachers who became the targets of attacks or stepped aside, would decide, say, in the morning and depart in the afternoon; rail tickets were not required anyway.) While my sisters and I were each gone with our own schoolmates, our mother was pleased to open our home to girls and boys from other provinces, as many Beijing residents did. In two hectic trips, I covered two-thirds of the country, from the north to the south, then from the east to the midwest. My group also went on foot for two hundred miles, on an imitative "long march" to honor the glorious undertaking of the Red Army (1934–1935), from the heart of the Jinggang mountains, where the Communist guerrillas created their first base in the late 1920s to Ruijin, the capital of the Chinese Soviet Republic (1931–1934).

That feverish period brought a further loosening and devaluation of family ties because of the intense "class struggle" that ruthlessly divided kin and, for that matter, other identities or communities. This becomes all the more interesting in light of the later revival of family solidarity, which served as a refuge for many people when political tyranny reached its height in 1975–1976. One may certainly ponder here the potentials and limits of the now formative analytical framework of separate public and private spheres when it is applied to China, where for decades politics regulated not only social but also personal life.

After two years of revolutionary activities in which classrooms were empty or only used for "struggle meetings," the three of us left home, quite willingly, for different places in the countryside during the campaign for "being reeducated by the peasants." My younger sister could have stayed with my parents (as policy permitted one child of each family to stay in the cities), but acting on their self-disciplined commitment to allow no room for selfish interests, they sent her away as well to the far north. She was barely fifteen. Later, as targets of criticism, they too went to a "cadre school" in rural Hubei, taking with them both my grandmothers who, however, failed to survive the unexpected emotional and physical difficulties (which they saw as a "great disorder under heaven") and died one after another within a few years. (My grandmother on my father's side had previously lived with my uncle's family in Beijing, and because they now had to move to another "cadre school" in a much more remote province, my parents took over the job of looking after her. I never met either of my grandfathers.)

Though they rarely talked about political ethics, my parents nonetheless taught us, simply by their deeds, what it was right to do. Their voluntary and total identification with what they believed to be a good cause had its historical origin in past experience, from which the revolution gathered its momentum and popular support. This identification survived the accusations against them during periodic "rectification" campaigns. It was gradually undermined only when the wrongs and sorrows within the revolution became so severe and so evident that they realized the necessity of clearing its name through conscious struggles – from inner-party actions to popular uprisings (such as the massive street demonstrations in Beijing and Nanjing in 1976). The goal was once again to find and devote oneself to a genuinely just cause "above" any individual interest.

The question of individuality and personal fulfillment, not to mention "separatist" identity, was, paradoxically, indistinguishable (if not excluded in standard theoretical formulations) from this pursuit of universal interests. Even the most noble and independent attempt at exercising citizenship did not consciously challenge communist degeneration at its root. The feminist thesis that "the personal is political" was no novelty for the Chinese, yet it oriented psychological conflicts far away from what that slogan clearly implies in a different social context. Having said this, I must add that it was not true that people in Communist China were merely obedient, their lives, therefore, lifeless. There were truly creative, emancipatory, and joyful moments in the lives of Chinese women and men, despite big and small tragedies. Nor was the system a monolithic bloc without any gaps, inner breakthroughs, and diversities. What is utterly wrong with Western mainstream liberal criticism of communist totalitarianism is its ignorance of the real complexity of communism (aside from the social achievements of the Communist regimes), which differs from country to country, party to party, period to period, situation to situation, believers to believers, even within the totalitarian territory. My parents, for example, both have strong personalities and remained so throughout the tortuous years of the "continuing revolution," which gradually lost its massive constituency.

I went to a village in northern Shanxi near the border mountains on which the "Smaller Great Wall" was built to obstruct nomadic tribes several centuries ago. Only by living with the peasants on that poor plateau during our formative years (in my own case, ages sixteen to twenty-one), did the group of us "city youth" develop a critical attitude toward reality. (Before then I did have some natural objections to the increasingly philistine Mao cult and was labeled a "reactionary student" for expressing them, but I never connected the cult to any systematic faults of existing socialism.) For the first time we learned how huge a gulf there was between material – including educational and medical – conditions in the cities and the countryside; how greatly the morale of real laborers, from time to time in hunger and despair, differed from the joyful folks singing of the harvest in familiar picture posters; how lucky we ourselves were compared with the often miserable life of rural women; and how unfair a fate was already prepared for our village friends.[4] On the other hand, since the peasants were hardly integrated into the state welfare establishment, it can be said that they also constituted the most independent (and the largest) portion of the population. Their tenacity, wit and unique perspective helped us to develop an outlook on life that was heavily influenced by egalitarian sentiments – against privilege, urban arrogance, and every form of elitist social bias.

Gaining its primary strength from the countryside, communism, as we began to see it then, ultimately failed the peasantry after seizing state power by subjecting the organization of agriculture to an "internal accumulation" for the sake of industrialization. This, almost a deliberate betrayal, was justified by the claim of necessity and sustained by a rigid system of urban–rural segregation that undermined the moral promise of Chinese socialism.

With a somewhat simplistic conviction of women's liberation through involvement in the labor force, we did promote some changes in local life. By working daily and competing in the fields with young male members of our production teams, and by playing a leadership role in organizing female hands, we set ourselves – inspired by the spirit of the day – to be role models for the young village women. We made every effort in other community activities as well to attract female participation, as part of our propaganda job. Having quite successfully brought women out of the home, however, we overlooked the typical problem of their "double burden." It was a neglect all the more regretable because the underdeveloped socialization of housework and the "feudal" attitude toward such work as gender specific were both especially severe in backward regions.

We also failed with another task: to alter the old custom of selling daughters in return for betrothal gifts. A widespread practice in the rural north, this frequently involved *huanqin* or direct exchanges of (underage) girls between families in order to get a son a wife. The price for a bride was so high that many young men could not afford marriage unless they were prepared to sacrifice their sisters – if they were "lucky" enough to have a sister who had, in turn, no luck to marry out to a town dweller. Under the government's strict residence control, few could ever escape the impoverished countryside. I was hurt, as a devoted women's team leader, not so much by the actual tears as by the passivity and even mindless contentment (over the gifts received, for example, which were made possible by the family's going into debt) on the part of the victims of those strange mercenary marriages. For the first time the "woman question" appeared to me as something of urgent contemporary relevance. It was immediately related to the situation of sheer poverty that overwhelmed men and women and erased even the most extensive and penetrating ideological influence.

Yet the question, which seemed merely rural, was in fact a pervasive one; and it might be approached very differently. Does tradition explain everything – as purely a matter of the "remnants of the old society," having nothing to do with a socialism that, almost by definition, would abolish these remnants in its irresistible forward march? Or maybe socialist policies and institutions are themselves severely limited by a certain cultural backwardness, hence unable to uproot deep forces of human indignity and misfortune? This latter doubt did bother me (as a dim passing thought) when I wondered why the official Women's Federation was powerless to confront those illegal acts of human trade[5] and, moreover, why the male-headed household should continue to be the norm, legitimated in a new society that thus rendered the exchange of women naturally acceptable. But without thinking much – that was an age for social change without philosophy or rational understanding of the world – we never fully understood the reality that struck our conscience and challenged our received education.

As privileged urban students "sent down" to learn from the peasants, we did not actually share some of their most fundamental experiences – such as hunger (we had grain subsidies from government reserves), early and undesired marriages, the closed world of a locally bound existence. That must be the reason, I admit, for our having sustained a naive idealism throughout the period, regarding personal feelings and affairs as ultimately unimportant in the great collective struggle. Socialism, often as an abstract ideal, was defended for the sake of socialism. Here the personal turned out to be not really political, except when private desires got in the way of ideological correctness and therefore were seen as politically offensive. So individuals, especially those of my urban generation, were highly politicized in the sense that their self-repressive mechanism worked effectively against "bourgeois" humanism and individualism in general and in support of communist puritanism in particular. Female self-repression was even stronger: strangely featured in a socialist culture, it existed side by side with an ideology of gender equality.

It was not accidental that a Soviet autobiographical novel called *How the Steel was Tempered* (by Nikolay Ostrovsky, English and Chinese trans., Moscow, 1952) about a young Bolshevik and his comrades fighting in the civil war had a tremendous influence on my entire generation. I still vividly remember every detail of the book, especially how a beloved revolutionary martyr was seen by his widow: falling in battle, dying in her arms on the vast Russian grasslands, his eyes forever gray, the color of steel, not blue, the color of love. Personal emotions and desires, including sexuality, appeared to be incompatible with the lofty, ruthless, and selfless revolution. It was not until much later that I would come to see the lack in our consciousness of two key notions tied to the very idea of liberation: freedom and happiness. We could indeed for a long while feel free and happy as so-called "successors to the cause of proletarian revolution," but not without profound blindness and prejudice, not without an immense feeling of alienation within ourselves. Critical of that past experience as I am now, I nonetheless also miss what I see as some of the most worthy, beautiful, and heroic expressions of "human nature" that are lost in the present age of cynicism, money fetishism, and single-minded pragmatism.

My life in the countryside came to an end when things began to change everywhere, as the country slowly recovered from the disruptions of the revolutionary 1960s. I left my village with mixed feelings of nostalgia and longing, also a sense of guilt for going to the university alone (only with a couple of my fellow city dwellers), leaving friends doomed to stay behind and to remain quasi-illiterate, some of whom were the smartest people I ever knew. Waving farewell to them on that golden autumn day has become for me a permanent reminder of naked inequality and minority privilege sustained by a proud socialist policy. I came to realize (as many others like myself did) that I had grown up physically and mentally not in Beijing where we were spoiled and deceived but in that northern corner of the great loess plateau, even though five years were not very long and we scarcely ever found a moment (or indeed a book – almost all we had were copies of *Anti-Dühring, And Quiet Flows the Don,* and *War and Peace* – apart from *200 Foreign Folk Songs*) to read in those days. Judging from what we gained from living with the peasants, Mao was right to hold the concept of education well beyond the reach of formal schooling.

But what was self-defeating with the Maoist educational revolution also became obvious as the new experiments failed to teach young people to appreciate, as critically as one should, the cultural heritage of human civilization. The emphasis on physical labor and on combining theory with practice did not work in an era when "knowledge" as such was totally unappreciated. In that year (1973) for the first time since the resumption of higher education, a rudimentary entry examination was required. The results of the exam were, however, cancelled later on after an applicant handed in a blank paper and stated in the *People's Daily* that such a bourgeois barrier to (academically unqualified but) politically qualified worker, peasant, and soldier candidates must be "smashed." So it was. Not surprisingly, then, the university students were composed of young (and not very young) people poorly prepared for any advanced study in any scholarly field. Even though in accordance with the principle of equality a great many more of them than ever before were from rural areas and female, they could not be provided with what they actually needed from a good primary and middle school education, despite great efforts by devoted teachers. Moreover, the purpose of attending university was not conceived as learning but simply as "occupying the educational arena" previously controlled by the "bourgeoisie" (a central category never coherently defined in the Chinese political language). Practically it was even simpler – the university became the single transitional place for anyone able to "get out" of the countryside and get on the state payroll, hence once and for all to lift one's status from the agricultural.

Reading was thus something odd, unfashionable, and even regarded as somehow politically incorrect. There was not much time to sit down to read anyway. Half of my three university years was spent on "social practice" in villages and factories, and at least another quarter on political activities. (By the way, sex was strictly prohibited and dating discouraged.) In the history department of the finest provincial university where I went, for example, the world history course (which, believe it or not, covered a time–space span from antiquity to the end of the Second World War over five continents) lasted a total of sixteen class hours in four weeks. There was no natural science taught to humanities majors. Foreign languages were not required. Examinations and the graduation thesis were altogether eliminated. Quite unusually, a group of friends and I still read as much as we could, including "big books" from the Chinese classics in the three volumes of *Capital*, with, of course, great gaps and difficulties in our understanding of them. Although not under pressure of exams or deadlines, we faced suspicion and even hostility from fellow students. (It is interesting to note that later in the 1980s the Chinese, after decades of isolation and ignorance, finally encountered some "new" intellectual trends in the West only to find them familiar. The Foucaultian "knowledge/power" thesis, for example, echoed well the Maoist preoccupation with bourgeois domination in the realm of cultural production; and indeed our university experience was not altogether bizarre if taken as part of the search for reinterpretations and innovations in an all-embracing project of cultural politics.)

I graduated in 1976, an eventful year, a second turning point, after 1949, in modern Chinese history. In April, in the form of mourning the late Premier Zhou Enlai, a popular revolt against the tyrannical regime – now in the hands of a handful of "ultra-left" careerists led by Mao's estranged wife – started in Beijing and spread to other urban centers. This movement, known as the Tiananmen Incident, was the first massive protest in the People's Republic, involving also numerous party members, against the ruling order. In July, in an unprecedented earthquake in Tangshan, an industrial city 80 miles from Beijing, 240,000 people perished overnight. I rushed to Beijing to be with my parents in their temporary shelter, which was in a sea of sheds while buildings were evacuated. My parents and their old comrades already knew, somehow, without accepting the traditional superstition that natural disaster is an omen of social-dynastic alterations, that significant changes would come soon. Mao died in September, and in a few weeks, a coup succeeded in overthrowing the "Gang of Four," an action supported ardently by almost everyone. A magnificent epoch, full of hopes and despair, glories and sorrows, was closed.

Today it seems rather remote, and indeed I am puzzled, to think of my mother as a liberated woman in the revolution and of the gender-blindness of my own generation growing up under communism. The whole question of women's liberation is all the more pressing because my daughter's generation is now being socialized in an environment in which the old socialist beliefs and policies concerning gender equality, however flawed themselves, are diminished by the overwhelming power of market forces. What has been a very positive development in China in the last decade, however, is the building-up of committed and autonomous movements for women's studies and women's interests. Moreover, these movements have rapidly expanded to make an impact on the entire course of the country's political liberalization and economic reform, primarily through strengthening the moral dimension of public discourse and actual policy formation.

Naturally I identify myself with the women's movements. My personal path leading to a feminist understanding is further related to the long, collective search for a synthesis of socialism and liberation, and hence at the present historical moment, to reform socialism. For me, feminism would inevitably link women's rights with citizens' rights, women's consciousness with democratic consciousness, women's liberation with social emancipation. This is a feminism aimed first and foremost at political democracy and full citizenship, and at self-realization and self-determination in harmony with social achievements. Perhaps a feminism bearing universal demands sounds too broad, but I do not see how it can be otherwise. Also, my own pathway has been shared by many others, and I know that there are many more who would join us even though their personal trajectories might have been very different.

NOTES

1   This article is a revised version of the first part of an introductory piece originally written for the author's book manuscript on the transformation of Chinese socialism.

2   Ding Ling was among a very few female Communist intellectuals who did express some criticisms of the sexual politics of Party life in the red bases. Cf. Ding, "Thoughts on March 8" (1942), in Tani E. Barlow, ed. *I Myself Am a*

Woman: Selected Writings of Ding Ling (Beacon Press, 1989). The article was publicly criticized in Yanan.
3   Lin Chun, "Love and hate: learning 'human nature' under Communism," in K. Gavroglu *et al.*, eds *Science, Politics and Social Practice* (Kluwer Academic Publishers, 1995).
4   There were of course richer areas and more successful communes, but the majority of the rural population evidently lived under poverty and compulsion in the two decades prior to the reform. Even William Hinton, the most formidable defender of Maoist agricultural socialism, accepted that two-thirds of the communes failed or stagnated by the late 1970s ("Mao, Rural Development, and Two-Line Struggle," *Monthly Review*, No. 9, February 1994).
5   The Marriage Law, adopted in 1950, outlawed child brides and mercenary and forced marriages, among other practices typical to prerevolutionary Chinese society.

Part II

GOING LOCAL

5

NEWSPAPERS AND NATIONALISM IN RURAL CHINA 1890–1929

Henrietta Harrison

In recent years, a great deal of exciting work in Chinese studies has focused on either newspapers (much of this emanating from the University of Heidelberg, where a long-term project on the medium's history in China is under way) or on nationalism. Some scholarship has moved between these two topics, which seems only natural given the emphasis that theorists of nationalism such as Benedict Anderson have placed on newspapers as molders of new forms of political and cultural identity. What this has meant, in the case of China, is that efforts have been made to explore the vision of the nation articulated in newspapers published in cities such as Shanghai, which from the 1840s through the 1940s were subdivided "treaty ports," containing mixtures of Chinese-run and foreign-run districts. These semi-colonial or quasi-colonial urban centers, which had been forced open to foreign trade and settlement by the Opium War (1839–1842) and subsequent conflicts, were the main places through which Western (and Japanese) ideas, products, and technologies of communication entered China. And there is broad agreement that, within them, a "public sphere" of sorts took shape, in which there were active debates on new ideas (such as imported concepts of nationalism) in new media (such as newspapers). The following chapter by Henrietta Harrison, while admitting that there is truth to this general idea, disputes some common assumptions about the prevalence of newspapers as sources of information and the spread of attachment to what she calls nationalism "in its modern form" into rural areas.

Her point of departure in making this argument is a close examination of the diary kept by a member of the local elite of a relatively isolated part of North China. If we analyze this text, Harrison argues, we can begin to understand that there were many ways that newspapers could be used, including quite skeptically (as no substitute for the "real" news of oral reports), as a source of information in the early twentieth-century Chinese countryside. We will also begin to gain an appreciation for the varied processes by which new ideas of the nation could mingle with other concepts of political identity and political loyalty. In presenting these arguments, Harrison has much of interest to say in passing about major political

83

events of the very late nineteenth and early twentieth centuries (the Boxer Uprising, for example), always focusing on how they affected and were understood by her diarist. In a sense, then, though her chapter begins a new section, it also picks up nicely on a theme discussed in the previous chapter. Harrison suggests, as Lin Chun does, that to understand fully the meaning of China's great transformations, we are best served by moving continually between different scales of analysis. We need to think about national processes and even about the flow of ideologies across cultural and linguistic borders, but we also have to make room for consideration of the complexities of individual experience. A key difference is that, for Harrison as opposed to Lin Chun, the individual is not herself but rather a figure whose views have come down to her via an unusual source, the peculiarities of which she describes in the pages to come as she introduces us to its contents.

* * *

In 1919 the *Shanxi Daily News* (*Shanxi ribao*) published an account by one of its readers who had visited some remote villages and had been impressed at how well informed the villagers were about recent government policies and reforms. He explained that the villagers now understood that certain traditional customs were wrong, because when they were resting, enlightened village leaders or schoolteachers often "hold a copy of this newspaper in their hands and read it aloud and explain it."[1] This image of the literate reading aloud to the illiterate, implying that the words of authors were injected verbatim into the minds of country folk, appealed for obvious reasons to the reformist newspaper writers of early twentieth-century China. It is also, however, a commonplace of studies of the impact of printing and print culture in European history.[2] Because of this image, historians of China have too often assumed that modern nationalism was transmitted to the countryside in precisely the terms of the newspaper modernizers, or not at all. We have thus assumed a shared vocabulary of nationalism that may never have existed, and dismissed as xenophobia nationalist behaviour that was not expressed in that vocabulary. This has obscured our vision of rural nationalism during the nineteenth and early twentieth centuries. Rural nationalism was formed not by the newspapers but by news. Until the 1920s that news was primarily oral and thus outside the control of the modernizing elites who dominated the newspapers.

Nationalism in its modern form was a Western import into China. However, modern nationalism was not the only form of state-centred identity available to nineteenth-century Chinese. China's long history as a political unit meant that its people had a strong sense of identity focused round the idea of the political and moral superiority of their culture over that of their neighbours. This type of identity, often called "culturalism," was seen both in ethnic relations (peripheral peoples were expected to assimilate to the dominant Han Chinese culture) and in the political order (peripheral states were expected to pay tribute to the Chinese emperor).[3] However, by the nineteenth century culturalism had been joined to the quite different political ideology of the Manchu dynasty that had ruled China since the seventeenth century. The Qing saw their empire as a state made up of many different cultures and peoples, whose assimilation to Han Chinese culture they not only did not encourage, but frequently tried to prevent.[4] The assimilation of these two world-views led to frequent policy disputes within the government, but it did provide a framework for an understanding of international events that allowed for interstate relations while preserving a strong sense of Chinese superiority.

Modern nationalism, which entered China from the 1860s onwards, was very different from the earlier forms of national identity both in its emphasis on the idea of competition between states and in its rejection of much of what previously constituted Chinese identity.[5] The Westernizers who introduced the new ideas were often under attack for selling out to the foreigners, while their personal commitment to modernity and reform on Western models initially made it hard for them to take a strongly anti-foreign line.[6] Consequently, the new national identity came to involve what Myron Cohen has called "a forceful and near-total rejection of the earlier traditional and culturally elaborated sense of nationhood."[7] By privileging modern nationalism over traditional forms of identity, elites, and the historians who follow their accounts, have been able to dismiss popular opposition to modernizing and Westernizing policies.[8] The claim that the majority of the population who lived in the largely rural interior were ignorant and their opposition to the new policies was therefore merely a product of xenophobia, or ignorant fear, was an important part of this process.

Newspapers like the *Shanxi Daily News* have been preserved for the historian in libraries and archives, often by men who shared their reformist agenda, while oral news is by its very nature transitory and largely inaccessible. This article uses one man's diary to look at how news was received in a village in north China. Oral forms of news transmission included both anonymous rumours and more accurate oral reports that contained a record of their chain of transmission from a source that could be presumed to be reliable. Soldiers were often cited as the original source of reports of major events, whereas items of economic and court news more often had their origins in the letters home of local merchants resident in Beijing and other major cities. In either case the news was generally transmitted by ordinary travellers, many of whom were merchants and traders. These primarily oral forms of news transmission interacted with the written news of the "Metropolitan Gazette" (*jingbao*) and modern-style newspapers, which were generally only available some time after oral reports of the events concerned. Written news sources did not replace oral news, but became part of a chain of transmission through which events were both reported and interpreted in ways that reflected the outlook of the rural recipients as much as the ideologies of the urban modernizers who composed the newspapers.

The diary of Liu Dapeng (1857–1942) is unusual among Chinese sources of this period in being written by a man who lived in the countryside, respected his neighbours' views, and shared their opposition to political change.[9] Liu Dapeng came from the village of Chiqiao, a day's journey south of Taiyuan, the capital of Shanxi province. The dusty track along which the little village straggled was also part one of the major north–south routes through the province, so the village was not remote. However, it was not particularly wealthy: the people made their living as papermakers and farmers, and the four rooms round a single courtyard inhabited by Liu Dapeng, his parents, and his five sons and their families was one of the largest homes in the village. Liu Dapeng had succeeded in passing the exams for the second level of degree and can thus be counted as a member of the local elite, but his family was unable to support him to study full time for the final level of exams that might have earned him an official position, and so for twenty years, from 1892 until the revolution of 1911, he also worked as a tutor in the village of Nanxi some thirty miles away. Nanxi was the home of a wealthy banking and trading lineage: high walls surrounded the spacious homes of the wealthy; dealers came out from Taigu county town to sell books; and Liu Dapeng ate meat every day and wished he could share his good fortune with his parents.

Although Shanxi was cut off from the rest of north China by the high mountains that surrounded it, there was a strong tradition of trade and banking on the central Shanxi plain which meant that local men travelled back and forth across north and central China. In terms of the transmission of news, this counteracted to some extent the effect of the poor roads in and out of the province that would otherwise have made it one of the more remote parts of north China. Both Chiqiao and Nanxi villages lay on the fertile central plain of Shanxi, and were richer and easier to get to than the remote hamlets scattered through the mountains that circled the plain. Each village had its own distinctive character, but neither Chiqiao nor Nanxi was in any way unusual among the villages of the plain. As a Confucian scholar and a respected if not particularly wealthy man, Liu Dapeng saw the identification of his own interests with those of the villagers with some dismay, exclaiming in mock horror after a day spent in the fields: "I am an old farmer."[10] His ambiguous position was an anomaly created by a rapidly changing society in which his traditional qualifications brought popular respect (he is still remembered in the village), but less and less access to power. In these circumstances he became an increasingly involved reporter of village talk and opinions.

On 31 April 1901, Liu Dapeng left his schoolhouse in Nanxi and went home to Chiqiao to take care of his family in the event of a foreign invasion. This was the consequence of a series of rumours and reports concerning the French and German forces then stationed along Shanxi's mountainous eastern border. Shanxi had been one of the provinces worst affected by the Boxer troubles of 1900, when the court, in response to a series of attacks on rural Christians which were seen as expressions of popular anti-foreign feeling, declared war on the foreign powers. Missionaries were executed in the provincial capital, while in villages across the province thousands of Chinese Christians were driven from their homes and murdered. Reacting to these events, the foreign powers sent a joint force which sacked Beijing and then moved inland towards Shanxi. On 22 April 1901, French and German troops launched an attack on the Guguan and Niangziguan passes into Shanxi. According to the provincial governor's telegrams, approximately two thousand foreign soldiers plus an unknown number of Chinese Christians attacked and captured the passes, but then withdrew. Shanxi losses were severe, and the telegrams refer to a Chinese retreat.[11]

Four days later, on 26 April, Liu Dapeng and a friend walked from Nanxi to one of the neighbouring villages for the day. Afterwards Liu wrote: "All along the road everyone was saying that the foreign marauders had attacked the Guguan pass, and the Christians had led the marauders in through the Niangziguan pass. I don't know whether it is true or not. If it is indeed the case then our Shanxi is in danger."[12] Next day he noticed soldiers passing Nanxi as if they were on their way to the Guguan pass, and commented that everyone was discussing what had happened and no one could agree on it, but the general impression was that the situation was dangerous. Soon the anxiety was severe enough for one of the other non-local employees in Nanxi to set off for home. This in itself worried people, and Liu sent his son to a neighbouring village to ask his father, who ran a timber-yard there, to return home and take charge. Then on the 30th he heard more detailed news of the engagement. This confirmed that there had indeed been an attack on the Niangziguan pass, but the Shanxi forces had repelled it, and seven to eight thousand foreign soldiers had been killed. News of a victory calmed people's anxieties somewhat, but nevertheless Liu returned home to Chiqiao to protect his family.[13]

These events show both the power and the unreliable nature of rumour. As Paul Cohen has shown, many rumours during the early period of the Boxer crisis were highly implausible, but were nevertheless widely believed.[14] People who heard rumours acted on them. The threat of a foreign invasion of Shanxi had existed for several weeks before the attack on the passes, but it was the reports of the attack that actually caused people in Nanxi to return to their homes.[15] At the same time, the news that was being received had been distorted by the hopes and fears of those who reported it. The provincial governor received reliable telegrams of a force of one thousand foreign troops; the people of Nanxi heard of a foreign force large enough to leave seven to eight thousand dead. And where the governor heard of defeat, the people of Nanxi heard of victory. As always, drought, rumour and unrest went together, for late rainfall left farmers anxious and with time on their hands to gather and talk.[16] When it finally rained some three weeks later, Liu commented that people were now busy planting and had no time to speak of the foreign troubles.[17]

The connection with unrest meant that rumour was regarded as a bad omen for the government. At times of crisis the provincial government would issue proclamations forbidding people to discuss state affairs, as it did in 1894 when it was being said that the emperor was dying.[18] This was untrue, but probably reflected popular concern about the weakness of the government. By issuing proclamations against the spreading of rumours, the government declared both its interest in, and its distrust of, the oral network of news which was hard to control and potentially a threat to law and order. Liu Dapeng shared the official distrust of rumour, but he made a distinction between rumour (*yao*) and oral reports (*chuan*). Later in 1901 he commented that although many oral reports were not true, those that described bad things usually deserved investigation; rumours on the other hand should not be looked into.[19] Indeed, the diary contains repeated, though clearly disregarded, injunctions to himself not to listen to rumours.[20] Oral reports, however, are recorded in detail and without apology, for this was the way in which Liu Dapeng, like most people of his time, learned about national affairs.

The working of the news network that combined rumour and oral report is well illustrated by the way the news of a minor uprising in the neighbouring province of Zhili reached Liu in Nanxi.[21] During the negotiations that followed the Boxer crisis the Chinese government agreed to pay a huge indemnity and to punish those who had joined in Boxer activities. The implementation of this agreement led to widespread resentment. When on 12 May 1902 Liu Dapeng heard that the people in Shulu county in Zhili had risen up against the foreigners who were forcing the officials to exact the indemnity, he saw the rumour as a form of expression of collective concerns: "Although it is a rumour, it is what is in people's minds."[22] Later that day a visitor to Liu's schoolhouse said that he had met a man who was returning from Beijing and had passed through the city of Zhengding, in Zhili, on the way. He had been told that there had been a revolt in the south-east of the prefecture in which 110 villages had united and fought against government troops. Liu guessed that this must be the same uprising described in the rumour. A few days later, a man who had just come to Shanxi from Manchuria reported seeing soldiers in Baoding who told him they had been fighting the rebels in Shunde and Guangping prefectures. This report provided further details: the rebels had killed a county magistrate; the revolt was caused by the indemnities; it had started in the winter, and there had been several battles between the people and the soldiers in March.[23]

Unsubstantiated rumour followed by detailed reports from travellers and soldiers was typical of the oral news network. These oral reports did not have written sources. Even today most news describes events which are seen and heard before they are written down, and this was even more true in early twentieth-century China. News stories were generated by things seen: foreigners being executed; city gates closing early. The traveller or passer-by then elicited further information from other onlookers: the foreign barbarians being executed were railway workers who had raped a woman; the city gates were closing early because of a mutiny.[24] Dependence on eyewitnesses meant that travellers, primarily soldiers and traders, many of whom journeyed long distances on foot, were central to the transmission of news; and that roads, which were also important public spaces, especially where they passed through villages like Chiqiao, were the principal sites of transmission. Soldiers could often provide detailed news of rebellions and bandits that they had been sent to suppress. Moreover, movements of soldiers were in themselves a major topic of news, since even government troops were a threat to any neighbourhood through which they passed. News from traders and bankers increased over the New Year when many returned home and then paid a series of obligatory New Year calls. Liu's understanding of the Zhili uprising was affected by a New Year visit from a friend who had visited Shanghai, Tianjin and Beijing that year, and reported that: "All the places he had passed through had been conquered by the ocean barbarians and there was nothing the dynasty could do."[25]

Letters formed part of this network of oral news. A letter home from a Nanxi man living in Beijing filled in the background to the uprising, giving details of the negotiations over the size of the Boxer indemnity and the demands made by the Catholic church hierarchy, as well as information about the foreign soldiers in Beijing and an uprising in Guangxi.[26] Letters could provide detailed accounts that would not be corrupted over long distances, and were a source of considerable general interest for this reason. However, surprisingly detailed accounts were also passed on by word of mouth: a book merchant coming out to Nanxi from Taigu county town told Liu the numbers of people attending a famine relief station there on three different dates that month.[27]

One week after hearing the first rumours of the Zhili uprising, Liu read an imperial edict concerning the revolt published in the "Metropolitan Gazette." The gazette was a daily report of court business provided by the Grand Secretariat and then issued by various publishers in Beijing. The origins of this practice can be traced back as early as the second century, and by the mid-nineteenth century the gazette was printed, though people continued to be employed in hand-copying abridged editions. Copies were sent to officials and others in the provinces who could afford the regular subscription, but it was also common for copies to be rented for a much smaller price.[28] Liu mentions reading the gazette in a shop in Taigu county town, which suggests that he may have rented copies in this way.[29] Samuel Wells Williams commented of the 1880s that the gazette was "very generally read and discussed by educated people in cities."[30] This would seem to be confirmed by Liu Dapeng, since he read the "Metropolitan Gazette" relatively frequently, recording the fact in his diary at least five times in 1901 and ten times in 1902.

Despite its wide circulation and somewhat misleading single title, the gazette was in several important ways different from the Western-style newspapers that were introduced into China in the nineteenth century. It has been said that one of the things that differentiates the print culture of newspapers from existing news networks is the distribution of identical items of information forming impersonal links between people unknown to each other.[31] It is also argued that such impersonal links are among the factors giving rise to modern nationalism.[32] The "Metropolitan Gazette," however, was created by several different publishers each of whom selected different documents from those provide by the government for circulation.

Thus the gazette did not have a single text that could have distributed uniform chunks of information, but rather a multiplicity of texts, each depending on the choices of the publisher and any later abridgers. These texts, moreover, shared a format and layout which linked them more closely to other printed books of the time than to Western-style newspapers. Each issue took the form of a small thread-bound volume which began with the court diary for the day, information which had negligible new value and was often omitted in provincial versions. The bulk of the text consisted of official memorials and the emperor's responses. The news thus followed the structure of official correspondence, with the emperor's decision coming at the end of the documentation. In the layout of the text, emphasis was given not to any aspect of the subject matter, but to references to the emperor, dynasty or court, which were placed at the head of the page.[33] The emphasis, in other words, was not on specific events but on the eternal structures of society. The layout also meant that the text required careful and consecutive reading, a practice which was in any case only suitable for the words of the reigning emperor. Thus format, layout and contents exacerbated the sense of closure and finality which is associated with printed works, even while the nature of the production process meant that any given text was the result of a series of selections.[34] The "Metropolitan Gazette" almost always arrived in the Shanxi countryside after important events had already been heard of through the oral news network, and it provided confirmation and clarification, as was the case when Liu read about the Zhili uprising. It was seen as providing the truth, a fact that associated it with the traditional texts of orthodox thought and was later to influence the readers and writers of Western-style modern newspapers.

That the "Metropolitan Gazette" provided a true account of events and opinions did not necessarily mean that readers agreed with government policy. When Liu Dapeng read about the Zhili uprising, the edict published in the gazette gave details of the trouble as it was viewed by the government, the name of the leader, and a summary of his offences: he had gathered crowds, killed fifty government officials and soldiers, burned churches, robbed Christians and murdered a French missionary. The edict ordered military suppression of the uprising and the protection of foreigners and Chinese Christians. Liu was highly critical: since the whole problem was caused by the foreigners and Christians, surely it was wrong to protect them at the expense of the ordinary people. To stigmatize as rebels those who opposed the Christian priests, and to send soldiers to oppress them, was blatantly wrong and thus bound to lead to trouble. Later entries mention that people are talking about the uprising everywhere and are angry about it.[35] People talked angrily about the uprising because, like Liu Dapeng, they shared many of the attitudes of the rebels and were critical of the government's response. The uprising was of interest because it gave people a focus around which to articulate grievances which may well be described as nationalist. They criticized both the central government in Beijing and individual local officials for complying with foreign demands, and sympathized with rebels who killed foreigners and their minions, the Christians.

The news network into which Western-style newspapers were introduced in rural Shanxi in the early twentieth century was thus primarily oral. News passed on by word of mouth was shared by the literate and the illiterate. The most common place for such conversations was the highway, a space open and available to all. The contents of the "Metropolitan Gazette" were passed on orally. Indeed, the gazette was part of the network of oral news just as letters and travelling merchants were. None of these elements defined a distinct elite sphere of news. In 1895, at the end of the Sino-Japanese war, Liu Dapeng noted that all the Chiqiao farmers were discussing the peace talks: "Everyone has the matter of the dwarf-pirate raids in their thoughts. Recently we heard that a peace was being negotiated. Even the farmers and country folk all say this is absolutely unacceptable. Since I came home my ears have been full of this talk."[36] The shared network of news provided the basis for an understanding of national politics among villagers that has been unreasonably dismissed as xenophobia by the Westerners and Chinese modernizers whom it opposed.

Newspapers of the kind we are familiar with – mass-audience, advertising-supported daily or weekly publications – were a Western import into China and followed a path of development that was only slightly linked to that of the existing "Metropolitan Gazette." Many of the early Chinese-language newspapers of the 1860s and 1870s were owned by foreigners, and in the early years most of their readers were connected with foreign trade. The origins of modern newspapers in the treaty-port world created a strong link between newspapers in general and Western-inspired ideas of modernity.[37] When Shanxi's first provincial newspaper, the *Shanxi Gazette* (*Jinbao*), was founded in 1902, it was backed by British missionary Timothy Richard as well as by the provincial government, and was printed on presses belonging to the printing classes of the newly founded Shanxi University.[38] Some of the contents of the *Shanxi Gazette* were drawn from the "Metropolitan Gazette" (imperial edicts and some memorials), but there was also a "Western learning" section which discussed such things as the distance of foreign countries, the depths of the sea and the advantages of planting trees to attract rain. The editorial of the first issue included advice to students leaving Shanxi to go abroad for study.[39] To the extent that both reform and revolution were essentially a matter of altering ways of looking at the world through creating and defining a new vocabulary, the modern press was one of the strongholds of such reform. However, this kind of background and ideology naturally meant that the nationalism promoted in the newspapers was very different from the nationalism of the oral news network.

The circulation of modern-style newspapers, previously negligible in comparison with China's vast population, rose rapidly during the early twentieth century. Newspapers kept their circulation secret, but indicators such as the number of newspapers handled by the government postal service, or the amount of newsprint imported, suggest that readership was increasing fast. The numbers of newspapers and magazines mailed at special cheap rates more than quadrupled between 1912 and 1924.[40] Studies of the history of the modern newspaper in China often argue that reader-ship rose because of the spread of modern ideas, but this was not necessarily the case.[41] When the *Shanxi Gazette* began publishing in 1902, it took the form of a single sheet issued every five days and cost three ounces of silver for a year's subscription, making it the most expensive in the country. Nevertheless, every magistrate in the country had to subscribe for thirty copies, a system that was later continued and enlarged. By 1908 Taiyuan county received one hundred copies which the villages were compelled to take and pay for. This system made the gazette a profitable enterprise and Liu Dapeng regarded it simply as a new tax to fund the reforms.[42] In Shanxi, newspaper circulation increased partly because of increased interest from readers, but also because of government pressure.

Calculations of newspaper readership in the early twentieth century usually assume that each copy of a newspaper sold was read by at least ten people.[43] The figures are based on contemporary guesswork, but this was certainly the category of reader into which Liu Dapeng fell. During the period of this study he mentions reading eight different titles, but he does not appear at any stage to have purchased a newspaper regularly. He mentions borrowing a copy of the *Shenbao*, the most widely read of the commercial Shanghai newspapers, and being given a copy of the *Shanxi Gazette* by his employer.[44] Before 1911 it is clear that he was much more likely to have access to both the "Metropolitan Gazette" and other news-papers in Nanxi than in Chiqiao, presumably because the concentration of wealthy families in Nanxi and other villages around Taigu made it more likely that someone would purchase a copy that might then circulate. That he was reading second-hand copies is also suggested by the time they took to reach him. In 1910 the *Cabinet Gazette* (*Neige guanbao*), a modernized version of the "Metropolitan Gazette," expressed the hope that copies should reach Taiyuan from Beijing in five days, and in 1912 the new republican *Government Gazette* (*Zhengfu gongbao*) was supposed to take four days to reach Taiyuan.[45] By contrast the newspapers Liu Dapeng read during the 1900s took an average of twenty days to reach him, and one copy of the *China News* (*Zhonghua bao*), which was written in a popular style with sensational stories ("The curious clothing of Mongolian women," "Japanese brothel burns down"), reached him more than two months after its date of publication.[46] Even the *Shanxi Gazette*, which was published in Taiyuan, took an average of eighteen days to reach Liu. This suggests that the late arrival of newspapers was indeed due more to multiple readers than to slow delivery.

The long time periods between a newspaper's publication and its arrival in the villages meant that oral report continued to anticipate published newspaper reports. When in 1914 the bandit White Wolf led his forces from Henan into Shanxi, Liu Dapeng knew of the events from oral reports six days before he received confirmation from the newspapers. When he did receive printed confirmation it was because his son read the newspapers on a visit to the county town and then sent a letter home with the news. This was followed by further oral reports and rumours which disturbed the villagers, and by Liu Dapeng's own observation of the ominous colours of the morning sky.[47] Similarly, Liu's first news of that greatest exemplar of modern nationalism, the May Fourth movement, in which student protesters demanded that China refuse to sign the Treaty of Versailles because it transferred control over German possessions in China to Japan, was when his son came home from Taiyuan and reported that: "The students of all the schools in the provincial capital were all holding little flags bearing the words, 'Denounce the traitors who are selling the country', and words like that, and were rushing around shouting, going towards the military governor's offices."[45]

Like other bearers of oral reports, Liu's son made enquiries on seeing this curious scene and found out that the students were angry because a student studying in Japan had pursued the Chinese ambassador to Tianjin, and shot at him, because he had sold Qingdao to the Japanese. Nineteen students had then been arrested. The details of this report were incorrect: the Chinese ambassador to Japan had been beaten up by students in Beijing, rather than shot at by a student in Tianjin. However, the general outline concerning the arrests and the attribution of the loss of Qingdao to the venality of the officials of the Beijing government, and especially the ambassador to Japan, was an accurate representation of the causes of the students' dissatisfaction.

Newspapers interacted with this network of oral news rather than replacing it. In 1923 Liu explained that he had "heard" that the newspapers had been promoting a statement made by Wu Peifu, a major central China warlord, that he would oppose any attempt to dislodge the Shanxi governor, Yan Xishan.[49] Here we see news that was originally written, moving from the newspapers into the oral network. Newspapers also reported news from travellers, giving the same kind of information that provided essential authenticity for the oral news network. So, for example, the *Shanxi Daily News* printed a report of a currency crisis in the county town of Pingyao in 1920, with the explanation that it came from a merchant who had travelled from Pingyao to Taiyuan the previous day.[50] The importance of oral news meant that governments continued to try and prevent it in times of crisis. When Yuan Shikai's government was about to fall in 1916, Shanxi officials banned the spreading of rumour on penalty of death, while at the same time ordering the local newspapers not to print any disturbing news.[51] Thus modern-style newspapers did not replace existing news networks, but became part of them. This naturally affected the way in which news was understood and interpreted. News of the May Fourth movement from an onlooker puzzled by students running around holding flags, was quite different from any of the interpretations, either positive or negative, published in the newspapers.

Interpretations of the newspapers were also affected by the continued existence of a style of reading that was in contradiction to the imported format and layout of the pages. The Western newspapers, on which the modern Chinese newspapers were modelled, were laid out not like a book in a series of consecutive paragraphs, but separated into articles with headings in contrasting typefaces. They were not intended to be read from cover to cover, but were designed for a new kind of inattentive reading.[52] But did people's reading habits correspond to those implied by the layout of the text? Ge Gongzhen, in his classic study of Chinese newspapers published in the 1920s, remarks that: "Some people say that when Chinese people read a newspaper they can usually read from the beginning to the end without missing a single word."[53] He then criticizes this as inappropriate for people who are truly concerned about public affairs, since they should not have enough time for such a thorough reading. An examination of Liu Dapeng's newspaper reading habits suggests that however much the producers of modern newspapers may have disapproved, this style of reading did indeed exist. Liu Dapeng was in the habit of rising well before dawn, lighting a lamp, and spending some time in meditation and the reading of history. In his youth, when he was studying for the state examinations, he had stressed the importance of reading history as a means of expanding one's knowledge and feelings.[54] When he later came to read newspapers, he usually read them during this same quiet time before the rest of the household rose. It was hardly an atmosphere conducive to the selective reading the modern newspapers were designed for. Moreover, it seems likely that he did indeed read the newspapers cover to cover, since on one occasion in 1914 he comments on a report of a shower of red rain in the Jiangsu town of Songjiang. This report was in the back pages of the *Shenbao*, in small print, and in the local news section, all of which related to towns far away in Jiangsu and Zhejiang.[55]

Liu Dapeng's comments on newspaper reports of the outbreak of war in Europe in 1914 suggest that his interpretation of the newspapers was affected by his reading habits and the attitudes and moral values they carried with them. The *Shenbao*, which Liu read at this time, provided considerable coverage of the war. However, the great majority of the material used consisted either of bulletins issued by the news services of the protagonists and forwarded by Reuters, or articles translated from the *North China Daily News*, the newspaper of the Shanghai British community.

These items naturally reflected their foreign sources. The newspaper's own interpretation of events was by and large restricted to the daily editorial. For some time after the war started, editorials dealt exclusively with it. Many of the editorials were intended primarily to explain what was going on: the tangle of alliances that had caused war on so many fronts, and the contradictions in the bulletins from each side. However, in the early days of the war, before the Japanese invasion of Qingdao, editorials still used the warring European nations as models for China: the British had laid aside their differences over Ireland when facing a foreign enemy; Serbia was a small country but had not given way to a great power.[56] In the autumn of 1914, *Shenbao* editorials criticized neither the war itself nor the attitudes, from which China had so long suffered, which had caused it.

Liu Dapeng's comments provide a completely different vision of events from that seen in the newspapers. In the 1890s his reading of history had caused him to note that generals should not allow indiscriminate killing.[57] Now his diary entries note the casualty figures and ignore the interpretations of the editorials: "The force of the war through all the European countries is still fierce, so I do not know how many lives and how much property have been lost. Alas! The supreme deity regards love of life as a virtue. But in the present Great War of the Western Ocean flesh and blood are scattered in the smoke of guns and the rain of bullets. Every day the bodies of the dead soldiers and officers are too many to count. Does it not hurt the supreme deity's love of life? Even I cannot avoid feeling pity when I think of it. Although the ocean people are outer barbarians their lives too are precious."[58] Other entries seek to make sense of the tragedy, and include ideas of the importance of technology and the oppression of China by the European states, explaining that the killing is because the foreigners have sought after technical ingenuity and conspicuous consumption, and that the disaster is Heaven's punishment of the barbarians for using the "power and wealth" of their countries to mistreat China.[59] Liu's understanding of the war is at once more nationalist than the newspapers in attributing the disaster to divine punishment for the foreigners' treatment of China, and at the same time completely divorced from the newspapers' understanding of nationalism as requiring imitation of Western countries.

The idea of the Europeans as "outer barbarians" in Liu's comments on the war, and the general sense of moral superiority, are part of a traditional culturalist outlook. The terminology was alien to modern Chinese nationalism and did not appear in the newspapers, which distinguished conscientiously between the various European nationalities. Another example of Liu's use of traditional terminology occurs in his reports of rumours of Sun Yat-sen's so-called Second Revolution, where he not only refers to Sun Yat-sen as "the chief rebel," but to Yuan Shikai, the president of the republic, as "the rebel minister."[60] The judgements implied in these terms would, of course, have been unprintable in the general press: but in any case the writers of the modern newspapers did not accept the value structure that lay behind them. On the other hand, Liu picked out and satirized modernizing vocabulary used by the newspapers. In his comments on the European War (1914–18) he criticizes the European countries for their emphasis on "power and wealth." Indeed, several years earlier when he had seen in the 1902 "Metropolitan Gazette" and the *Shanxi Gazette* that the government was to emphasize "wealth and power," then a key idea behind the reforms, he had commented grumpily that what the officials were actually doing when they talked about economic rights, and set up mines and other enterprises, was to take the people's property.[61] Thus although Liu read the national newspaper, he did not during this period adopt any of the terminology that indicated their understanding of nationalism, but this was not because he was ignorant. It was simply that his sense of national identity and pride was part of his existing moral framework, and the knowledge he acquired from the newspapers was fitted into this.

The May Fourth movement changed the relationship between the Chinese newspapers and nationalism. Scholarship that touches on the impact of newspapers on popular nationalism in China too often assumes that the aims of the press had always been nationalist. This follows Liang Qichao, the famous reformist journalist of the 1900s, who suggested that newspapers should translate world news and write about current affairs so that readers would be spurred to action by knowledge of China's humiliation.[62] However, contrary to what is often imagined, newspapers of the 1900s and 1910s did indeed translate world news, but most of them seldom did so in a way that explicitly urged their readers to nationalism. This was very different from subsequent Chinese newspaper practice. A recent Chinese study of the *Shenbao*'s coverage of the Boxer crisis expresses understandable shock at the discovery that during the foreign invasion the *Shenbao* published such literal translations of Western reports that the Chinese military forces were referred to as "the enemy."[63] Newspaper journalists and publishers still perceived themselves as arguing for Western-style modernity, which prevented them from expressing strong criticism of the Western powers. Newspaper reports of the Boxer crisis carried far less sense of injury to national pride than the oral news network, which spoke of "foreign barbarians" and sympathized with rebellions against the imposition of the indemnities. This situation changed partly as a result of the rising student nationalism of the 1910s and 1920s that affected newspaper staff and partly as a result of the politicization of newspaper ownership. Modern newspapers in China had been primarily commercial enterprises in their early years. But after 1916 the combination of student nationalism and warlord politics made favourable publicity a necessity for any group seeking national political power. Beijing in 1920 is said to have had seventy-seven daily newspapers, most of them subsidized by political groups.[64] Only the great newspapers of the treaty ports, like the *Shenbao* and

Dagongbao, produced in Shanghai and Tianjin respectively, could afford to remain independent. By the 1920s the promotion of modern nationalism, and with it power for one or other of the various nationalist parties, had become central to the activities of most of the periodical press.

In Shanxi the provincial press was tightly controlled by the provincial governor, Yan Xishan. The *Shanxi Gazette* had folded before the 1911 revolution, but its place was taken by a series of other provincial newspapers, and the practice of requiring county and village governments to purchase these newspapers continued. However, distribution was a problem with this system: newspapers tended to accumulate in the county government and then be sent on to the villages in large bundles.[65] In 1919 the Shanxi government held a drive to encourage the setting-up of newspaper reading-rooms in towns and villages. The aim of one such reading-room was explicitly stated to be to assist the implementation of government policy.[66] Several planned to provide staff to explain the contents of the newspapers to the illiterate.[67] People were interested in news, and some of the reading-rooms were successful. However, outside the county towns the rooms were expected to make do with the second-hand copies of the newspapers purchased by shops, schools and village offices, most of which would have been likely to have circulated round interested local readers in any case. In addition, some of the reading-rooms set up under pressure from the government never actually functioned. One that was set up in a sub-county town in Qixian had tables and chairs but no newspapers. The district head explained that newspapers were not worthwhile since there were no newspaper readers.[68] The campaign to set up newspaper reading-rooms was only one of a series of reforms that marked Governor Yan Xishan's consolidation of his personal power in 1918. The newspapers were intended to promote these campaigns against such things as foot binding and opium smoking, and included many articles on exemplary practice. The campaign for newspaper reading-rooms indicates the close links that were perceived to exist between provincial government policy and the newspapers.

At the same time as the newspapers became more politically oriented, they also became much more readily accessible to Liu Dapeng, now living in declining circumstances in Chiqiao. Instead of writing the diary on plain paper as had done in the past, Liu now began to write on the backs of scraps of paper pasted together and folded into a book. For several months in 1926 and 1927 the diary is written on the backs of sheets of the *Jinyang Daily* (*Jinyang ribao*). In addition, the delay between the date of publication and the date on which Liu received the newspapers he read dropped to an average of two days for newspapers published in Taiyuan and eight days for national publications from the coastal cities. This suggests that someone in Chiqiao or nearby was having a newspaper delivered. This could have been Liu himself, but might equally well have been the village office under pressure from the provincial government. The effects of the increased politicization of newspapers, combined with their wider and more rapid circulation, can be seen in Liu's comments on the fighting between the armies of Yan Xishan and Feng Yuxiang that took place in the north of Shanxi in the summer of 1926. Feng Yuxiang had been driven from a brief spell of national power in Beijing by a coalition of warlords that included Yan Xishan. His army needed to pass through Shanxi during its retreat from Beijing to its bases in north-west China. As the army came south across the mountainous border into Shanxi, Yan Xishan's forces opposed it and the fighting was intense.[69] In some ways the fighting and the locations were similar to the threatened foreign invasion of 1901, but the way the news reached Liu in Chiqiao was quite different. For one thing the first news now came through the newspapers rather than through rumour.[70] When soldiers passed through the village he already knew that they were on their way to the north of the province, and why.

This is not to say that oral report no longer played a part in the transmission of news. On various occasions during the campaign Liu notes rumours that grain has been shipped out of the province by train, that the Shanxi troops have been defeated in a battle north of Datong, and that there are more than ten thousand dead on each side.[71] What the majority of oral reports like these share is that they concern aspects of the war that were not being printed in the provincial newspapers controlled by Yan Xishan. After reading a report of the battle north of Datong in the *Jinyang Daily*, Liu records the newspaper's statement that the Shanxi forces won and that many of the enemy soldiers were killed. From this he then deduces that many of the Shanxi soldiers must also have been killed. About two weeks later, after seeing newspapers from Beijing and Tianjin, he notes their statements that the Shanxi forces have in fact been defeated.[72] This much more critical attitude to the factual content of the newspapers was a direct result of their political affiliations. But the distrust of the content of the newspapers had brought a new role for the oral news network. In the past, it had anticipated the printed news and interacted with it. Now it was beginning to take up a quite different and very powerful role as a voice of opposition and criticism against government actions defended and promoted in an increasingly politically dominated press.

Newspaper news did not simply replace oral reports, but became a part of the existing network of communications. In the same way, the kind of nationalism promoted by the newspapers did not simply replace the existing nationalism of the rural population. Instead, as people learned about provincial, national and international events through rumour, oral report, letters and newspapers, so their understandings of the nation shared the characteristics and concerns of all these different sources. A concern with the language of nationalism promoted through the newspapers has obscured our perception of a continuing rural nationalism. Nationalism was not injected into the countryside verbatim by an urban elite, but was transformed and reinvented by the concerns and interests of those who saw and reported local and national news.

NOTES

1 *Shanxi ribao*, 20 June 1919, 4.
2 For example, David Cressy, *Literacy and the Social Order: Reading and Writing in Tudor and Stuart England* (Cambridge, 1980), 14; Jeremy D. Popkin, *Revolutionary News: The Press in France, 1789–1799* (Durham, NC, 1990), 80. In the only detailed justification of this view, Roger Chartier and Daniel Roche, "Les Livres ont-ils fait la Révolution?", in Fréderic Barbier and Daniel Roche (eds), *Livre et Révolution* (Paris, 1987), embed reading aloud in public in the specific context of revolutionary France, thus implying that such a culture was not necessarily characteristic of other times and places.
3 John King Fairbank, *Trade and Diplomacy on the China Coast: The Opening of the Treaty Ports, 1842–1854* (Cambridge, Mass., 1953), 26–32; Stevan Harrell, *Cultural Encounters on China's Ethnic Frontiers* (Seattle, 1995), 18–20.
4 Pamela Kyle Crossley, *Orphan Warriors: Three Manchu Generations and the End of the Qing World* (Princeton, 1990); James L. Hevia, *Cherishing Men from Afar: Qing Guest Ritual and the Macartney Embassy of 1793* (Durham, NC, 1995), 29–49.
5 Benjamin Schwartz, *In Search of Wealth and Power: Yen Fu and the West* (Cambridge, Mass., 1964), ch. 4; Joseph R. Levenson, *Confucian China and its Modern Fate: The Problem of Intellectual Continuity* (London, 1958), 98–104.
6 Paul A. Cohen, *Between Tradition and Modernity: Wang T'ao and Reform in Late Ch'ing China* (Cambridge, Mass., 1974), 230–5.
7 Myron A. Cohen, 'Being Chinese: The Peripheralization of Traditional Identity', in Tu Wei-ming (ed.), *The Living Tree: The Changing Meaning of Being Chinese Today* (Stanford, 1994), 88.
8 Prasenjit Duara, *Rescuing History from the Nation: Questioning Narratives of Modern China* (Chicago, 1995), ch. 3.
9 Liu Dapeng, *Tuixiangzhai riji* [Diary from the Study for Retreat and Contemplation] (1892–1942), Shanxi Provincial Library, Taiyuan, MS (hereafter Liu Dapeng MS). Parts of Liu Dapeng's diary have been published: *Tuixiangzhai riji*, ed. Qiao Zhiqiang (Taiyuan, 1990); *Tuixiangzhai riji (xuanlu)* [Diary from the Study for Retreat and Contemplation (Selections)], in *Yihetuan shiliao* [Historical Materials on the Boxers] (Beijing, 1982). Where possible I refer to the published versions.
10 Liu, *Tuixiangzhai riji*, ed. Qiao, 262.
11 *Yihetuan dang'an shiliao* [Archival Materials on the Boxers], ed. Ming Qing dang'anguan [Ming Qing Archives], 2 vols (Beijing, 1959), ii, 1056–7.
12 Liu Dapeng MS, 8 Third month 1901.
13 Liu, *Tuixiangzhai riji*, ed. Qiao, 95–6; Liu Dapeng MS, 10, 14 Third month 1901.
14 Paul A. Cohen, *History in Three Keys: The Boxers as Event, Experience, and Myth* (New York, 1997), ch. 5.
15 For the threat, see Wang Baoshu, *Tai xing zu zhan ji* [A Journey to Wutaishan to Prevent Battles], in *Yihetuan shiliao*.
16 *North China Herald*, 13 July 1906, 112; 10 June 1916, 571; Cohen, *History in Three Keys*, 71–9, 156. For similar reactions in India, see Anand A. Yang, "A Conversation of Rumors: The Language of Popular *Mentalités* in Late Nineteenth-Century Colonial India," *Jl Social Hist.*, xx (1987).

17 Liu Dapeng MS, 24 Third month 1901.
18 George Farthing to Baynes, Taiyuan, 31 Oct. 1894: Baptist Missionary Society Archives, Regents Park College, Oxford, CH 9 (George B. Farthing).
19 Liu Dapeng MS, 28 Eleventh month 1901.
20 Liu, *Tuixiangzhai riji*, ed. Qiao, 66.
21 For similar arguments with relation to Europe, see Richard Cust, "News and Politics in Early Seventeenth-Century England", *Past and Present*, no. 112 (Aug. 1986); Roger Chartier, *The Cultural Uses of Print in Early Modern France* (Princeton, 1987), 5–9; Adam Fox, "Rumour, News and Popular Political Opinion in Elizabethan and Early Stuart England", *Hist. Jl*, xl (1997).
22 Liu, *Tuixiangzhai riji* (*xuanlu*), in *Yihetuan shiliao*, 817. For rumours and collective concerns, see Yang, "A Conversation of Rumors".
23 Liu, *Tuixiangzhai riji* (*xuanlu*), in *Yihetuan shiliao*, 817. March is an approximation for the second month of the lunar calendar.
24 Liu, *Tuixiangzhai riji*, ed. Qiao, 155, 194.
25 *Ibid.*, 105.
26 Liu, *Tuixiangzhai riji* (*xuanlu*), in *Yihetuan shiliao*, 816.
27 Liu Dapeng MS, 1 Third month 1901.
28 For the history of the gazette, see Ge Gongzhen, *Zhongguo baoxue shi* [A History of Journalism in China] (Shanghai, 1927), ch. 2; Yin Yungong, *Zhongguo Mingdai xinwen chuanbo shi* [A History of News Transmission in Ming China] (Chongqing, 1990), ch. 2; Roswell S. Britton, *The Chinese Periodical Press, 1800–1912* (Shanghai, 1933), 7–13. The standard English translation for "Metropolitan Gazette" is "Peking Gazette."
29 Liu Dapeng MS, 4 Eleventh month 1901.
30 S. Wells Williams, *The Middle Kingdom: A Survey of the Geography, Government, Literature, Social Life, Arts and History of the Chinese Empire and its Inhabitants*, 2 vols (London, 1883), i, 420.
31 Elizabeth L. Eisenstein, *The Printing Revolution in Early Modern Europe* (Cambridge, 1983), 94.
32 Benedict Anderson, *Imagined Communities: Reflections on the Origin and Spread of Nationalism* (London, 1983).
33 *Dichao quanlan* [A Complete Overview of the "Peking Gazette"] (1897–1900), Bodleian Library, Oxford, Backhouse collection.
34 See Walter J. Ong, *Orality and Literacy: The Technologizing of the Word* (London, 1982), 132.
35 Liu, *Tuixiangzhai riji* (*xuanlu*), in *Yihetuan shiliao*, 817–19.
36 Liu, *Tuixiangzhai riji*, ed. Qiao, 43.
37 For modern newspapers and their links with the treaty ports, see Ge, *Zhongguo baoxue shi*, chs. 3–4; Britton, *Chinese Periodical Press*; Rudolf G. Wagner, "The Role of the Foreign Community in the Chinese Public Sphere", *China Quart.*, cxlii (1995); Joan Judge, *Print and Politics: "Shibao" and the Culture of Reform in Late Qing China* (Stanford, 1996).
38 Sun Yuxiang, Chen Xungang, Li Hongqi and Zhang Suhua, *Shanxi chuban zhi* [A Survey of Publishing in Shanxi] (Taiyuan, 1983), 47; Shi He, Yao Fushen and Ye Cuidi, *Zhongguo jindai baokan minglu* [A Handlist of Modern Chinese Periodicals] (Fuzhou, 1991), 282–3.
39 *North China Herald*, 27 Aug. 1902, 420.
40 Joan Judge suggests a newspaper readership of 1 percent of the population in the 1900s: Judge, *Print and Politics*, 41. This is probably too high. According to Ge Gongzhen, the number of newspapers handled by the post office rose from approximately 37 million in 1912, to more than 137 million in 1924: Ge, *Zhongguo baoxue shi*, 241, 255.

41 Judge, *Print and Politics*, 41.
42 *North China Herald*, 27 Aug. 1902, 420; 18 Feb. 1903, 318; 30 Apr. 1903, 822; Liu, *Tuixiangzhai riji*, ed. Qiao, 171; Shi, Yao and Ye, *Zhongguo jindai baokan minglu*, 282–3.
43 Lin Yutang, *A History of the Press and Public Opinion in China* (Chicago, 1936), 148; Judge, *Print and Politics*, 41, estimates fifteen readers per copy.
44 Liu, *Tuixiangzhai riji*, ed. Qiao, 114, 297.
45 Ge, *Zhongguo baoxue shi*, 53, 61.
46 *Zhonghua bao*, 1 Second month 1906, 9. I have been unable to find a copy of the First month edition that Liu Dapeng read.
47 Liu Dapeng MS, 21 Second month; 20, 26, 29 Third month; 12, 25 Fourth month 1914.
48 Liu, *Tuixiangzhai riji*, ed. Qiao, 277.
49 *Ibid.*, 310.
50 *Shanxi ribao*, 8 Jan. 1920, 2.
51 Liu, *Tuixiangzhai riji*, ed. Qiao, 228; *North China Herald*, 27 May 1916, 444.
52 Stanley Morison, *The English Newspaper: Some Account of the Physical Development of Journals Printed in London between 1622 and the Present Day* (Cambridge, 1932), 184–5.
53 Ge, *Zhongguo baoxue shi*, 221.
54 Liu Dapeng MS, 12 Fourth month 1892.
55 *Ibid.*, 8 Fifth intercalary month 1914; *Shenbao*, 19 June 1914, 7.
56 For example, *Shenbao*, 1 Aug. 1914, 7; 9 Aug. 1914, 2.
57 Liu Dapeng MS, 14 Fourth month 1892.
58 *Ibid.*, 15 Eleventh month 1914.
59 *Ibid.*, 21 Seventh month 1914; 3 Ninth month 1914.
60 *Ibid.*, 21 Second month 1914.
61 Liu, *Tuixiangzhai riji*, ed. Qiao, 117.
62 Liang Qichao, *Yinbingshi wenji* [Collected Works from the Ice Drinker's Studio], 16 vols (Shanghai, 1936), i, 102.
63 Xu Daiping and Xu Ruifang, *Qingmo sishi nian Shenbao shiliao* [Historical Materials on the *Shenbao* in the Last Forty Years of the Qing] (Beijing, 1988), 149.
64 Andrew J. Nathan, *Peking Politics, 1918–1923: Factionalism and the Failure of Constitutionalism* (Berkeley, 1976), 70–1.
65 *Shanxi ribao*, 4 July 1919, 2; interview conducted by the author, Chiqiao, 11 Sept. 1997.
66 *Shanxi ribao*, 30 June 1919.
67 For example, *ibid.*, 26 Oct. 1919, 3.
68 *Ibid.*, 24 Sept. 1919, 3; 6 Jan. 1920, 3.
69 *Shanxi dashi ji (1840–1985)* [A Record of Major Events in Shanxi (1840–1985)], ed. Shanxi sheng difangzhi bianzuan weiyuanhui [Shanxi Provincial Gazetteer Editorial Committee] (Taiyuan, 1987), 131–2.
70 Liu, *Tuixiangzhai riji*, ed. Qiao, 316–18.
71 *Ibid.*, 319, 323, 327.
72 *Ibid.*, 326, 328.

6

CONTOURS OF REVOLUTIONARY CHANGE IN A CHINESE COUNTY, 1900–1950

R. Keith Schoppa

In addition to the 1949 divide alluded to above, there has also been a Nationalist/ Communist divide in revolutionary studies, which has led to separation of discussion of the causes and the effects of the rise of the GMD (in the late 1920s) and of the CCP (two decades later). This separation, which is encouraged by the patriotic myths of both the GMD and the CCP that present the other party in a harshly negative light, can be seen, and recently has been seen, as problematic in several different ways. For example, as noted in Chapter 1 this volume, one can argue that thinking of separate National and Communist revolutions obscures the organizational and symbolic links between parties that shared a common attachment to Leninist principles and a vision of Geming as a sacred quest. Differentiating sharply between the GMD and the CCP also hinders understanding of how the two parties could have collaborated, albeit never easily, in a First United Front (1924–1927) formed to fight warlord rule and then again in a Second United Front (1937–1945) formed to oppose Japanese aggression. Specific political factors help explain the origin of each of these brief alliances. In the 1920s, Sun Yat-sen's personal interest in the coalition was key. And in the late 1930s, Sun's successor, Chiang Kai-shek, had to be kidnapped by a non-Communist general who was convinced that all Chinese needed to work together to fight Japan before he agreed to join forces with the Communists. Still, without some shared goals, these specific factors would not have been enough to create even the admittedly tenuous alliances in question.

In this chapter, R. Keith Schoppa argues against the Nationalist/Communist divide in study of the Chinese Revolution. He insists that we need to think of the transformations that swept through China in the first half of the twentieth century as comparable to a war "made up of innumerable engagements" taking place over a long stretch of time. Hence, it is dangerous to focus exclusively on the battles of the years either leading up to or following the Northern Expedition (1926–1928)

103

and think one has a sense of the overall course of the struggle. Schoppa also insists, though, that the Revolution was too complex a phenomenon to lend itself to analysis on a scale as large as that of the nation. Or, rather, before analyzing it on this scale, one has to have a very good feel for the way "congeries of countless local revolutions, some only loosely link to national-level goals," unfolded.

The chapter that follows is a first-step toward a style of analysis that connects the revolutionary upsurges of the very early twentieth century to those of the 1940s, while staying attentive to regional variation. It does so primarily by focusing on a single county, showing us how the ecology and social structure of one of the smallest of the main Chinese administrative units shaped and was shaped by the events of the day. Here, though, as in the previous two chapters, the story of an individual life (in this case a revolutionary activist and political leader of great local and some national significance, Shen Dingyi) is given a good deal of attention. This is not surprising, since Schoppa's article was written soon after he had completed a book-length local history and as he was beginning work on a biographical study that explored the mysterious death of Shen.

* * *

Most local studies of the "revolution" in pre-1949 China have focused on Communist successes and failures during the 1930s and 1940s in the base areas of north and central China. It seems obvious, however, that in its more complete meaning the Chinese revolution in this century has been more than the story of Communist Party fortunes. On the national level, it has been the process of casting off politically enervated and/or discredited systems (the imperial, warlord, and Republican) and moving toward the vision of a fundamentally new state and society. The first major blow in this process was the abolition in 1905 of the civil service system that had served as the foundation for the political and social structure of traditional China. The revolution, which has often focused on struggles for political power and prerogative, has continued throughout the country in a number of phases, with varying actors, agendas, timing, and dynamics. Like a war made up of innumerable engagements, it has been a congeries of countless local revolutions, some only loosely linked to national-level goals. If, as a recent work put it, "[a] new generation of scholarship is emerging [in the study of the Chinese revolution] which promises to resolve old debates, bridge old dichotomies, and join formerly separate strands of analysis" (Hartford and Goldstein 1989:3), then it must take into account the larger chronological sweep of the revolution at the same time it burrows deeply into its local bases. This essay is an exploration of the contours of revolutionary change in the half-century from 1900 to 1950 in Xiaoshan County, Zhejiang Province, a county in the Lower Yangzi region that was for most of this period in the Guomindang, not the Communist sphere (see map).

More than two decades ago, Roy Hofheinz sought the secret of Communist success through county environmental and ecological analysis: what social and economic structures and what sort of political culture were most likely to give rise to a flourishing Communist movement? Though he concluded that the "proper mixture of contextual and motivational factors" was impossible to determine (Hofheinz 1969:76), analysis of the spatial context to help explain social structure and behavior in historical studies of China has not diminished in importance but has become more significant. Part of this is attributable to the marketing and regional systems models of William Skinner in the 1960s and 1970s (Skinner 1964–65 and 1977). But treatment of social and political topics grounded deeply in local context is not yet the norm; a recent state-of-the-field essay suggested that "a spatial dimension will become requisite" in studies of society "[s]hould further research substantiate Skinner's model" (Lavely, Lee, and Wang 1990:821). The two most recent county-level studies of revolution and change during the Republican period give brief sketches of their counties' natural and social ecology, but these sketches are relatively undifferentiated, and the focus remains on structures and institutions (Averill 1990; Barkan 1990).

In its exploration of the sources and direction of change in Xiaoshan County, this essay examines the significance of the natural and social

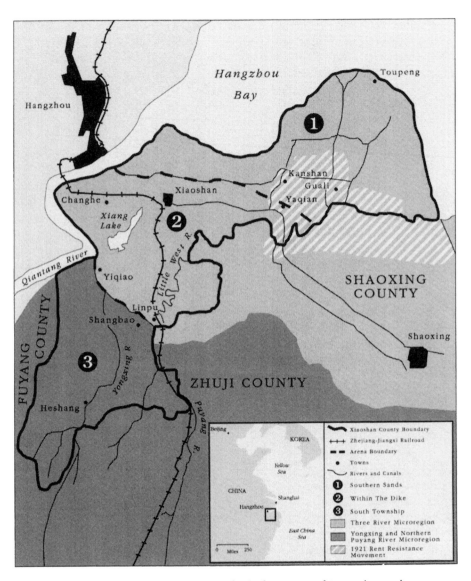

Xiaoshan County, showing three main ecological arenas and two microregions

contexts for revolutionary change. Are there relationships between context and the shape of county political and social change and, if so, what forms do they take? Within a specific context, which cultural structures and values seem most significant? Beyond context, what forces and dynamics best explain such change? Since the agency and stimulus for change are keys to understanding change itself, who are the agents and what are the structures of change in the half-century?

In this study, though the focus is the administrative unit of Xiaoshan County, the actual units of analysis are natural subcounty ecological arenas, parts of natural microregions. In Hofheinz's analysis, in Skinner's regional systems analysis, and in my analysis of Zhejiang elites, the county became the unit of analysis because it was the lowest administrative unit on which economic data was available (Schoppa 1982:23). If it does nothing else, this analysis of Xiaoshan County should show the error of generalizing the development and nature of a county unit as a whole. While Xiaoshan County falls within the inner core of both Skinner's and my classification, in reality the differential development of the three subcounty arenas (each comprising about one-third of the county's area) more accurately matches the levels of development in three different zones: inner core, outer core, and near periphery. Such differential development contributes, as we will see, to the dynamics of revolutionary change itself.

Natural and social ecology in subcounty arenas of Xiaoshan County

Within the Dike (*Tangli*). This arena's designation comes from its location within the original North Sea Dike on the southern shore of Hangzhou Bay and the West River Dike on the north bank of the Puyang River. In Skinner's classification, it would clearly be an inner-core area. It was part of the Three River microregion, a hydrological system that included the plains in Shaoxing County to the east. That close, natural relationship bolstered the links that Xiaoshan historically had to Shaoxing as part of the latter's prefectural administration (*SX* 1937:12, *passim*). The mercantile region of the county, Within the Dike is on the main transportation routes between Hangzhou and Ningbo (*XXZ* 1931:35, 38). Containing the county seat, the largest commercial town, and seven of the other fourteen higher-level market towns during the Republican period, the area Within the Dike enjoyed a flourishing commerce supported by financial institutions. It contained thirteen (and possibly eighteen) of the county's twenty-one pawnshops in 1939 and all ten of the native banks remaining in the county in 1949 (*XX* 1985:12:41). When Chambers of Commerce were established early in the century, the central chamber (in the county seat) and its three branches were all in Within the Dike (*XXG* 1935:7:32b–33a). Its population comprised 50.7 percent of the county's total in 1910, making it the county arena with the highest population density (*XXG* 1935:5:4a–5a). All the county police posts at the end of the Qing and all the main post offices in the county from the late Qing to the 1940s were in Within the Dike (*XXG* 1935:7:29b–30b and *XG* 1947:39).

According to the county gazetteer, the land in this arena, generally flat with occasional outcroppings of hills and small mountains, was the most fertile and productive in the county, producing primarily rice and rapeseed but with a wide range of subsidiary crops (*XG* 1947:9). When the great heat of late summer called for irrigating the paddies, water was obtained from the Little West River and from Xiang Lake, a reservoir in disrepair during the Republic (Schoppa 1989). With security from floods dependent on the condition of river and sea dikes and the harvest dependent on the reservoir and internal waterways, many of the arena's elites had management experience in conservancy matters. Water control and management were the dominating agendas of the county government, based, as it was, in this arena.

Landholding statistics are not differentiated according to subcounty arenas. In the county as a whole before the Communist victory, landlords made up 2 percent of the population but held 16.9 percent of the land; peasants (poor, middle, and rich) made up about 82 percent of the population but farmed 68.3 percent of the land (*XX* 1985:4:5). The degree of landlordism was high in Within the Dike, where great lineages were most concentrated and where commercial wealth served as a bulwark to landed affluence. The primary system of rent was sharecropping, with a fixed percentage of the actual harvest allotted to landlord and tenant, usual tenant shares ranging from 30 percent to 40 percent (*XX* 1985:4:2).

The arena Within the Dike was oriented to Hangzhou, the provincial capital, less than ten miles across the Qiantang River. A treaty port after 1896 but never an important entrepôt with the West, Hangzhou functioned for this arena as an important source of modern changes (*MR*, November 28, 1922, and *XXZ* 1931:78). Looking toward Hangzhou as model and political-economic center, the county took the first steps toward industrialization with the establishment of textile factories in the county seat in 1898 and 1899; the founding of the first higher-level elementary school in the county seat came in 1901; and organization of the first Western-style hospital came in 1909 (*XX* 1985: *Dashiji* 17–18).

The Southern Sands (*Nansha*). This arena, which lay outside the original North Sea Dike, had once been situated north of Hangzhou Bay. It became part of Xiaoshan County in the mid-Qing dynasty when Qiantang River currents shifted sharply northward. The almost cataclysmic work of the river did not cease then, for the shifting currents continued to drop tons of alluvium, building up new land along the coast, at the same time eroding and immersing land that farmers had previously turned into productive plots (*XX* 1985:6:2–6 and *ZSN* 1929:80–83). One of the region's native sons,

Shen Dingyi, described in a 1923 essay the horrifying sounds of the land and houses of poor farm families collapsing into the river when heavy rains made the Qiantang a torrent (*JW*, May 6, 1923). This ongoing environmental tragedy made life in the Southern Sands precarious and became its critical agenda in the twentieth century.

The alluvial deposits that make up this arena constituted good soil for the cultivation of cotton, jute, rape, and mulberry. But exacting social and economic structures seemed only to compound the potentially devastating natural threats for the area's farmers. The Southern Sands had the highest concentration of landlords of the three ecological arenas of the county, and the various kinds of rents extracted produced almost continual hardship for tenants. The two most common methods of assessing rent were setting a fixed rate before the crop was planted and, harsher, requiring the payment of a fixed rate before the planting (*XX* 1985:4:2). In years of drought or flood, many farmers became refugees. An economic investigation of a village in the 1930s showed that, even in good crop years, more than 20 out of 170 households had to resort to begging. Many households were threatened annually with loss of fuel for cooking, and many survived only by traveling to Shaoxing for short-term work, making tinfoil for funeral rituals (*XX* 1985:23:8–9).

The arena's production of cotton and silk made it a natural center for the textile industry in the county. Traditional cottage industry declined during the Republic as modern mills began to be established (*XX* 1985:7:11). Yet the area's economic development was retarded by its location north of critical transportation and communication routes, by considerable social unrest spawned by the unpredictable but frequent ravages of nature, and by the threat of destruction by the Qiantang currents. As late as August 1947, for example, large areas of the Southern Sands near the important town of Toupeng, a local industrial center, collapsed into the river and sea with immense loss of life and property (*XX* 1985:6:6).

Linked by waterways to the Three River microregion, this arena, which probably would be placed in the outer core of the regional systems model, seemed in the early twentieth century to have great economic potential if the natural ecological threats could be controlled. Containing one-third of the county's population in 1910, it was in many ways a frontier area of new land and possibilities. The educational and cultural level of the population was reportedly low. One other noteworthy aspect of the cultural scene: it was the center of Christian missionary efforts in the county. Almost all of the forty-eight county churches in 1950 were in the Southern Sands (*XX* 1985:23:41). The area's orientation was to Hangzhou and the outside world – with its Hangzhou entrepreneurs, its Western missionaries, and, as new land formed along the coast, large numbers of Chinese moving in from other counties for the chance to better their livelihood. The Southern Sands was, perhaps more than many arenas, a world in flux.

South Township (*Nanxiang*). A greater contrast than that between the Southern Sands and South Township would be hard to imagine. South Township, an area of mountains and forests, had been physically separated from the rest of the county since the 1460s, when a large-scale conservancy project rechanneled the Puyang River across it to the northwest to meet the Qiantang River (Schoppa 1989:43–44). The fast-flowing river in effect isolated the area: the only bridge until 1948 was a floating bridge from Jianshan on the west bank of the river to the county of Shaoxing on the other side; there were no bridges to Within the Dike (*XX* 1985:9:30). The two main communication centers for South Township, Linpu and Yiqiao located in Within the Dike, could be reached only by boat. A third of the county in area, the township held only 15.3 percent of the population in 1910. Though there were letter boxes, there were no post offices or branches in the township; there were no pawnshops or native banks (*XX* 1985:23:42; *XG* 1947:29). The environmental, social, and economic reality of the area approximates that of the near periphery in the Skinnerian scheme.

The land was the least fertile in the county, producing relatively meager crops of wheat, barley, beans, and rice. Although the number of landlords and the land they owned were less than in the other arenas, the most common method of collecting rent was the merciless system of requiring it before planting. During a calamitous drought in 1934, when there was no harvest at all in South Township, landlords collected their preplanting rent while hundreds of tenants reportedly became starving refugees (*XX* 1985:4:2–3).

South Township paper manufacturing flourished from the beginning of the Ming through the Qing dynasties. A report to the Hangzhou government in 1930 indicated that 90 percent of all households in the township (a total of roughly 50,000 people) were involved in some way in this cottage industry. The impact of imported machine-made paper and the decline in demand for paper used in religious rituals led to a severe economic decline in the 1920s and 1930s. Under such conditions, workers' livelihoods could not be sustained, and this came at a time when paper workers already worked more hours for less wages than any county industrial workers (*XZH* 1930:31, 49–50; *XX* 1985:7:1; 23:1).

South Township's natural environment and social ecology were more like northern Zhuji County to its south and the eastern part of Fuyang County to its west than to the rest of Xiaoshan County. With these areas, it was a part of microregion centering on the northern reaches of the Puyang River and the Yongxing River, which drained into it. Unlike the Southern Sands and Within the Dike, then, South Township was not oriented primarily to Hangzhou, with its ties to Shanghai, the presence of foreigners (there was no missionary activity here), and an array of modern changes. Instead, it faced Linpu, the county's largest non-administrative town on the Puyang River. Linpu's orientation, in turn, was also not primarily to Hangzhou but to central and eastern Zhejiang. One of the province's largest rice markets, in 1912 Linpu had sixty rice firms whose decisions determined the price of rice in Xiaoshan and counties east and south in Shaoxing and even Ningbo prefectures. The presence of large numbers of outside merchants, shippers, and brokers involved in the rice trade contributed to an unrestrained atmosphere where commercialism, opium, and prostitution flourished. During the Republic, the merchant establishment of the town compiled a notorious record of price gouging and corruption that helped spawn a series of anti-merchant riots centering on the price of rice, salt, and the collection of paper taxes (Schoppa 1990a:145).

South Township showed evidence of a culture of poverty and dependency. With low agricultural output and a declining paper industry, the people lived hand-to-mouth. Women foraged in the hills for each day's cooking fuel. Ninety-five percent of its people had to buy rice, which came from Linpu, often at elevated prices. At the same time, timber products and paper were sold at the Within the Dike entrepôt of Yiqiao at prices that helped make Yiqiao merchants prosperous (*XXZ* 1931:39, 47, 67–68).

According to Chinese commentators, these three different natural contexts gave rise to specific personal and social attributes which they assigned (or by which they stereotyped) people from each area. They noted the strong influence of Hangzhou in Within the Dike, even to the point of suggesting that its inhabitants lacked a spirit of their own, tainted as they were by the allure of urbanization. The people of the Southern Sands were characterized as hard-working, patient, and, above all, able to bear suffering. South Township people were said to be firm of purpose and overbearing (*XG* 1947:26; *XXZ* 1931:75–78). Though there is in this stereotyping more than a little of the Confucian disdain for commerce and perhaps an elite's idealization of the masses' stoic acceptance of poverty, the categorization underscores the perceived significance of the three natural arenas for social and cultural realities beyond economics and the environment. The question before us is how significant and in what ways.

Contours of revolutionary change

In examining the shape and direction of political change in Xiaoshan County, I will use shifts in the nature and composition of non-official functional elites (local leaders providing public services or serving in non-bureaucratic positions in the community) as one measure of change over time. Despite differences among the three arenas, the key sociocultural unit in Xiaoshan was the lineage, a group that traced its ancestry to a common patriarch; many villages and even towns in Within the Dike and South Township were lineage bases where all the inhabitants shared a single surname. Such lineages might build ancestral halls, publish genealogies, and set up lineage estates to further their interests. In many cases, lineage funds were used to train precocious males for the civil service examination, success in which further enhanced lineage stature. The wealthiest lineages in the county were in Within the Dike. Lineages in South Township were significant social units but were not notably well off: there were no recorded lineage estates in the township. Southern Sands, undergoing continual environmental transformation, had fewer lineages of importance, as migrants moved rapidly onto the area's new land and out again when floods wreaked their destruction (*XXG* 1935:7:38a–b; *XXS* 1984:39–45; *XX* 1985: 23:15–20).

The number of civil service degrees attained in each arena in the period 1870 to 1911 suggests their late-Qing social and economic situation. The Southern Sands produced only three upper-degree holders (one *juren* and two *gongsheng*) from two lineages (Shi and Wang), a total reflecting the arena's relative poverty and greater social heterogeneity (*XXG* 1935:13 *passim*; *XXS* 1984). In contrast, a comparison of upper degrees attained by just the seven most important lineages (in terms of producing functional elites) shows that Within the Dike lineages (Chen, Han, He, Huang, Lai, Kong, and Ni) produced six *jinshi*, thirty *juren*, and thirty *gongsheng* degrees, while South Township lineages (Xie, Hu, Lou, Shen, Yu, Wei, and Zhu) produced four *jinshi*, fourteen *juren*, and nine *gongsheng* degrees. Since the number of degree holders in South Township was produced by a much smaller population, the relative production of degree holders there may be equal to or even exceed that of Within the Dike. There are several possible interpretations of these figures that on their face run counter to the hypothesis that economically flourishing areas produced more degree holders than poorer areas (Schoppa 1982:52). One could argue that the modern economic change which would reshape Within the Dike had not yet begun to stimulate a marked differential between the two arenas. As for the late-imperial economies, the Taiping Rebellion had devastated Within the Dike while South Township was much less touched; the paper industry in the latter had, in addition, not begun its precipitate Republican-period decline. One could also argue that economic change in Within the Dike had provided elites more opportunity outside the traditional examination system and that, concurrently, South Township, like other poorer, near-periphery areas in the province, produced elites more intent on traditional values, including examination success (Schoppa 1982:112–18, 127). Whatever the case, both Within the Dike and South Township continued substantial traditional elite production in the last decades of the Qing.

The Beginnings of Change, 1900–11. Mary Rankin has shown that local elite activism following the Taiping Rebellion began to transform local society and the elite itself (Rankin 1986). Reconstruction and reforms undertaken through elite initiative at a time of state impotence gave rise to an expanding public sphere of elite contributions to the community that were neither state directed nor primarily for private ends. It is not surprising that the first responses to the revolutionary change of the abolition of the civil service system – the founding of modern schools – were initiated in the locality by these local elite activists.

In the years from 1906 to 1911, fifty-nine schools were established in the county: twenty-five in Within the Dike, twenty-nine in South Township, and five in the Southern Sands. The leadership of South Township in this regard, where all but three of the schools were financed and run by lineages, reflects, I would argue, the strong traditionalist commitment in less commercialized areas to the Confucian value of education by lineages. In contrast, though lineages also strongly supported schools in Within the Dike, twelve of the twenty-five there were funded by other means – by businesses and by special taxes assessed by local government. Similarly, four of the five Southern Sands schools received their support from non-lineage sources (*XXG* 1935:10 *xia*:4b–12b).

Social background data on the schools' organizers, administrators, and teachers are too fragmentary for meaningful generalizations. Even the meaning of the school numbers is difficult to assess because we do not know whether the content of the education matched the institutional newness of the schools. At least one school in the county seat lived up to its modern billing, offering courses in geography, economics, and English (*S*, October 12, 1910). At most we can draw only a few tentative conclusions in evaluating the patterns of change. All three county arenas were involved in this first step toward the remaking of Chinese society, with the Southern Sands least involved. Importantly, while the underlying perceptions of the meaning of the new schools may have differed, much of the initiative and support for the action came from lineage elites of town and village. Although the potential of the educational change was revolutionary, the traditional cultural base of the lineage was its foundation.

Of the eighty-seven principals and teachers from Within the Dike, nineteen were traditional upper-degree holders and three were graduates of modern schools outside the county. Six in South Township were such modern graduates. The return of modern-school graduates and of upper-degree holders (many of whom had held official positions outside of Xiaoshan) to their hometowns and villages points to the significance of native place for those who had been to higher arenas and probably were motivated by the common early twentieth-century elite desire to remake their community. The return of those who had been away also probably served as the stimulus or at least the occasion for local elites to support the development of the new schools. The culture-based magnetism of the ancestral home had a multitude of practical effects on local political attitudes, agendas, and decision-making. When ideas and sentiments based on this attachment were transposed to higher levels of the polity, they created obviously important political dynamics in the county and beyond.

In this regard, from the early years of the century (and probably before) the nine separate subdistricts (*xiang*) of South Township gave evidence of a sense of identity as a unit. Shortly after the establishment of the Xiaoshan County Education Association in 1906, for example, self-government committee members of South Township subdistricts established their own education association in the town of Linpu (*XXG* 1935:10 *xia*: 10b–11a). No other similar subcounty association was formed in the county. The sense of separate identity in this arena probably was borne of a sense of isolation and relative political weakness, but it was supported and reinforced by a common sense of native place. The association also underscores the seriousness with which these elites dealt with educational issues. Finally, the location of the association in Linpu *outside* of South Township points again to the arena's particular urban orientation and to the lack of commercial centers within itself.

The growth of a civil society, 1912–19. The revolution that brought the Republic to Xiaoshan seems more akin to a palace coup, restricted to government offices in the county seat. Though specific details are unavailable, reports indicated that it was the work of about a dozen respected modern educators, old-style gentry, and merchants (*S*, December 4, 1911). The 1911 revolution clearly, however, did not reach far into the countryside. Reports *from as late as 1930* indicated that people in South Township and even in the flourishing southern part of Within the Dike – fifteen to twenty miles from Hangzhou – were still wearing queues, the distinctive coiffure of Chinese under the old regime (*NCH*, May 31, 1913; *XZH* 1930:19). Clearly, economic development in itself was no certain indication of a modern consciousness or its correlatives. In this context, there is no evidence that South Township experienced any "revolutionary" activity in the 1911 period.

In the period between the overthrow of the Manchus and the May Fourth Movement, Within the Dike and to some extent the Southern Sands experienced the growth of a civil society, that is, the development of a society marked by voluntary associations unconnected to and unsponsored by the state (Esherick and Rankin 1990:384, n. 52; Strand 1990:224–26; Rowe 1990). Political party branches and various reform organizations sprang up, stimulated by a sense of newness welling up from the abolition of the monarchy (Schoppa 1982:155–57) or, in the case of political parties, from agents dispatched from Hangzhou or Shanghai (*MLB*, January 22, 1912; *S* June 5, 1912, April 11, 1913, November 30, 1913; March 26, 1916; *XX* 1985:*Dashiji*:19–20). These social and political developments were stimulated by the revolutionary surge of 1911, and, in the longer process of revolution, they set the stage for subsequent developments in the May Fourth era.

Such groups met alongside already established professional associations and the self-government bodies established by the Qing. Though the full membership rolls of the county assembly are not extant, the backgrounds of the assembly's leaders indicate that elites from Within the Dike formed the core of the county elite and that they came from an old-gentry/modern-educated coalition based on longstanding and important lineages. The chair, Tang Cairong, was a *juren* degree holder who had been instrumental in educational reforms in the county seat in the years before the revolution. The vice chair was Wang Zhao, a *juren* degree holder but also a graduate of Beijing University's institutional forerunner who had served as a magistrate in Shaanxi Province before the revolution (*XXG* 1935:10 *xia*; 13 *passim*). The county assembly met from 1912 to 1914 and from 1916 to 1918; while the institutional structures overseeing change were new, it seems that the agents of political change were a continuation of late-Qing elites and their early Republican transmutation, the modern-school graduate.

Of Xiaoshan County's five representatives to the provincial assembly, which met in 1913–14 and 1916–18, three (from the old Han, Huang, and Ni lineages) were from Within the Dike and two (Shen Dingyi and Sheng Bangyan) came from the Southern Sands (*S*, January 12, 1913). They joined other native sons from Within the Dike (such as important military figures Lai Weiliang and Han Shaoji) in key provincial positions. With connections to these men came access to the networks of power, if not to power itself. It is no coincidence that a number of Lais and Hans were able to move into provincial ministries and boards in the early Republic (*S*, August 24, 1917; December 1–30 *passim*). Men like Assemblyman Ni Zian moved from his career as significant local elite to assemblyman and in 1930 was still serving as key local leader; his connections to men of power and his knowledge of politics at a higher level served to put his home area near Yiqiao in good stead (*XZH* 1930:36 and *XXG* 1935:10 *xia*:6b). Shen Dingyi, who will be discussed at greater length, established networks among lawyers, politicians, and educators in Hangzhou that provided him both provincial and local support in various undertakings. Local agendas could be more successfully pursued with connections to men who had connections to higher levels in the system. It was a resource that South Township lacked.

Another aspect of change in these years that had great impact on Within the Dike and the Southern Sands was the dramatic rise in the fortunes of the bourgeoisie and the beginnings of industrial development. Again, South Township was not touched by this economic development. The years of the early Republic saw the emergence of new entrepreneurs, some from within the county, others from outside, willing to invest in business enterprises and to develop land for profit (Bergère 1989). The catalogue of business and industrial activity in Within the Dike is lengthy – from the first motorized boat company to rice mills, which doubled as power plants to the expansion and renovation of the Donghui Cotton Mill, one of the three most important in the province (*XX* 1985:*Dashiji*:20–21 and *CIHC* 1935:483). The Southern Sands also saw industrial expansion in machine and iron works, soy sauce brewing, grain oil production, and boat manufacture, which continued into the 1920s (*XX* 1985:7:18–21). Its most notable industry, lace making,

115

began with the investment of a Hangzhou capitalist in 1919 and produced what became one of the county's distinguishing products (*XX* 1985: *Dashiji*:21).

These projects changed the socioeconomic environment, providing new jobs and fundamentally new social relationships between employers and workers. Although the industrial work force was small, new economic and political issues and conflicts obviously began to emerge in the process (*SH*, May 15, 30, June 7, 1927). Although some of the entrepreneurs came from prerevolutionary merchants with roots in the locality, many were based outside the county, dependent on connections to elites in the locality but not necessarily as concerned for the locality as locals might be. They were entrepreneurs like Jin Yuan'ao, who set forth plans to build an industrial complex at Linpu to manufacture a variety of finished products (*S*, April 24, 1919). They were land developers whose reclamation of local lakes, ponds and streams stood to make corporations they headed reap substantial profits (Schoppa 1989; *XHT* 1920). It is clear that after 1912 a new monied leadership emerged. It is not that they replaced the gentry-modern educated political and social leadership, but they became a force to be reckoned with in discussions of political and social issues and, in terms of the historical process, a force to be opposed by later revolutionaries. Their presence underscored ever more clearly the orientation of Within the Dike and the Southern Sands to Hangzhou, Shanghai, and other cities where monied investors were based.

One other new agent of change in this period was the specialist, the trained professional, primarily in engineering or entomology who could come as expert, bringing the latest scientific and technological knowledge to bear on local problems. Although the data are fragmentary, it appears that those who peopled local conservancy and entomology boards and land-surveying teams were often native sons (many of them from key lineages) who returned after training outside Xiaoshan to deal with local problems (*XZH* 1930:*Zhiyuan yilanbiao* 1–14; *ZSL* 1933:17–20). These specialists joined the bourgeoisie, the new urban working class, the modern schools, and the new associations in the arenas of Within the Dike and the Southern Sands. It is clear that developmental change, in many ways facilitated by central government weakness in the early Republic, created situations that fostered increasingly rapid changes in local society. In contrast, in South Township, the culture of economic decline and the world of the cottage paper industry saw no similar agents of change or signs of social and economic diversity.

The Beginnings of Revolutionary Mobilization, 1920–28. The formation in the 1920s of revolutionary parties and programs in the context of May Fourth thought and of local differential development and varying natural and social ecology brings us directly to one of the central questions of this essay: the relationship between context and revolutionary change. If one posits that revolutionary activity is probably linked to contexts of greatest diversity and openness to modern change, we would expect to find it first in Within the Dike; or, if it is assumed to be probably linked to the most traditional, closed, or economically poor context, then we would expect to find it in South Township. In fact, the first revolutionary program and party in the county appear in the Southern Sands, neither the most nor the least affected by modern change. Further, while a sufficient condition for the beginning of revolutionary activity was indeed a particular situation fostered by the area's natural and social environment, the necessary condition was an agent of change – in this case, Shen Dingyi, a native of Yaqian, on the border of the Southern Sands. It is worth looking in some detail at this episode of revolutionary activity to probe the relationships between context, agent, and contingency. A brief biographical sketch of Shen is thus necessary at this point (*SDSX* n.d.; Gao 1972).

Born in 1883 into an important landholding lineage as the son of a *jinshi*-degreed magistrate, Shen inherited great wealth. Spending large sums of the family fortune on revolutionary activities in the 1911 Revolution, he emerged in the early Republic as an important provincial assembly leader and a strong spokesman for constitutional government. In 1916, Shen was elected chair of the provincial assembly, assuming a role that brought him substantial provincial prestige as a leading opponent of the Northern warlords. He became a key figure in a network of what might be called liberal constitutionalists, advocates of the powers of elected assemblies against civil and military autocracy. A number of this group, many of them lawyers and educators, became significant members of the provincial Guomindang in the early 1920s. In 1919 and 1920, Shen became editor, writer, and chief financial supporter of the *Weekly Review* (*Xingqi pinglun*) in Shanghai. Near the end of his editorship, he participated in discussions that were precursors to the founding of the Communist Party (Chang 1971:1:103). Shen's politically progressive ideas were further liberalized through his May Fourth experiences and his association with other future Guomindang and Communist leaders.

In the fall of 1920, Shen returned to Yaqian. Using various material and metaphorical symbols, he assumed the role of protector and supporter of the area's farmers, forging a strong link to his potential followers. He donned farmer's clothes and, using the local dialect, began to talk with farmers about their living conditions. He reduced the rent of his tenants, in some cases refusing to accept any at all. He established and funded the Yaqian Village School, which farmers or their children could attend at no cost. In addition to class lectures on revolutionary themes, the teachers visited farmers on their land and investigated farm conditions. To teach at the school, Shen brought a number of talented graduates of the most famous progressive institution in Hangzhou, the First Normal School. The teachers came from his social and educational networks, and most shared his general native place as well, hailing from Xiaoshan and neighboring counties in Shaoxing Prefecture (*YNY* 1985:68–82; Zhao, Xu, and Li 1986:88–89).

In April 1921, Shen was brought into the larger Southern Sands arena when a number of households represented by an elderly Yaqian farmer sought his help in recovering money owed them by an unscrupulous merchant. Though unsuccessful in this effort, Shen in the process began to build patron–client bonds with farmers beyond his own tenants. When rice merchants arbitrarily began to raise prices late in the spring, Shen encouraged farmers to form an association (*nongmin xiehui*), spurring them on to successful confrontations with particularly notorious merchants in a nearby market town. Shen continued to serve as patron for the farmers' efforts, prodding them to work toward realizing farmers' rights through careful organization. That he was a powerful provincial assemblyman and a native son only enhanced the impact he had on the farmers. By late September, the Yaqian Farmers' Association was established, with Shen drafting a declaration of principles, regulations, and goals, the chief of which were rent reduction and abolishing the system of preplanting rent payments.

Word of the organization and its goals spread rapidly across the southern coastal area of Hangzhou Bay in the canal-crossed plains of the Three River system. Throughout the fall, similar organizations sprang up in villages and towns in this microregion in a sixty-to-seventy-square-mile area in the counties of Xiaoshan, Shaoxing, and Shangyu. Delegations of farmers came to Yaqian to learn organizational procedures and tactics; Yaqian became the center and symbol of a movement which led to the establishment of farmers' associations in eighty-two villages. Chinese historians today point to Shen's movement as the first such rural revolutionary action in the nation after the founding of the Communist Party (Shao 1985:458). In mid-December, however, frightened Shaoxing landlords met with the county magistrate at the county self-government office (an indication of which class self-government was designed for) to plan strategy to deal with what they saw as an increasingly serious threat. Their appeals to the provincial government led to the dispatch of provincial soldiers who crushed the movement and arrested the effort's leaders (*XX* 1985:*fulu*: 1–6).

It is worth noting that the farmers' associations spread into areas with similar environmental and ecological structures and concerns, not primarily into a larger area of Within the Dike (which was contiguous and much closer than Shaoxing and Shangyu counties). This pattern is not only a result of similar natural context and concerns but probably stems from the social, economic, and labor networks of Yaqian-area farmers. Many participating villages were located along the Grand Canal, which linked them by various economic ties directly to Yaqian. Marriage networks between lineages in the Southern Sands and northwestern Shaoxing County were well developed. In addition, many farmers from the Southern Sands had traveled for part-time subsistence work to the cottage tinfoil industry in Shaoxing. Thus, the agency for revolutionary change in this episode was not only the individual but even more the network – whether the rural networks which helped spread the resistance movement or Shen's Hangzhou political and educational networks, on which he relied for teachers or for personal support when the movement was repressed (Schoppa 1990b).

The episode of the rent-resistance movement points to several important aspects of revolutionary change in the 1920s. While context was indeed formative in shaping social reality, it was obviously not predictive of any certain reality. There was no compelling developmental reason to bring educated and radical youths to the small village of Yaqian or, after the rent-resistance failure, to have them begin a May Fourth-style journal in the small nearby town of Kanshan in 1922 and 1923. There was no cogent county political rationale for Shen to establish the county's first Guomindang branch in Yaqian in 1924 (XX 1985:Dashiji:24). The sites for these three revolutionary steps were chosen because this was Shen's native place. While previous political associations and key political change had occurred at the county seat in Within the Dike, Shen's intervention altered the previous pattern of change. In his essay on ecology and Communist success, Hofheinz notes the intriguingly random geographic distribution of Guomindang membership. He asks rhetorically: "Are we justified in assuming that the distribution of KMT [Guomindang] recruitment ... resulted mainly from the importance of personal ties rather than basic social conditions?" (Hofheinz 1969:65). From the record of Xiaoshan County, the answer would appear to be yes.

In addition, the episode suggests the importance of certain aspects of Chinese society at this time. The pivotal nature of Shen's incitement of the farm population with his reliance on symbols and his patron–client ties, the importance of his personal connections, and the varied and sometimes overlapping networks through which organization and mobilization seem to have been achieved – all point to the critical role of the leader in mobilizing a dependent population through charisma and the power of social connections. Finally, the repressive alliance of officialdom and the local socioeconomic elites, many of them members of powerful lineages, points to the reality of class in rural society and places the constructive school-building and modernization roles of lineage elites in the early years of the century in a fuller social context.

In the mid-1920s, the two northern arenas of Xiaoshan County, like much of the country, were rocked by wave after wave of nationalistic fervor. Various Japanese depredations in treaty port cities, the May 30th incident and its tumultuous aftermath, and the June 1925 killings in Guangzhou all stimulated protest demonstrations in Yaqian and the county seat (XX 1985:Dashiji:24–25). The united front between the Guomindang and Communist parties was established in 1922, and, although there was initially considerable cooperation in common goals, the death of Sun Yat-sen in early 1925 began a polarizing period of increasing animosity and distrust.

During these years, Shen Dingyi played various roles on the national and provincial stages as a member of both parties, while members of his local and provincial networks continued to play dominant roles in Xiaoshan County politics (*MR*, April 2, June 29, 1925; *XZH* 1930:9, 55; *ENX* 1940:10). When the Northern Expedition under Chiang Kai-shek began to unite the country, Shen emerged as one of the main leaders of the provincial Guomindang party organization. His role in provincial politics ended abruptly, however, in December 1927 when a national party faction seized power in Zhejiang (*SH*, June 20, June 23, July 3, October 3, November 5, 28, December 18, 1927).

Utilizing the base of the 1921 rent-resistance movement, Shen returned to the Southern Sands to undertake his own self-government project. Though the revolutionary surge of seven years before had seemingly been extinguished, the earlier process had forged common local memories that generated support for Shen. Despite the hiatus of seven years, for the son of one of the leaders of the earlier movement, the 1921 campaign and the effort in 1928 were part of one revolutionary process: he told an interviewer in the 1930s that, though the Yaqian Farmers' Association was established in 1921, its most active days came in 1928 (Lin 1935:74). In reality, they were not at all the same organizations. The revolution of the 1920s in the Southern Sands moved by fits and starts, building on earlier successes and from earlier failures in a process that expanded both the views and roles of the local populace.

The Southern Sands plan centered in Shen's native Yaqian and extended through much of the arena, an area frequently referred to as East Township (*Dongxiang*). Setting forth an alternative policy to the increasingly centralized vision of the national government, Shen emphasized a reform agenda tailored to the arena's environmental needs: solving the devastating problem of coastal erosion through the construction of strategically placed jetties, establishing educational and charitable organizations, reforming the sericulture industry, building roads, and setting up credit cooperatives to assist farmers in their financial difficulties. Shen argued that the prerequisite for reconstruction was imbuing the masses with power, and that, to make a difference, that power had to be structured in effective organizations. Therefore, he specifically based his efforts on mass organizations; he mobilized an estimated 30,000 farmers in the agriculture association and about 2,000 businessmen in the merchants' association (Kong 1934).

In sum, this reconstruction project envisioned substantial transformations in the subcounty ecological arena. Directed by a native son returning from many years' action on higher political stages, it involved substantial mobilization of sectors of the arena's populace and resources. Shen's assassination in August 1928, however, led the next year to the sudden end of the promising East Township project. The historical contingency of Shen's death in his forty-fifth year ended any further development or revolutionary activity in the Southern Sands in the Republican period. There was no one of comparable stature from the area to succeed Shen, even though a number of people from his local party network remained in key county party and government positions into the 1930s and 1940s.

After Shen's death, a Shanghai newspaper published a commemorative piece written by one Feng Zhifang, a Southern Sands native, detailing the nature of the Southern Sands and the role Shen played there (*MR*, September 2, 1928):

> In East Township on the land along the river, where there are frequent floods, the people are desperately poor. Apart from Yaqian, communications are inconvenient; therefore the general environment and customs are backward. In this kind of backward place, the Nationalist Party flag was very much in evidence by 1925; early on, even women and children knew what it was. Slogans like "down with imperialism," "down with warlords," and "unify the farmers, workers, merchants, educators, and military" were on the lips of every elementary student. As in Shanghai, revolutionary songs were sung everywhere. . . . If it had not been for the leadership of Shen, among Xiaoshan people, who would know the party? I fear that they would still be wearing queues and speaking about the Qianlong and Jiaqing emperors [from the mid-Qing].

In an interview in the mid-1930s, a Yaqian farmer argued that, although Shen's movement had collapsed, any farmer in the area could now talk with outsiders about the Three People's Principles or the Five Power Constitution – so significant was the impact of Shen's leadership (Lin 1936:75).

In dealing with causation in historical processes, it is not fashionable to focus on single individuals as determinative. Explanation which "postulates a set of structures that supervene upon the behaviors of many individuals and that in turn constrain and direct the behaviors of individuals" is the most acceptable analytical mode (Little 1989:248). Indeed, one of the goals of this essay is to probe the influence of structures and elites in the three arenas to detail the shape of revolutionary change in the county. But in this case it seems clear that, had there been no Shen Dingyi, there would have been no revolutionary activity and change in the Southern Sands.

While the Guomindang had its base in the Southern Sands the county Communist Party branch bureaus were first established in Within the Dike, the wealthiest county arena, in early 1927. Unlike previous agents of change who were generally natives of Xiaoshan, Communist organizers were uniformly county outsiders, mostly hailing from the province and with many from nearby counties. This pattern was unlike that of many other early Communist organizers, who returned to their native places for their revolutionary efforts (see, e.g., Galbiati 1985:68–9, 99, 178–79 and Sheel 1989:136–59). The Communist leaders in Xiaoshan until 1929 had been educated at the First Normal School in Hangzhou, and the initial recruitment targeted teachers, students, and textile workers in the county seat (*XX* 1985:24:26–27; 14:2–3). The party grew quickly in Within the Dike, especially around Changhe, home of several of the county's most prosperous lineages. A full-fledged county party bureau was established in October, and by the spring of 1928, Xiaoshan had 150 Communist Party members, more than in any other Zhejiang county (*XX* 1985:14:1).

From the beginning, the Communist Party experienced continual repression, its members facing arrest by the Nationalist government. During the Guomindang purges, or "white terror," in 1927 and early 1928, many Communists were imprisoned and executed. In March and April 1928, violence erupted around Changhe when Communists (some of them members of important local lineages) fomented rent protests among tenants, action which stirred powerful landlords in some of the same lineages to call on authorities to crush the effort. The rapidly expanding Communist movement in Within the Dike was thus fairly easily quashed (*SH*, March 31, May 1, 1928; *XX* 1985:*Dashiji*:28–29).

The emergence of South Township as political base. The collapse of the Changhe rent protests opened the way for South Township to surface for the first time in the twentieth century as the base for county political activity – in this case, of the Xiaoshan Communist Party. There had been no substantial shifts in political or social structures in the area. Analysis of a twenty-seven-man relief board of key elites established in the town of Heshang in early 1929 to deal with disastrous floods in all South Township shows that 78 percent (twenty-one) came from the old established lineages. In addition, the homogeneity and continuity of leadership from a quarter of a century earlier is shown by the occupations which are given for twenty-two: 45 percent (ten) were principals and teachers at local elementary schools and 27 percent (six) were paper manufacturers or shop owners (*ZZ*, January 8, 1929:16–18).

For the Communists, the focus on South Township seems more tactical and pragmatic than ideological. They tried once more in 1930 to recruit supporters and rebuild the base near Xiang Lake, but repression in Within the Dike made recruitment and work there difficult if not impossible. Government records of county landlord–tenant disputes in 1929 show that from 57 percent to 69 percent (20 to 24 of 35) of the confrontations came in Within the Dike, a likely indication of the power (and perhaps arrogance) of landlords in that area (and also perhaps of tenant feistiness left from the early Communist organizing) (*XZH* 1930:32). Whatever the motive, by

1929 the Xiaoshan party seemed to be moving away from a focus on the intelligentsia, proletariat, and tenants in the prosperous agricultural areas of the county near the county seat and turning to the rural poor in South Township.

The first Communist activity came with the efforts of agents to organize farmers' associations in the northern part of the township. Landlords resisted these associations and their demands, but the secular decline of the paper industry and the predominant rent system that demanded preplanting payment created a desperate situation for paper workers and tenants. The floods of late 1928 created many refugees from these groups. In early January 1929, the remnants of the county Communist Party decided to use Shangbao Village, across the Puyang River from Linpu, as the base for a rural uprising – the "Fell the Bamboo Uprising." The leader, one Zhong Ama, a thirty-five-year-old paper worker, had been active in the local farmers' association and was elected to the party's county committee in December 1928. Landlords and paper manufacturers got wind of the plans and notified authorities. Provincial forces arrested the planners, and Zhong and ten others were executed in Linpu in 1930 (*XX* 1985:24:24; 14:3).

Despite the failed uprising, the county party headquarters remained at Shangbao Village; the area of Within the Dike never figured prominently in the Communist movement in the 1930s and 1940s. As South Township continued to serve as the base, Linpu, the important urban center for the township and its rough-and-tumble commercial entrepôt, became a focal point for Communist activity in 1929 and 1930. A Nationalist government report noted that if one "goes to the villages around Linpu at festival times, there are many Communist announcements and placards." Reports indicated that mail inspections had turned up evidence that these were sent from Shanghai to Linpu (*XX* 1985:14:3). The plans of the county committee in the summer of 1930 to join with Communists in Zhuji and Fuyang counties to the south and west in an armed uprising underscore the northern Puyang River microregional orientation of both Linpu and South Township. The plans disintegrated when the Guomindang government completely suppressed the county organization in November. From then until October 1938, there was no county Communist Party (*XX* 1985:14:4).

The years 1928 to 1930 were pivotal for Xiaoshan County. For the first time since rapid political and social change had begun early in the century, South Township came to be seen by progressive political forces – at that time, the Communist Party – as the base for the revolutionary movement. It is important to note that the Communist initiative for change, like that brought by Shen Dingyi, came to both South Township and Within the Dike from the outside, not from among then current residents of the ecosystem. The events in South Township hinted at another pattern of change as well. While those in the forefront of change since the beginning of the century had been members of elites educated in either the old examination system or the modern-school system, the emergence of men like Zhong Ama, an illiterate paper worker, serving as a key member of the party's county committee, was a harbinger of a new-style elite and the social revolution that would come.

The period of Guomindang statism, 1929–40. One measure of the differences in the elite political culture of the three arenas at the beginning of Guomindang rule from Nanjing comes from a government report of local elites in 1930 (*XZH* 1930:*Zhiyuan yilanbiao*:29–50). The Nationalists initially divided county units into wards containing groups of villages or urban neighborhoods; these were controlled by headmen who were appointed (likely with the advice of key men in each locality) by the magistrate. This system provided the administrative structure in Within the Dike and South Township. In the Southern Sands, the self-government system of Shen Dingyi continued in effect to 1930.

The statistics on these headmen underscore the findings from the composition of the Heshang relief board of 1929 on the nature of South Township elite culture. That arena, not surprisingly, reflected a greater degree of traditional structures than did Within the Dike. The earlier seven key lineages in South Township produced 43 percent (46 of 107) of the arena's headmen compared to 27.5 percent (55 of 200) produced by earlier key lineages in Within the Dike. The number of leaders coming from a wider range of lineages in Within the Dike probably reflects the greater degree of modern change there associated with its more diverse social and economic opportunities. South Township leaders tended to be older than those in Within the Dike: the average age in the former was 59.8 years, with a median of 50; in the latter, the average was 45.6, with a median of 46. Occupational categories – farmers, businessmen, and educators – reveal that in Within the Dike, 29 percent (58) were farmers, 45.5 percent (91) were businessmen, and 22 percent (44) were educators. In contrast, South Township had 21.4 percent (23) farmers, 43 percent (46) businessmen, and 34.5 percent (37) educators. The relatively large number of businessmen and educators in South Township is striking. From other materials, we know that the businessmen were paper manufacturers. The larger number of educators points to the continuing traditional association of elite roles with educational functions, an association seen also, but to a lesser degree, in the greater diversity of leadership in Within the Dike. While the persistence of lineage control, the marked linkage of elite status with education, and the more advanced age of the headmen do not in themselves necessarily translate into traditional or conservative approaches, taken together and placed in the context of the absence of modern changes in South Township life and circumstances, they stand as important indicators of the more traditional nature of its elite culture.

This relationship comes into even sharper focus from the data on Southern Sands elites. The average age of the self-government leaders in Shen's East Township experiment was 28.5, with a median age of 29;

furthermore, fully two-thirds of the men were outsiders to the county, hailing from neighboring counties. The data point to a leadership born at the turn of the century rather than from fifteen to twenty years earlier, with substantially different life experiences from the leaders in the other two arenas. The significance of the individual – Shen the charismatic reformer – for this area's developmental mobilization is once again obvious in these appointments. Also obvious is the significance of the context: it is likely that outsiders were acceptable as leaders of local self-government bodies because of the more open nature of social structures in the Southern Sands, relatively recently formed and with an absence of longtime lineages. It is difficult to imagine a similar degree of acceptance of outside elites in Within the Dike or South Township. With Shen dead, however, the self-government bodies were dismantled in 1930 and replaced by the ward, village, and neighborhood structures of the rest of the county.

The 1930s in Xiaoshan saw the end of local mobilization – of the elites, as had been seen in the last years of the Qing and into the 1920s, and of the masses, seen in the mid to late 1920s. The Guomindang government's chief goal in these years was to achieve political stability and control. This meant reining in the unpredictable masses and obstreperous elites with bureaucratic structures (Miner 1975:92, 101). Mass organizations of farmers, workers, and women were curtailed or taken over by the Guomindang (*XX* 1985:14:57–58, 63). The earlier openness and voluntarism that were hallmarks of civil society in the northern arenas were no longer allowed. The government, aware and fearful of the revolutionary potential of modern schools, began to control and even close suspected radical centers (Schoppa 1989:205–10). The various government experiments in local administration – Xiaoshan saw three significant county reorganizations in the six years from 1928 to 1934 – produced no basic reforms and certainly nothing remotely resembling revolutionary change (*XX* 1985: 1:28).

The decade saw minimal modern developmental change: the introduction of telephone service in Within the Dike, the construction of an airfield in the Southern Sands, and road construction and repair in all three arenas (*XX* 1985:*Dashiji*:30–33). The economic depression seriously damaged industries which had earlier been successful. Prices plummeted and production declined in the silk textile, silkworm cocoon, lace, and paper industries. The stagnant or declining economies in all three arenas compounded the statist halt of social and political change to produce a peculiarly static period in the sweep of early twentieth-century change. But the revolutionary process had not come to a halt. This was simply a hiatus that war and revolution would end.

The impact of the Japanese invasion and occupation. As we have seen, county elites from Within the Dike and the Southern Sands, which dominated the county political scene, were oriented politically and economically primarily to Hangzhou and Shanghai, with a subsidiary orientation to the natural microregion of the Three River drainage system. South Township, in contrast, faced the interior of the province. The incipient shift of the county political center, initiated with the Communist efforts in South Township in 1929, was ultimately brought to fruition from outside by the Japanese invasion. The invasion and occupation for the first time militarized the political agendas and society of Xiaoshan. If the period of the 1930s saw a halt to the developmental change of the century's first three decades, the Japanese actions destroyed much of the development that had occurred, as it also ended the statism and stagnation of the 1930s.

At the end of November 1937, Japanese air attacks on the county began, striking first at the county seat and then at other targets in Within the Dike. By June 20, 1938, the Japanese had struck sixty-eight times, destroying over four thousand homes and causing almost three thousand casualties, including about six hundred fatalities, The county had been involved in the construction of forts and defensive outposts along the coast, and the populace had been mobilized in anti-Japanese nationalist organizations at least in the Southern Sands (where the coastal defenses were erected) and Within the Dike. But in the face of the ferocious air attack, there began an exodus of mostly wealthy elites and several institutions farther into the province's interior (XX 1985:Dashiji:34–36).

The Japanese attack gave the moribund Communist Party a chance to revive itself in South Township. In the summer of 1938, the CCP provincial committee sent two students from Resist Japan University (Kangda) in Yan'an to the township to begin to organize anti-Japanese Self-Defense Corps (XX 1985:Dashiji:35). In October, the Ning(bo)-Shao(xing) Special Party Committee established a county Work Committee to develop the anti-Japanese movement and a party organization. In the fall of 1939, the Ning-Shao Committee set up a full-fledged party committee to be headquartered in South Township and to develop an anti-Japanese guerrilla base (XX 1985:14:4–5). With Hangzhou occupied by the enemy, the initiative for the effort came from party cadres to the east and southeast in the region of the Ning-Shao Plain. The Communist agents sent to work in South Township were all outsiders from neighboring Zhuji County and from Jiangsu Province.

In January 1940, the Japanese army crossed the Qiantang River, capturing and occupying the Southern Sands and the northern two-thirds of Within the Dike, including the county seat. The county government fled to Heshang in South Township, where it remained until August 1945. For the first time, South Township became the base of county political power. At the first administrative conference of county leaders in Heshang in June 1940, of the 71 percent whose native place is known, 49 percent (19) hailed from South Township, with 38 percent (15) from Within the Dike, and 13 percent (5) from the Southern Sands. The degree of representation of South Township elites in county affairs was unprecedented.

For the first time in county counsels, the situation in South Township seemed to get a hearing, as county elites became aware of the context in which contingency had placed them (*ENX* 1940). At the conference, there was frank talk about the contrasts between South Township and the other two natural county arenas. Speakers pointed out, for example, that Within the Dike and Southern Sands had experimental farms (for rice and cotton cultivation, respectively) to assist in reforming agriculture. But there had been no county response to pleas and even specific modernizing plans concerning the paper industry from township elites and villagers in the period from 1927 to 1930 (*S*, August 31, 1927; *XZH* 1930:31, 49–50). When a chronic flooding problem on the Yongxing River became severe in 1939, there was no county response despite efforts of local committees to initiate action (*ENX* 1940:28).

Others at the conference pointed to the lack of economic infrastructure in the mountainous township and thus to the fact that the new headquarters of Xiaoshan's county government had few economic resources. The serious issue was how this area – "more important than ever for the military and the economy, for politics and culture – could support the county government (*ENX* 1940:28). Already by mid-1940, an estimated 90 percent of the rich households and great merchants who might have been expected to offer economic support had moved out of the county into interior areas of the province (*ENX* 1940:14). The financial difficulties of the Heshang government were further exacerbated by the Japanese capture of Linpu, South Township's urban center, in January 1942.

For Within the Dike and the Southern Sands, the Japanese war and occupation were devastating. Setting up a puppet government in June 1942 at the old county seat, with a scion of the wealthy Lai lineage from Changhe serving as magistrate, the Japanese continued to gut the handiwork and hopes of the reformers and revolutionaries of the previous four decades (*XX* 1985:15:40). Those under Japanese control faced an almost intolerable life: commerce and industry came to a halt; food was scarce and, when available, was exorbitantly priced; the scarcity of fuel for cooking and heating forced farmers to cut mulberry and tea plants – acts that by the end of the war had brought the silk and tea industries to the point of extinction. The commercial prosperity and incipient industrialization of the area were destroyed, as the Japanese dismantled the textile mills to produce spare parts for their military machine. The physical destruction of Within the Dike was the worst in all of eastern Zhejiang Province (Schoppa 1989:222). The Japanese had not only made necessary the shift of the political power base in the county by forcing the evacuation of county offices to South Township, but they destroyed the economic base for political power in the other two arenas.

The Guomindang county government's South Township base was continually under siege by the Japanese army. Japanese raiders struck

Heshang in July 1942, and major forces of Japanese and Xiaoshan puppet troops attacked the county seat in January 1943 and May 1944. All three attacks were repulsed, but they kept the county government, starved for funds and resources, weak and able to do little more than wring its hands over the serious problem of refugees (*XX* 1985:*Dashiji*:37–38). That the Japanese were able to seize and build a fort on Jianshan Mountain on the west bank of the Puyang River only a few miles from Heshang indicates the precariousness of Heshang's security (*XXD* 1984:492).

The Heshang government was also concerned about the Communist threat. Within a year after the move to South Township, in January 1941, it succeeded in destroying an incipient CCP county committee that had been directing a slowly growing anti-Japanese movement. There would be no county committee again until 1949, but considerable Communist activity continued, along with the expected Guomindang suppression. In 1942, as the Japanese began sustained attacks along the Zhejiang–Jiangxi Railroad, which passed through Xiaoshan, the provincial CCP committee, working to establish a three-county base, set up the Zhu(ji)-Xiao(shan)-Fu(yang) West Route Work Committee, whose scope of activity included South Township (*XX* 1985:14:5). All along the railroad, anti-Japanese organizations sprang up, with townships and county subdistricts setting up their own self-defense corps. Details of the work of this committee are not available, but it is very clear that, as in north and central China, the Communists were active in building support for their cause beyond simply repelling the Japanese (Zhong 1982:17–18, 29; Jin 1985:118).

In early January 1944, the Jin(hua)-Xiao(shan) detachment was formed, unifying previously separate self-defense units and becoming a force for building Communist support as it battled the Japanese army. By May 1945, the support (or, at least, given the precarious state of South Township's food supply, the marshaling) of subdistricts in South Township was evident in their sending 20,000 catties of rice to supply units of the Communist 4th Route Army attacking an important market town in Fuyang County. An important point for our purposes is that in every case of Communist organizing, South Township became part of a larger regional undertaking – whether it was accepting directions from the Ning-Shao Special Committee, the Zhu-Xiao-Fu West Route Work Committee, or the Jin-Xiao detachment. In the years before the war, the township was frequently isolated from the advances of the two other county arenas. Now South Township, joining forces from the northern Puyang and Yongxing rivers microregion, was in the vanguard of military mobilization. The bourgeois and socialist agendas of educational progress, industrial development, and mass social mobilization of earlier periods had been swallowed up by defensive nationalism and a military ethos.

Politics and change in the three arenas, 1945–50. Although the Japanese finally seized Heshang in late May 1945, the Guomindang county government had already begun to establish institutions for the postwar world. In October 1944, the provisional county assembly (*canyihui*) was established at Heshang by the Xiaoshan Guomindang County Bureau (*XX* 1985:15:38–39). The twenty-five-man assembly chose leaders who clearly represented the important position that South Township had taken in county counsels: Lou Guancang, from the old South Township lineage, as chair and Ge Shiyou of the town of Linpu as vice chair.

But when the assembly moved back to the county seat in Within the Dike, the county Guomindang acted as though the years in South Township had not existed. When the assembly was formally established in June 1946, Ge was chosen chair, but the vice chair went to Chen Yuehuan from the county seat. The assembly was composed of representatives from a variety of occupational and organizational categories; proportional representation on the basis of area population was not a consideration. The native-place composition of the body was 55 percent (36) from Within the Dike, 23 percent (15) from the Southern Sands, and 20 percent (13) from South Township (*CYH* 1946). The politics of the subordination of South Township continued. Seven of the thirteen from the township had participated in the 1940 administrative conference, whereas only three of the other fifty-one had served in that body. The South Township figure suggests again the greater continuity of that arena's leadership. But the other statistic means that 94 percent of the assemblymen from Within the Dike and the Southern Sands had no personal memory of the years based in South Township and no personal awareness or understanding of the environmental and economic difficulties that arena faced.

It seems clear that this county assembly, which met for nine sessions before the Communist victory in May 1949, represented the public values of elite Guomindang society as it had evolved into the late 1940s. It was composed of an array of types: rural and urban administrative heads; schoolteachers and administrators; various professionals: doctors, lawyers, bankers, and industrialists; government and party functionaries; journalists; and professional association (agricultural and educational) leaders. In its diversity and its degree of specialization, it seems light-years away from the gentry leadership of four decades earlier or from the South Township Flood Relief Committee of less than two decades earlier. The diversity of family background in county leadership positions also stands in contrast to the situation at the end of the Qing. Only nine of the earlier designated fourteen key lineages from Within the Dike and South Township produced assemblymen, and there were forty-five surnames among the sixty-five members.

The assembly's all-male membership had an average and median age of forty-three. Born on average in 1903, it was a group for whom the formative national events in their public lives would have been the May Fourth Movement and the Nationalist Revolution, men who entered adulthood

amid the 1920s ethos of nationalism, capitalist development, and profes-
sionalism and expertise. It was also a notably educated group. Of the sixty
men about whose educational backgrounds we know something, 15 percent
(9) had graduated from a university; 50 percent (30) had graduated from a
high school or normal school; five had attended special institutes or courses;
three had graduated from elementary school; one had a traditional civil
service degree; and twelve – all of them government functionaries – had
some unspecified degree of education.

But for all its modernity and promise, this leadership would not endure.
By 1947, the Communist armies had begun to sweep out of Manchuria to
north China in what seemed an inexorable flow south. In Xiaoshan,
beginning in August 1948, the Jin-Xiao detachment, revived from the anti-
Japanese war, began guerrilla raids against targets in South Township,
attacking Guomindang police and military outposts. In February 1949 the
political committee of the Jin-Xiao detachment organized Xiaoshan territory
into the Heshang and Linpu districts to mobilize farmers, paper workers,
and others against the Guomindang. It seems clear that here guerrilla
military action preceded social mobilization. By mid-April, when Nanjing
was on the verge of falling to the Communist armies moving south from
their great victory at Xuzhou, the Jin-Xiao detachment set up the Xiaoshan
Office to prepare for the seizure of power. On May 5, that detachment
entered the county seat, the object of the county military campaign, bringing
Communist rule to Xiaoshan (XX 1985:Dashiji:40–43).

The formal county committee was established on May 16, in control of
nine district (qu) committees. In evenhanded fashion, probably evidence of
the influence of South Township forces, each of the three natural arenas
held three district committees. Altogether there were only 120 party cadres
at the time of "liberation." Sources stress that the leaders and important
cadres were from South Township, that they were military men hardened
by local struggle against the Guomindang (XX 1985:14:6). They did not have
to give up their military roles quickly. Through April 1950, determined
Guomindang resistance forces in all three of the county's natural arenas
attacked the regime. The resistance was reportedly especially strong in the
Southern Sands, the old base of Shen Dingyi and the Guomindang. The
Communists followed the bombings, assassinations, and guerrilla attacks
with mass arrests and executions (XX 1985:Dashiji: 43–45).

Analysis shows the face of the new county elite, which shared two
characteristics with the ousted elite of the Guomindang county assembly.
It was almost completely male (115 out of 120). And the cadres were
predominantly middle-aged (the precise limits of the categories are not
given): 61 percent (73) were so designated; 32 percent (38) were classified
as young; and 8 percent (9), old. But this was a starkly different county elite
– in their military ethos and in their educational and social backgrounds.
Fully 32 percent (38) were illiterate or had never attended any school; none

had attended a university; only 3 percent (4) had graduated from high school, while 11 percent (13) had attended some high school; and 54 percent (65) had an elementary school education (*XX* 1985:14). The table below gives a clear picture of the change in the educational backgrounds. Together with obviously correlative social backgrounds and the shift to a military orientation, they produce a change in elite profile that could perhaps not be more revolutionary.

Although developments in the People's Republic are beyond the scope of this chapter, there are important indications that "liberation" meant also the liberation of South Township from the subordination to the other arenas under which it had existed for many years. Although the magistrates of the county since 1949 came from outside the province, twelve terms of the vice magistracy have been served by Xiaoshan residents – nine of them by men whose native place was South Township (*XX* 1985:15:18–21). Most important, the urgent, political and economic agenda of South Township was addressed. The paper industry, which, after years of decline, suffered greatly during the civil war because of price fluctuations and transportation disruptions, was reformed and, by 1984, employed over three thousand workers in forty-seven firms. Official sources indicated a substantial profit that year (*XX* 1985:4:32–33).

In addition and perhaps more significant, the county water conservancy agenda was extended after 1949 for the first time to South Township. Though the arena had frequently experienced flood damage in the years before 1949, there had been no serious county efforts at flood control, the county's attention and funds being directed instead to the Three River system. Apart from small-scale mountain dikes in the township, there were, in fact, no water-control facilities. Dike construction began in 1952 along the township's two main rivers and was completed during the decade. Irrigation reservoirs were also constructed for the first time. Nine of the fourteen county reservoirs holding at least 100,000 cubic meters of water

Educational backgrounds of county elites, 1946–49

	Guomindang County Assembly, 1946–49	*Communist Cadres, 1949*
University	9 (15%)	–
High school	30 (50%)	17 (14.1%)
Elementary	3 (5%)	65 (54%)
Institutes	5 (8.3%)	–
Old degree	1 (1.6%)	–
Educ. unspecified	12 (20%)	–
Illiterate	–	38 (32%)
Total	60	120

Sources: CYH 1946 and *XX* 1985

built since 1957 have been in South Township. During this time, nineteen pumping stations have also been constructed. The Communist success, led in the county by South Township men, clearly helped provide the access to power that the township had lacked, and with that access came also some of the benefits of power (*XX* 1985:5: 11–12, 18–19).

Conclusion

The revolution that swept China in the first half of the twentieth century was not only about "the search for modern China" represented by themes of modernization and efforts to enunciate a new ideological and social orthodoxy. It was a process made up of myriad local struggles with their own dynamics and ultimately their own meanings. Defined by its relationship to the past, a revolution proceeds dialectically with the past, reacting to or building on changes wrought in the process of revolutionary developments. The *process* of revolution was composed not only of the national revolutionary surges of 1911, 1927, and 1949, but it also involved periods of evolutionary and even devolutionary change upon which subsequent surges were built.

In Xiaoshan County, the revolutionary process brought different realities in the three major ecological arenas. While social and economic change came rapidly in Within the Dike and to a lesser extent in the Southern Sands in the first three decades of the century and then slowed and ground to a halt in the 1930s and 1940s, South Township saw little modern change until the 1950s, when it was made possible by events in the 1930s and 1940s. A central result of this process was a change in the patterns of county political power that had at base no necessary ideological identity with the triumph of the Communists over the Nationalists. For the people in South Township, the central political meaning of the revolution may well be not so much that Communist forces prevailed and embarked on ambitious programs of social and economic experiments but that, by dint of circumstances and contingency, they were able finally to acquire the political connections and legitimacy for power in local affairs that Within the Dike and Southern Sands had enjoyed in the Republic.

What does this analysis of revolution in Xiaoshan County suggest about our study of the countless other revolutions that make up the Chinese revolution? We must begin by underscoring Daniel Little's contention that "there exists no a priori way to identify the factors relevant to a given process, and certainly no ultimate . . . theory to which all types of social change can be reduced" (Little 1989:216). Revolutionary potential and reality could not have been accurately predicted in Xiaoshan County's three natural arenas through causal models that focus on such explanations as degree of economic development, the nature of social behavior, or the structures of economic and social class relationships. As Hartford and

Goldstein have rightly put it, the revolution was "not the predetermined working out of structural factors or the inevitable Big Boom emanating from the mixture of revolutionary preconditions and revolutionary conscious-ness" (Hartford and Goldstein 1989:33).

While it is clear that there is not one formula for analyzing the course of the revolutions in China, the case of Xiaoshan County suggests key sources of revolutionary change: context, culture, human agency, and contingency. Only the latter cannot be factored with certainty into other revolutionary processes. The random event of Shen's assassination and the unpre-dictability of the Japanese invasion and its particular degree of violence in this county, for example, would not be replicated elsewhere. The remaining sources, however, are central in analyzing the contours of the revolutionary process.

This study suggests that the significant contexts for penetrating the patterns of long-term political and social change were natural units – microregions (e.g., the Three River system and the Yongxing and northern Puyang river basins) and their components, here called arenas. Micro-regions shared a sufficient commonality of natural ecological conditions to give rise to similar public agendas (e.g., water-control interests or economic orientation) and to some similar social, economic, and cultural structures (e.g., agricultural strategies, rent systems, lineage structures). A micro-region's commonalities helped shape the scope and nature of political and social action as in Shen's Southern Sands-based rent-resistance movement in 1921 and in the anti-Japanese guerrilla activity of South Township and the areas to the south and west in the 1930s and 1940s.

Microregions were internally differentiated into ecological arenas that were sometimes overlapping, perhaps even multioriented. Though the integrity of the Three River microregion was naturally maintained in its defining dimension of water control, in urban and some aspects of economic orientation, for example, a western arena faced Hangzhou, while an eastern arena faced Shaoxing. Such dual orientation could bring conflicting allegiances in political and economic goals and policies that might affect the common agenda of water control. Historical, cultural, and some natural factors further divided the western arena into Within the Dike and the Southern Sands. These arenas helped shape the social-political structures and processes that contributed to the nature of local revolutionary action. The revolutionary self-government effort in the quasi-frontier Southern Sands, for example, could not have been effectively replicated in Within the Dike or, for that matter, in South Township.

The dynamism of the relationships among the three natural arenas which made up Xiaoshan County points to the interpretative dangers of relying on the county (or indeed any political unit) as the analytical unit of change. Analysis of political and social developments and specifically of the differential revolutionary process requires primary attention to the natural context, here the county's three arenas and the microregions of which they were a part. Yet the essential political reality remained that, for these natural arenas of Xiaoshan County, political resources for achieving goals, position, and power lay in the county seat, not in microregional centers and not in subcounty or subregional arenas. South Township could have participated indefinitely with arenas of neighboring counties to the south and never achieved a share of political power in Xiaoshan County. Because a revolution is ultimately a struggle for political power and prerogative (Aya 1984: 326), the relationship between natural and administrative contexts becomes a crucial element. Studies of the revolutionary process must then consider not only elements of and dynamism among microregions and their component arenas but also the relationships between these natural contexts and the administrative units that exercised political power. Thus, this study points to the need for more extensive local research into the contextual dynamics of twentieth-century revolutionary change.

If context is an essential element in detailing the setting and structures of this change, cultural forms and structures are indispensable for helping to explain the dynamics, direction, mode, and pace of change. Some traditional cultural and social forms had determinative power in mediating the revolutionary process. In new circumstances, they were like powerful new wine in old wineskins. Some of the most important – native-place ties and social connections to people and positions of power – crossed local contexts and cultures and provided the cohesive power for significant sociopolitical networks during times of revolutionary flux.

The importance of other cultural forms and values varied according to context. Lineages remained the most important bases of power throughout these revolutionary years, though the nature and extent of their control varied according to context and effective leadership. The traditional cultural value that emphasized education contributed to dynamic change in Within the Dike: as the practice of education evolved, schools became centers for the restructuring of local society and sources for the emergence of a multifaceted elite. In contrast, in the sharply different context of South Township, those same cultural values produced a system that sustained the traditional lineages and militated against change. As yet another example, existing traditional marriage and socioeconomic networks in the Southern Sands became vehicles for revolutionary mobilization. In South Township, these same networks were either conservative or ineffectual forces when change was demanded.

The third essential – indeed, critical – element for the analysis of the revolutionary process in Xiaoshan County is human agency, which, like contingency, is unpredictable but potentially determinative. It is this factor that revolutionized the traditional networks of the Southern Sands and stimulated that arena's revolutionary involvement. Shen Dingyi's personal leadership and charisma captured the imaginations and mobilized the energy of the farmers in 1921, an experience that in turn garnered their support in 1928. The farmers in 1921 did not organize themselves to redress grievances but approached Shen for counsel and leadership. Similarly, the paper workers and farmers of South Township, though suffering severe deprivation, did not act until outside Communist agents initiated farmers' associations in 1928. Even such a potential local leader as Zhong Ama, who directed the ill-fated 1929 uprising, had not been emboldened to act until the spark of outside agents ignited his zeal. Though one can point to contextual and cultural structures and situations as shapers of the reality of change, in almost every case the intervention in the particular ecosystem of individual agents from the outside (returned students, entrepreneurs, Shen, Communist agents) or of mass agents from the outside (the Japanese and Communist armies) was the catalyst for change. Though some of the individual agents were originally natives of Xiaoshan, they came as catalysts with ideas and instruments of change gained not in their native ecosystem but in the world outside, through schooling or links to powerful connections or business interests.

In sum, the revolution in Xiaoshan County suggests a number of sources critical to understanding the twentieth-century process of revolutionary change. In revolutionary episodes, the particular nature of context, culture, and catalyst and their dynamic interrelationships disclose the contours of the local process. Their variation in episodes across the Chinese countryside reveals the contours of the Chinese revolution.

REFERENCES

Averill, Stephen C. 1990. "Local Elites and Communist Revolution in the Jiangxi Hill Country." In Joseph W. Esherick and Mary Backus Rankin, eds, *Chinese Local Elites and Patterns of Dominance*. Berkeley: University of California Press, 282–304.

Aya, Rod. 1984. "Popular Intervention in Revolutionary Situations." In Charles Bright and Susan Harding, eds, *Statemaking and Social Movements*. Ann Arbor: University of Michigan Press, 318–43.

Barkan, Lenore. 1990. "Patterns of Power: Forty Years of Elite Politics in a Chinese County." In Joseph W. Esherick and Mary Backus Rankin, eds, *Chinese Local Elites and Patterns of Dominance*. Berkeley: University of California Press: 191–215.

Bergère, Marie-Claire. 1989. *The Golden Age of the Chinese Bourgeoisie 1911–1937*. Cambridge: Cambridge University Press.

Chang Kuo-T'ao. 1971. *The Rise of the Chinese Communist Party, 1921–1927*. Lawrence: University of Kansas Press.

CIHC. *China Industrial Handbooks, Chekiang*. 1935. Shanghai: Bureau of Foreign Trade, Ministry of Industry.

CYH. *Xiaoshan xian canyihui diyijie dierci dahuiyi* [The second meeting of the first session of the Xiaoshan County assembly]. October 1946. N.p.

ENX. Xiaoshan xian ershijiu niandu diyici xingzheng huiyi jilu [Records of the first administrative conference for Xiaoshan County in 1940]. 1940. N.p.

Esherick, Joseph W., and Mary Backus Rankin. 1990. *Chinese Local Elites and Patterns of Dominance*. Berkeley: University of California Press.

Galbiati, Fernando. 1985. *P'eng P'ai and the Hai-Lu-Feng Soviet*. Stanford: Stanford University Press.

Gao Yuetian. 1972. "Shen Dingyi xianshengde yisheng" [The life of Shen Dingyi]. *Zhejiang yuekan* [Zhejiang monthly] 4.3:5–8; 4.4:8–13.

Hartford, Kathleen, and Steven M. Goldstein, eds, 1989. *Single Sparks*. Armonk, N.Y.: M. E. Sharpe, Inc.

Hofheinz, Roy, Jr. 1969. "The Ecology of Chinese Communist Success: Rural Influence Patterns, 1923–45." In A. Doak Barnett, ed., *Chinese Communist Politics in Action*. Seattle: University of Washington Press, 3–77.

Jin Pusen. 1985. "Zhedong kangRi genjudide chuangjian" [The construction of an anti-Japanese base in eastern Zhejiang]. *Hangzhou daxue xuebao* [Journal of Hangzhou University] 15.3:116–23.

JW. Juewa [Awakening]. 1919–25. Shanghai.

Kong Xuexiong. 1934. "Dongxiang zizhi shimo" [An account of the East Township self-government movement]. In *Zhongguo jinri nongcun yundong* [The rural movements in China today]. N.p.

Lavely, William, James Lee, and Wang Feng. 1990. "Chinese Demography: the State of the Field." *Journal of Asian Studies* 49.4:807–34.

Lin Weibao. 1936. "Yaqian yinxiang ji" [Impressions of Yaqian]. *Zhongguo nongcun* [Rural China] 1.7:72–75.

Little, Daniel. 1989. *Understanding Peasant China*. New Haven: Yale University Press.

Miner, Noel. 1975. "Chekiang: The Nationalists' Effort in Agrarian Reform and Construction, 1927–1937." Ph.D. diss., Stanford University.

MLB. Minlibao [The People's Stand]. 1911–13. Shanghai.

MR. Minguo ribao [The National Daily]. 1916–29. Shanghai.

NCH. North China Herald. 1911–29. Shanghai.

Rankin, Mary Backus. 1986. *Elite Activism and Political Transformation in China*. Stanford: Stanford University Press.

Rowe, William T. 1990. "The Public Sphere in Modern China." *Modern China* 16.3:309–29.

S. Shibao [The Eastern Times]. 1909–37. Shanghai.

Schoppa, R. Keith. 1982. *Chinese Elites and Political Change*. Cambridge: Harvard University Press.

——. 1989. *Xiang Lake – Nine Centuries of Chinese Life*. New Haven: Yale University Press.

——. 1990a. "Power, Legitimacy, and Symbol: Local Elites and the Jute Creek Embankment Case." In Joseph W. Esherick and Mary Backus Rankin, eds, *Chinese Local Elites and Patterns of Dominance*. Berkeley: University of California Press, 140–61.

——. 1990b. "Rent Resistance and Rural Reconstruction: Shen Dingyi in Political Opposition, 1921 and 1928." Unpublished manuscript.

SDSX. Shen Dingyi xiansheng shilue [A narrative account of Shen Dingyi]. N.d. N.p.

SH. Shenbao. 1923–31. Shanghai.

Shao Weizheng. 1985. "Yaqian nongmin xiehui shimo" [A complete account of the Yaqian farmers' association]. In *Dangshi yanjiu ziliao* [Party history research materials]. Chengdu: Sichuan Renmin Chubanshe.

Sheel, Kamal. 1989. *Peasant Society and Marxist Intellectuals in China*. Princeton: Princeton University Press.

Skinner, G. William. 1964–65. "Marketing and Social Structure in Rural China." *Journal of Asian Studies* 24:3–43, 195–228, 363–99.

———. 1977. "Regional Urbanization in Nineteeth Century China." In G. William Skinner, ed., *The City in Late Imperial China*. Stanford: Stanford University Press, 211–249.

Strand, David. 1990. "Mediation, Representation, and Repression: Local Elites in 1920s Beijing." In Joseph W. Esherick and Mary Backus Rankin, eds, *Chinese Local Elites and Patterns of Dominance*. Berkeley: University of California Press, 216–35.

SX. Shaoxing xianzhi ziliao diyi ji [A compilation of materials for a gazetteer of Shaoxing County]. 1937. N.p.

XG. Xiaoshan gailan [A general examination of Xiaoshan]. 1947. N.p.

XHT. Xiaoshan hetang jinianlu [A remembrance of the affair of Xiaoshan rivers and ponds]. 1920. N.p.

XX. Xiaoshan xianzhi [A gazetteer of Xiaoshan County]. 1985. Xiaoshan.

XXD. Xiaoshan xian dimingzhi [A gazetteer of place-names in Xiaoshan County]. 1984. Xiaoshan.

XXG. Xiaoshan xianzhi gao [A draft gazetteer of Xiaoshan County]. 1935. N.p.

XXS. Xiaoshan xingshi [A directory of surnames in Xiaoshan]. 1984. Xiaoshan.

XXZ. Xiaoshan xiangtu zhi [A gazetteer of the Xiaoshan locality]. 1931. N.p.

XZH. Xiaoshan xian zhengzhi huibian [Political compendium of Xiaoshan County]. 1930. Xiaoshan.

YNY. Yaqian nongmin yundong [The Yaqian farmers' movement]. 1985. Xiaoshan.

Zhao Zijie, Xu Shaoquan, and Li Weijia. 1983. "Xuan Zhonghua" [Xuan Zhonghua]. In *Buxiude zhanshi* [Immortal Warriors]. Hangzhou: Zhejiang renmin chubanshe.

Zhong Fazong. 1982. "Huiyi Jin-Xiao zhiduide zhandou licheng" [Recollections of the wartime progress of the Jin-Xiao detachment]. In *Zhejiang geming shiliao xuanji* [A compilation of historical materials on Zhejiang revolutionary history]. Hangzhou Zhejiang renmin chubanshe.

ZSL. Zhejiang sheng shuiliju zhiyuan lu [Directory of functionaries in the Zhejiang conservancy office]. 1933. N.p.

ZSN. Zhejiang shuiliju niankan [Zhejiang conservancy office yearbook]. 1929. Hangzhou.

ZZ. Zhejiang sheng zhengfu gongbao [Government gazette of Zhejiang Province]. 1929–37. Hangzhou.

7

PERSPECTIVES ON THE CHINESE COMMUNIST REVOLUTION

Kathleen Hartford and Steven M. Goldstein

The CCP was founded in 1921 by a group of young intellectuals who had taken part in the May 4th Movement of 1919 – so named for the first day when protesters shouting out nationalistic slogans clashed with police. The specific trigger for that struggle had been a widespread sense in China that the terms of the Treaty of Versailles signed after World War One were unfair, since they transferred to Japanese control pieces of Chinese territory that had formerly been claimed by Germany. Why, these young Chinese nationalists asked, had the territories in question not been given back to China, when their country too had sided with the Allies? In addition to agitating against the Treaty of Versailles and taking part in related mass protests, patriotic youths of the "May 4th Generation" and radical professors who shared their beliefs spent a great deal of time looking abroad for inspirational works that might help them solve China's problems. One particularly attractive set of texts, for those desperate to find some way to get a revolution derailed by corrupt warlords back on track, was Marxist. And these took on a special appeal after the Bolsheviks took power in Russia, apparently proving that Marxist ideas could be useful in helping a backward nation to modernize rapidly. This, in the most basic of terms, is how the Chinese Communist Party began. At first, though, it was only one of many radical organizations, competing not just with the Nationalist Party but also with various anarchist groups. It was only in the mid-1920s that it began to establish itself as the main competitor to the GMD on the Left.

There is nothing very mysterious about this bare-bones tale of the origins of the CCP, since the milieu of Chinese society at the time was conducive in many ways to the formation of radical groups, but what requires much more explanation is its eventual rise to power. After the First United Front collapsed and Chiang Kai-shek turned against his erstwhile Communist allies, the CCP was almost completely destroyed. In the early 1930s, a fierce series of battles was waged against those remnants of the CCP that had survived the White Terror of 1927 by the GMD, and there was also intense infighting within the Communist ranks. In addition, support *from the Soviet Union was sporadic at best. How this battered organization managed to take control of the entire country in 1949 has perplexed analysts ever since that year, and this chapter is a tour-de-force survey of all of the various answers that have been proposed to solve the conundrum. Kathleen Hartford and Steven M. Goldstein take us through a series of debates that centered on the differential significance of CCP appeals to nationalism and to social justice and its internal organizational strengths in accounting for its rise. Their main emphasis, though, is on the limitations of all efforts to find a single explanation for the phenomenon. Writing in 1989, just as a series of impressive studies of individual CCP base areas had been completed, they argue against one-size-fits-all interpretations. The first step toward making sense of the Communist Revolution, they insist, is to break it down into many smaller revolutions. In this sense, though he breaks with them when it comes to temporal divides, their chapter complements Schoppa's.*

* * *

We are at a new juncture in the study of the Chinese revolution. A new generation of scholarship is emerging which promises to resolve old debates, bridge old dichotomies, and join formerly separate strands of analysis. We are accumulating a rich body of empirical data making possible a fruitful exchange between those studying the Chinese revolution and those attempting comparative generalizations. We are gaining a clearer sense of the interrelations of domestic and international factors, of the Communist movement and its opponents, of spontaneous peasant impulses and revolutionary organization and leadership. These strands are being joined by intensive studies of the Chinese Communist revolution in local contexts. Although these local studies deal with milieus far more limited in geographical and, at times, chronological scope than much of the earlier work on the revolution, such limitations have allowed more comprehensive examination of relevant actors and causal factors than has heretofore been possible. The result is a seemingly paradoxical development. The exceptions to previous generalizations on China, the catalogue of "local idiosyncrasies," are pointing to a pattern that promises a new set of tentative general hypotheses on the revolution. In this pattern one finds a greater consonance between the Chinese revolutionary process and the generalizations of comparativists than was evident in earlier, more general works on the revolution.

Clearly these are large claims to make for a body of work that is still maturing. In support and elucidation of them, we provide here an overview of studies on the Chinese revolution and on comparative revolutions.

The study of the Chinese revolution: early images, 1932–1949

Not until the CCP's forced removal to China's rural hinterlands did it emerge as a significant object of study by Westerners. Before 1927, most observers regarded the Guomindang (GMD) under Chiang Kai-shek as the (pejorative) extreme in Chinese radicalism. But once the GMD achieved control of the national political apparatus, Westerners reporting on China's military, political, and social upheaval turned their attention to the growing Communist movement. They tended to find the sources of its dynamism in three factors: popular (especially peasant) support for the CCP, partisan warfare, and organization.

In 1944, the Shanxi warlord Yan Xishan accounted for CCP strength in an apparent tautology: "The reason why the Communists today have such powerful forces is that so many people are following them."[1] The Western reporter who recorded this comment accepted popular support as central to an explanation of the CCP's strength, a view that figured in almost all discussions of the Communist movement in the pre-1949 period. For most authors, one question was paramount: Why do the peasants so enthusiastically support the CCP?

The reasons for this preoccupation lie, in part, in the prior experience of analysts assessing the Communist areas: most knew Guomindang China well. Whatever their political leanings,[2] these Western observers were overwhelmed by the country's massive social dislocations and disgusted by the GMD's continuing inability to respond to these problems. Popular dissatisfaction in the Nationalist areas highlighted the perceived enthusiastic peasant support in the base areas.[3] Even by the mid-1930s most accounts (primarily of the Jiangxi Soviet) located the sources of Communist success in the party's ability to address rural economic hardship.[4] This approach figures in perhaps the earliest systematic discussion of the Communist movement, written in 1932 by O. Edmund Clubb, then a young American vice-consul. Clubb saw the Guomindang's 1927 break with the CCP as an important watershed. The GMD had lost its "roots in the great body of the people" and had turned to a policy of "grasping militarism." It was simply unresponsive to China's worsening socioeconomic problems. By contrast, the Communist program – land redistribution, fiscal reform, and labor legislation – had created "considerable popular support."[5]

A second factor focusing observers' attention on peasant support was the type of warfare conducted by the Communists. "Partisan warfare," later to be known as "people's war," was to many observers a new and exciting phenomenon. And those who wrote in the 1930s and 1940s agreed that the key to success in such warfare lay in popular support.[6]

Popular enthusiasm was needed if the CCP's armies were to get the recruits, supplies, and intelligence they needed to fight. But enthusiasm was of little use unless there was an organization in place to channel and deploy it.[7] Almost all visitors to the Communist areas commented upon the pervasiveness of organization. Organization was the vehicle for the education, discipline, and further indoctrination that helped elicit support. But organization did more than this: it transformed propaganda into popular policies. Relief from military threat or economic insecurity was impossible without the intercession of party-led or sponsored organizations. Peng Dehuai made this point to Edgar Snow in 1936 when he asserted that only by "constant political and organizational work" could the CCP "fulfill the promise of its propaganda." Foreign residents of the GMD areas had seen how government venality and brutality sapped popular support. In the CCP areas, they concluded that the reverse was true: organization was essential to building support.[8]

Few authors during these years would have denied that strong and constant organization was needed to avoid a return to peasant passivity and indifference. And even fewer would have quibbled with the United States War Department, which asserted that the CCP was "the most effectively organized group in China."[9] All these writings recognized that the Communists had created organizations that had generated the commitment of the masses, channeled it into apparently popular policy directions, and so created policies, and institutions that a growing proportion of the population considered worth fighting for.

Some analysts saw power in Communist organizations flowing primarily from the top down. Traditionally passive peasants had to be organized, and the resultant bodies were intended to implement the will of the party leadership.[10] Others spoke of "democracy" in the base areas, suggesting that they saw more mass spontaneity and popular control in these organizations.[11] Some traced the sources of peasant support to the CCP's socioeconomic policies, while others, during the Anti-Japanese War era, tended to stress the mobilizing effects of the war. The major differences of emphasis are illustrated by three works: Edgar Snow's *Red Star over China*, George Taylor's *The Struggle for North China*, and Theodore White and Annalee Jacoby's *Thunder out of China*.

For Taylor, writing in 1941, the emphasis is clearly on the importance of the Japanese invasion and Communist resistance organizations: "[Japanese] brutality was, of course, an excellent argument for the guerrillas, *but only* on condition that they were there to state it, that they had been in a district long enough to organize and infuse a new morale and political outlook into the peasantry."[12] In Taylor's view, socioeconomic reforms were a secondary but complementary factor stimulating peasant involvement. He sees the war not merely as a catalyst but as a crucial intervening variable which generated a peasant consciousness unprecedented in Chinese history. He suggests, however, that peasants might lapse into apathy again once the war had passed and, further, that classes brought together to fight the Japanese might divide again along economic lines. Maintaining the momentum, Taylor believed, took considerable political acumen. The Communist movement was not a passive beneficiary of GMD decay and Japanese invasion. Rather, the basis of Communist success lay in organizations able to channel mass dissatisfaction and implement ameliorative policies.

Snow's contrasting view of the Communist movement was decisively conditioned by his visit to the border areas before the Japanese invasion. The CCP leaders with whom he spoke were naturally tentative about the new policy of promoting anti-Japanese nationalism. Indeed, Snow's conversations with the Communist leaders suggest their belief that a conservative, parochial peasantry could only be incorporated in the movement for national liberation if their immediate economic needs were first addressed. The CCP leaders remained skeptical of the efficacy of anti-Japanese resistance policies as a mobilizational device. Zhou Enlai, for example, spoke of food and land as "the primary demands of the revolutionary peasantry."[13]

For Snow the Communist movement was part of an inexorable process fueled, for the most part, by China's serious, long-standing economic ills. The war was a catalyst, not a precondition of revolution. It would speed the growth in awareness of the Chinese people. The CCP, of course, would benefit from popular mobilization brought about by the war; Snow certainly recognized the importance of nationalist appeals in building Communist support. But in contrast to Taylor, he argued that a socioeconomic reform program had to draw the peasants into Communist organization *before* the issue of anti-Japanese nationalism could become salient.[14]

White and Jacoby viewed the Communist revolution from the very different vantage point of the immediate postwar era. Theirs is the perspective not only of economic misery and brutal Japanese occupation but also of a degenerating, and to them thoroughly corrupt and reprehensible, Guomindang. For them, the simple act of bringing an alienated people into the governing process created support crucial to party success. The reason for this success, they wrote,

> could be reduced to a single paragraph: If you take a peasant who has been swindled, beaten, and kicked about for all his waking days and whose father has transmitted to him an emotion of bitterness reaching back for generations – if you take such a peasant, treat him like a man, ask his opinion, let him vote for local government, let him organize his own police and gendarmes, decide on his own taxes, and vote himself a reduction in rent and interest – if you do all that, the peasant becomes a man who has something to fight for, and he will fight to preserve it against any enemy, Japanese or Chinese.[15]

Thus we see their strong emphasis on Communist political institutions as an integral part of the movement's appeal. The role of international forces is unclear in their analysis. They saw the Japanese invasion as an important event, as was the postwar rivalry between the Soviet Union and the United States and the growth of Asian nationalism. Still, the Chinese revolution remained essentially a domestic phenomenon.[16]

If one pauses at the 1949 juncture for a retrospective look at evaluations of the Communist movement, several qualities of the literature stand out. One is struck first by the diversity of those writing on the Communist movement. In contrast to later years, academics played a secondary role. Although George Taylor and Laurence Rossinger, for example, made important contributions, they were overshadowed by newspaper reporters and free-lance writers who introduced the Communist movement to the public outside China. This was quite natural. Most academics were historians, and the Communist movement was current events, to be described by participant observers on the spot.

Second, a clear evolution in sources of evidence took place. The movement was, until the mid-1930s, largely inaccessible to foreigners. During the period of the Jiangxi Soviet, commentators such as Clubb and Harold Isaacs had to rely on scarce written sources or hearsay. Snow changed all that. After 1936, and until the final Civil War, studies of the Communist movement relied heavily on firsthand observations which circulated among a small community of CCP-watchers in China. This factor not only provided a means by which the reporting of diplomatic personnel like John S. Service and John Payton Davies influenced public writings but also contributed somewhat to the uniformity of themes in writing about the CCP during these years. Indeed, some would argue that the dependence on such shared impressions and conversations with Communist leaders, to the neglect of examination of party publications, presented a somewhat misleading image of the CCP.[17]

Finally, the reliance on on-the-spot observation meant that conditions within China – primarily Guomindang corruption and lack of purpose – were the major determinants shaping Westerners' views of the CCP. Distaste for the GMD conditioned a tendency to see the Communists as an indigenous revolutionary movement responsive to the grave social problems being ignored by the GMD. As the only major force pressing for change in a steadily deteriorating China, the CCP was assumed to have deep indigenous roots. The Soviet tie was thus viewed as quite secondary when compared to the CCP's links to the Chinese revolution.[18]

Such was the mainstream view of the nature of the Chinese Communist movement, characterized by a common set of preoccupations but distinguished nonetheless by considerable internal pluralism. It by no means went unchallenged. Many within the American government, and outside of it, felt that the strength, popular following, democratic nature, and military effectiveness of the CCP had been overstated. The Communists, this school asserted, made only a slight contribution to the war while maintaining their hold over the population by means of propaganda backed up by organized coercion. They viewed the Guomindang as making the major contribution to the war against Japan. Charges of undemocratic practices and corruption were largely dismissed with reference to the exigencies of war. How, Walter Judd asked, could freedoms be extended to people during wartime?[19]

In the eyes of many who subscribed to this view, the prevailing drift of analysis was part of a deliberate plan to misrepresent the Chinese situation by discrediting the Guomindang. This argument presaged what was known during the cold war era as the "conspiracy theory."[20] But as Ross Koen has argued, until 1947 those defending the Guomindang from its critics made little headway. Paradoxically, they began to win out only as the tide of civil war turned against the increasingly corrupt and inept Nationalists. Perceptions of the Chinese Communist movement were coming under the pressures of the growing cold war mentality and the "who lost China" debate that it spawned.[21]

"The organizational weapon," 1949–1962

During the 1950s many who wrote on the Communist revolution ignored earlier insights regarding the relationship between Chinese Communism and China's ongoing revolution.[22] Many also discarded the analytical categories – party/mass relations, people's war, organizational ties with the populace, etc. – that had dominated earlier discussions. Treatments of the emergence of Chinese Communism were thus intellectually detached not only from China's earlier history but also from the scholarship of less than a decade earlier. They were now written against a preoccupation with three immediate issues: the prevailing scholarly view of Communist revolutions, the cold war, and the nature of the Communist system.

Scholarly studies of Communist revolution passed through two stages during the period from 1949 to 1962. In the first, which lasted until the mid-1950s, conceptualizations of Communist revolution were largely post-facto extrapolations from the takeovers in Eastern Europe. In the second stage, starting with the mid-1950s, Communist revolution became associated with the emergence of the third world and the movement of Marxism eastward. Communism became a "disease of the transition" to economic takeoff, a "problem of development."[23] Despite this shift, the intellectual categories used to study Communist revolution remained remarkably consistent throughout the thirteen-year period.

The most striking consistency was the propensity for the study of Communist revolution to become the study of Soviet foreign policy. It was assumed that national Communist parties were best understood as instruments of Soviet foreign policy. Some writers spoke of Soviet "fifth columns" in various states, and Sigmund Neumann asked the concept of "international civil war" where "a central revolutionary authority . . . can direct its orders by remote control."[24]

Commentators throughout these years recognized, however, that the quality and strategy of national Communist organizations were also crucial to the revolutionary success. Most important was the creation and proper use of what Philip Selznick called "the organizational weapon." Those emphasizing this instrument referred to the Leninist prescriptions for a thoroughly disciplined, professional organization seizing power through ruthless manipulation.[25] Success, in the view of earlier analysts of the Chinese revolution, had to be *created*; in the view of these later commentators on Communist revolutions, it had to be *engineered* through such techniques as bogus coalition governments or the seizure of crucial ministries.[26]

The mid-1950s shift toward a study of Communist revolution as a species of anti-imperialist, nationalist revolution only added a new variant to this tendency.[27] Most who looked at Communist movements in these areas argued that the crucial revolutionary factor in third world countries was the intellectuals who were attracted by the Soviet foreign policy stance and socialist developmental model. An understanding of their nature, aspirations, and ideology as well as their ties with the Soviet Union, it was believed, provided the most important insights into Communist revolution.[28]

Obviously the trend of scholarship was related to the political currents of the decade. As the cold war mood grew in the United States, so did the intellectual currency of the conspiracy thesis. The conspiracy thesis found its greatest acceptance in the Congress and in the mass and international affairs media. Two elements are present in all the variants of the conspiracy thesis. First is the argument that the outcome of the Chinese revolution was determined primarily by international factors rather than domestic ones. The Communist movement, the argument ran, prevailed only because Soviet aid to the CCP, combined with grievous deficiencies in American aid and damaging diplomatic concessions to Moscow, had crippled the Guomindang's ability to fight. With the Communist movement now depicted as the surrogate and beneficiary of Soviet policy, it was no longer important to study its domestic roots. The second common element is the assumption of conscious conspiracy. Different proponents of the thesis identified different villains, but all assigned some blame to short-sighted American policy makers misled by traitorous advisers seeking to bring the Communists to power.[29]

Both the organizational weapon argument and the conspiracy thesis imply that a model of elite politics is more appropriate for studying the Chinese revolution. Communist revolutions were by and large considered not to command the following or loyalty of the majority of the populace; they were illegitimate. Organization, Selznick argued, was a way "of eluding the need to win consent."[30] Success lay in the party's ability to manipulate legitimate mass needs and aspirations, particularly for agrarian reform and national independence so as to weaken the established authorities and promote seizure of power.[31] In the fifties, most commentators seemed indifferent to what attracted the masses to Communist movements; their thoughts or aspirations were considered to bear little relationship to the actual course of the revolution.[32]

The actions of the Chinese themselves helped foster this view. Not only did China, until the late 1950s, closely follow the Soviet lead in foreign affairs and contend that Soviet aid had been indispensable for victory but also, beginning in the early 1950s, a series of mass movements culminating in agricultural collectivization suggested the sovietization and regimentation of China. The People's Republic of China bore little superficial resemblance to the old base areas. Many fell easily into viewing the past history of the party through the prism of its present, more nearly Soviet form.

The work of one group of scholars – David Rowe, Richard Walker, Franz Michael, George Taylor, and Karl Wittfogel – seems to reflect the conspiracy thesis. Like the thesis, their work often reads like an exoneration of the

Guomindang. The CCP, we are told, was victorious in the first instance because a viable Nationalist government was grievously weakened by the Sino-Japanese War, and second, because its own strength was augmented by Soviet aid, both direct and indirect. These writers see the Communist Party using such devices as the united front to seize power by exploiting popular demands for anti-Japanese resistance and for social reforms, after which time the organization became "dictatorial," imposing leadership preferences on the masses.[33]

The emphasis on the Soviet connection so permeated the scholarship of the 1950s that it appeared in the very important and certainly non-conspiracy thesis studies of Benjamin Schwartz and Robert C. North. For both authors the focus of attention is on CCP policy and personnel shifts on the elite level. They agree that these shifts were the key to understanding the nature of the Chinese Communist movement, a key that could not be understood without reference to Soviet influence.

The emphasis on broad policy questions and elite struggle – views from the top – is quite consistent with the other emphasis in the work of these two men, the organizational question. In this respect, however, their views differed somewhat. North's study remains close to the typical 1950s view of the organizational weapon. He is concerned with the use of united front tactics and front organizations as a means of building support within China and isolating the party's enemies. This "program for revolt," North makes clear, was a Russian product applied to Chinese conditions with only minimal changes.[34]

Schwartz, while recognizing Mao's debt to the Leninist conception of organization, found the principle given rather un-Leninist applications in China. He argued that Mao's willingness to develop his revolutionary formulae independently of Moscow and in response to national conditions was demonstrated by the movement to the countryside and by the CCP's reliance on a base of "peasant discontent." Although emphasizing the importance of organization, Schwartz thus also touched upon the "needs" of which the Communists made themselves "spokesmen." He wrote of the amelioration of peasant grievances and the CCP's ability to harness "national sentiment to its own cause."[35]

Schwartz's work thus called for scholars to focus more on the indigenous Chinese development of the Leninist organizational weapon and its application to peasant warfare and revolution. In his extraordinarily skillful hands the Soviet connection figures as not an alternative but an aid to understanding the indigenous roots of the CCP.

John King Fairbank, Schwartz's colleague at Harvard, also stressed the indigenous roots of the Chinese revolution. Fairbank's argument was atypical of the 1950s. Rejecting the premises that the Japanese invasion could exonerate the Guomindang from responsibility for its failure, he argued that "historical trends" were "no one's monopoly and may be ridden by alternative power groups."[36] In other words, the inability to meet the crisis of the war had highlighted the limitations of the Guomindang just as it had brought out the political prowess of the CCP. What, then, explained the Communist victory? Fairbank emphasized the CCP's "grip on the two essentials of power – agrarian revolution as the dynamic of the peasantry and national regeneration as the dynamic of the intellectuals."[37] He was returning to those interpretations – including that of George Taylor himself – that explored the popular appeal of the Communist movement in China.[38]

Perhaps the most striking characteristic of the 1950s scholarship, with Fairbank the only exception, is the general emphasis on the impact of international events. Earlier authors had recognized the Japanese invasion's crucial impact on the fortunes of the CCP, but under the influence of the conspiracy thesis some placed this event and the diplomacy surrounding it at center stage. More strikingly, it was during these years that the nexus between Soviet foreign policy and the CCP was most exhaustively explored. Soviet intervention in CCP policy and leadership was thoroughly documented; on these points much of the scholarship of these years remains definitive.

The related emphasis on elite politics focused attention on high-level leadership conflicts over personalities and policies. Intraparty disputes over policies concerning relations with the GMD, approaches to the peasantry, and emphasis on rural or urban areas were the subject of extensive research and writing.[39] The effects of those policies in practice were largely ignored.

What of the masses? In keeping with the elite politics approach, the common view was that the party's leadership was indispensable to a mass of peasants clearly unable to organize themselves.[40] There were general discussions of the appeals made by the Communist Party for popular support. All seemed to agree that national resistance to Japan and moderate economic reforms were the principal rallying cries used by the CCP.[41] Yet the actual details of party/army organization and, most importantly, party relations with the people were rarely discussed. The masses and their attitudes played a decidedly secondary role in studies of the Chinese Communist movement.

The debate on appeals, 1960s and 1970s: nationalism versus social revolution

The terms of debate began to change with the publication of the most important study of the Chinese revolution in the 1960s, Chalmers Johnson's *Peasant Nationalism and Communist Power*.[42] Johnson argued that the roots of Communist success in 1949 are to be found in the bond the party forged with the mass of Chinese peasants during the Anti-Japanese War of 1937 to 1945. The brutality of the Japanese occupation spurred the development of anti-Japanese nationalism among the peasants, championed by the

Communist Party. The party's anti-Japanese stance, rather than the peasants' economic grievances and the party's platform of socioeconomic reform, gave the CCP the popular mandate that carried it to victory. Johnson's evidence of mass support for the party is found simply in the fact of successful guerrilla warfare, a strategic mode, he asserts, that could not possibly have succeeded without broad mass support. The CCP thus came to power with legitimate (but conditional) authority based on popularly supported nationalist goals.

The influence of contemporaneous events on this analysis is obvious. Johnson is exploring the nexus between nationalism and communism. This, along with the comparison with Yugoslavia, clearly demonstrated the impact of the Sino-Soviet conflict. In addition, as Johnson mentions briefly in a contemporary article, his interest in guerrilla war was to some extent a reflection of growing American concern with Asian manifestations of what the French in Algeria had called *la guerre révolutionnaire*.[43]

But if Johnson was responding to current events, he was also self-consciously writing in reaction to the scholarship of the 1950s. He argued strongly against the "organizational weapon" approach, rejected the conspiracy thesis, and criticized those who would focus on mass discontent based on economic deprivation.[44] In doing so, he returned to hypotheses suggested by works of the 1930s and 1940s. Johnson's focus on guerrilla warfare led him, like Taylor and Evans Carlson, immediately to the issue of popular support and, like many others, to the mobilizational potential of Japanese brutality. As he himself would later admit, he was merely using different sources (Japanese intelligence reports) to substantiate hypotheses generated earlier by others.[45]

Still, certain central elements in the analyses of the 1930s and 1940s are absent from Johnson's study. Although he spends some time describing the broad outlines of the CCP's military organization, he shows little of the appreciation of the centrality of organization that one finds in the works of Snow or Taylor. There is no clear sense of the concrete organizational nexus that linked the people and their leaders. Instead, in this and later works Johnson depicts this linkage in the ephemeral terms of an authority relationship.[46]

Johnson also omits any systematic treatment of an element typical in the analyses of the 1930s and 1940s: the role of the party's socioeconomic program in generating support. To be sure, he does not deny that agrarian reform might have played a secondary role in heightening the party's appeal. Nor does he deny that, given time, festering economic problems might have brought revolution. He simply asserts that since the CCP failed when it advocated "radical" agrarian policies and succeeded when it abandoned these and promoted nationalist policies, the nationalist policies were essential to Communist success.[47] Earlier authors rarely had been ready to treat the nationalism issue in such a one-sided fashion.[48]

It was on this point that Johnson came under attack by Donald Gillin, whose review of the book took issue with what he saw as Johnson's major thesis: that the CCP was successful among the peasants only when it "virtually ceased advocating revolution." Gillin argued that appeals to nationalism found a responsive audience only among the elite. The peasantry was involved by policies aimed at alleviating their social and economic distress.[49]

The Gillin article, forcefully argued and widely read, was a natural starting point for a major debate over the sources of Communist success. However, there was no response by Johnson, or others, until the late 1960s.[50] The Cultural Revolution in China and the concurrent radicalization of the political mood in the United States changed this situation. Some were moved by the Cultural Revolution to seek the roots of the apparently bitter elite conflict in the policies of the revolutionary era.[51] Others saw the Cultural Revolution as a Maoist attempt to revive China's revolutionary thrust by reintroducing many of the policies of the base areas.[52] Some, proceeding from this point, were drawn to the pre-1949 period because it was then, they felt, that the bases of an attractive and humane form of society were laid, and it was from this perspective that the peasant nationalism thesis came under renewed criticism.

Those who attacked *Peasant Nationalism* initially proceeded from the assumption that the singular contribution made by Chinese Communism to socialist theory was "uninterrupted revolution" intended to secure an egalitarian, just society. And revolution was to be the work of the masses. In one respect they were sympathetic to Johnson's analysis: they too believed that the "organizational weapon" approach obscured the close spiritual bonds that linked the party to the people. However, they differed strongly with Johnson on the bases for the authority relationship. Socioeconomic deprivation, not nationalism, was the fuel of genuine mass revolution. To suggest that Communism had to "disguise" itself as nationalism in order to be successful was, in their minds, to deny the revolutionary quality of Communism or the legitimacy of the Chinese revolution. Johnson's book was attacked as a "political tract in social science guise."[53]

Similarly, the emphasis on the war was seen as a way of exonerating a reactionary GMD regime and denying the validity of the Chinese revolution. In short, the major issues of analysis for the 1960s and 1970s became the role of socioeconomic factors, the role of organization, and the impact of the war. We will consider each of these in turn.

With Johnson himself surprisingly sounding the charge (or perhaps blowing the retreat), the nearly monocausal analysis of *Peasant Nationalism* was revised. Five years after the book's publication, without so much as mentioning how great a change in his orientation it signified, Johnson stated simply that *both* "appeals to nationalism and mild reform of agriculture [rent and interest reduction]" constituted "the twin faces of Mao's mass line." Johnson seemed to be suggesting that economic appeals, insufficient by themselves to bring about revolution, required war-generated nationalism.[54] He thus quietly returned to the double appeal analysis of the 1930s and 1940s, minus any real discussion of organization. Other authors joined the discussion, arguing for both kinds of appeal rather than one.[55]

Some scholars remained dissatisfied, considering the double-appeals approach a compromise that waffled on the key issue. The most prominent expression of this view was Mark Selden's study of the central party base of Shaan-Gan-Ning, *The Yenan Way in Revolutionary China*.[56] Selden divides his analysis into three periods: pre-1936, 1936–1941, and 1942 and after. He argues, contra Johnson, that in the early period "agrarian revolution" was the very popular and necessary first step to engage peasant support and "[pave] the way for the increasingly effective military and political participation of the rural population" (p. 79). During the second period, the imperatives of the united front against Japan necessitated moderation of land policy, but land revolution was not the only way to solve peasant economic distress. Rather, Selden argues that peasants' support for the CCP stemmed from its meeting their basic needs and integrating them into responsive political organizations (pp. 119–20).

The final period was a response to leadership concerns over the loss of revolutionary fervor and the need to solve new economic problems facing the base area. It required directing the "creative energies of the people" toward "transforming the fabric of social and particularly economic life at the village level" (p. 209). Peasants' egalitarian, participatory efforts to meet the economic and political problems of daily life constituted the "Yenan way" to revolution (ch. 6). Emerging out of the Communist revolution in China was a "humane" alternative to the alienating systems spawned by "technocratic liberalism and Bolshevism."[57]

There is much that is extremely valuable in Selden's study. His was the first case study of a base area since George Taylor's work. Besides providing a wealth of data regarding broad shifts in CCP political and economic policies, Selden focused on the dynamics of party/peasant interaction at the local level. In contrast to Johnson, Selden was concerned with the kinds of exchanges between peasants and the CCP that gained involvement in and support for party programs. He seemed acutely sensitive to the importance of meeting immediate peasant needs as a prerequisite for the continuation of such involvement. Like Snow before him, Selden believed that the simple act of participation in the political process met an important peasant need and constituted an occurrence of revolutionary quality in rural China.

Here Selden's analysis, unlike Johnson's, moves into the area of organization. However, there are real limits to that movement. Because the point of his argument is to deny the necessity or efficacy of elite or administrative authority during the Resistance War period, he reacts even more strongly than Johnson against the organizational weapon view. However, like Johnson's, his alternative explanation – the mass line – is ephemeral. The emphasis throughout is on the participation, "creativity," and "dedication" of the masses.

After the early 1970s authors such as Kataoka and Thaxton, like Selden, emphasized the importance of socioeconomic restructuring in building support for the CCP. With this came a greater sensitivity to the enormous changes that seemingly "moderate" policies could effect in the country-side.[58] Yet work in this area of CCP policies slowed as most analysts settled for the path of least resistance and recognized the importance of both nationalist and socioeconomic appeals in generating support during the Resistance War period.

The question of organization proved less tractable; it became difficult even to define its contours. Scholars increasingly emphasized the contribution of organization to CCP growth in the pre-1949 period, but agreement on the nature of that organization was hard to come by.[59]

In his study of the Jiangxi Soviet, Ilpyong Kim argues that Mao's success stemmed from his appreciation of the importance of organization in mobilizing "passive and irresponsive" masses toward revolutionary ends – in other words, the mass line.[60] Participation roused peasants from their usual apathy, exposed them to party propaganda, and gave them the opportunity to vent their frustrations and to have the sense of shaping their sociopolitical environment (pp. 131–33). Peasant participation in organization, Kim suggests, was an appeal in itself. The feeling "that they were participating in bringing about revolutionary change and economic well-being" was "as important to revolutionary strategy as was peasant nationalism" (p. 89). However, in contrast to Selden, Kim suggests that mass organizations were more important in enhancing party awareness of mass feelings and eliciting popular participation in policy implementation than in allowing mass control over leadership selection or basic policy.

Tetsuya Kataoka's *Resistance and Revolution in China*, published in 1974, presents the strongest brief since the 1950s for the centrality of organized leadership in the Chinese Communist revolution.[61] His analysis portrays a highly traditional and parochial peasant. In contrast to Johnson, Kataoka sees the war provoking peasant reaction along quintessentially traditional lines. In response to outside threats, traditional defense organizations are formed and the peasantry prepares to defend the locality. There is no war-induced organizational void; the CCP must vie with traditional elites and other groups (bandits, secret societies, and so forth) for leadership in the countryside (pp. 279–302). Always ready to defend local or self-interest, the peasantry is not easily drawn to the party calls for self-sacrifice in the name of anything beyond the local community.

Thus the Communist Party's problem was to use economic incentives (land revolution, albeit by moderate means) to gain initial peasant involvement and then through military organization to create a structure to coordinate disparate local fighting groups. Such organizational control was essential; without it, the peasants deserted the Communist cause and slipped back into parochial attitudes. Moreover, local control could be lost to traditional leadership groups. In contrast to both Selden and Johnson, Kataoka sees no natural community of interests between the peasants and the CCP (p. 116).

Kataoka's picture of rural revolution, stressing difficult organizational work in the face of peasant apathy, is directly related to his view of the war's role in bringing party success (ch. 8).[62] In essence, he argues that the force of Communist-led rural revolution was insufficient before 1937 to bring victory. The urban areas, controlled by the Guomindang, had the strength to defeat rural revolution. Without the respite provided by the war, and without Wang Ming to call the party's attention to the cities, the rural Communist movement would have been crushed by the growing urban power centers. No war, no Communist victory.[63]

Given the research findings of Johnson and Kataoka, it was increasingly difficult to gainsay the impact of the war on the CCP's revolutionary success. But for the most part, the question of the precise role of war was resolved during the 1970s in a manner reminiscent of the settlement of the appeals question. Most scholars admitted that the war played a crucial, catalytic role in creating a vacuum in the countryside which the CCP could fill, weakening the GMD and laying the basis for Communist appeals to nationalism in the city and the countryside. But almost all tried to avoid categorical statements.[64]

The scholarship of the 1970s, then, provides something of a cyclical, perhaps even dialectical, quality to the past four decades' scholarship on the Chinese revolution. In the 1930s and 1940s the dual-appeal concept was advanced, only to be largely ignored in the 1950s and dichotomized in the 1960s. In the 1970s it was recombined. Few issues in the field of Chinese politics had generated as much heat and light as the nationalism versus socioeconomic appeals argument. Yet in the end the debate was never really resolved. On one level, it ended in a draw on terms somewhat reminiscent of the 1930s. On another level, the terms of resolution in the late 1970s seem disturbingly abstract and parochial.

In fact, the earlier conflict between Chalmers Johnson and his critics was often more apparent than real. Most of Johnson's critics shared with him a largely identical conception of the explanation for Communist success: widespread peasant support. Both sides very clearly assumed both a radical transformation in peasant mentality and pervasive, consistent support of the Communist movement, But their conclusions proved as abstract as those offered by the scholars focusing on elites: the translation of popularity into action, or support into power, and the relation of action or power to victory remained to be demonstrated precisely. To the level of abstraction was added the problem of parochialism in the body of research as a whole. Studies that did concentrate on limited geographic areas focused on the central base areas (Jiangxi and Shaan-Gan-Ning); those that chose a broad field were confined primarily to the Anti-Japanese War period. Thus hypotheses about the sources of the Communist movement's success were tested on atypical cases and limited periods of time. The combination of abstractness and parochialism may explain why, despite their fruitfulness for sparking more research, the generalizations simply do not square with a good deal of information on the relationship between the peasants and the Communist movement that was available at the time and has been plumbed since.

A second type of parochialism characterized the debate as well. Although scholars of comparative revolutions drew generously upon the empirical findings of specialists on the Chinese revolution, the flow of information and ideas remained essentially unidirectional. Whereas some scholars in the 1950s and 1960s had drawn on theories or models in comparative fields, that sincerest form of flattery was never exercised on the work on comparative revolutions. Even in the 1970s, Elizabeth Perry's was the only major work on the Chinese revolution to draw upon hypotheses and generalizations advanced by that body of comparative scholarship.[65] Most China specialists remained largely ignorant of or unconcerned with the different problematiques and conclusions being drawn by comparativists out of the empirical findings on China. China scholars' contributions to generalizations on comparative revolutions thus remained largely passive, and they drew no intellectual profit from the uses to which those contributions were put.

Comparative theories of revolution

One finds in the "third generation" of scholarship in comparative revolutions[66] a concern with the major issues so hotly debated by the China specialists: the appeals of revolution or revolutionaries to the peasantry, the role of revolutionary organization, and the impact of international factors. These factors, however, have been rather differently conceived by the comparativists, particularly in view of their attempts to derive some general statement valid for a variety of revolutionary histories.

Most attempts at studying revolutionary causation fall into two types: structural and volitional approaches. The structural approach draws upon such concepts as social structure, economic forces, and world systems in an endeavor to trace the sources and dynamics of revolutionary events. To the structuralist, although individuals and groups may act consciously for particular ends, motivations and attitudes must be traced to structural factors and therefore matter not one whit as independent explanations of either the occurrence or the outcome of revolutions. For those taking the volitional approach, on the other hand, the motivations of participants in revolutions are key, whether these are understood as primal urges propelling *levées en masse*, as the development of a group consciousness making collective action possible, as responses to revolutionary leadership or organization, or as the ideology and strategy of a revolutionary elite.

Few attempts at explanation of revolutions have avoided resort to both such approaches at some point in their analysis, and a number of explanations are self-consciously eclectic in resorting deliberately to both. Nonetheless, most can be said to rely predominantly on one or the other approach. A handful of recent studies seminal for debates in the comparative field offer sufficient examples of the current generalizations about revolutions. Two of these, Theda Skocpol's *States and Social Revolutions* and Jeffrey Paige's *Agrarian Revolution*, fall on the structuralist side of the spectrum. Two other works, James C. Scott's *The Moral Economy of the Peasant* and Samuel Popkin's *The Rational Peasant*, fall on the volitional side.[67]

Structural approaches

Theda Skocpol takes an explicitly structuralist tack in her comparative study of the French, Russian, and Chinese revolutions. For Skocpol, the key process in the great revolutions was the collapse of state power, coupled with "widespread peasant revolts from below." Skocpol traces the crisis of the state to "international structures and world-historical developments" – wars and economic crises situated within the system of competing states and the developing world capitalist economy. The *ancien regime* state, seeking to respond to such challenges, encounters obstacles raised by the dominant classes within its own society, and it is this impasse that precipitates its collapse.

In the Great Revolutions examined by Skocpol, the collapse of state power was crucial in permitting "*widespread* and *irreversible* peasant revolts against landlords" to develop (p. 117). Peasant rebellions in this crisis environment may finish off the old regime or propel a new revolutionary elite into power. For Skocpol, the peasantry's capacity for revolutionary collective action depends upon its "internal leverage," which "is explained by structural and situational conditions that affect: (1) the degrees and kinds of solidarity of peasant communities; (2) the degrees of peasant autonomy from direct day-to-day supervision and control by landlords and their agents; and (3) the relaxation of state coercive sanctions against peasants [*sic*] revolts" (p. 115). Social revolution, then, becomes the "conjunctural result" of a crisis in the affairs of the dominant class and the potentially autonomous state structure on the one hand, and the rebellious activities of the peasantry, on the other.

Jeffrey Paige's study of social movements in export agricultural settings concentrates on structural factors as well. Paige focuses on features of the social structure that, in his view, determine both the motivations of and the capacity for effective action by the masses of cultivators and the noncultivating elite. Paige distinguishes several types of agrarian social structures, each characterized by a particular combination of interests of the noncultivating elite and the cultivators, depending upon their sources of income (land or capital for the elite, land or wages for the cultivators). These sets of interests determine the type of agrarian class conflicts that may arise in each environment. Paige finds that it is primarily in a wet-rice sharecropping system that a coincidence of instability of tenure, cooperative reward structure, and independence from the noncultivating elite gives rise to a combination of radical ideology, collective action, and strong solidarity. Here one finds the growth of strong revolutionary communist movements. Other social structural settings are conducive only to nationalist revolutionary movements (the migratory labor estate), to reformist labor movements (the plantation), to agrarian revolts (the commercial hacienda), or to reform commodity movements (the smallholding system) (pp. 42–43, 45–48, 63–69).

Volitional approaches

James Scott locates the rebellious potential of a peasantry in the perceived violation of a "moral economy" grounded in traditional values. Scott argues that not objective exploitation but peasants' indignation fuels rebellions. That indignation stems from trespasses against traditional principles of rights and obligations. These include a "norm of reciprocity" calling for exchanges of equal value in social relations, and a "subsistence ethic" dictating that all are entitled to a living out of village resources (in the form of a floor below which none should fall). Scott, exploring the 1930s depression rebellions in South Burma and central Vietnam, contends that with colonialism and commercialization of agriculture, landlords and the state claimed resources at the expense of cultivators. Peasant reaction stemmed not from the magnitude of the exactions, but from the decline of social insurance as landlord or state demands eroded the subsistence floor. Peasants' adherence to a moral economy knit together rural communities in condemning and acting against these perceived illegitimate demands.

The implication of Scott's argument is that one may expect to find peasant collective action in those places where, first, the subsistence ethic and norm of reciprocity are being violated, and second, there is still a strong village community accustomed to acting according to such principles.[68] Scott is well aware, however, that even under such conditions, rebellion may be the exception rather than the rule. First, the societies in a better position to act collectively in rebellion may be less inclined to do so because they are less exposed to "economic shocks" than the "more differentiated and atomistic villages." Thus, in Scott's view, generalizations "relating peasant social structures to the potential for rebellion would be questionable" (pp. 201–3). Second, alternative survival opportunities may deflect rebellious potential, while also eroding the communal solidarity of peasants (pp. 223–25). Finally, effective repression by the state serves to drive peasants away from rebellious activity – just as the erosion of state power may attract them to the standard of rebellion (pp. 229–30). Despite these contingencies, Scott's approach offers a framework for comprehending peasant participation in rebellions, linked to revolutionary movements or not, as tied to peasant conceptions of justice and legitimacy rooted in the traditional village order.

Samuel Popkin, contrary to Scott, suggests that "peasant politics" is not so very different from any other kind of politics. He argues for a "political economy" interpretation of revolutionary causation, seeing participation in a revolutionary movement as an "investment decision" which a peasant weighs along with other options for balancing costs and benefits (p. 244). For Popkin, class grievances or norms of justice are beside the point. The central problem for a revolutionary movement is to provide the incentives and leadership that will induce peasants to participate in the movement, and not to participate against it. The key, he argues, lies in "organization, particularly communication and coordination" – or, if one will, the presence of a revolutionary, nationally based leadership (p. 251). Organization in such settings provides sufficient incentive to overcome individuals' resistance to collective action. In short, in Popkin's world, peasants do not automatically act to further group or common interests; social structures and cultural values do not preprogram their responses, and motivating them for collective action is much the same type of leadership problem as motivating any other group.

Here the free-rider problem enters the picture. Collective action aims at achieving certain "collective goods" in which all may – indeed, must – share regardless of contribution to the action. "Free-riders" are thus an endemic problem; if all make the free-rider's calculation of maximum benefit for minimum effort, of course, no one will act at all. Therefore collective action "requires conditions under which peasants will find it in their individual interests to allocate resources to the common interests – and not be free riders" (p. 253). The "political entrepreneur" – read, new leadership, or even old – is essential in solving this problem. The political entrepreneur demonstrates to peasants the efficacy of collective action; applies selective incentives to elicit participation or prevent defection; and selects the issues and offers goods most suitable for initial mobilization (pp. 253–64).

Common emphases

Exploring the differences among these works in detail would no doubt teach us much about the orienting assumptions of each author, but for our purposes what are instructive are not so much the obvious differences as the less obvious similarities. For there are common threads of findings and interpretation running through all four of these works.

First, all these authors tend to assume the lack of natural consonance between the goals of revolutionary leadership and their potential peasant following. Only Paige appears to entertain the possibility of a close correspondence, and then only in one type of agrarian setting. Skocpol explicitly states that the outcomes of revolutions frequently bear little resemblance to the original goals of the revolutionaries, let alone to the "peasant rebellions" that help propel the revolutionaries into power. Scott implies in his book, and elsewhere makes into his central thesis, that rebellious peasants' intentions are far afield of those of any revolutionary organization that rides the tide of rebellion into a takeover of state power. And Popkin, whose line of argument certainly suggests that peasants and revolutionary leaders may find points of agreement, nevertheless makes it clear that finding those points and turning them to the benefit of a revolutionary organization is neither easy nor certain.[69]

Second, while all these authors are concerned with the question of "what makes peasants revolutionary,"[70] they are concerned as well with the role of opportunities and countervailing factors. Skocpol indeed makes these the centerpiece of her argument, but it is remarkable to find that even in those works primarily seeking the sources of revolutionary/rebellious impulses among the peasantry, the presence or absence of countervailing forces, revolutionary opportunities, and non-revolutionary opportunities is eventually acknowledged as key in explaining peasant responses.[71]

The countervailing factors are of two types: the strength of the state apparatus, and the strength of the rural elite. In Skocpol's analysis, one may as well not bother talking about revolutions if these are omitted; the weakness of both is the only opening permitting peasant rebellions to blossom into full-scale revolutions. Only the inability of the state to suppress challenges to its own power, only the relative autonomy of peasant communities from elite control, will permit the forces of revolution to build up to a successful climactic confrontation. But although Skocpol treats these as structural factors, and therefore as givens in a revolutionary situation, the others introduce them in one form or another as the contingent factors that help determine a revolution's success. Paige recognizes that the "weakening of the repressive power of the landed aristocracy" can create the opening for revolution in a hacienda system; Scott acknowledges that the ease of repression may cancel the inherent potential for rebellion; and for Popkin, the calculation of likelihood of repression by state or elite is an integral part of the cost/benefit considerations weighed by peasants contemplating participation in a revolutionary movement.[72]

But the availability of opportunities is also crucial. Even Skocpol's structuralist approach must break away from a strictly structural explanation when she reaches the Chinese revolution, to find that a relative lack of autonomy of peasant communities was compensated for by the presence of able revolutionary organizers. For Skocpol, voluntarism thus creeps in by the back door. In a later article, she posits the presence of a revolutionary leadership as a key explanatory factor for most third world revolutions. Paige likewise must allow for chance or voluntarism in trying to account for revolutionary movements outside the lone social setting he considers conducive to a natural congruence between peasant and revolutionary purposes. He admits, for example, the possibility of revolution arising out of a situation ordinarily conducive only to agrarian revolt, if somehow the peasantry is linked to outside leadership by revolutionaries.[73]

The others note not only the strong incentive effect of revolutionary organizations, but also the potentially derevolutionizing effect of alternative opportunities for solution of peasants' dilemmas. For Popkin, of course, the cost/benefit calculation always weighs other opportunities against participation in a revolutionary movement. Popkin recognizes as well that there is a contest of action here, where the opposing side's ability to mobilize interests and resources changes the effectiveness of the incentives offered by the political entrepreneur. But both Scott and Paige offer examples of alternatives: Scott, in the possibilities for outmigration, technical modernization of agriculture, individual or state patronage, and local self-help; and Paige, in the "deal" that is offered by the agrarian elite (which, however, he sees as determined by their structurally defined interests).[74] Markets, migration, cooptation, and compromise thus all offer peasants solutions undercutting their propensity for integration into a revolutionary movement.

Third, and in large part due to the factors discussed above, all these authors offer basically the same roster of relevant actors in a revolutionary situation. The obvious central actors are there: peasants and revolutionary leaders, defined in varying degrees of clarity and precision. It is instructive that all recognize in one form or another the importance of the variety of peasants or peasant communities: Skocpol, in the relative autonomy of the peasant communities; Scott, in the difference between cohesive and atomized communities; Popkin, between corporate and open villages; and Paige, in a comprehensive inventory of peasant social structural types and corresponding interests.[75] But not one of the authors assumes that the proximate combination of peasantry and revolutionary leadership alone provides the powder keg that will blow away the old order and bring in the new. Rather, their appreciation of countervailing factors and alternative opportunities sensitizes them to three other key actors: the state, the rural elite, and international forces.

The state is crucial primarily as the repressor of rebellious or revolutionary activities. What constraints it faces on the uses or sources of its power, what alternatives it may offer to those contemplating rebellion, are therefore essential to a full consideration of revolutionary causation. If only

Skocpol attends fully to this actor, it is because only she claims to be considering revolution as a unitary phenomenon. But clearly the state hovers in the wings as a critical player as Scott's peasants contemplate rising up in just rebellion, Popkin's peasants assess their risks, and Paige's square off in a contest against agrarian elites. The rural elite is another key actor whose responses to revolutionary or rebellious challenges must be anticipated by peasants and revolutionary leaders alike. And finally, the international forces of capitalist markets and military conflict play crucial roles: first in reshaping the peasantry in the modern era, second in defining the needs and interests of the state, third in shaping the rural elite, and finally in precipitating the collapse of the state or fatally undermining its capacity to weather domestic challenges to its power.

These common threads – the resort to opportunities and countervailing factors to complete historical explanations, the longer roster of relevant actors in a revolutionary situation – suggest that the scope of studies of the Chinese revolution should be widened. To be sure, we can find appreciation of each of these elements in some past work on the Chinese revolution. The difference for the comparative studies is that they find it necessary explicitly to define and acknowledge the role that each plays in determining the final outcome. And Skocpol's and Paige's studies go a step further also in suggesting that an understanding of the role of the state, the rural elite, and international forces is indispensable for understanding the options and actions of the peasantry and (for Skocpol) revolutionary organizations. Rarely in previous studies of the Chinese revolution do we find these conjoined, and never before the present generation of scholarship (though often in the writings of revolutionaries themselves!) do we find their interactions explored with any care [. . .]

[Recent case studies by William Wei, Gregor Benton, Kathleen Hartford David M. Paulson, and Steven I. Levine point in a new direction and illustrate the analytical paths taken in] much of the scholarship of the late 1970s and 1980s, which brings to life the interactions of elements stressed by comparativists.[76] It is paradoxical that we find such correspondence, because, far from actively seeking grand generalizations, the new generation of China scholars would seem almost to have fled to the opposite extreme. Dissatisfied with debates in the China field, debates that ordinarily offered sweeping generalizations with little close testing in actual situations, they immersed themselves in detailed studies of local revolutionary milieus, tracing the birth, life, and sometimes death of the revolution in these locales. Their findings have tended to call into question not only the resolutions but the very terms of the earlier debates in the China field. Yet although we find considerable divergence between generations in the China field, there is a remarkable convergence between the answers (if not the questions) of these newer scholars and the approaches current in comparative revolutions.

[. . . The five aforementioned authors have produced works that are diverse in nature but they] display a remarkable unanimity on the terms of debate. And it is here that we find their strong correspondences with the comparative work.

First, they tend to agree that it is very difficult to get peasants integrated into a revolution; or, having gotten them involved, to keep them that way. This departs significantly from the thrust of the preceding generation of work on the revolution.

[. . .] Second, all five of these authors are painfully aware of the key importance of countervailing factors in defining the revolutionary (or counterrevolutionary) situation. This is perhaps inevitable in a group of studies, all of which focus on areas or periods where the CCP was either on the defensive or just gaining a foothold. But some of these are the very areas or periods for which it has heretofore been thought that the CCP was on the offensive or that any opposition was easily turned to the party's benefit. However, more is at issue than whether the Communist movement was on the way up or down. If we may invoke a homely image for illustration, previous studies have tended to convey the sense of a conflict in which two sides lined up their forces and then slugged it out. These essays offer the flavor more of a dimly patterned general melee where the punches thrown at any particular point determined the way that the sides *would* line up. What the CCP's opponents did at each juncture determined both the way peasants could or would act and how the party could act in the next round.

In this vein, two essays argue explicitly that counterrevolutionary repression can indeed succeed against a mobilized peasantry. Wei, for example, suggests that the critical turning point in Jiangxi came not as a result of the massive military pressure of the encirclement campaigns, but rather as a consequence of the GMD's lining the rural elite up on its side. But the timing of this development may have been crucial, for the GMD's changed attitude to the rural elite coincided with the radicalization of CCP land policy and violent attacks on landlords and rich peasants. With the assistance (and accompanying material blandishments) offered by the GMD, the elite were then able to extend counterrevolutionary security organizations into the countryside and gradually to root out those who supported the revolutionary side. Hartford, on the other hand, while arguing that repression can succeed, also contends that it can be intelligently countered by the revolutionary side if it is willing to use methods that can lower the calculated risks to its potential mass supporters – even if that means lowering the calculated benefits as well. In both these situations, Jiangxi as well as Hebei, the implication is that the strength of repression by state or rural elite is key in determining the outcome; but the potential for repression can be altered at least marginally (and the marginal difference may be critical) by the revolutionary side.

But so can that potential be dissipated by the counterrevolutionary side, which is what Paulson suggests occurred in Shandong. In this case, the CCP's opponents on the GMD side diluted their own strength through internecine quarrels, ignored the very real opportunities for developing a mass base of support, and then vitiated their claims to legitimacy by joining the Japanese camp for instrumental purposes. Levine's analysis also affords some grounds for attributing the failure of repression to avoidable errors, in pointing out that the Japanese occupation undermined the capacity of the indigenous rural elite to mobilize effectively against the postwar communist land reform.

In this respect, therefore, while our studies confirm the comparativists' emphasis on the importance of countervailing factors for the revolutionary outcome, the local research indicates that those countervailing factors are no more static a given than is the revolutionary potential of the peasantry. We are, rather, viewing a dialectical process of contest among contenders for power, in which the *rules* may be written by the environment (local, domestic, and international), but the *moves* are subject to the intelligence, acumen, aims, and will of the contenders.

We come, finally, to the third point of correspondence with the comparative approaches, the central importance of alternatives open to those contemplating support of a revolutionary movement. Seldom in a revolutionary situation are most potential participants faced with such bald alternatives as land or starvation, liberty or death. Usually the opportunities are arrayed along a continuum, and most of the reasonable (or attractive) ones fall into the middle range of the spectrum. The winning side is usually the one that manages to stake out the middle range as its own territory; often, it does so because its opponents have left that area untended.

[. . . What, then, does this new work] offer in the way of generalizations? It suggests, first, that the China field must take seriously the interpretations advanced by comparativists, and the patterns detected in other revolutionary situations. But it suggests in fact that these are almost automatically taken into account by those who immerse themselves in a local situation and attempt to trace the development of the revolutionary process there. In making the necessary connections of cause and effect, one is led inexorably to trace the interactions among peasants, party, state, rural elite, and various manifestations of international forces, and to recognize the malleability of the fortunes of revolutionary war.

Second, the new work suggests that, in making these connections, the boundary lines between appeals and organization, domestic and international factors, structures and motivations, break down; that posing either–or questions for explanation points one either toward ambiguity or away from half the answer. The question, rather, is how all these factors are linked in the revolutionary process.

Third, with respect to this linkage, the new studies suggest that revolution at the local level – without which no revolution would succeed; therefore, that The Revolution – is a political process, not the predetermined working out of structural factors or the inevitable Big Boom emanating from the mixture of revolutionary preconditions and revolutionary consciousness.[77]

Finally, they offer not so much a generalization as a proposition on the direction that future research should follow. That is to trace, with sensitivity to the different possibilities offered in different situations, just where are the boundaries of the givens, what is the leeway for political action, and what general patterns of interaction across diverse environments we can find. We may, in the process, discover that some locales of the Chinese revolution bear far more resemblance to local revolution in other countries than to other parts of China itself. We will be, at that point, much closer to an understanding of the Chinese revolution and of revolutions in general.

NOTES

The research assistance of Barat Ellman, Julia Erickson, Donna Milrod, and Christine Torre is gratefully acknowledged as is the financial assistance of the Ida and Louis Katz Foundation. This chapter has also benefited from helpful readings by Lloyd Eastman, Craig Malone, Michel Oksenberg, Elizabeth Perry, and Stanley Rothman.

1 Gunther Stein, *The Challenge of Red China* (New York: Whittlesey House, 1945), p. 54.
2 Tang Tsou, *America's Failure in China 1941–1950* (Chicago: University of Chicago Press, 1963), p. 223.
3 Edgar Snow acknowledges that his view of the base areas would have been quite different had he come directly from the United States rather than via Guomindang China. Edgar Snow, *The Long Revolution* (New York: Vintage Books, 1972), p. 177. Archibald T. Steele, who visited Yan'an, makes the same point. *The American People and China* (New York: McGraw Hill, 1966), ch. 2.
4 See, for example, G. E. Taylor, "Reconstruction After Revolution: Kiangsi Province and the Chinese Nation," *Pacific Affairs* 8, 3 (September 1935): 302–11, and Dorothy Borg, *American Policy and the Chinese Revolution, 1925–1928* (New York: American institute of Pacific Relations, 1947).
5 O. Edmund Clubb, *Communism in China: As Reported from Hankow in 1932* (New York: Columbia University Press, 1968), pp. 71–73, 81–87.
6 See, for example, Evans Carlson, *Twin Stars of China* (New York: Dodd, Mead, 1940); George Taylor, *The Struggle for North China* (New York: Institute of Pacific Relations, 1940), p. 101.
7 A good statement of this view can be found in Michael Lindsay, "The North China Front," *Amerasia* 8, 7 (31 March 1944): 105.
8 Edgar Snow, *Red Star over China* (New York: Grove Press, 1961), p. 299. Snow perceived this apparent bond between the people and their political organizations as "something new in rural China" (p. 237).
9 Lyman P. Van Slyke, ed., *The Chinese Communist Movement: A Report of the United States War Department, July 1945* (Stanford: Stanford University Press, 1968), p. 1.

10 A good statement of this view is Taylor, *The Struggle*.
11 See, for example, Harrison Forman, *Report from Red China* (New York: Henry Holt, 1945), and Stein, *The Challenge*.
12 Taylor, *The Struggle*, p. 78. Emphasis added.
13 Edgar Snow, *Random Notes on Red China, 1936–1945* (Cambridge, Mass.: East Asian Research Center, Harvard University, 1974), p. 37.
14 This was also clear in Snow's later *Battle For Asia* (New York: Random House, 1941). Our thanks to Christine Torre for this insight. The view that the Communist movement was in the mainstream of an ongoing Chinese revolution against domestic ills was an important factor causing Snow to minimize the influence of the Soviet Union on the Chinese Communist movement.
15 Theodore H. White and Annalee Jacoby, *Thunder Out of China* (New York: William Sloane Associates, 1946), pp. 201–202.
16 See White and Jacoby, *Thunder Out of China*, chs 20 and 21.
17 Tang Tsou suggests this in his *America's Failure*.
18 On the mood in Chongqing, see Steele, *The American People*, ch. 2.
19 An eloquent statement of this view can be found in Lin Yutang, *Between Tears and Laughter* (New York: John Day, 1941). See also his exchange with Edgar Snow in *The Nation*: Snow, "China to Lin Yutang," 160 (17 February 1945): 180–83; Lin, "China and Its Critics," 160 (24 March 1945): 324–27; Snow, "China to Lin Yutang – II," 160 (31 March 1945): 359. For a discussion of pro-GMD elements within and without the government, see Michael Schaller, *The U.S. Crusade in China, 1938–1945* (New York: Columbia University Press, 1979); Schaller, *The United States and China in the Twentieth Century* (New York: Oxford University Press, 1979), chs 4 and 5; and Ross Y. Koen, *The China Lobby in American Politics* (New York: Macmillan, 1960). Walter Judd's 1945 speech to the House of Representatives is in *Congressional Record*, vol. 91, pt. 2, 79th Congress, 2d session, pp. 2294–2301.
20 Koen, *The China Lobby*, pp. 156–58.
21 See ibid., and Kenneth E. Shewmaker, *Americans and Chinese Communists, 1927–1945: A Persuading Encounter* (Ithaca: Cornell University Press, 1971).
22 H. Arthur Steiner, "Foreword," *The Annals of the American Academy of Political and Social Sciences* 277 (September 1951): vii.
23 The first term is W. W. Rostow's and the second, Lucien Pye's. W. W. Rostow, *The Stages of Economic Growth: A Non-Communist Manifesto* (Cambridge: Cambridge University Press, 1960), p. 162; and Lucien Pye, *Guerrilla Communism in Malaya: Its Social and Political Meaning* (Princeton: Princeton University Press, 1956), p. 349.
24 Sigmund Neumann, "International Civil War," *World Politics* 1, 3 (April 1949): 346.
25 Philip Selznick, *The Organizational Weapon: A Study of Bolshevik Strategy and Tactics* (New York: McGraw Hill, 1952); Ivo Duchacheck, "The Strategy of Communist Infiltration: Czechoslovakia 1944–1948," *World Politics* 2, 3 (1950): 345–71. See also Josef Korbel, *The Communist Subversion of Czechoslovakia 1938–1948: The Function of Coexistence* (Princeton: Princeton University Press, 1959), and Stefan Possony, *A Century of Conflict: Communist Techniques of World Revolution* (Chicago: Henry Regenry, 1953).
26 Isaac Deutscher, "The French and Russian Revolutions," *World Politics* 4, 3 (April 1952): 378. The best overview of the Eastern European takeovers from this period is Hugh Seton-Watson, *The East European Revolution* (London: Methuen, 1950.
27 See, for example, Ronald Scheider, *Communism in Guatemala, 1944–1954* (New York: Frederick A. Praeger, 1958).

28 Eduard Heimann, "Marxism and Underdeveloped Countries," *Social Research* 19, 3 (September 1952): 322–45; Robert V. Daniels, *The Nature of Communism* (New York: Random House, 1962), ch. 6; Eugene Staley, *The Future of Underdeveloped Countries: Political Implications of Economic Development* (New York: Harper and Brothers, 1954), part 2; A. V. Sherman, "Nationalism and Communism in the Arab World: A Reappraisal," in *The Middle East in Transition: Studies in Contemporary History*, ed. Walter Z. Laqueur (New York: Frederick A. Praeger, 1958), pp. 452–61; and Walter Laqueur, *Communism and Nationalism in the Middle East* (New York: Frederick A. Praeger, 1956).

29 The above is based on Koen, *The China Lobby*.

30 Selznick, *The Organizational Weapon*, p. 318.

31 See, for example, Feliks Gross, *The Seizure of Political Power in a Century of Revolution* (New York: Philosophical Library, 1958), pp. 187–295; Dinko Tomasic, *National Communism and Soviet Strategy* (Washington. D.C.: Public Affairs Press, 1957); Mario Einaudi, Jean-Marie Domenach, and Aldo Garosci, *Communism in Western Europe* (Ithaca: Cornell University Press, 1951); Walter Crosby Eells, *Communism in Education in Asia, Africa and the Far Pacific* (Washington. D.C.: American Council on Education, 1954), Schneider, *Communism in Guatemala*; and Laqueuer, *Communism and Nationalism in the Middle East*.

32 There is one significant qualification to this statement. During these years there was some work done on the "appeals of Communism" to either the masses or middle-level cadres. This was, however, the exception to the rule in a field where leadership strategies received the lion's share of attention. See Adam B. Ulam, *The Unfinished Revolution: An Essay on the Source of Influence of Marxism and Communism* (New York: Random House, 1960); Gabriel Almond, *The Appeals of Communism* (Princeton: Princeton University Press, 1954); Lucien Pye, *Guerrilla Communism in Malaya*; and Richard V. Burks, *The Dynamics of Communism in Eastern Europe* (Princeton: Princeton University Press, 1961).

33 George Taylor, "The Hegemony of the Communists, 1945–1952," *The Annals of the Academy of Political and Social Sciences* 277 (September 1951): 13, 14, 21. See also David N. Rowe, *Modern China: A Brief History* (Princeton: Van Nostrand, 1959); Karl Wittfogel, "The Influence of Leninism-Stalinism on China," *The Annals of the American Academy of Political and Social Sciences* 277 (September 1951): 28, 30–34; Franz Michael, "The Fall of China," *World Politics* 8, 2 (January 1956): 300–306; and R. L. Walker, "How to Misunderstand China," *Yale Review* 40, 3 (March 1951): 437–51.

34 Robert C. North, *Moscow and the Chinese Communists* (Stanford: Stanford University Press, 1953), ch. 1.

35 Benjamin I. Schwartz, *Chinese Communism and the Rise of Mao* (Cambridge: Harvard University Press, 1951), pp. 199, 200–201. See also Schwartz, "Marx and Lenin in China," *Far East Survey* 17, 15 (27 July 1949): 176–78.

36 John K. Fairbank, "Past and Present," *The New Republic* 136, 19 (13 May 1957): 14. See also Fairbank, *The U.S. and China* (Cambridge, Mass.: Harvard University Press, 1958), ch. 13.

37 John K. Fairbank, "Revolutionary Asia," *Foreign Affairs* 29, 1 (October 1950): 102–104. Note should also be taken of the work of Mary Wright, who also explored the indigenous roots of the Communist movement. See her "Modern China in Transition, 1900–1950," *Annals* 321 (January 1959): 1–5; and "The Chinese Peasant and Communism," *Pacific Affairs* 24, 3 (1951): 256–65.

38 Fairbank, "Revolutionary Asia," pp. 107–108.

39 See, for example, Hsiao Tso-liang, *Power Relations Within the Chinese Communist Movement, 1930–1934* (Seattle: University of Washington Press 1961); Schwartz, *Chinese Communism*; and North, *Moscow and the Chinese Communists*.

40 Most forcefully stated in Ygael Gluckstein, *Mao's China: Economic and Political Survey* (Boston: Beacon Press, 1957).

41 For example, Theodore Hsi-en Chen, "China: Communism Wins," *Current History* 19, 108 (August 1950): 78–82; Conrad Brandt, Benjamin Schwartz, and John K. Fairbank, eds, *A Documentary History of Chinese Communism* (Cambridge, Mass.: Harvard University Press, 1952); Mary Wright, "Modern China in Transition," pp. 3–5; and Tilman Durdin, "The Communist Record," *The Atlantic Monthly* 204, 6 (December 1959): 41.

42 Chalmers Johnson, *Peasant Nationalism and Communist Power: The Emergence of Revolutionary China, 1937–1945* (Stanford: Stanford University Press, 1962).

43 Chalmers Johnson, "Civilian Loyalties and Guerrilla Conflict," *World Politics* 14, 4 (July 1962): 646–61.

44 Johnson, *Peasant Nationalism*, ch. 1.

45 Chalmers Johnson, "Peasant Nationalism Revisited: The Biography of a Book," *The China Quarterly*, no. 72 (December 1977): 766–67.

46 Chalmers Johnson, "The Changing Nature and Locus of Authority in Communist China," in *China: Management of a Revolutionary Society*, ed. John Lindbeck (Seattle: University of Washington Press, 1973), pp. 34–76. In his review of Johnson's book, Benjamin Schwartz was critical of the vagueness with which Communist organization was discussed. *The China Quarterly*, no. 15 (June 1963): 169–70.

47 Johnson, *Peasant Nationalism*, pp. 17–18.

48 Donald G. Gillin, "'Peasant Nationalism' in the History of Chinese Communism," *Journal of Asian Studies* 23, 2 (February 1964): 269, also makes this point.

49 Ibid., pp. 274, 283–85.

50 Most prominently, John E. Rue, *Mao Tse-tung in Opposition 1927–1935* (Stanford: Stanford University Press, 1966); and Shanti Swarup, *A Study of the Chinese Communist Movement* (Oxford: Clarendon Press, 1966).

51 For example, Stuart Schram, "Mao Tse-tung and Liu Shao-ch'i, 1939–1969," *Asian Survey* 12, 4 (April 1972): 274–94; and John Lewis, "Leader, Commissar, and Bureaucrat: The Chinese Political System in the Last Days of the Revolution," in *China in Crisis*, ed. Ho P'ing-ti and Tang Tsou (Chicago: University of Chicago Press, 1968), vol. 1, book 2, pp. 449–81.

52 See, for example, Richard H. Solomon, *Mao's Revolution and the Chinese Political Culture* (Berkeley: University of California Press, 1971); Benjamin I. Schwartz, "China and the West in the 'Thought of Mao Tse-tung,'" in *China in Crisis*, ed. Ho and Tsou, vol. 1, book 1, pp. 365–489; and Peter Seybolt, "The Yenan Revolution in Mass Education," *The China Quarterly*, no. 48 (October–December 1971): 641–69.

53 Johnson himself reports this last criticism in his "Peasant Nationalism Revisited: The Biography of a Book," *The China Quarterly*, no. 72 (December 1977): 784. The quotation is from an article by Richard Pfeffer in *The Nation*, 27 April 1970, p. 506.

54 Chalmers Johnson, "Chinese Communist Leadership and Mass Response," in *China in Crisis*, ed. Ho and Tsou, vol. 1, book 1, pp. 397–437. Johnson later claimed that he still stood by the original argument of *Peasant Nationalism*. Johnson, "Peasant Nationalism Revisited," pp. 766–85.

55 James Sheridan, *China in Disintegration: The Republican Era in Chinese History* (Glencoe: Free Press, 1971), esp. pp. 264–69; and Maurice Meisner, "Yenan

Communism and the Rise of the Chinese People's Republic," in *Modern East Asia: Essays in Interpretation*, ed. James Crowley (New York: Harcourt, Brace and World, 1970). The most masterful synthesis can be found in the work of the French historian Lucien Bianco, *The Origins of the Chinese Revolution 1915–1949*, trans. Muriel Bell (Stanford: Stanford University Press, 1971), ch. 6.

56 Mark Selden, *The Yenan Way in Revolutionary China* (Cambridge, Mass.: Harvard University Press, 1971).

57 See Mark Selden, "People's War and the Transformation of Peasant Society: China and Vietnam," in *America's Asia: Dissenting Essays in Asian–American Relations*, ed. Edward Friedman and Mark Selden (New York: Pantheon Books, 1971), and *The Yenan Way*, p. 277.

58 Ralph Thaxton, "On Peasant Nationalism and National Resistance," *World Politics* 30, 1 (October 1977): 24–57; Tetsuya Kataoka, *Resistance and Revolution in China* (Berkeley: University of California Press, 1974), chs 4 and 7; and Meisner, "Yenan Communism."

59 Roy M. Hofheinz, Jr. is often credited with laying the greatest stress on the determining role of organization, based on his conclusion in "The Ecology of Chinese Communist Success: Rural Influence Patterns, 1923–45," in *Chinese Communist Politics in Action*, ed. A. Doak Barnett (Seattle: University of Washington Press, 1969), p. 77. However, Hofheinz's later study of the early years of the Communist peasant movement casts doubt on the efficacy of organization or leadership alone as "the yeast of revolutionary growth." *The Broken Wave: The Chinese Communist Peasant Movement, 1922–1928* (Cambridge, Mass.: Harvard University Press, 1977), p. 286.

60 Ilpyong J. Kim, *The Politics of Chinese Communism: Kiangsi under the Soviets* (Berkeley: University of California Press, 1973), p. 3.

61 Of course, Kataoka's argument does not carry the ideological baggage typical of some Western works published in these years.

62 A very strong case for the importance of organization as a factor contributing to Communist success can be found in Bianco, *Origins of the Chinese Revolution*, ch. 6.

63 For a summary of his argument see Kataoka, *Resistance and Revolution*, introduction and conclusion.

64 Some scholarship on the GMD tends to favor those who minimize the role of the war, suggesting, in contrast to Kataoka, that the power of the GMD was not growing in the prewar period. See Lloyd Eastman, *The Abortive Revolution: China under Nationalist Rule, 1927–1949* (Cambridge, Mass.: Harvard University Press, 1974); and Hung-mao Tien, *Government and Politics in Kuomintang China, 1927–1937* (Stanford: Stanford University Press, 1972). In a later study, Eastman does underscore the importance of the war in contributing to the Guomindang collapse, while by no means granting it the sole determining role. *Seeds of Destruction: Nationalist China in War and Revolution, 1937–1949* (Stanford: Stanford University Press, 1984), esp. pp. 216–26.

65 Elizabeth J. Perry, *Rebels and Revolutionaries in North China, 1845–1945* (Stanford: Stanford University Press, 1980).

66 Jack A. Goldstone, "Theories of Revolution: The Third Generation," *World Politics* 32, 2 (April 1980): 425–53.

67 Theda Skocpol, *States and Social Revolutions: A Comparative Analysis of France, Russia, and China* (Cambridge: Cambridge University Press, 1979); Jeffrey M. Paige, *Agrarian Revolution: Social Movements and Export Agriculture in the Underdeveloped World* (New York: Free Press, 1975); James C. Scott, *The Moral Economy of the Peasant: Rebellion and Subsistence in Southeast Asia* (New Haven: Yale University Press, 1976); Samuel L. Popkin, *The Rational Peasant: The*

Political Economy of Rural Society in Vietnam (Berkeley: University of California Press, 1979).

68 He does not exclude the possibility that political action may occur in rural settings where these notions never had, or no longer hold, currency, but he suggests that for many such, we are no longer discussing "peasant" action at all. Cf: his discussion of the effects of migration, p. 213.

69 Skocpol, *States and Social Revolutions*, p. 171; Scott, "Revolution in the Revolution: Peasants and Commissars," *Theory and Society* 7 (1979): 97–134; Popkin, *Rational Peasant*, p. 259.

70 Skocpol enshrines this question as the title of a review on the subject, "What Makes Peasants Revolutionary?" *Comparative Politics* (April 1982): 351–75.

71 For China, by contrast, the only major attempt to apply these factors in an analytical fashion was a paper by John Wilson Lewis. The paper dealt primarily with peasant rebellions in traditional China but linked the same patterns with the Chinese revolution. Lewis, "Memory, Opportunity, and Strategy," paper for the Research Conference on Communist Revolutions, St. Croix, V.I., January 1972. Lewis argues that the historical memory of repression of rebellion in a locality reduced the propensity to revolt.

72 In Skocpol's words, "Revolutionary situations have developed due to the emergence of politico-military crises of state and class domination. And only because of the possibilities thus created have revolutionary leaderships and rebellious masses contributed to the accomplishment of revolutionary transformation." *States and Social Revolutions*, p. 17. Paige, *Agrarian Revolution*, p. 42; Popkin, *Rational Peasant*, pp. 42–43; Scott, *Moral Economy*, pp. 229–30.

73 Skocpol, "What Makes Peasants Revolutionary?" p. 363. Interestingly, she does not see this as boding ill for peasant interests; rather to the contrary: "Because of this direct mobilization, peasant resources and manpower have ended up participating in the building of new-regime social institutions and state organizations. Peasant participation in this revolutionary pattern is less 'spontaneous' and autonomous than in the first pattern, but the result can be much more favorable to local peasant interests, because during the revolutionary process itself direct links are established between peasants and revolutionary political and military organizations." For Paige's position, see *Agrarian Revolution*, p. 44.

74 Popkin, *Rational Peasant*, p. 259; Scott, *Moral Economy*, pp. 223–25; Paige, *Agrarian Revolution*, pp. 45–49.

75 Scott, *Moral Economy*, p. 236; Popkin, *Rational Peasant*, pp. 43–46, 64, 176–77, 236.

76 The current essay was originally written as an introduction to a collection of short pieces by the five scholars referred to above, in which these China specialists summarized the findings of recently published books and dissertations.

77 In line with this perspective on revolution as a political process, see the masterful essay by Rod Aya, "Popular Intervention in Revolutionary Situations," in *Statemaking and Social Movements: Essays in Theory and History*, ed. Susan Harding and Charles Bright (Ann Arbor: University of Michigan Press, 1984), pp. 318–43.

8

SUSPECT HISTORY AND THE MASS LINE: ANOTHER "YAN'AN WAY"

Chen Yung-fa

The local turn in study of the first half of the China's twentieth century has pulled scholars in many directions, most of which have led away from the traditional concerns of political history and away from focusing on the lives of the best-known government leaders. As the last three chapters have illustrated, to "go local" has led to increased interest in everything from the ecology of specific counties to the thoughts of little-known members of provincial elites. It has also often meant, where the rise of the CCP is concerned, reduced attention to Mao Zedong and other famous personalities who loom large in famous works on the period such as countless Chinese language books and Western accounts such as Edgar Snow's **Red Star over China.** *This has had a salutary effect, if for no other reason than that the single figure of Chairman Mao, presented either as a saint or as a personification of evil (and, much more rarely, as a multifaceted human being), has loomed so large in writings on the period. No revolution is the work of just one person, or even a small circle of people. Hence bringing in more actors and settings other than Yan'an, the mountainous base area that served as the main center of operations for Mao and his closest comrades-in-arms during the Civil War, has been a very good thing for understanding the process that led to the establishment of the PRC. Widening our vision of the period to include struggles in diverse rural areas and also in China's cities has led to a sense of the rise of the CCP much richer than that conveyed in hagiographic tales of Mao and films that use Yan'an as a metonym for the nation.*

In this chapter, though, Chen Yung-fa argues that one crucial aspect of the local history of the Chinese Revolution that deserves close scrutiny is Yan'an itself and the experiments that Mao carried out there. Even before 1949, Yan'an had been elevated to the status of sacred site in Communist Party historiography, with Mao's activities there shrouded in a mythic aura. After the CCP took power at the national level, the sanctification of Mao, and by extension those closest to him in Yan'an and that physical space itself, reached a new intensity. Chen is one of the recent scholars who has tried hardest to convince his readers that nearly every aspect of the official

CCP vision of Yan'an as a holy spot and the Yan'an period of Communist history as utopian should be treated with extreme skepticism. For example, he has argued elsewhere, in a revisionist essay that complements the one included here and in his book Yan'an's Shadow, *which he cites below, that opium sales played an enormously important role in funding activities in the base area. Since the CCP derided the GMD's turning of a blind eye to the drug trade, and since opium had long been linked to images of national humiliation, Chen's argument took aim at a key feature of Maoist mythology. In the chapter presented here, he attempts to undermine another part of the official CCP history of Yan'an, namely, the tale of campaigns carried out there to rid the base area of "traitors" in its midst. These were not necessary efforts to keep the Revolution on track, Chen insists, but brutal and petty affairs that prefigured the purges of the Cultural Revolution era (1966–1976) that official histories now present as having had catastrophic effects.*

* * *

After the Cultural Revolution, historians in the People's Republic began to reexamine the policies of the Chinese Communist Party from 1942 to 1945, the period that had given birth retrospectively to the much-praised "Yan'an Way." The reexamination begun in the 1970s was selective, however. When Mao Zedong's staunch supporter Kang Sheng was officially dubbed "the devilish advisor" of the fallen Gang of Four, Chinese authors began to ask questions about his role in the Yan'an period, particularly his leadership over the cadre-screening campaign. In the subsequent reevaluations of Kang, no one has dared examine Mao's role nor question the wisdom of the mass line. Chinese historians invariably praise Mao for his policies on rectification and cadre screening. They ignore Kang Sheng's leadership of the rectification campaign, but treat the spy-hunting campaign of 1943 as a political aberration and attribute it to Kang's sabotage of Mao's policies. Had Mao failed to intervene in time, they say, the hunt for enemy spies might have turned into a disaster.[1]

The spy-hunting campaign grew out of Mao Zedong's application of the mass-line technique to cadre screening. However, it was not Kang Sheng's "wrong" line against Mao's "right" one; both closely followed the "mass line" principle. Kang Sheng's "deviation" from the Maoist path was no different from the "left excesses" inherent in any mass campaign and was deliberately condoned to encourage mass activism and participation.

Rectification

Mao's concern with the prevalence within the Party of "undesirable tendencies" – in his terms, "dogmatism, sectarianism, and bureaucratism" – led him in early 1942 to launch an investigation of cadres and a program of "rectification." The ultimate goal of rectification differed little from that of earlier ideological struggles, but the methods prescribed and developed for it differed markedly. The key difference was that while earlier ideological struggles were waged as if engaging an implacable enemy, rectification was in theory carried out in the spirit of comradeship. In Mao's terms, criticism was necessary for progress, but within the Party it should be practiced with unity as starting point and as ultimate goal. Mao urged Party members to criticize one another with two guidelines in mind: cure the sickness to save the patient, and learn the lessons of the past in order to avoid repeating them.[2]

Another main difference from past campaigns was the intensive study of prescribed documents and articles written primarily by Mao and his chief supporters. These documents related to the general situation in the Party. Abstract in their diagnosis, they offered detailed guidance for behavior and concrete examples as illustration.[3] Mao instructed all cadres to study them and practice criticism and self-criticism in their light. Cadres studied the assigned articles intensively for several months, carried out endless rounds of criticism of comrades and relentlessly "exposed" and criticized themselves along prescribed lines. Only presiding cadres were allowed to call an end to study sessions.

Study groups were formed within each organizational unit (*danwei*).[4] Since senior cadres were in charge, the Party tended to make more stringent demands on lower and middle cadres than on them. Senior cadres were asked to undergo rectification, but studying Party history took up so much of their energy that they had little time left to criticize themselves.

It is curious that Mao appointed his security chief Kang Sheng to take care of cadres' spiritual transformation. John K. Fairbank once commented that Chiang Kai-shek's appointment of his security chief as minister of education was as absurd to American minds as having the FBI's J. Edgar Hoover appointed as chancellor of the University of California. At least Chiang Kai-shek's security chief was a university-trained mining engineer from the University of Pittsburgh. Kang Sheng, in contrast, was founder of the Communist security system and professionally trained as a security expert by the NKVD.[5] Loyal but suspicious, Kang was chosen not merely for his theoretical understanding and moral rectitude. His appointment was a veiled threat. The implied message: "Hide nothing from the Party" because Kang Sheng will sooner or later sniff it out.

"Cadre screening" was not a new practice of the Chinese Communist Party. In 1939 the Party's Central Committee rebuilt its security apparatus and ordered it to work together with the Organization Department to collect personnel data and screen all Party members. To avoid creating unnecessary anxieties, it instructed investigative departments not to work through mass campaigns but to screen Party members individually. Investigative departments were told to secure first the cooperation of heads of the *danwei* and order all Party members to report on their class background, social contacts, political connections, and – where relevant – periods during which they had lost contact with the Party or had been arrested by enemy authorities. In suspicious cases, security agents were to make a thorough check on Party members' testimony.[6] The whole screening process resembled security clearance in Western countries; conducted by specialists, it would have created little disruption.

Mao, however, wanted more. The start of rectification was an opportune moment for another round of cadre screening. Criticism and self-criticism, both written and oral, yielded a bonanza of personnel material that provided the basis for thorough study of each Party member. Kang Sheng also routinized the filling up of "small broadcasting forms" and required every Party member to report periodically on anything the member was regretful of (*duibuqi*), such as any remarks or revelations considered damaging to Party interests and any social connections outside the Party. Mao obviously considered the added sources of information valuable for cadre screening.[7] He thus secretly formed a committee to investigate Party and non-Party cadres and put Kang Sheng in charge of it.[8] Inevitably, security cadres uncovered more "enemy spies" in the process.

After one such investigation, Kang Sheng "discovered" that one Zhang Keqin (Fan Dawei) was a Nationalist spy. Zhang was nineteen years old. His father was an underground Communist; he himself joined the Party at the age of just fourteen. In 1942 he was in Yan'an studying in an intelligence school. His dossier included two pieces of damaging information: his father had joined the Communists suspiciously soon after being arrested and released by Nationalist authorities, and Zhang had once criticized his Party superiors. So during the rectification campaign when a friend denounced Zhang as a Nationalist agent, the security department accepted the testimony without further ado. Zhang was arrested and interrogated. Five high-ranking security cadres, including two future political upstarts of the Cultural Revolution, Wu De and Wang Dongxing, were assigned to the case. They eventually got Zhang to admit the charges. One of the interrogators has recently revealed that Zhang's confession was involuntary; it came from more than forty hours of ceaseless questioning. The interrogator also has revealed for the first time in Party history that the security apparatus widely used round-the-clock interrogation instead of physical torture. The use of such interrogatory techniques against Zhang Keqin was permitted and encouraged by Li Kenong, Kang Sheng's right-hand man in security. Kang Sheng was not directly involved, but the case of Zhang Keqin enabled him to argue for a vigorous cadre-screening campaign in Yan'an.[9]

Although Kang Sheng never urged his underlings to extort false confessions, the pressure he put on them, together with their desire to ingratiate themselves and their inclination to follow orders blindly, gave rise to the widespread use of round-the-clock interrogation and similar practices. According to a technical manual, interrogators were to regard the political prisoner as a cunning and deceitful class enemy, who awaited a chance to counterattack. This was class war – the interrogators would be damaging their own interests if they treated the enemy leniently.[10] The result was disaster. The definition of suspect was now much looser. An underlying assumption that a true Communist would never make false confessions – under any circumstance – encouraged Kang Sheng's security personnel to see uninterrupted interrogation as an effective test of Party loyalty. It was a way of mentally "exhausting" the enemy and making him vulnerable, but it would have no effect at all on a comrade, for comrades could endure such treatment without compromising their integrity.[11] Unfortunately the premise was untrue. Many comrades admitted to being spies and Party interrogators saw this as confirmation of their original suspicion. A vicious circle developed. The number of victims began to multiply.

The day after Zhang Keqin made his confession in November 1942 he appeared at a mass meeting, publicly confessed his "heinous crimes," accused the Nationalist government of duping him, expressed gratitude to the Party for delivering him from the Nationalist "hell," and urged other enemy spies to confess and repent too. Afterward, he also went from unit to unit making the same confessions, accusations, and pleas. His case later grew to implicate the underground Party of more than ten provinces, including Henan, Sichuan, Gansu, Zhejiang, Hubei, and Guizhou. Because the implicated supposedly "used the red banner to fight the red banner," it was referred to as the case of "the red banner party."[12] Though rehabilitated in 1950, Zhang was again jailed as a Nationalist spy for ten years during the Cultural Revolution. He proved to be a model repenter. Many Party members, younger ones in particular, were so moved by his "sincere" confession that they responded to his call enthusiastically. Other Yan'an institutions found their own Zhang Keqins and turned them into antiheroes. Many victims exaggerated their former Nationalist ties in order to outdo Zhang Keqin or please their Party superiors.[13]

If round-the-clock interrogation was necessary to break Zhang Keqin, we can imagine how hard it was for the Party to get what its security people regarded as necessary materials for cadre screening. Even if Zhang Keqin had been a Nationalist spy, his case demonstrated the limits to the call for rectification. The Party leaders in charge of the rectification campaign found similar resistance to their call for criticism and self-criticism. Later developments revealed that they believed many cadres still refused to dig deep in their souls and practice criticism and self-criticism according to Party wishes.

The hunt for enemy spies

Only from this perspective can we understand why the Party arrested more than 260 suspects in one night in April 1943.[14] In Kang Sheng's judgment, resistance to criticism and self-criticism was still far too strong. Mao agreed. In March 1943 Mao won the newly created chairmanship of the Politburo and the Secretariat. Entrusted with power to make final decisions in the Party hierarchy, he also won support to simplify the powerful Secretariat into a triumvirate (including himself) and to reorganize the Party's functional departments.[15] In a sense, this was a coup against the Comintern, Wang Ming, and his staunch supporter Zhou Enlai. The Comintern representative Peter Vladimirov once confronted Kang Sheng with a question about the arrest of the 260.[16] Kang Sheng told him angrily that the decision came from his Party superiors. We have no reason to doubt that this was true. It would have been imprudent for Kang Sheng to make the massive arrests without the permission of the Party center – of Mao in particular, immediately after Mao's seizure of supreme power.

The arrests happened at the same time as a new campaign to disseminate the experience of Zhang Keqin. No sooner had Kang made the arrests than the Party announced its intention to start a campaign to eradicate nonproletarian thought and to root out hidden counterrevolutionaries.[17] This directive, referred to in Communist documents as the Second April 3 Decision, remains classified more than four decades after its issuance. The tidbits that have been revealed suggest Mao's exaggeration of the Japanese and Nationalist success in infiltrating Communist organizations. In his words, "they succeeded in implanting a large contingent of spies in our Party and affiliated organizations, their methods being extremely ingenious and their numbers being large enough to horrify people." He thus urged cadres to plan the rectification campaign afresh. In his new view, rectification was to go through three stages. The first emphasized study of documents and the second, criticism and self-criticism of either persons or units (danwei). These stages repeated the early rectification and extended it by attacking a selected few for erroneous thought, presumably taking the ideological struggle against Wang Shiwei as an example. The third stage was to use accumulated personnel materials to study every Party member's life history. In this stage, the danwei heads were authorized to use mass meetings to struggle against chosen spies and mistaken cadres. Mao instructed Party leaders to plan to spend at least five more months for the first and second stages and hoped to enter the third stage in late 1943 and to conclude the whole campaign within one more year.[18] Two months later, he readjusted the schedule to reflect the slow progress of the work, asking top cadres to finish the first and second stages within 1943 and devote the whole year of 1944 to the third stage with emphasis placed on a spy hunt.[19]

The Second April 3 Directive also revealed Mao's keen awareness of ordinary Party members' resistance to cadre screening and spy hunting and he therefore urged senior cadres to talk only in terms of correcting erroneous thought and inspecting assigned tasks. He also urged top cadres to distinguish the combating of nonproletarian thought and the unmasking of hidden counterrevolutionaries, each possessing distinct goals, targets, and methods. But in actual practice, they were urged to learn how to facilitate one job by pursuing the other without mixing them up.

Six days later, on April 9, Ren Bishi, the Party's number three leader, and Kang Sheng transmitted Mao's message and started rectification anew by calling to several separate mass meetings more than 20,000 people from danwei affiliated with the Party center. This provided the necessary impetus to transform what had first been cadre screening of limited scale into a spy-hunting spree throughout the Yan'an area. Riding on a horse with a large red flower on his chest, Zhang Keqin appeared at the mass meetings as a model repenter and urged other "spies" to follow his own example.[20]

The mass meeting introduced a new method for dealing with those suspected to be spies. At the urging of Mao, the Party heads of danwei began to take cadre screening and spy hunting into their own hands and many of them endeavored to imitate and improve upon Kang Sheng's exemplification. Zhou Yang, famous for his staunch support of Mao's literary policy, reviewed the personnel materials of Yan'an University and persuaded some suspects to be model repenters like Zhang Keqin. Imitating Kang Sheng, he used immunity to prompt them into a tense competition with one another in confessing and exposing new suspects. Party members and activists were assigned to pressure them to outdo each other. Zhou surpassed Kang by urging the so-called masses, in this case rank and file in his *danwei*, to form "persuasion" groups, charged with finding their own spy suspects and using whatever means over several days to persuade them to confess. No legal experts were on hand to scrutinize evidence that ostensibly justified the targeting of suspects. Persuaders followed their targets day and night, persuading not only by reason, but also by veiled threat. The pressure was so intense that two people chose suicide. But afterward Zhou Yang claimed to have found 27 more spies, in addition to 25 he had found earlier.[21]

Hu Yaobang, who would later become the secretary-general of the Communist Party, and who was then the organization chief of the Eighth Route Army's political department, also contributed to the political fervor.[22] He devised a new method of detecting suspects: he dispatched trusted Party activists to mass confession meetings after telling them to watch for changes of color in suspects' faces and to use every possible means of persuading them to confess whenever their color changed. Kang Sheng also sent his wife to the villages around Yan'an to experiment with cadre screening and spy hunting. Kang's wife demonstrated the feasibility of cadre screening outside Yan'an and accumulated enough experience for a new model. This approach is what Mao later called "harmonizing general policy and concrete experience."[23]

On the basis of such model experiences, Mao jotted down the famous nine guidelines for cadre screening and cautioned specifically against "torture, confession, and credulity" (*bi-gong-xin*). These guidelines are (1) the unit leader takes charge, (2) the leader personally undertakes the campaign, (3) strive for unity between cadres and masses, (4) make general policy but implement it with specific examples, (5) conduct research and investigate, (6) distinguish the innocent from the guilty and the serious from the trivial, (7) rescue the fallen, (8) cultivate activists and transform them into cadres, and (9) educate the masses. Without elaboration and clarification, these nine guidelines remained impracticably vague.[24]

No sooner had Kang Sheng made known the nine guidelines than he launched the now infamous "rescuing-the-fallen" campaign in Yan'an.[25] For three days from July 15 to July 18 he held a mass meeting in Yan'an. After Kang reiterated the policy of "treat the confessor leniently, punish the recalcitrant severely," model repenters began to testify to their rebirth through confession. Suspects were paraded on a stage and urged to emulate model repenters. If they followed Zhang Keqin's example, they were given encouragement and pronounced rehabilitated; otherwise, the audience shouted slogans at them. Members of the audience came forward to testify against them and make fresh accusations. The whole process continued until the suspects gave in and satisfied the audience, especially the presiding cadre.[26]

In May 1943 the Comintern announced that it was being disbanded and the bad news caused some panic in Yan'an. Taking advantage of the changed international situation, the Nationalist government moved troops nearer to Communist territory. The Communist Party found it necessary to gear up for possible attacks by mobilizing anti-Nationalist public opinion. In an attempt to drum up passion in a mass meeting of 30,000 people on July 9, the Party center called for further mobilization against spies. Although the Nationalists by July 15 had decided to call off the attack, Mao still endorsed the move by calling a ten-day "rescue-the-fallen" mass meeting. Criticism from other Party leaders led Mao to shorten the schedule to only three days, but when the limelight dimmed from Kang Sheng's mass meetings, the mass line approach to cadre screening and spy hunting gained momentum in all the *danwei*.[27]

The goal of rescuing the fallen was to transform waverers and spies. Here Mao admitted that the majority of 2,000 people suspected to be spies were actually the ones who had suffered moments of delirium, but he saw nothing wrong in Kang Sheng's method of unmasking them. He also mentioned Kang Sheng's efforts to recruit 10 to 20 percent of the participants for the tasks of cadre screening and spy hunting; he emphatically urged the use of these "defected" spies, presumably people like Zhang Keqin, for the campaign. Mao never specified how to use the defectors, but he congratulated Kang Sheng for his achievements in this task. Equal emphasis was put on the efforts of *danwei* leaders to involve and educate the masses in the process. Mao considered spies a problem of "mass nature," by which he seemed to mean that spies operated in a social context. He therefore urged cadres to awaken the masses to the urgency of spy hunting and cadre screening, and to recruit and train activists for the two tasks.

The *danwei* heads only sent 10 percent of their suspects to the security apparatus (e.g., Society Department or Security Bureau) and 10 percent to the "self-reflection organizations" (e.g., Central Party School, Northwest Public School, Administrative College). The rest were people suspected of light transgressions; they were to stay in their own *danwei*, rectifying themselves and awaiting their colleagues' scrutiny. Near the end of the campaign, Mao made an adjustment in his earlier timetable for rectification and allowed its extension to include the entire year of 1944. He also allowed *danwei* heads to start cadre screening and spy hunting as they saw fit. But fully aware of the danger of free mass mobilization, he made it crystal clear that no *danwei* were allowed to undertake cadre screening and spy hunting unless under the tight control of loyal cadres.

"Left excesses"

Common sense seemed to have taken leave. For example, both cadres and ordinary people believed the confession of a teenage student that he was the leader of a Nationalist assassin squad and his weapon was a bagful of stones. They also believed adolescent girls who confessed that the Nationalists had instructed them to seduce their schoolteachers and cadres. A district and a county cadre whom the *Jiefang ribao* had just commended for his achievements turned out to be simultaneously a Nationalist and a Japanese spy. Imitating the earlier rescue-the-fallen meetings, Xi Zhongxun allowed underlings to mobilize family members to admonish their relatives to confess publicly. Despite their complete ignorance of the facts, many suspects' parents, children, brothers, sisters, or friends were mobilized to urge their beloved to confess and repent. When they met silent resistance, they even threatened to cut off relations. Yet no one seemed to have noticed the absurdities.

The situation in jails was far worse. Before the "rescue-the-fallen" mass meeting of July, round-the-clock interrogation had already developed further. A nineteen-year-old girl who had traveled thousands of miles to Yan'an was suspected to be a Japanese spy simply because one of her relatives had joined the puppet government. After being arrested, she was interrogated without stop for three days and three nights. Interrogators threatened that if she continued to resist, they would release two big snakes into the cave that was her jail cell. Interrogators also improved their craftsmanship and invented all sorts of methods to extract confessions. For example, they would ask suspects to write down a personal chronicle month by month and use the inconsistencies found as grounds for further suspicion. Physical torture, simple or sophisticated, began to reappear. Security people generally stayed behind the "masses," pitting prisoner against prisoner, but often ignored the niceties of the mass line and took over the job themselves.[28]

In early October 1943 the Party called a mass meeting in Yan'an against traitors and spies in which the policy of "killing none and arresting few" was reiterated and immunity from legal action was promised to self-confessors.[29] The Party center even responded to a request from Suide and invited a group of model student repenters from there, the youngest of whom was only twelve or thirteen years old. They were treated as heroes freshly returned from battle, given accommodations in the guest houses for the Party's prominent visitors, and dined with meals full of such delicacies in the impoverished Northwest as white rice, flour noodles, pork, cabbage, and snow peas. The students went to different *danwei* to testify to the Normal School's success in the spy hunts. Some units even followed Zhang Keqin's example and treated repenters like production heroes, pinning red flowers to their chests and throwing parties for them.[30]

On the other hand, pressure from superiors and colleagues was so intense as to make unit leaders amazingly innovative and inventive; they concocted all sorts of ways of detecting suspected spies and of pressuring them into publicly accusing the Nationalists. Measures to persuade the "fallen" took every imaginable form: persuasion by individuals or by groups; by friends or superiors; by small meetings, private conversation and public meetings; and so on. "Persuasion" was applied also by passionate plea, private admonishment, public exhortation, friendly advice, or veiled threat. It could be by day or night; some persuaders followed suspects everywhere and never stopped "helping and persuading" them. One waverer-turned-activist was promoted to be head of the subregion organization department because he allegedly did not sleep for fifteen days in order to maintain surveillance over a spy.[31] And under curfew, suspects had no way of escaping the pressure.[32]

Years later, after his posthumous disgrace, Kang Sheng was criticized for stipulating at this time that a percentage of cadres were spy suspects.[33] Whether Kang did this or not, a mass campaign created pressure few *danwei* cadres could withstand. Not only did superiors expect results, but other *danwei* also generated pressure. Many cadres lost both appetite and sleep in their anxiety about failure to unmask suspects and spies. In one *danwei*, the leader one night blew his whistle as if in an emergency. When his underlings jumped from bed to the appointed gathering place, he began to lecture them on their failure to confess. Intimidated by the screaming and the threatening voice, some people stepped out and confessed. As if confirming his suspicion, he became even more emphatic in his insistence on turning out more spies and suspects. In another case, the underlings mostly peasants, were so sympathetic to their superior's predicament that they decided to confess together. In their view, such a move not only saved their boss from humiliating criticism but also enabled them to enjoy a reward for confession – in this case, just a party featuring crackers.

In mid-October, Kang Sheng allegedly sent a work team to the Anti-Japanese University (Kangda) and the work team leader Huang Zhiyong (a future lieutenant general) improved on earlier models. The president of the university, Xu Xiangqian, recalled:

> [Huang and his work team] turned the rectification of the Anti-Japanese University into a mess. Their methods varied, including "instant confession," "exemplifying confession," "collective persuasion," "five-minute's persuasion," "private talks," "report in mass meetings," "catch the water turnip [outwardly red but inwardly white]." The most ridiculous one was the so-called taking pictures, so named because they would parade people by groups and invite the audience to "take their pictures." If the person who was paraded before them did not show a change

in the color of his face, he was regarded as innocent beyond question; otherwise, he became a suspect who required further scrutiny. They widely practiced "tortures" and used round-the-clock interrogation. In the end, they turned out 602 suspects, about 57.2 percent of the cadres above platoon level. The cadre corps had 496 people, but 373 of them, more than 75 percent, turned out to be spies and suspects. It was horrible.[34]

Similar outcomes were found outside the Yan'an area, too. In Jin-Sui, a rectification class of about 200 cadres above district level was instructed to undertake cadre screening in August 1943. Kang Sheng conveyed his findings from the Yan'an area, and for one month, from December 1943 to January 1944, the local Party secretary divided the class by squads and scrutinized every cadre's personnel materials. A large portion of the cadres were found to be "spies" or "counterrevolutionaries."[35]

In many more cases, unrestrained mass mobilization yielded still more suspects. False accusations and confessions reinforced each other and created a momentum once the authorities accepted them. In the Yan'an border area in late 1943 and early 1944, it was no longer news for a unit to declare that more than 70 percent or even 90 percent of its cadres were "suspects" to be saved. In the Military Communication School, attached to the Military Commission's Third Bureau, 170 spies were uncovered from among slightly more than 200 students. Of 88 people who participated in rectification in the Guanzhong Normal School, 62 turned out to be "spies." The Praetorian Regiment had 80 to 90 percent of its soldiers and officers suspected of spying. Even the Department of the Secretary of the Central Party Office unmasked more than 10 "spies" among a staff of about 60. In an eastern Gansu county, the Party uncovered a spy ring of 200 people within only two weeks.[36] The most shocking was that half of the representatives to the Seventh Party Congress were suspected of spying.[37]

"Left excesses" obviously went too far and caused a backlash, and Mao had to respond. From December 1943 on, Mao began to centralize the power of calling for confessional mass meetings. First, he merely asked that *danwei* leaders to be "more careful and more prepared" in using this tool; later, he banned the meetings completely. Mao urged *danwei* leaders to stop ceaselessly questioning and pressuring suspects, unless evidence merited such action. He also wanted them to make periodic inspections to make sure that there would be no more "physical torture," "mental torture," "round-the-clock interrogation," "hitting and scolding," "binding and hanging," and "humiliating" of suspects. Mao specifically forbade emulation of the Self-Reflection Institutes, such as the Northwest Public School.[38] Here we see Mao's pattern of shifting blame, already noted by scholars of the Hundred Flowers and Great Leap Forward, but fifteen years earlier.

Mere injunctions were insufficient. Mao needed to do more to defuse dissatisfaction. By the end of 1943, the Third Bureau, which was responsible for communications between Yan'an and other base areas for the Military Commission, could no longer discharge its normal function. The bureau used stringent standards to recruit its more than one thousand cadres, but the majority of them had been accused of being spies. Fortunately for the victims, the New Year was near. To extricate himself from difficulties, the bureau chief, Wang Zheng, asked his underlings to wish Mao a happy New Year. When Mao saw the gloomy crowd, he immediately understood the real intention for the invitation to pay a visit. He compared cadre screening to bathing and apologized for pouring in an excessive amount of "manganese oxide" which hurt their skins. Mao then cheered them up with a salute. In hearing the humorous remark, many were unable to control their feelings. As Mao asked them to return the salute, they responded accordingly.[39]

Mao criticized cadre screening and spy hunting for the lack of "investigation and research" as well as the adoption of an indiscriminate approach, which confused other anti-Party behavior with spying.[40] In fact, Kang Sheng made a similar but longer self-criticism in his summary report on the two campaigns. Whether he got hints from Mao or not, he characterized the shortcomings as "a by-product of [making historical] progress." In Kang's view, they were what Stalin might term "left excesses in carrying out correct policies," or, in other words, a result of cadres' failure to faithfully enforce Mao's correct policy of the nine guidelines.[41] By "progress," Kang did not merely mean the handful of spies uncovered; he meant all the waverers and their reform.

By participating in cadre screening and spy hunting, *danwei* leaders and activists took the law into their own hands. They would find the occasion opportune for showing devotion to the Party, currying favor with superiors, and even settling private scores. But as long as "left excesses" were deemed necessary for mass mobilization, the Party instructed cadres to condone them. Only after the goals of mass mobilization were achieved would the Party tighten discipline and weed out unredeemable activists. Such a view of mass mobilization required Mao Zedong to forbid physical and mental torture and to condone them at the same time – forbidden in order to leave room for later maneuverability and condoned in order to stir up mass activism. In spite of his emphasis on the power of persuasion, Mao never completely renounced the use of compulsory methods. In his view, "left excesses" were always a necessary evil for effective persuasion.

Placed in this perspective, the Party policy of leniency acquires a much overlooked dimension. It was a safeguard against the extreme forms of left excesses. The Party used it to prevent the degeneration of tolerable left excesses into full-fledged Red Terror, which Mao had personally witnessed in the early 1930s. Mao had built his personality cult on the solid support of senior cadres who had suffered cruel and relentless struggle under the Internationalist leaders; he had to repudiate the resort to naked power in ideological struggles. Leniency was the badge of his leadership. He foresaw a second stage of mass mobilization in which enough materials would have been accumulated for a different sort of cadre screening. So he invariably stressed the need for research and investigation in order to win back the falsely accused. The stricture against execution gave him enough leeway to remedy mistakes. It is difficult to say exactly when mass mobilization moved from the first to the second stage, for it happened at different times in different units and places. In late 1943 spy hunting peaked.

Party review

Soon the Party found it could no longer afford an isolationist approach: "Close doors to hit [entrapped) dogs." The Japanese offensive in China proper of April 1944 was a golden opportunity for the Party to expand. To launch this offensive, the Japanese army had to wind down its campaign against the Communists. The consequent losses of the Nationalists at the hands of the Japanese created a power vacuum for the Communists to fill. To win the sympathy of both Chinese patriots and American liberals, the Party had to work hard to return to normality. This required a cessation of spy hunting.

Kang Sheng instructed those in charge of cadre screening to reexamine all the materials they had accumulated and make correct judgments on each implicated Party member. In Kang's view, Party members had undergone "rectification"; if they saw their mistakes, they should have the courage to say so and remedy them. Mao shared Kang's optimism. But developments did not confirm his optimistic view. Mao constantly had to criticize the security personnel in public and to apologize for them to people who had been falsely accused. He held no cadres responsible for so-called deviation from the official policy, let alone penalizing them. Virtually the same people were asked to review the materials accumulated during cadre screening and spy hunting.[42]

Despite all efforts, the reviews took much longer than expected. Meanwhile, Mao still found it necessary, as he had earlier, to apologize to different *danwei*, including the Central Party School and the Administrative College. On the eve of the Seventh Party Congress, he again apologized in a mass meeting of cadres of the border government and Party center.[43] Interestingly, when Mao offered his apologies, most of the falsely accused immediately accepted them. Some *danwei* leaders followed suit. They might have felt guilty but they were never held responsible for their deviation.[44] Indeed Mao Zedong never held anyone responsible, because he knew very well "leftist excesses" were inherent in any mass campaign that he himself blessed. On the other hand, victims might have participated in the mass mobilization in villages, but the majority seemed unable to see the link between mass mobilization and their personal woes. Mao decentralized responsibility just as he decentralized the power of rectification, cadre screening, and spy hunting. Because he constantly stressed his opposition to physical and mental torture, victims concluded that what had gone wrong was the implementation of policy rather than its formulation. Mao was not wrong; the problem instead arose from his *underlings'* failure to understand his correct instructions. Strangely enough, victims seemed to make no move against these underlings either. Only after Kang Sheng's posthumous disgrace in official circles did they dare to pin all blame on him. Kang Sheng was a perfect scapegoat.

In 1945, after about one year's study of Party history, senior cadres finally reached a consensus. More importantly, the Internationalist leader Wang Ming succumbed to Mao and signed a confession. Immediately afterward Mao convened the long over-due Seventh Congress, at which the Party canonized Mao's thought. In principle Kang Sheng should have reported on rectification, cadre screening, and spy hunting to the Congress, but Mao decided for the sake of internal unity to drop the issue from the agenda. In his work report, he affirmed the accomplishments in these three fields, though without going into detail, and again he apologized to those people who had been wrongly accused.[45]

If the review only justified the detention of about 100 suspects, the figure might mean at least 10,000 people were falsely accused. The calculation is based on the assumption that only 1 percent of confessors were detained. A much lower estimate was 3,000 victims, excluding all those implicated outside Yan'an. In spring 1944 Kang Sheng reported that throughout the Northwest 20,000 cadres, and 140,000 peasants, had participated in spy hunting and cadre screening. I suspect one-half to one-seventh of these cadres were falsely accused.[46] Mao and Kang considered the cost justifiable in terms of combating waverers and spies, particularly the former, though they nominally focused on spies. Jiang Nanxiang took a negative view and called 1943 and 1944 a waste of time.[47]

In the 1940s the mass line in practice meant mobilizing Party activists to detect suspects and to use group pressure to force them to confess and repent. Behind this effort was a desire to locate nonconformists and subject them to ideological remolding. Little attention was paid to possible excesses. As the Yan'an experience shows, the Party center was fully aware that untrained cadres and ordinary citizens would be unable to penetrate the often contradictory evidence to pass correct judgments on people's loyalty. The involvement of the masses in cadre screening was a political maneuver rather than a case of sincere belief in their power of discrimination.

In the 1940s leaders of chosen units were empowered to define and detect suspects and persuade them to confess in public. The decentralization of power and bureaucratic pressure for results encouraged these leaders to do their best but often led to "left excesses." These people had no legal training and the guidelines issued to them were vague and contradictory. Yet the Party demanded results, so they tended to condone "left excesses" or even the abuse of power to meet their superiors' expectations. The policy of killing none and arresting few kept undesirable tendencies in bounds. There were no bloody scenes as in the hunt for anti-Bolsheviks in the early 1930s. In justifying the strictures against killing, Mao Zedong blamed the Internationalists for the earlier purges and conveniently ignored his own responsibility in the Futian Incident.[48]

Party veterans mostly went along with Mao's directives in these campaigns. Even when alienated by Kang's heavy-handedness, they restricted their criticism to his interpretation and implementation of Mao's correct policy. Kang insisted, however, that he had faithfully performed Mao's assignments and quickly admitted that many mistakes had been made in the process. The crucial point mainland Chinese authors ignore in studying the problem is Mao's refusal to settle the dispute. Mao left the ambiguity of his directives unresolved and chided cadre-screening authorities only for what he called "technical" mistakes, while continuing by other means to push for maximum exposure of Party members inner-most secrets. Unable to see the campaign from this perspective, Party members could only have their respective unit heads and, at most, Kang to blame. Because Mao's directives stated that the campaign should proceed according to the principle of "research and investigation" and of comradely persuasion and self-criticism, when Mao apologized Party members were so moved that they immediately regained faith and confidence in the Great Leader and the Party. When they failed to understand was that Mao's directives included many "dialectical" elements, the balance of which the Party was not always able to maintain. In other words, in a mass campaign "left excesses" were inevitable, regardless of precautions.

This was also true of the Cultural Revolution that crowned the series of mass campaigns that unfolded in Mao Zedong's People's Republic of China. In the name of combating "capitalist roaders," Mao let Lin Biao and the Gang of Four mobilize young students and other radicals and implicitly empowered them to detain suspects, encourage confessions, and even stage mass trials for the purpose of "remolding" suspects. This mobilization bypassed the Party and targeted many senior cadres. Mao made little effort to limit the geographical scope of the campaign, which extended to the whole of China. On the basis of the Yan'an experience, abuses of power were inevitable. Red Guards (for convenience' sake, here I include in this term "rebels" of every unit), roused by idealism and untrammeled by legal constraints, training, experience, or supervision, invented mental and physical tortures worse even than those used in the spy hunts of wartime Yan'an. Party veterans accepted Mao's explanation that Red Guard attacks were an ordeal to test their loyalty; since they were absolutely loyal, they need fear nothing. What they did not realize was that Mao was determined to push them from power. The Gang of Four, with Mao's tacit support, colluded with security people to ransack personnel data collected through the rectification, cadre-screening, and spy-hunting campaigns. With the help of these materials, they and their followers could move easily to discredit "capitalist roaders."

In Yan'an top leaders were not subject to excessive mass criticism; instead their unhappy experience under the Internationalist leadership was conjured up to solidify Mao's attack mounted against Wang Ming and his cohorts. The Party therefore survived and expanded. In the Cultural Revolution, top leaders – even Liu Shaoqi – were subject to such tactics as political smearing and public beating. Thus the Party was shattered. Rectification had not changed from the 1940s to the 1960s, only its victims and its scale of victimization. The Yan'an Way was lit not by beacons of hope but by storm lamp and danger signals.

NOTES

I am as indebted to Professors Gregor Benton and Timothy Cheek for their editorial comments on an earlier, fuller version of this chapter as I am to my classmate Randy Stross for his abridgment.

1 See Li Weihan, "Jianchi Makesi Liening zhuyi pubian zhenli tong Zhongguo juti shijian de jiehe he tongyi" (Insisting on the unification of the universal truth of Marxism-Leninism with concrete Chinese practice), in Zhonggong zhongyang dangshi yanjiushi tushu zhiliaoshi (Party History Research Office Library of the Chinese Communist Party Center), ed., *Zhonggong liushinian jinian wenxuan* (Selected articles in memory of the sixtieth anniversary of the Chinese Communist Party) (Beijing: Zhongyang dangxiao chubanshe, 1982), 51; Su Kechen, "Kang Sheng he Wang Ming luxian" (Kang Sheng and the Wang Ming line), *Jindaishi yanjiu* 1 (1981): 117–30; Shi Zhe, "Women dang de guanjiaren – huiyi Ren Bishi tongzhi" (The chamberlain of our party – my memories of comrade Ren Bishi), in Zhonggong zhongyang dangshi yanjiushi tushu zhiliaoshi, ed., 366–76. Peter Seybolt has regarded the cadre-screening campaign to be a "counterespionage campaign," but his 1986 article has been rendered somewhat outdated by subsequent Chinese Communist Party revelations. Peter Seybolt, "Terror and Conformity: Counterespionage Campaigns, Rectification, and Mass Movements, 1942–1943," *Modern China* 12, 1 (Jan. 1986): 39–73.
2 Chen Yung-fa, *Yan'an de yinying* (Yan'an's shadow) (Taibei: Zhongyang yanjiuyuan jindaishi yanjiusuo, 1990), 24–30.
3 Lu Cheng *et al.*, eds, *Dang de jianshe qishinian jishi* (A chronicle of seventy years of Party building) (Beijing: Zhonggong dangshi chubanshe, 1991), 178.
4 Mao started with the Central Party School and gradually pushed rectification elsewhere in Yan'an. Even after he decided to launch a rectification campaign outside Yan'an, he confined his major efforts to Shaan-Gan-Ning, where no Japanese military threat was in sight.

5 *Jiefang ribao*, June 5, 1942. Lin Qingshan's work, *Kang Sheng waizhuan* (An informal biography of Kang Sheng) (Hong Kong: Xingchen chubanshe, 1987), is quite useful, though politically motivated and biased.

6 See for example (Zhonggong) Zhongyang zuzhibu (Organization Department of the Chinese Communist Center), "Zhongyang zuzhibu guanyu shencha ganbu jinyan de chubu zongjie" (Preliminary summary concerning the cadre-investigation experience of the Organization Department of the Chinese Communist Center), *Dang de shenghuo* 7 (1941): 38–42; Shi-zhengzhibu (Divisional-level Political Department), "Shi-shengshibu chubu shencha ganbu de jingyan jiaoxun" (Experiences and lessons at the beginning of cadre investigation), *Dang de shenghuo* 7 (1941): 45–51; Wang Youzhi, "Ganbu shencha gongzuozhong jidian shiji jingyan jieshao" (Some experiences in cadre investigation), *Dang de shenghuo* 7 (1941): 52–58; Cheng Ming, "Shi weisheng ganbu shencha gongzuo de jingyan jiaoxun" (Experiences and lessons from the investigation of division-level medical cadres), *Dang de shenghuo* 7 (1941): 58; Wang Guangli, "Xianji ganbu shencha de yixie jingyan" (Some experiences in the investigation of county-level cadres), *Dang de shenghuo* 9–10 (1941). Cadre screening can be traced to the August 7th Emergency Meeting. See Wang Zhangling, *Zhongguo gongchanzhuyi qingniantuan shilun, 1920–1927* (A critical history of the Chinese Communist Youth Corps) (Taibei: Guoli zhengzhi daxue dongya yanjiusuo, 1973), 519.

7 Chen Yung-fa, 61–62.

8 Ibid., 77, 128; Peter Vladimirov, *The Vladimirov Diaries: Yanan, China, 1942–1945* (New York: Doubleday, 1975), 77, 221. Su Kechen (p. 122) confirms the existence of this secret committee, although his dating differs from Vladimirov's. Zhonggong Miluo xian weiyuanhui (The Miluo County Party Committee of the Chinese Communist Party) ed., *Ren Bishi* (Changsha: Hunan renmin chubanshe, 1979), 230, emphasizes the effect of Ren Bishi's protest against Kang Sheng's "save-the-fallen" mass meeting and the formation of the committee. These materials also emphasize that Chen Yun was the one in charge, but to my knowledge Chen was forced to take a sick leave in the spring of 1943 and later, when returned to active duty, he was appointed as a deputy in He Long's Finance and Economics Office under Gao Gang's Northwest Party Bureau. See Chen Yun, *Chen Yun wenxuan* (Selected works of Chen Yun) (Beijing: Renmin chubanshe, 1984), 304.

9 Li Yimin was the interrogator. For his revelations see Li Yimin, "Canjia Yan'an qiangjiu yundong de huiyi" (Reminiscences about participating in Yan'an's Rescue-the-Fallen Campaign), in *Gemingshi ziliao* 3 (1981), and also *Li Yimin huiyilu* (Li Yimin's memoirs) (Changsha: Hunan renmin chubanshe, 1986). See also Gong Gujin and Tang Peichang, *Zhongguo kangri zhanzheng shigao* (Draft history of China's Anti-Japanese War) (Wuhan: Hubei renmin chubanshe, 1984) 2: 157; Hua Shijun and Hu Yumin, *Yan'an zhengfeng shimo* (The rectification campaign of Yan'an) (Shanghai: Shanghai renmin chubanshe, 1985), 66.

10 Tan Zhengwen, *Shenxunxue* (Manual on interrogation), revised ed. (Jin-Sui border region: Jin-Sui bianqu ganganju bianweihui, 1944). This book was written by Tan, but revised thoroughly in light of the review of a group of security experts. Kang Sheng endorsed the publication of an abridged version during the high tide of the spy-hunting campaign. The version consulted here was published by the security department of the Jin-Sui base area. See esp. pp. 36, 117–18. On the wide use of round-the-clock interrogation in Yan'an, see Jin Cheng, *Yan'an jiaojichu huiyilu* (Reminiscences from the Yan'an Public Relations Office) (Beijing: Zhongguo qingnian chubanshe, 1986), 180–81.

11 Tan Zhengwen, 36.

12 Hua Shijun and Hu Yumin, 68. Li Zhaobing dated the case November 1942 and according to him Kang Sheng used the case to warn senior cadres at a Party bureau conference in December 1942. See Li Zhaobing, "Yanan dangxiao zhengfeng suoji" (Recollections of the rectification campaign in Yan'an's Party School), in Zhongguo geming bowuguan dangshi yanjiushi (The Office of Party History of the Chinese Revolutionary Museum), ed., *Dangshi yanjiu ziliao* (Materials for Party history research) (Wuhan: Hubei renmin chubanshe, 1983), vol. 4.

13 Li Yimin, 33–35. Zhang was rehabilitated by the Party committee of his home province in 1950.

14 Tongyi chubanshe, ed., *Zhonggong zuijin de douzheng neibu* (The inside story of power struggle within the Chinese Communist Party) (hereafter *ZZDN*) (Chongqing, 1944), 78; Shi Zhe, *Zai lishi juren shenbian: Shi Zhe huiyilu* (On the side of a historical giant: Shi Zhe's memoirs) (Beijing: Zhongyang wenxian chubanshe, 1991), 249–50, and *Feng yu gu: Shi Zhe huiyilu* (Mountain peaks and valleys: Shi Zhe's memoirs) (Beijing: Hongqi chubanshe, 1992), 5–6. The excuse that the Party gave for the arrests was that they prevented "suspects" from making contact with a secret Nationalist mission to Yan'an. Shi Zhe participated in the arrests and according to his testimony, the Party soon arrested at least 200 more.

15 Tan Zongli, "Yijiusisannian sanyue zhongyang zhengzhiju huiyi" (The Politburo meeting of March 1943), *Dangshi yanjiu* 2 (1980): 77. I suspect that Mao Zedong used the case of the "Red Banner" to implicate Zhou Enlai and force him to denounce the Wang Ming line, of which Zhou was an integral part. Otherwise, it is difficult to explain Zhou's ouster from the Party center. Zou Fengping, Zhou's underling in the Sichuan underground Party, was falsely accused; he wrote Mao several times to plead his innocence. Zou later committed suicide because of his failure to receive any attention. See Wang Suyuan, "Shaan-Gan.Ning bianqu 'qiangjiu yundong' shimo" (The rescue-the-fallen campaign in the Shaanxi-Gansu-Ningxia border region), *Zhonggong dangshi ziliao* 37 (1991): 210; Zhonggong dangshi renwu yanjiuhui (The Association for the Biographical Studies of Chinese Communism), ed., *Zhonggong dangshi renwuzhuan* (Prominent figures of Chinese communism) (Xi'an: Shanxi renmin chubanshe, 1980–92), 14: 311–12.

16 Vladimirov, 112.

17 *ZZDN*, 51–58.

18 Ibid., 162; Lu Cheng *et al.*, 191. The directive was misdated April 23, 1943, in the second source.

19 Mao Zedong, "Mao Zedong guanyu Yan'an zhengfeng de yizu handian" (A set of Mao Zedong's letters and telegrams concerning Yan'an's rectification campaign), *Wenxian he yanjiu* 8 (1984): 23.

20 *ZZDN*, 79; Wang Suyuan, 212.

21 Chen Yung-fa, 193–211.

22 Ibid., 229–43, esp. 230–31.

23 Ibid., 245–309.

24 Mao Zedong, "Mao Zedong guanyu Yan'an zhengfeng de yizu handian," 7.

25 Kang Sheng, "Qiangjiu shizuzhe" (Rescue the fallen), July 15, 1943. Four versions are extant: one printed by Jiefangshe (The Liberation Press), one by Zhonggong Huazhongjunqu (The Military Region of Central China of the Communist Party), one by Disanjunfenqu zhengzhibu (The Political Department of the Third Military Subregion) under the title *Qiangjiu shizuzhe de kuanda zhengce*) (The policy of leniency in rescuing the fallen), and one by an unknown authority. Here I refer only to the first version. Also see Vladimirov, 129–31.

187

26 Zhonggong Miluo xian weiyuanhui, 229–30.

27 Chen Yung-fa, 83–87. The Nationalist decision to call off the attack was reported to Yan'an by a Communist spy on July 10, 1943, and by July 13 Mao told his colleagues in a Politburo meeting that an attack was improbable. See Xiong Xianghui, *Dixia shi'ernian yu Zhou Enlai* (Twelve years' underground work under Zhou Enlai) (Beijing: Zhonggong zhongyang dangxiao chubanshe, 1991), 26; and Zhonggong zhongyang wenxian yanjiushi (The Research Office of Documents of the Party Center), ed., *Zhu De nianpu* (Zhu De's chronological biography) (Beijing: Renmin chubanshe, 1986), 259.

28 Wang Suyuan, 215–17, 219.

29 Zhonggong zhongyang dangshi yanjiushi, *Zhonggong dangshi dashi nianbiao* (A chronology of the history of the Chinese Communist Party) (Beijing: Renmin chubanshe, 1987), 164.

30 One should not underestimate the combined inducement of "good meals" and "red flowers." For another example, see Shi Zhe, *Zai lishi juren shenbian*, 258.

31 Kang Sheng, "Sanshisannian fanjian zhengfeng hou zhi zongjie chengji ji quedian" (The deficiencies and achievements of the rectification campaign of 1944), Bureau of Investigation collection, 1944, p. 2.

32 *ZZDN*, 80.

33 Wang Soudao, *Wang Soudao huiyilu* (Wang Soudao's Memoirs) (Beijing: Jiefangjun chubanshe, 1988), 208.

34 Xu Xiangqian, *Lishi de huigu* (My memoirs) (Beijing jiefangjun chubanshe, 1987), 685–86. Huang was later a political chief of an army corps during the civil war and reached the rank of lieutenant general in 1955. On his career, see the index on Huang Zhiyong in Junshi kexueyuan junshi tushuguan (The Military Library of the Academy of Military Science), ed., *Zhongguo renmin jiefangjun zhuzhiyange he geji lingdao chengyuan minglu* (A handbook on the organization and personnel of the People's Liberation Army of China) (Beijing: Junshi kexue chubanshe, 1987). Huang was Xu's political enemy during the Cultural Revolution. Xu therefore had a reason to vilify him, but after studying the relevant materials on cadre screening and spy hunting, I am inclined to believe his testimony. On Xu's grudge against Huang, see Xu Xiangqian, 841.

35 Gao Kelin, *Gao Kelin huiyilu* (Gao Kelin's memoirs) (Neimenggu renmin chubanshe, 1987), 138–39.

36 Lin Qingshan, 92. Ren Bishi was praised for his efforts to restrain Kang Sheng but both the Praetorian Regiment and the Department of the Secretary were under his control. The Guanzhong case implicated the subregional commander's wife and her brother and the commissioner-cum-security chief. See Shi Zhe, *Feng yu gu*, 8–9.

37 Shi Zhe, *Feng yu gu*, 3.

38 Chen Yung-fa, 134–35.

39 Ibid., 125–26.

40 *ZZDN*, 164–65.

41 Kang Sheng "Guanyu fanjian douzheng de fazhan yu dangqian renwu" (Concerning the development of the anti-spy campaign and our current task), Bureau of Investigation collection Mar. 29, 1944, pp. 8–9; Jiang Nanxiang, "Guanyu qiangjiu yundong de yijianshu" (My opinions concerning the rescue-the-fallen campaign), *Zhonggong dangshi yanjiu* 4 (1988): 65.

42 Wang Suyuan, 224. Wang cited the review committee of the Shaan-Gan-Ning Border Region government as an exception to this general rule. But the committee still drew its members mostly from the ranks of senior cadres who had indulged in the earlier "left excesses."

43 Li Weihan, 514; Wang Suyuan, 229. Wang mentions four apologies.

44 For example, see Li Weihan, 514–15; Wu Xiuquan, *Wode licheng* (My past) (Beijing: Jiefangjun chubanshe, 1984), 164.
45 See Hua Shijun and Hu Yumin, 72–77.
46 Lin Qingshan, 99; Kang Sheng, "Guanyu fanjian douzheng de fazhan," 6.
47 Jiang Nanxiang, 67.
48 Chen Yi and Xiao Hua *et al.*, *Huiyi zhongyang suqu* (Reminiscences of the central soviet area), 1st ed. (Nanchang: Jiangxi renmin chubanshe, 1981), 200; Chen Yung-fa, "Zhonggong zaoqi sufan de jiantao: A B tuan an" (Purges in early Chinese communism: The case of the Anti-Bolshevik League), in *Zhongyang yanjiuyuan jindaishi yanjiu jikan* 17 (1988): 219–24.

Part III

SYMBOLIC TURNS

9

THE LANGUAGE OF
LIBERATION

Gender and *jiefang* in early Chinese
Communist Party discourse

Harriet Evans

The term jiefang, *which is usually translated "liberation" but sometimes "emancipation," has very specific and powerful connotations in Chinese. The Revolution, especially in CCP rhetoric but also in that of other groups at various points, was presented as a war waged on many fronts to free the people of the nation from varied forms of oppression. Each particular battle against a particular enemy was portrayed as a struggle to "liberate" or "emancipate" a given group or save all Chinese from a given form of bondage. But, in addition, all of these battles were seen as part of a single great move toward Liberation, conceived of as singular and upper case. In deference to this sense of* jiefang, *before 1949 base areas were described as constituting China's Liberated zones and the most important newspaper for this section of the country was known as the* Jiefang ribao *(Liberation Daily). Then, after 1949, though the* Liberation Daily *began to take second place to the new* Renmin ribao *(People's Daily) as the CCP's leading newspaper, the term* jiefang *remained in the name of the military (the People's Liberation Army) and became a shorthand for the moment the PRC was founded. Thus, for example, people were encouraged to draw a sharp contrast between their experiences "before Liberation" and "after Liberation," and celebrations held in various cities in 1959, on the anniversaries of the arrival of the PLA, were described as marking the passage of ten years since Liberation.*

This chapter by Harriet Evans explores the complex question of how exactly specific moves to liberate groups fit within this larger vision of Liberation as a sacred quest and transformational moment. Many radicals of the early twentieth century, Communist and non-Communist alike, saw the oppression of Chinese women as of special symbolic import, representing in some sense all of the ways that China had remained backward, its people held down. This showed through in works that used the rape of Chinese women by foreign men to stand for the rape of China by imperialism. It also showed through in one of Mao Zedong's most famous early writings, the 1927 "Report on an Investigation of the Hunan Peasant Movement." In this essay, which Evans cites in her chapter below, Mao argued that all rural Chinese were constrained by three forms of bondage (those linked to class, religion, and lineage). But, he added, women in the countryside chafed under a fourth kind of oppression as well (due to the power that husbands had over wives in the traditional family system). There was no way to uproot the old order, Mao and others assumed, without radically altering the position of women within Chinese society, and women's liberation and national Liberation were intimately linked. It is one thing, however, to describe two processes as necessarily entwined, as Evans shows, and quite another to place equal weight upon them so that one cannot be deferred until a more propitious time for pursuing it comes along. To note that the CCP often moved to defer the liberation of women is nothing new, but what Evans does that is novel and important is show how post-1949 policies were foreshadowed by pre-1949 discourse.

* * *

Debates about feminism and socialism have long ceased to occupy centre stage in feminist analyses of approaches to women's liberation.[1] If the events that shook the socialist "bloc" in 1989 finally sealed the fate of socialism, the suggestion that socialism could somehow provide an answer to feminism's concerns had been discredited long before. As Deng Xiaoping's market-oriented reform programme progressed in the 1980s, Chinese feminists became increasingly critical of the vertical approach to the "woman question" pursued between 1949 and the late 1970s.[2] Evidence had long demonstrated the fallacies of the classical Marxist formula that women's participation in "social labour" was the key to women's emancipation. The entry of women into the labour force did not significantly alter the customary domestic division of responsibilities, with women as the prime carers and servicers of husbands, children and often parents-in-law.[3] Scholars writing in English about women in socialist states, in particular China and the former Soviet Union, repeatedly pointed to the contradictions between the official promise that women would be liberated by proletarian revolution and the realities of women's continuing social and economic subordination to men.[4] Unable to counter this barrage of criticism, the canon of "socialist feminism" now reads as testimony to a particular historical moment far removed from the aspirations and desires of young feminists today, whether in the US, Europe or in China. Echoes of it continue to resonate in official Chinese analyses of gender disparities under the current system.[5] At the other extreme, it serves as a reminder of a vertically constructed programme of "women's liberation" that in many key respects had little to do with women's identification of their own needs.

Given the failure of communist states' programmes of "women's liberation", discussion about the gendered meanings of *jiefang* (the Chinese term for liberation) might appear as something of an irrelevance.[6] "Liberation" now represents ideas and projects which, as Apter and Saich wrote with reference to contemporary understandings of "Yan'an" as a political experience, have, in the eyes of many, been "trivialized by history."[7] To many Chinese women, the notion of "liberation" belongs to their mothers' and grandmothers' generations. For those older generations, it often recalls a nostalgia for the shared ideals of a purer past when policies of sexual equality seemed to offer women unprecedented and empowering opportunities of social action.[8] The term and practice *"funü jiefang"* [women's liberation] for them signified a positive challenge to the conventional male/female dichotomy according to which gender and sexuality were the main signifiers of female experience.[9] Younger women, by contrast, associate the term with a denial of feminine self, with a subjugation of self to masculinist interests, and to political and social constraints belonging to another time and another place. For them, the failure of policies of *funü jiefang* to eradicate the commercial exploitation of women's bodies, for example, speaks much more eloquently than their mothers' memories.

In the context of these suggestions, the political and ideological positions invoked by the term "liberation" of course seem condemned to historical ignominy. From another perspective, however, unravelling the different layers of meanings and effects associated with the word *jiefang* is important because of the formative influence the term had in shaping public articulation about women's and gender issues in China for a very substantial part of this century. Many of the ideological values inscribed in the term *jiefang* as it was developed in the first two decades of the Chinese Communist Party's (CCP) history continue to occupy an influential position in contemporary debates about, for example, the distinctions between Chinese and Western approaches to feminism.[10] The collectivist priorities signified by the word "liberation" have by no means been rejected by contemporary thinkers and activists, even if the term itself is no longer common usage. Within the dominant discourse of the revolution, the term *jiefang* exercised extraordinary authority as the set of dispositions that informed women's subjective positioning of themselves as well as others' positioning of them.

Critiques of the Party's failure to live up to its promise to women have largely started out from socio-economic and political analyses of empirical data – for example, of discriminatory employment and remuneration practices, unequal access to education at different levels of the educational system, unequal representation in political bodies, and gender discrimination in the formulation and implementation of population control policy. Many of these analyses have also drawn attention to the inadequacies of Marxist theories of women's emancipation. Recent analyses of dominant discourses of sexuality in the People's Republic of China (PRC) have broadened the debate to argue that a hierarchical biological essentialism has been a persistent constraint on the conceptualization and implementation of gender policies since 1949.[11] This paper adopts another approach through focusing on the term and concept of "liberation" [*jiefang*] as a central component of the Communist Party's discourse on women. On the basis of analysis of CCP and related documents produced between the early 1920s and 1950s, I argue that the texts written about and often for women produced fixed and hierarchically arranged meanings of *jiefang*, which consistently denied identification of women as agents of gender transformation, and which insisted on the absolute privileging of class over gender in analyses of gender inequalities. The effect of this was not only to subordinate the "women's movement" to the goals of social and national revolution as a whole. It established the only language in which gender issues could be publicly discussed. *Funü jiefang* thus became a discursive and ideological tool of Communist Party authority, always and necessarily indicative of pre-ordained approaches to women as social agents. The word produced and reinforced many of the hierarchies that its integration into the rhetoric of revolution ostensibly sought to challenge.

The Party and "women's liberation"

Normative uses of the term *jiefang* between the 1920s and the early 1950s identify different fields of revolutionary discourse and action, in which those of the nation/society (led by the proletariat) and women were particularly prominent. As part of the linguistic capital accumulated by the Communist Party during these decades, the former was arguably the principal one, as was evidenced by its symbolic place in the moment of the Communist Party's ascension to state political power after its defeat of the Nationalists in 1949. From the earliest days of the CCP and before, national liberation [*minzu jiefang*] referred to the linked tasks of overthrowing imperialist and feudal control as the condition for national independence. Liberation, in this context, signified a release from the controls of a past system of socio-economic and political power as well as from colonial domination, and the possibility, therefore, of formulating new structures and practices to sustain the benefits of that release.[12] It simultaneously signified the removal of constraints and the creation of a new future. Liberation was also a class process, in which only those constituents identified with the social sectors integrated into the term *renmin* [the people] could participate.[13] Linked through *renmin* to the concepts of democracy and dictatorship, it further signified the possibility of extending democratic rights to those within the category of the *renmin*, and of denying them, through exercising the controls of the dictatorship of the people, to classes deemed unassimilable to the revolutionary purpose.[14]

With reference to women, liberation signified a particular aspect to the struggle envisaged for the nation as a whole. Women's liberation [*funü jiefang*] was generally defined between the 1920s and the early 1950s as liberation from the patriarchy [*zongfa*] as well as from feudalism and imperialism. At first glance, it brought a gendered range of meanings into the concept of liberation, to identify the point at which women's particular situation and experiences departed from, or were distinct from those of the nation and society as a whole. Another gloss on the concept of "women's liberation" of course derives from Mao Zedong's famous analysis, set out in 1927 in his "Report on an Investigation of the Hunan Peasant Movement." Mao argued that while "men generally are subject to the control of three systems of authority (political authority, clan authority and religious authority) . . . women in addition are also subject to the control of men (authority of the husband) [*fuquan*]. These four kinds of authority represent the entire ideology and system of feudal patriarchy [*fengjian zongfa*]."[15] From this perspective, patriarchy – here defined very generally to refer to the system of oppression which accounts for women's gendered subordination – emerges as a term which conflates gender and class issues in describing a past system of authority associated with the socio-economic forces that the national application of liberation was oriented to overthrow.

From its earliest days, CCP policy toward women was unequivocal in its formal commitment to women's equal rights with men. Before the founding of the Party in 1921, individuals who were to become communist activists such as Li Da, Chen Duxiu and Li Dazhao had published a number of articles about women's issues.[16] In its Second Congress, held in July 1922, the young party passed a resolution committing itself to women's liberation as an integral part of the proletarian revolution. It also stipulated a series of laws concerning women's economic, social and educational rights.[17] The following year, in its Third Congress, it reviewed the development of the women's movement, with particular focus on women's participation in the burgeoning labour struggle, and called for the formation of a Women's Committee and the publication of a women's organ.[18] In both congresses, the Party made reference to the need to integrate the women's movement with the anti-imperialist and anti-feudal struggles. Just as significantly for presaging future approaches to gender issues in *funü jiefang*, the Third Congress also pointed out that patriarchal "habits" among the male workers were producing conflicts between women and men which threatened the unity of the labour movement.

In this early stage of the communist women's movement, *funü jiefang* was one – albeit increasingly authoritative – among a number of terms applied to the diverse tasks associated with the women's struggle. *Nüquanzhuyizhe* (lit. women's power-ism activists), *nüquan yundong* (lit. women's power movement), *nüxingzhuyizhe* (female/woman-ism activists) were all terms used by Communist Party sympathisers and members to denote different aspects of the women's movement.[19] Even *jiefang* was far from being used uniformly during this period. Li Da's 1919 use of *nüzi jiefang* referred to a kind of humanistic re-integration of women into the political demand for "persons' rights" (*renquan*, also translated as "human rights"].[20] Li Dazhao, writing in 1922, called for "great unity throughout the world" [*shijie de da lianhe*] as the condition of women's full *jiefang*.[21] Again, Xiao Chunü in 1923 called for liberation to start with the "essential self" [*ziji de xing*], with the "essential female" [*nüxing*] in women. In an essay entitled "The basic meaning of women's liberation," she argued that women should not demand liberation from society in the expectation that society would grant it to them, but should "take it" [*qu*] through liberating themselves from customary expectations and practices.[22]

However, Party expositions on women increasingly clarified the positions associated with *funü jiefang*, with the simultaneous effect of marginalising other potentially contesting terms outside the boundaries of ideological legitimacy. Hence, by 1925 *nüquanzhuyi* was clearly identified with a partial and implicitly divisive approach to the whole notion of persons'/human rights.[23] By 1926, articles appeared denigrating the gains of the previous stages of the women's movement, even to the point of questioning women's sincerity in struggling for women's rights.[24] "Women's activists" [*funüzhuyizhe*] came in for attack on the grounds that they were too narrowed-minded in their perspective on the "struggle between the sexes" [*liangxing douzheng*].[25] By 1926 communist appropriation of *jiefang* seems to have eclipsed contesting terms defining the women's movement. Henceforth, renewed invocation of women's rights [*nüquanzhuyi*], *ipso facto* signalled a challenge to the Party's version of "liberation." After 1927, though the specific referents of *funü jiefang* often shifted according to moment and political need, the discursive range and authority associated with the term settled into a stable relationship with other aspects of communist practice and language.

In its customary use in the language of Chinese communism, *jiefang* had little to do with the notions of individual and personal rights inscribed in the Western humanist tradition. As Li Xiaojiang has pointed out, whereas liberation and liberty in English are etymologically the same, and signify similar fields of meaning, the Chinese words for liberation and liberty are contrastive; liberation has little to do with freedom in any philosophical or humanist sense, but denotes liberation from particular shackles through collective action with the oppressed class(es).[26] It is thus in the historically specific context of the nation-state, and with particular reference to the twentieth-century formulations of national liberation struggle, that the Chinese word *jiefang* matches its usage and development elsewhere.[27] In England, the women's movement started using the term "liberation" through its association with political movements from 1940. The common earlier word had been emancipation, a term which was more associated with freeing from the legal powers of the paterfamilias in Roman law, from slavery, and then by the nineteenth century with "the removal of legal and political disabilities of women".[28] The subsequent shift from emancipation to liberation, in Williams' analysis, seemed to "mark the shift from ideas of the removal of disabilities or the granting of privileges to more active ideas of winning freedom and self-determination."[29]

In her study of women's activism and gender issues in the CCP of the 1920s, Christina Gilmartin uses the term "emancipation" for *"jiefang"* "to remain faithful to the historical tenor of the 1920s" when women's emancipation was the dominant term used in the English women's movement.[30] Though this infers some of the early European influences on the May Fourth women's movement, I prefer to stick to the term "liberation" in the discussion that follows for a number of reasons. First, its meanings were far from fixed in its early appearance in communist discourse, and though it was often quite loosely applied to a diversity of tasks and goals, it rarely seemed to refer to Western experiences of struggle for the political participation and representation without the mediating textual presence of other terms such as "women's-rights-ism" [*nüquanzhuyi*]. As more and more documents were published about the women's movement, *funü jiefang's* ideological association with the women's labour movement, with the communist-directed challenge to economic structures sustaining private ownership and with the liberation of the proletariat as a whole, became increasingly clear. At the same time, as the above discussion has noted, contrasting terms became increasingly identified with unacceptable ideological positions. Henceforth *jiefang* was the only legitimate term to apply to the broad goals of "woman-work" both before and after 1949. Use of the term "liberation" thus serves to identify the discursive trajectory through which *funü jiefang* came to identify the legitimate meanings associated with "woman-work" against its potential contenders. "Liberation" also identifies the common ideological parameters the CCP used to define the goals and processes of the women's and general social and national struggle.

Texts and terms of *funü jiefang*

In a very broad sense, the following discussion about *jiefang* is informed by my reading of an extensive range of materials written about and often by women in China between the 1920s and the present.[31] My analysis of the key meanings of "liberation," however, is based on a more focused examination of specific documents and articles from the communist movement between 1919 and the early 1950s. Though the dominant meanings of the term were clearly established by the time the first united front with the Nationalist Party (GMD) collapsed, reference to this longer period better demonstrates the full range of its discursive positions as they were established through time as well as through linguistic, symbolic and ideological structures. As the overall goal of all "woman-work," *funü jiefang* of course never identified exactly the same commitments and acts, regardless of moment. In implementation, *funü jiefang* – and the particular meanings it acquired in political processes – varied in very specific ways at different moments and periods, at different levels of political authority and activism and in different localities. Hence, at the level of central policy formulation, in the form of congressional resolutions for example, "liberation" could identify a general programme or strategy. In more deliberative or polemical texts, *funü jiefang* could just as well function as a marker of a particular political position at a particular moment. It was also subject to some modification in interpretation in accordance with policy fluctuations and factionalisms at the central levels of the Communist Party's command structure. A more detailed examination of the specific synchronic meanings of the term within the context of particular strategies and policy orientations would undoubtedly yield some interesting variations. Yet, while as Michael Schoenhals has pointed out, the "use and abuse, currency and obscolescence of individual terms" invalidates the possibility of any absolute fixing of meaning, *funü jiefang* rapidly became an instance of discursive closure.[32] Its range of meanings shifted within parameters that were firmly established in the early years of the Communist Party. The dominant significations of the term acquired a hegemonic status within the official discourse on women which transcended policy changes and factional interests.

The following analysis falls into two main parts. The first draws out particular readings of the word *jiefang* through its political and ideological references, and through its semantic and collocational associations within the narratives of the text. The second contains a more reflective discussion about the meanings inscribed in the various uses of the term to position women as particular subjects within the processes of social transformation.[33]

Funü jiefang *as destruction of the past and creation of the future*

One of the dominant and most frequently applied of *funü jiefang* before 1949 identified a dual process of "liberation from" as the condition and basis for the creation of a new future. Women sought liberation from the feudal shackles of the past, from abuse by husbands and mothers-in-law, from ignorance and illiteracy, and from patriarchal constraints on mobility and social activity. As the Hubei activist Xiang Ying (1898–1941) put it in 1940, "Women's liberation is the thorough destruction of the old and the creation of the new. Progress means getting rid of the old and creating the new."[34] Though its meaning as a release from the constraints of the feudal past diminished in prominence as the socialist transition gathered steam in the mid-1950s, this theme of *jiefang* corresponded with the Party's exposition of its "anti-feudal" struggle in approaching the past as a source of reaction, constraint and burden. Destruction of this past thus became the necessary condition for forging a new future, as Deng Yingchao, one of the most important communist women's leaders, speaking at the Second National Congress of Women in 1953, noted. "The central tasks the Central Committee has put to the people of the nation ... are the reform of the old society in all its aspects and the construction of new democracy. These [provide] the economic and political basis necessary to fundamentally eradicate the feudal system which shackles women and to create the social conditions for the liberation of women."[35]

Funü jiefang *as social liberation*

A second very common assumption about *funü jiefang* apparent in its earliest communist usages concerned the links between women's and societal liberation as a whole. The Second Congress of the CCP held in 1922 made this clear when it stated that "the Chinese Communist Party thinks that women's liberation needs to be carried out through relying on the liberation of the labouring people as a whole, because only if the proletariat obtains political power will women be able to achieve full liberation."[36] Another document argued that the women's movement was "an indispensable arm of the revolutionary struggle as a whole." Raising women's specific demands was therefore an appropriate strategy to encouraging the development of the revolutionary struggle as a whole.[37] Or again, in 1940, an editorial article in the *New China* publication in Yan'an commented that "In order to demand their own liberation, Chinese women of today must participate in all movements that benefit the state and nation."[38]

Here *funü jiefang* was defined in a dual and complementary sense, on the one hand, as a necessary part of "social liberation as a whole," dependent on it and doomed to defeat without it, and, on the other, as essential to the success of the broader movement. The particular campaigns or policy objectives of which *funü jiefang* was expected to become a part shifted at different moments between the 1920s and 1949, to correspond with the particular policy emphases given the revolutionary movement as a whole. Thus, in the Yan'an base area of anti-Japanese resistance, women's participation in the broader movement of "liberation" took concrete form in setting up co-operative production associations to support frontline activities.[39] In 1948, it took the form of encouraging women to actively participate in the struggle against "American imperialism, feudalism and bureaucrat-capitalism."[40] By the early 1950s, with the CCP's successful consolidation of state power, it referred more to the classical Marxist formula according to which women's liberation lay in women's equal entry into the public sphere of production and labour. As Deng Yingchao indicated in 1953, "Ten years of practice has proven that mobilising the masses of women to participate in production is the basic key to improving equality between men and women and to achieving the thorough liberation of women."[41]

The gendered and the general applications of "liberation" are here conflated in a single process of struggle and change. In these first two glosses on the term, the distinctions between its general and the gendered applications emerge not with reference to their implied goals and ideals, but to the mode of their interrelationship and the means used to encourage women's participation across the two. The main distinction was therefore instrumental and tactical, as the CCP's commentaries made clear. However, this collapsing of the two fields of reference of the term did not presuppose a relationship of mutuality, but rather of hierarchy, as a 1941 document made clear.

> In our view, mobilising women to participate in the war is the basic task of the current women's movement. However, if we are to increase women's enthusiasm for participating in the war and want to enable them to participate spontaneously and self-consciously, then we have no option but to take appropriate steps to remove their feudal fetters, raise their social position, protect their personal interests and improve their lives.[42]

Women's liberation was dependent on social liberation. In epistemological and material terms, society and the revolution pre-existed women, and moulded women's gendered struggle for transformation within a political context that privileged class and nation.

Funü jiefang *as a process of class and gender unity*

As a potentially gendered process, *funü jiefang* rarely referred to release from male controls on grounds of gender. Typically, it called for a challenge to male authority only when this was associated with class oppressors. Within the social classes and sectors to which the term *funü jiefang* applied, women's liberation could not be divisive. It could only target men of the non-revolutionary classes, men not included within the ranks of *renmin*, the People. Though in the aftermath of the May Fourth movement until the mid-1920s, communist commentators on women's issues from time to time drew attention to the necessarily gendered aspect of women's demands, official policy documents distributed by the Party made its own position absolutely clear.[43] The Resolution of the CCP's Third Congress, for example, referred to the "crisis" [*weiji*] produced by gender conflicts between male and female workers which threatened disunity within the labour movement.[44] Or as a 1928 provincial report on woman-work in Henan unequivocally put it,

> women's liberation is only one part of the broad movement of labour liberation. The target of women's liberation in the rural areas are not the men of the same class, but the gentry and landlords. So the women's movement in the rural areas must not impede the broad peasant movement, and rural women must stand on the same battle front as the men of their class, to carry out the revolutionary struggle. Only in this way will they be able to attain liberation.[45]

In this light, *funü jiefang* could only become an explicitly gendered process when associated with a struggle against the past in the form of male class enemies. As a term central to the political language of the communist-led revolutionary struggle, *funü jiefang* was thus divested of notions of conflict, contestation and challenge, except where these invoked class as distinct from gender. The hegemonic paradigm of class struggle determined a vocabulary of revolution that had uniform and universal applicability.

> Approaching the women's movement in separation [from the broader movement] gives rise to the "women's rights" [*nüquanzhuyi*] tendency. Of course we all know in theory that it is mistaken to emphasize the antagonistic position between the sexes [typical] of the women's rights movement. But in fact, some people cannot avoid committing this error. They fail to examine the roots of women's oppression from a socio-economic basis but explain women's suffering and oppression by referring to men.[46]

The idea that gender might be treated as a marker of difference in addition to or alongside class resonated too closely with the "individualist" pitfalls of "women's-power-ism" [*nüquanzhuyi*] for the Party's comfort.

This particular aspect of *funü jiefang* signified a closure on the possibilities of gender as an experimental arena of debate; it also established the parameters of the state's policy towards women after 1949. Apart from a brief period after 1949 when women were urged to take advantage of their new rights as enshrined in the 1950 Marriage Law, women were disenjoined from entering into conflictual relationships with men of their class.[47] By the same token, they were unable to insist on the specificity of a range of gender issues through uniting with women as a gendered rather than class or social category. Logically, therefore, women had to forge the conditions of their own liberation in unity with the rest of the *renmin*. This construction of *funü jiefang* by definition precluded the possibility of treating it as an explicitly gendered process, rather than as a bunch of particular effects of other processes on women. The association between an emphasis on gender (as opposed to class) and a "bourgeois" political stance – already well in place in CCP texts of the mid-1920s – effectively invalidated any plea for a gendered approach.

Funü jiefang *through the liberation of the majority*

A common criticism of the individualist potential of "gender" as an analytic category was that it suggested the possibility of liberation of a social minority of women. The "errors" of *nüquanzhuyi* in large part lay in the latter's elite social positioning, and its elitist separation from the demands of the majority of labouring women.[48] Not only, moreover, was a social minority of women unable adequately to represent the interests of the majority, but as He Xiangning put it in 1925, "there are too few educated women to rely on them alone for liberation. We have to rely on peasant and worker women if we are to obtain liberation."[49] The "misses and ladies from the upper classes" would make little progress through peaceful means; "women's liberation is a very pressing need, particularly in the countryside. To incorporate all women and not just women from petty bourgeois backgrounds must include several specific aims, including organizing female cadres in factories and villages, demanding equal wages for equal work, giving allowances for childbirth and pregnancy."[50] Xiang Ying also stated the position very clearly:

> Women's liberation is not the liberation of a minority, for the liberation of a minority is actually no more than the desire of lower level slaves to ascend to the status of higher level slaves, in which even though the situation of the slaves is different, the basic essence of slavery remains the same. So the thorough liberation of women must be the liberation of the great mass of lower class [*xiaceng*] women. Our female comrades should not only demand their own individual liberation but ought to contribute all their strength to the struggle for the liberation of the great mass of women, particularly working class and peasant women. Women's individual liberation can only be guaranteed through the thorough liberation of the great mass of women.[51]

As a class-based process, the signifieds of the term *funü jiefang* identified the appropriate class context establishing the legitimate approaches to women's liberation. In this meaning, *funü jiefang* identified the worker and peasant women masses as the social carriers of its project. As a category which applied to the political and social tasks of the *renmin*, *funü jiefang* by definition could not include interpretations which contradicted its association with the collectivist, class-based principles of those agencies responsible for defining it. In itself, *funü jiefang* could mean none other than a mass-based approach to woman-work.

Jiefang *as external process*

The language of *funü jiefang* in the texts examined so far almost exclusively denoted acts and processes in which women were actively encouraged to participate but in which that participation was discursively removed from women's agency. Women "are encouraged," "are mobilized," "are educated" and "are liberated" – women are "done to" – without being active agents of the processes involved. The acts and processes of liberation were defined by authorities external to women, in voices speaking on women's behalf, and defining their good. Of course, this did not mean that women did not act, nor that their actions did not have profound effects on their self-identification as women. The concept of active participation in itself identified women's active efforts in the processes of change. However, textual representation of the efforts involved suggested a collective activity defined and directed by other sources of authority. "Women's liberation" acquired meaning and possibility not through its links with the experiences and voices of material, living women but through its articulation by a supposedly non-gendered authority which stood outside and above women. Though centrally premised on the massive participation of women in active struggle, *funü jiefang* thus identified women, first of all, as vehicles of interests, designs and strategies formulated by others.

Of course, the issue of agency was neither necessarily nor specifically gendered; the *renmin* were also denied agency in the textual processes of their own transformation. However, the Party's claims to legitimacy rested on a kind of organic link with the people; in its own self-definition, the Party's success in 1949 was the inevitable culmination of its self-appointed role as the vanguard and the voice of the People. Women may have been part of the People, but the texts of *funü jiefang* positioned women in a relationship with the Party that could only be hierarchical – the women's movement was "under" the leadership of the Party – rather than organic as well. In its idealised self-definition, therefore, the Party did not, and could not, represent women in the way it did the People; by the same token, the lack of women's agency was not simply another discursive rendering of the lack of people's agency.

Readerly and writerly positioning of women in texts of funü jiefang

The Party's insistence that the women's movement be integrated into the revolutionary movement as a whole had particular effects on the textual and syntactical organisation of *funü jiefang*. The term often appears at the end of a sentence or paragraph, or in a subordinate clause, structurally and discursively privileging other terms of the narrative. *Funü jiefang* also appears in fixed places, notably in contexts which invoke the "People," the "labouring masses," the proletariat. It is also significant that with a few exceptions in the early 1920s, women's *jiefang* is never associated with women positioned as *nüren, nüzi,* or *nüxing*.[52] As a project defined and implemented by the Party and assimilated into the People's [*renmin*] struggle as a whole, *jiefang* could only refer to the officially sanctioned category *funü*. Documents about general issues also typically listed references to women after other items, often including young people.[53] In all, the rhetorical and political status of the term *funü jiefang* as both goal and process of the women's movement did not give it a particularly privileged place in the narrative organisation of CCP texts.

A Fujian directive of 1930 pointed out that "in the past in Fujian, only a few young women have joined the struggle, in part because of the fact that we have not thrown off the shackles of the feudal past but also because we have not given adequate attention to women's needs."[54] Despite frequent criticisms of the Party's failure to pay adequate attention to the women's movement, and exhortations to male cadres to treat woman-work more seriously, the texts of *funü jiefang* invariably targeted a female audience. Many of the more detailed texts, particularly those which specified tasks to be undertaken in work with women, were drawn up by women's organisations, and intended for women activists. General texts also implied that the responsibilities and tasks of "women's liberation" were principally women's. It was women who were asked to refrain from undertaking acts that would impair revolutionary unity between women and men.[55] It was women who were expected to correct past mistakes in the struggle for sexual equality, such as thinking that the "struggle between the sexes" was an important aspect of women's liberation, or that the anti-imperialist struggle was irrelevant to the women's struggle. It was also women who were asked to "liberate their thought" [*jiefang sixiang*], despite references to men's attachment to "feudal customs." Women were thus given almost exclusive responsibility for conducting processes of transformation which, by definition, were those of society as a whole. Between the writing and the reading of these texts, therefore, women were thus caught between contradictory positions: on the one hand,

207

fixed, ideologically bound and displaced from privilege, while on the other charged with the major responsibilities of their own and society's liberation.

To summarise these points, women were encouraged to "liberate their thought" [*jiefang sixiang*] in contexts of anti-feudal struggle and to "liberate out from" [*jiefangchulai*] conditions of feudal oppression. Liberation appeared as a process and goal to which not all women could aspire, but rather women [*funü*] identified with particular socio-economic and political positions. If liberation was associated with notions of struggle, then the targets of that struggle were first of all defined in class terms, and never in gendered terms which transcended or ignored those of class. Hence, men from the oppressor classes appeared as the missing element of the gender struggle; men from the revolutionary classes, from "the broad masses of the people," were discursively excluded from the agenda for transforming gender relations, except when they were urged not to ignore women's issues.

Reflections

The fixing of *jiefang* as a keyword of the Communist Party's language was a necessary component of its project of national unification and control. The formation of such a language was both part of and synonymous with a political process. Arif Dirlik has suggested that the "learning of a new language and forgetting the old has been a basic problem in Chinese politics, as is evident in the radical shifts in the language of socialist ideology."[56] He went on to argue that a revolution, to be authentic, has to create a new language of its own, in order to assert hegemony over history, and as an indispensable part of the attempt to discover new ways to think about social relationships and structures. Such a new language was simultaneously a language of vision and a language of control.

Dirlik's argument about the radical shifts in the CCP's language of socialist ideology is certainly relevant to the deployment of words such as revolution, class, struggle and transformation, the meanings of which have been profoundly transformed (as well as rewritten) since the Party's founding. It is not, as I understand it, so relevant to *jiefang*, at least in its reference to women, though *jiefang* was key to the CCP's "hegemony over history." As one component of the new revolutionary language, *funü jiefang* was not subject to radical changes of signification. While its specific relationship to liberation as a general process was constantly modified to correspond with the changing priorities the Party authorities gave to the national revolutionary project, depending on moment and political need, its core identification with a class-based and collectivist process of transformation that involved the *renmin* as a whole did not change. As a politico-linguistic term, *jiefang* was fixed in distinctive relationships. *Jiefang* could only be obtained and experienced by *funü*, which itself, as Tani Barlow has argued, was a word which produced woman as a category belonging to the communist state and to the political category of *renmin*.[57] Within this language, *nüren* and *nüxing* could not go through the processes of *jiefang*, for these signified other meanings to woman which were excluded from the legitimate language. By the same token, *jiefang* could not signify an individualist search for gendered identities; its textual and semantic associations with the nation, society, mankind and class produced only collective women positioned within particular class parameters.

Whatever the tasks and visions inscribed in the word *jiefang*, it denoted a series of fixed positions and relationships with other words and phrases, which in themselves identified the processes and possibilities of its operation. *Jiefang* was not a trope – a device to explore possible meanings – but rather a figure denoting fixed structures and positions in a closed discourse, in which fixed associations – for example, in the use of pronouns and adjectives – and fixed distinctions between wrong and right were repeatedly made through invoking the same set of practices, the same kinds of people, and the same kinds of class characteristics. As a keyword in this discourse, *funü jiefang* limited the range of subject positions it offered women by marginalising everything that did not correspond with its fixed positions to the realms of the unacceptable, the "bourgeois," "individualist" and "counter-revolutionary." Through explicit and implicit oppositional devices, it set out clear lines defining the appropriate approach to any particular course of action. Through its fixed associations, textual relationships and exclusions, *jiefang* itself identified the range of meanings it incorporated.

Contestation of the meanings given to *funü jiefang* by the Party centre were specific, isolated and short-lived. If occasional writings between 1921 and 1926 featured alternative meanings, through use of contested categories such as *nüxing*, or through less fixed versions of the tasks of "women's liberation," the dominant meanings of *funü jiefang* were clearly established by the formal organs of the Party early on in the 1920s. Criticisms of the Party's inscription of the term in its practice of woman-work, most famously associated with Ding Ling's critique in 1942, came to very little.[58] One way of explaining this would be to use Bourdieu's notion of complicity and Henrietta Moore's analysis of dominant discourse. Bourdieu argued that the generalised use of legitimate language depends not only on formal institutions of political and legal power, but on the complicity of those who use it, a relation-ship between the users and the language which presupposes neither "passive submission" nor "free adherence."[59] Discourses become or are dominant by virtue of their power to define and articulate social processes; and as Moore has argued, material subjects – living persons – have no alternative but to negotiate their own identities with reference to those terms, whether through conscious or unconscious means and processes, and whether to support them or to contest them.[60] In this light, Ding Ling's self-criticism and her adoption of the language of her authorities in Yan'an may be seen not only as an individual response to sanctions used to silence her, but also as the impossibility of following through a critique, the development of which depended on the substitution of the legitimate language for another. Her critique implied an attack on the only terms available within the legitimate language of the revolution that women could use to identify the processes of their own transformation. The approach to women and gender which her critique demanded logically implied the substitution of a new language of women's liberation for that which was already essential to the Party's project. It was, in this light much more than an attack on the Party's authority, for it signified a challenge to the language that its users – whether they believed in the Party's version of revolutionary truth or not – were obliged to use to maintain their association with the revolution.

The texts presented above demonstrate that the dominant usages and referents of *jiefang* were the nation, the collective, the labouring masses and society – words and concepts which in themselves were removed from gendered meanings. As such, *jiefang* excluded the possibility and experience of gendered difference, and constructed women as the same kinds of subjects as men. Here it is useful to refer to Meng Yue's discussion about the ways in which narratives about issues of gender and sexuality in *The White Haired Girl* were divested of gendered and sexual meanings and reinscribed with class meanings.[61] The dominant significance of the successive revision of Xi'er's image was to represent her as a subject of class struggle and its effects, and not of gender struggle and transformation. These notions may be extended to the analysis of the term "liberation" to grasp the ways in which, as associated with the tasks of "woman-work," "liberation" either brought gender, class and nation together into a single, indivisible bunch of meanings, or subordinated specifically gender tasks to those defined for class and nation. It rarely – at least in the terms of central party policy pronouncements – identified debates and practices associated with gender as autonomous and principal sites of strategic thinking about policy. Meng Yue's analysis is therefore useful for approaching ways in which, though formulated and used as a rhetorical device to signal the Party's commitments to gender equality in public and domestic life, the term itself collapsed its specifically gendered references into the hegemonic meanings of class and nation. Though explicitly linked with a range of tasks which sought to transform women's social and political practice, the term was discursively developed without reference to women's articulated experiences of gender as daughters, wives and mothers.

Funü jiefang was defined by centres of power which in their gendered composition, social and political commitments, and vision of revolutionary need, had little to do with women's articulation of their own interests. It simultaneously produced women through voices mediated not by their own experiences but by Party perceptions of revolutionary strategy. *Jiefang* was a keyword of a discourse which offered the dominant and necessary terms in which material women could publicly identify themselves.

Conclusion

Apter and Saich have looked at Yan'an and the rectification movement in Yan'an as the triumph of an exercise of exegetical bonding, in which subjects of the revolution came together through uniform identification with a key body of texts. They have argued that the main significance of the Yan'an experience within the totality of the Party's political trajectory was the "point during the Chinese Revolution when the discourse community was reformed and generated sufficient power to change the course of China's history." In their terms, Yan'an signified the transformation of the CCP from a political movement into an established discourse community which defined fixed boundaries, primary affiliations, obligations and powers, by cementing loyalties to shared myths and ideals through "acknowledgement of the need to observe methods of discipline (exegetical bonding) and through subscription to and drawing down from cultural, educational and moral forms of power (symbolic capital)."[62]

Their analysis, however, did not include an examination of gender, and my reading of the term *funü jiefang* suggests different conclusions to theirs. The main parameters delineating the possible meanings of "liberation" in its references to women seem to have been established almost as soon as the word made its appearance in the language of revolution, when the dominant features and principles of the Party authorities' interpretation of "liberation" as an organisational, social and political principle were set down. Between the 1920s and the Yan'an period, the term was subject to limited contestation, which famously exploded in Mao Zedong's attacks on Ding Ling for her criticism of the Party's approach to women in 1942. In particular, meanings were debated and contested around the mediating influence of the individualist strains of the May Fourth legacy on the more collectivist-oriented principles of the communist-led women's movement. The debate was never an equal one, though, for despite the extraordinary influence on the early communists' lives and ideological outlooks of the May Fourth movement, "individualism" was almost from the outset used as a synonym for selfish, morally suspect, and eventually bourgeois and reactionary tendencies. The dominant meanings and tasks signified by the word were clearly established in its early usage, when tight links – to the point of total overlap – were established between the meanings inscribed in women's and social/national liberation. The specific referents of liberation were, of course, modified to correspond with the changing definitions of the Party policy priorities and emphases. However, the overriding collectivist and social principles which gave the term liberation its essential meanings in Party discourse were rarely disturbed.

From this perspective, the Yan'an condemnation of Ding Ling and her own recantation reinforced meanings and practices associated with *funü jiefang* that were already well established. If Mao Zedong's response to Ding Ling was to emphasise the "unity" of women with men in the processes of women's liberation, then this signalled a consolidation of previous tendencies within an episteme already established in the early stages of the communist movement and which continued as part of communist rhetoric, with only momentary disruptions until the late 1970s. The place of *jiefang* as a keyword within the Communist Party's exegetical lexicon signified not a change of course from previous usage and application, but rather the definitive reinscription of women in positions already established for them as vehicles of others' power.

One of Li Xiaojiang's principal arguments concerning the different stages of the women's movement in China concentrates on a key distinction between the revolutionary (1921–1978) and reform periods. She argues that the shortcomings in achievements of gender equality in the first period were the necessary effect of an understanding of women's liberation as something to be bestowed or imposed by the Party authorities, and not as a process formulated in autonomous spaces defined by women themselves. To use the terms of a recent article of hers and Zhang Xiaodan's, the "stumbling block in Chinese women's progress toward their own emancipation, in fact, has been that many Chinese women have been wholly passive in the liberation process."[63] The term liberation as I have analysed it brings an additional element to her argument. For it suggests that while the Party consistently defined the principal aims and processes of the women's movement, and stressed the importance of women's agency in accordance with its strategic identification of the goals and processes of the revolution as a whole, its "bestowal" of policies and practices defined as furthering women's interests in their own liberation did not, fundamentally, construct women as agents of their own transformation. Indeed, the Party's conservative response once ordinary women did treat themselves as agents, in seeking divorce, for example, or in selecting a marriage partner, suggests that female agency outside officially sanctioned parameters was seen to disturb women's capacity to function as vehicles of power.[64]

This analysis of the term *jiefang* suggests that the Party's limitations in implementing its commitment to achieving gender equality were fully inscribed in the meanings of the word itself. The term positioned its users in such a way that they had no alternative but to support it, or be rejected by it. The intersection between the gendered and societal associations of liberation severely limited women's capacity to identify themselves as agents of a process of transformation of gender relations. To a certain extent, by contrast, it positioned them as what Foucault called "vehicles of power," to realise aims that had no more than an indirect bearing on gender relations. Its identification of particular goals and objectives, its disqualification of others, and its dissociation from the possibility of formulating a gender analysis in language, all determined the outcomes of its application. The term "liberation" was associated with "women" in various practices and policies, but was rarely linked to notions of gender as a site of struggle. So, while, for example, "women's liberation" was often presented as a yardstick measuring the success of social and national liberation, this did not, in itself, invoke gender relations as a site of social transformation.

In this light, this analysis of *funü jiefang* clarifies a familiar paradox which long preoccupied Western feminist commentators.[65] For years, Western feminists treated with incredulity Chinese women's frequent claims to be liberated. How could they be, without sexual autonomy, or without the individual freedom to choose not to marry, for example? Western feminist objections, however, derived from a very different conceptualisation of "liberation", situated with the liberal Western discourse of individual rights and freedoms, permitting a significant but, at the time unacknowledged, slippage between Chinese and Western uses of "liberation." The boundaries of meaning of "liberation" within which Chinese women were working excluded such matters to another site of political identification. From this perspective, the assertions of Chinese commentators were much nearer to the "truth" in claiming that they had been liberated than their Western sisters were prepared to countenance.

NOTES

1 A first draft of this paper was presented at a conference on Keywords of the Chinese Revolution, held at the Centre for Pacific Asia Studies, Stockholm University, 27–28 February, 1997. I would like to thank Michael Schoenhals and Jeffrey Wasserstrom for supporting the initial research for this paper through inviting me to participate in the Keywords project. I would also like to thank both of them, as well as Stephanie Donald, Stephan Feuchtwang, Gail Hershatter and Steve Smith for their many thoughtful comments and suggestions on the arguments developed in this paper.

2 I am using "feminists" in this context as a term of convenience to refer to women's studies scholars, activists in the Women's Federation and in the emerging NGOs – a diverse range of women committed to discussing and resolving issues of gender discrimination.

3 For further discussion about women's complaints about their "double burden" in the "Maoist" period, see for example Elisabeth Croll, *Feminism and Socialism in China*, London: Routledge and Kegan Paul, 1978, pp. 266–7, 328–9.

4 Phyllis Andors, *The Unfinished Liberation of Chinese Women, 1949–1980*, Bloomington: Indiana University Press, 1983; Kay Ann Johnson, *Women, the Family and Peasant Revolution in China*, Chicago: University of Chicago Press, 1983; Marilyn Young, "Chicken Little in China: Some Reflections on Women", in Arif Dirlik and Maurice Meisner (eds), *Marxism and the Chinese Experience*, M. E. Sharpe, 1989, pp. 253–68; Maxine Molyneux, "Family reform in socialist states; the hidden agenda", *Feminist Review*, 21 (1985): 47–66.

5 Women's Federation analyses suggest, for example, that higher rates of female unemployment, or factory managers' preference for male or unmarried female labour, are at root caused by economic constraints, the effect of which are gender disparities.

6 Of course, women's equality with men [*nan'nü pingdeng*] continues to be invoked in the relevant laws of the People's Republic of China, such as the Constitution, the Marriage Law (1981), the Law on the Protection of Women's Rights (1992). But as the effects of marketisation of the economy continue to exacerbate gender inequalities and divisions in China, official references to '*nan'nü pingdeng*" and "*funü jiefang*" are becoming noticeably fewer in official policy pronouncements and commentaries.

7 David Apter and Tony Saich, *Revolutionary Discourse in Mao's Republic*, Cambridge, Mass.: Harvard University Press, 1994, p. 6. Yan'an, in Shaanxi province, was the communist base area and centre of the communist-led movement of resistance against Japan between 1936 and 1944. It is particularly associated with Mao's consolidation of power over his rivals, through his speeches on art and literature (which established the principles of artistic and literary creation that were to dominate during the following decades) and the famous "rectification campaign" of 1942–43, which in Apter and Saich's terms, sought to create an "exegetical bonding" – an exercise in intellectual and moral remoulding designed to produce ideological uniformity – within the Party.

8 In personal interviews, a number of Chinese women who identify with the "masculinist" images of female gender of the 1950s–1970s have told me that the gender "sameness" of dress in those days contributed to a sense of being first and foremost "persons" rather than women. While this view clearly demands more analysis than I can give it here, it also indicates some of the main lines of women's memories of that past. See also Rae Yang's memory of her appearance as a Red Guard in her recent *Spider Eaters: A Memoir*, Berkeley:

University of California Press, 1997, p. 213. In a recent special issue of *boundary* 2, Dai Jinhua has also written about the "imagined nostalgia" for the gendered positioning of this earlier revolutionary discourse. Various women who are now actively involved in establishing new organisations to represent and defend women's interests in China have in private conversation with me indicated their dismay at the way In which young women are now obsessed with interest in appearance, with romance and wealth. A number of them seem to feel that the commercialised and sexualised images of femininity which abound in China's current media and advertising and film industries impose much greater constraints on the possibilities for women's full liberation than the supposedly gender-neutral images of the 1950s to the 1970s.

9 Ample evidence from interviews, autobiographical accounts and other writings also indicates the excitement many women felt when given the possibility of engaging in public activities through challenging the association between women and the private sphere. See, for example, Rae Yang's *Spider Eaters* or Yue Daiyun and Carolyn Wakeman's *To the Storm: The Odyssey of a Revolutionary Chinese Woman*, Berkeley: University of California Press, 1985. *Jiefang* certainly did signify such a challenge, but not in ways that could withstand the reassertion of sexualised and domesticised femininity that re-emerged together with the market in the 1980s.

10 The appropriate "naming" of the Chinese word for "feminism" was a particularly heated aspect of debate at a conference on Chinese Women and Feminist Thought held in Beijing by the Institute of Philosophy and the Sino-British Summer School in Philosophy in June 1995. Some contributors to the debate felt that *"nüquanzhuyi"* (lit. women's power-ism) resonated too closely with the pejorative "bourgeois" ideology so long associated with it in communist discourse to be able to use it in a new context. Despite the participants' critiques of the practices associated with *funü jiefang*, and despite their commitment to broadly feminist goals, few of them identified themselves as "feminists."

11 Harriet Evans, "Defining difference: the 'scientific' construction of female sexuality and gender in the People's Republic of China", *SIGNS: Journal of Women in Culture and Society*, 20, 2, (Winter 1994–5): 357–96; Harriet Evans, *Women and Sexuality in China: Dominant Discourses of Female Sexuality and Gender since 1949*, Cambridge: Polity Press, 1997; Frank Dikotter, *Sex, Culture and Modernity in China*, London: Hurst and Company, 1995.

12 In correspondence with me, Steve Smith has pointed out that the term *"jiefang"* was not tied exclusively or even mainly to national liberation in the early days. In his 1915 "Address to Youth," *Duxiu wencun* [Chen Duxiu's Collected Works], Vol. 2, Hong Kong, 1965, Chen Duxiu talked of *"jiefang"* in terms of liberation from monarchy, from oppressive government, religious tyranny and economic exploitation. Later, in another essay in January 1920 entitled *"Jiefang"* [Liberation], he talked about breaking old forms and liberating new ones. In this sense, "liberation" emerges as a polyvalent notion applicable to different contexts and capable of forging discursive links between different political struggles. While I agree that it was applied distinctively in different contexts, I argue that the general/social/national aspects of *"jiefang"* consistently occupied a more privileged position in the CCP's political discourse than the other, more focused, applications of the term.

13 Michael Schoenhals discusses the key political distinctions between "People" [*renmin*] and *"fei renmin"* [non-people], which together constituted the indefinite category of persons ("men and women indefinitely"). See Michael Schoenhals, "'Non-People' in the People's Republic of China", Indiana East

Asian Working Paper Series on Language and Politics in Modern China, Paper 4, July 1994.

14 This gloss on the class aspects of national liberation derives from Mao Zedong's 1949 essay "On the People's Democratic Dictatorship", *Selected Works*, Vol. 4, Beijing: Foreign Languages Press, 1969, pp. 411–24.

15 Mao Zedong, "Report on an Investigation of the Hunan Peasant Movement", Selected Works, Vol. 1, Beijing: Renmin chubanshe, 1968, p. 31.

16 See Christina Gilmartin's *Engendering the Chinese Revolution*, Berkeley: University of California Press, 1995, pp. 24–30, for a discussion about the male activists in the early stages of the communist-led women's movement. A number of the early essays of these male participants are included in Vol. 2 of *Zhongguo funü yundong lishi ziliao* [Materials on the history of the Chinese women's movement], Beijing: Renmin chubanshe, 1988, and in *Wusi shiqi funü wenti wenxuan* [Selected documents on women's issues during the May Fourth period], Beijing: Zhongguo funü chubanshe, 1981.

17 See "Zhongguo gongchandang di'erci quanguo daibiao dahui guanyu funü yundong de jueyi" [Resolution of the Second National Congress of the CCP concerning the women's movement], in Vol. 2 of *Zhongguo funü yundong lishi ziliao*, pp. 29–30. See also Lü Meihe and Zheng Yongfu (eds), *Zhongguo funü yundong, 1840–1921*, Henan: Henan renmin chubanshe, 1990, pp. 378–9.

18 "Zhongguo gongchandang disanci quanguo daibiao dahui guanyu funü yundong de jueyi an" [Decision of the Third National Congress of the CCP concerning the women's movement], in Vol. 2 of *Zhongguo funü yundong lishi ziliao*, pp. 68–9.

19 In many ways, the literal translations of these terms offer as partial an understanding of their meanings and uses as would simple use of the word "feminism" to translate the entire bunch. For example, *nüquanzhuyi*, here literally rendered as "women's power-ism," was much more closely linked with the liberal notion of women's equal rights with men than with women asserting their power over, or against men. I here offer these literal translations as a way of indicating the range of words used for similar projects and principles. The distinctions between the terms also overlap with Tani Barlow's discussion about the different terms in Chinese for "women." *Nüquan* refers to concepts of women's rights, whereas *nüxing* leans more to an essentialist gender position for women, according to which notions of womanhood are grounded in basic, natural gender differences. See Tani E. Barlow, "Theorizing Woman: Funü, Guojia, Jiating", in Angela Zito and Tani E. Barlow (eds), *Body, Subject and Power in China*, Chicago: University of Chicago Press, 1994, pp. 253–89.

20 Li Da, "Nüzi jiefang lun" [On women's liberation], (1919) in *Li Da wenji* [Li Da's Writings]. Vol. 1, Beijing: Renmin chubanshe, 1980, pp. 9–11.

21 Li Dazhao, "Xiandai de nüquan yundong" [The modern women's movement], in *Zhongguo funü yundong lishi ziliao*, Vol. 2. pp. 49–52.

22 Xiao Chu'nü, "Nüzi jiefang' de genben yi" [The basic meaning of women's liberation], in *Zhongguo funü yundong lishi ziliao*, Vol. 2, pp. 98–101.

23 "Guangxi funü lianhe hui chengli xuanyan" [Declaration on the establishment of the Guangxi Women's Federation], October 1925, in *Zhongguo funü yundong lishi ziliao*, Vol. 2, pp. 408–9.

24 For example, "Guangdong funü jiefang xiehui diyici daibiao dahui ji yijue an" [Decision of the First Congress of the Guangdong Women's Liberation Association], in *Zhongguo funü yundong lishi ziliao*, Vol. 2, pp. 672–5.

25 Yang Zhihua, "Zhongguo funü yundong zuiyan" [The errors of China's women's movement], in *Zhongguo funü yundong lishi ziliao*, Vol. 2, pp. 555–61.

26 Li Xiaojiang, "With what discourse do we consider women: who created the concept and defined it?", paper prepared for conference on Chinese Women and Feminist Thought, Beijing, June 1995.

27 In its political sense, "liberation" (or liberty and liberator) makes occasional appearances in the sixteenth century but became more common in the middle of the nineteenth and especially the twentieth centuries, when it became the name for movements of resistance to Fascism and then against occupying powers or forces. See Raymond Williams, *Keywords: A Vocabulary of Culture and Society*, London: Fontana Press, 1988 (1976), pp. 181–2.

28 Williams, *Keywords*, p. 183.

29 Williams, *Keywords*, p. 183

30 Gilmartin, *Engendering the Chinese Revolution*, pp. 7–8. My reading of the term *funü jiefang* differs from Gilmartin's in another significant way. While the Chinese Communists of the early 1920s did not reject the *nüquan yundong*, their dominant definitions of *funü jiefang* clearly eclipsed alternatives by the mid-1920s.

31 Though not specifically included in the present discussion, my analysis here also draws on detailed readings of writings about women and gender issues between the late 1940s and the post-Mao reform period. See, in particular my unpublished doctoral dissertation "The Official Construction of Female Sexuality and Gender in the People's Republic of China, 1949–1959", and *Women and Sexuality in China*.

32 Schoenhals, " 'Non-People' in the People's Republic of China", p. 1.

33 My theoretical approach draws on the work of Bourdieu, particularly with reference to his concept of "habitus," and to his work on legitimate language, interpretation and social change. I also draw on Henrietta Moore's discussion about dominant discourses and the ways in which they produce social and gendered subjects. See Pierre Bourdieu, *The Logic of Practice*, Cambridge: Polity Press, 1990; *Language and Symbolic Power*, Cambridge: Polity Press, 1991; Henrietta Moore, *A Passion for Difference*, Cambridge: Polity Press, 1994.

34 Xiang Ying, "Women de nü zhanshi" [Our female comrades-in-arms] (1940), in *Zhongguo funü yundong lishi ziliao*, Vol. 4, pp. 409–10.

35 Deng Yingchao, "Zai Zhongguo funü di'erci quan guo daibiao dahui shang de gongzuo baogao" [Work Report to the Second National Congress of Women], 16 April, 1953, in *Zhonghua quanguo funü lianhehui sishi nian*, 1991, p. 387. Deng Yingchao became vice-head of the All China Women's Federation in 1949.

36 "Zhongguo gongchandang di'erci daibiao dahui de jueyi" [Resolution of the Second Congress of the CCP], 1922, *Zhongguo funü yundong lishi ziliao*, Vol. 2, pp. 29–30.

37 "Zhonggong zhongyang tonggao dibashiwu hao" [Circular 85 of the Chinese Communist Party's Central Committee], 21 July 1930, in *Zhongguo funü yundong lishi ziliao*, Vol. 3, pp. 63–4.

38 "Jinian guoji funü jie guangfan kaizhan funü yundong" [Commemorate international women's day and extensively develop the women's movement], in *Shaan-gan-ning bianqu funü yundong wenxian ziliao xuanbian* [Selected materials on the women's movement in the Shaanxi-Gansu-Ningxia border region], Shaanbei sheng funü lianhehui, 1982, pp. 80–2. Xiang Ying elaborated a bit more on this aspect of *jiefang* In her "Our female comrades-in-arms": "Women's liberation and social liberation cannot be separated, and it is inappropriate to seek women's liberation detached from social liberation . . . Women must participate in the revolutionary struggle and must unite with all revolutionary forces to struggle for the victory of the revolution, for only with revolutionary victory can the victory of women's liberation be won . . .

Women's liberation is the glorious future to social progress and the progress of mankind. See *Zhongguo funü yundong lishi ziliao*, Vol. 4, pp. 409–10.

39 Shi Xiuyun, "Bianqu funü yundong de renwu" [The tasks of the women's movement in the border area], March 1938, in *Shaan-gan-ning bianqu funü yundong wenxian ziliao xuanbian*, pp. 17–22.

40 "Zhongguo gongchandang zhongyang weiyuanhui guanyu muqian jiefang qu nongcun funü gongzuo de jueding" [Decision of the CCP's Central Committee on current work among rural women in the liberated areas], December 1948, In *Zhongguo funü yundong zhongyao wenxian*, Beijing: Renmin chubanshe, 1979, p. 20.

41 Deng Yingchao, "Work Report at the Second National Congress of Chinese Women".

42 Zhang Qinqiu, "Dongyuan funü can zhan yu baohu funü qieshen lieyi de guanxi" [The relationship between mobilising women to participate in the war and protecting women's personal interests], in *Zhongguo funü yundong zhongyao wenxian* [Important documents of the Chinese women's movement], Beijing: Renmin chubanshe, 1979, p. 131.

43 In fact, the *"jiefang"* position was clear in numerous documents from the early 1920s. For example, a 1923 article on the origins and influence of the "women's liberation movement" [*funü jiefang yundong*] published in *Women's Weekly* argued that earlier proposals for the women's movement were not, in themselves, bad, but their "individualistic tendency" to stress women's particular position in matters concerning marriage and love, for example, seemed more prominent than attention to collective issues such as the welfare of humanity, and were having fragmentary and divisive effects. See Hui Daiying, "Funü jiefang yundong de youlai he qi yingxiang" [The origins and influence of the women's liberation movement], October 1923, in *Zhongguo funü yundong lishi ziliao*, Vol. 2, pp. 94–6. Another 1925 article from Guangxi Province argued that the "women's rights movement" was both unreasonable and divisive, for it ignored that fact that men were as oppressed as women. "Guangxi funü lianhehui chengli xuanyan" (Declaration on the establishment of the Guangxi Women's Association], *Zhongguo funü yundong lishi ziliao*, Vol. 2, pp. 408–9.

44 "Zhongguo gongchandang disanci quanguo daibiao dahui guanyu funü yundong de jueyi an", in Vol. 2 of *Zhongguo funü yundong lishi ziliao*, pp. 68–9.

45 "Henan funü gongzuo dagang" [An outline of woman-work in Henan], August 1928, in *Zhongguo funü yundong lishi ziliao*, Vol. 3, p. 27.

46 Ou Mengjue, "Lüe tan funü gongzuo zuofeng" [Talking about the work style of woman-work] November 1941, *Shaan-gan-ning bianqu funü yundong wenxian ziliao xuanbian*, p. 136.

47 For further discussion of the "gender retrenchment" in implementing the Marriage Law after 1953, see Evans 1991, and Croll 1981, pp. 184–8. See also Evans, *Women and Sexuality*, pp. 129–34, 195–8. It is only relatively recently, with the rapid increase in women's demands for divorce from abusive and violent husbands, and revelations about domestic violence and marital rape, that a more conflictual tone has entered into discussion about gender relations.

48 "Guangdong funü jiefang xiehui diyici daibiao dahui ji jueyi an" [Documents of the First Congress and Resolution of the Guangdong Women's Association], May 1926, in *Zhongguo funü yundong lishi ziliao*, Vol. 2, p. 674.

49 He Xiangning, "Guomin geming shi funü weiyi de shenglu" [The national revolution is the only lifeline for women], 1925, in *Zhongguo funü yundong lishi ziliao*, Vol. 2, pp. 285–6. Though this article does not include analysis of Guomindang approaches to the women's movement, it is interesting to note

that though He Xiangning was a member of the Guomindang, her views on the positioning of women through *funü jiefang* were similar to those of contemporary CCP activists. Contrary to retrospectively applied arguments that the CCP was alone in denying the individual political space in the course of revolution, her interpretation of *funü jiefang* is one example of the ways in which the GMD's emphasis on national unity and its understanding of national and social need in this early period intersected with that of the CCP. An early activist in Sun Yatsen's Revolutionary Alliance in Tokyo, and married to Liao Zhongkao, He Xiangning was appointed to the directorship of the Nationalists' Central Women's Department in 1924.

50 "Hunan gongzuo jihua dagang" [Outline for a work plan in Hunan], 1929, *Zhongguo funü yundong lishi ziliao*, Vol. 3, pp. 55–6.

51 Xiang Ying, in *Zhongguo funü yundong lishi ziliao*, Vol. 4, pp. 409–10.

52 As references in earlier sections of this chapter indicate, these terms reinscribed liberation with notions of individualism, femininity and elitism which were anathema to the Party's collective emphasis. See Tani Barlow's "Theorising Woman: Funü, Guojia, Jiating" for a detailed discussion about the different positioning of women through deployment of these different terms. Tani Barlow's frequently cited analysis was arguably the first of its kind with reference to the contemporary women's movements in China to look at the importance of language and discourse in defining gender subject positions for women.

53 While conducting research for this chapter, it became obvious to me that compilations of Party documents that did not specifically refer to women contained virtually no references to women in their contents pages. See for example the authoritative *neibu* collection published in two volumes as the *Zhongguo gongchandang xinwen gongzuo wenjian huibian*, Beijing: Xinhua chubanshe, 1980. At the risk of pushing the argument too far, the editorial exclusion of women's issues from compilations on central political matters could be seen as a further subordination of women's issues from the significant affairs of state.

54 "Minxi suweiai zhengfu tonggao diqi hao" [No. 7 circular of the Fujian Soviet government], December 1930, *Zhongguo funü yundong lishi ziliao*, Vol. 3, pp. 97–9.

55 Ou Xiamin, in May 1926 suggested, for example, that it was women's responsibility to stop thinking about their conflicts with men. *Zhongguo funü yundong lishi ziliao*, Vol. 2, p. 548.

56 Arif Dirlik, "Revolutionary Hegemony and the Language of Revolution" in Dirlik and Meisner (eds), *Marxism and the Chinese Experience*, p. 27.

57 Borrowing from Tani Barlow's analysis, *funü jiefang* could not position *nüxing* or *nüren*, except possibly as class elements excluded by *fenü jiefang*'s association with the *renmin* as defined by the Party. For the most of the period under analysis here, *nüxing* or *nüren* denoted gendered behaviours, aptitudes and attitudes which were considered ideologically unsound by the Party exponents of *funü jiefang*.

58 The well-known and radical novelist and short-story writer Ding Ling wrote an essay entitled "Thoughts on March 8" which appeared on the literary page of *The Liberation Daily* in Yan'an on 9 March 1942. In it she criticised the Party's policy of gender unity, and drew attention to its failure to live up to its claims to liberate women. Women, she wrote, were still subject to contempt and misery, were overworked, were expected to play a double role, and were criticised if they failed in either. The Party attacked her for her "narrow feminist standpoint" and for ignoring the difficulties in forging new social and

economic roles for women. Later, in an interview with Gunther Stein Ding Ling retracted her position and agreed that the first priority for women and men was to co-operate and work together for the revolution. See Croll, *Feminism and Socialism in China*, pp. 212–24, and Delia Davin, *Woman-Work: Women and the Party in Revolutionary China*, Oxford: Clarendon Press, 1976, pp. 36–9.

59 Bourdieu, *Language and Symbolic Power*, pp. 50–2.

60 Moore, *A Passion for Difference*, pp. 49–66.

61 Meng Yue, "Female Images and National Myth", in Tani E. Barlow (ed.), *Gender Politics in Modern China*, Durham, NC, and London: Duke University Press, 1993, pp. 119–22. The earliest version of *The White Haired Girl* was a *yangge* opera created in the late 1930s by teams of writers and musicians doing anti-Japanese war propaganda. The first published version was an opera script in 1942 in Yan'an, and English-language translation of which was published by Yang Xianyi and Gladys Yang in 1954, as *The White Haired Girl*, Beijing: Foreign Languages Press, 1954. The first film of the story was made by the Northeast Film Studio in 1950, directed by Shui Hua. It was later produced as a ballet by the Shanghai Ballet Institue, and became one of the approved eight model plays during the Cultural Revolution.

62 Apter and Saich, *Revolutionary Discourse in Mao's Republic*, pp. 66–7, 300.

63 Li Xiaojiang and Zhang Xiaodan, "Creating a Space for Women: Women's Studies in China in the 1980s", *SIGNS*, 20, 1 (Autumn 1994): 146.

64 Here, I am referring to the Party leadership's response to the disruption of families and local communities which followed the initial encouragement to women to make use of their new rights as set out in the 1950 Marriage Law. By 1953, alarming evidence about the numbers of divorces, women's suicides, and acts of violence against women, resulted in a radical modification in the implementation of the Marriage Law to discourage women from disruptive acts and to insist on their responsibilities to maintaining family and social stability.

65 I would like to thank Gail Hershatter for suggesting this last point. In a recent private discussion about her own work on women and gender in the rural sector in the 1950s, she also suggested that the interpretation of "liberation" I have offered in this chapter might contribute to elucidating other arguments put forward by Chinese women about the non-existence of gender in the Maoist period as a category of understanding social relations and transformation.

10

REVOLUTIONARY RUDENESS

The language of Red Guards and rebel workers in China's Cultural Revolution

Elizabeth J. Perry and Li Xun

Throughout the twentieth century, in China as elsewhere, political activists in opposition (as well as people in positions of power) sometimes used very harsh rhetoric to castigate those with whom they disagreed. And in China, again as in other settings, violent language was sometimes accompanied by physical assaults, but sometimes seems to have served instead as a substitute for them. One important time when rhetorical and physical violence were particularly closely linked was the Cultural Revolution era, a decade that remains in many ways the least well-understood part of China's twentieth century. Was the "Great Proletarian Cultural Revolution" (its full official title) that was launched in 1966 a bold effort to keep the Geming from ossifying, in the way that the Russian Revolution had? Was it instead a desperate effort by Mao and those close to him, including his wife, Jiang Qing, to settle scores with political rivals? Was it a top-down or bottom-up initiative, or a strange combination of both things, with student Red Guards inspired by devotion to Mao sometimes leading and sometimes being led by those much further up the CCP hierarchy? Was it, almost from the moment it began, more a civil war, fought by opposing sets of urban guerrillas, than a mass movement, or was it a complex amalgamation of both of these things? And, as with pre-1949 upsurges, was the Cultural Revolution so differently inflected in various parts of China that we need to think of multiple overlapping cultural revolutions? These are just some of the questions that remain unsettled.

One thing that is clear about the period, though, as Perry and Li demonstrate very effectively below, is that it was a time when words mattered, serving alternately as weapons and as shields in battles that could begin with polemics and end with bloodshed (or vice versa). This was a time when, as novelists and the authors of memoirs have made clear, what you said or wrote could make the difference between whether you were seen as a member of the proletariat or a member of the bourgeoisie. This was true even though, according to Marxism, social classes are not supposed to be determined by language but rather by relations to the means of production.

Class struggle was exalted by the student Red Guards and their laboring counterparts, but it was transmogrified into something very different from a battle between economically defined groups. Rather, as Perry and Li show, it became a struggle between sets of people divided into "classes" on the basis of everything from their beliefs to their patterns of speech. In analyzing some aspects of this discursively driven form of class struggle, Perry and Li highlight both the peculiarities of the Cultural Revolution milieu and its parallels to other settings in which rhetorical and physical violence have become linked. This takes them backwards into China's past and out toward France, a country whose revolution has received a great deal of attention of late from historians interested in the politics of language and the language of politics. The result is a short essay that covers a great deal of ground in terms of both textual analysis and laying out an agenda for future comparative and China-specific research.

* * *

Introduction

Revolutions spark fundamental changes in the way people think about the world. Since people generally think with words, one measure of a movement's revolutionary impact is the extent to which it generates new wordings. Thus recent reappraisals of the French Revolution, for example, have focused considerable attention on the language of the participants.[1]

In the case of the Chinese Revolution scholars are also beginning to devote serious consideration to the question of linguistic change.[2] But the Chinese case is particularly complicated. Unlike the French Revolution – which is usually dated rather narrowly as the events surrounding the storming of the Bastille in 1789 – what we refer to as the Chinese Revolution is usually said to have begun a century and a half ago (with the Opium Wars of the mid-nineteenth century) and to be still underway today.[3] The linguistic issues surrounding such a long and momentous period are obviously complex. To try to cut into this unwieldy subject, this chapter will examine but a small temporal slice – the decade of the Cultural Revolution (1966–76), especially its early years, 1966–68. The choice is not entirely arbitrary, for as one student of the subject points out, "rhetoric played a more integral role in the Cultural Revolution than in previous movements."[4]

Even when we delimit the time period, however, a further difficulty remains: the substantial cultural and linguistic gap that separates China from the West. Although Western scholars are increasingly interested in Chinese revolutionary discourse,[5] seldom are they linguistically and culturally equipped to do the topic justice. The co-authorship of this paper – joining a Chinese participant in the Cultural Revolution with a Western student of the Chinese Revolution – is an attempt to help bridge the abyss.

As a very preliminary foray into uncharted waters, this paper will briefly consider several aspects of Cultural Revolution language as it took shape in the writings and speech of young Red Guards. We touch upon the use of military terminology, the techniques of slandering one's opponents, the conventions of color coding, and the like. Although each of these features has received some attention from previous analysts, earlier studies have overlooked an important thread linking these rhetorical practices: a striking characteristic of Red Guard language – at least to the native Chinese ear – was its *vulgarity*. The use of curses and other crude expressions was a conscious effort on the part of rebellious young students to adopt what they took to be the revolutionary language of the masses.

Recent approaches to revolutionary culture, in contrast to an earlier generation of scholarship,[6] highlight its socially *variegated* character. Thus Robert Darnton, in his masterful study of *l'histoire des mentalites* in eighteenth-century France, devotes separate chapters to peasants, urban artisans, bourgeois, police, and intellectuals.[7] Each social group, it turns out, exhibited distinctive modes of thought, talk, and action.

In the case of the Chinese Cultural Revolution, this sort of social differentiation remains relatively unexplored.[8] The comparison, which we draw toward the end of this paper, between students and workers is intended to open a discussion on this important issue. As we will suggest, however, the term "Great *Proletarian* Cultural Revolution" is something of a misnomer. Important as workers were in the later stages of the movement, the cultural transformation of this era – reflected in linguistic change – was largely the work of brash young students. Despite their pretense of embracing proletarian rhetoric, these fledgling intellectuals were in fact advocating a type of language that was rather far removed from that of the Chinese working class.

Red Guard crudeness

One of the more arresting features of the language of the Chinese Cultural Revolution was simply how crude and rude it was. The trend was prefigured in a seminal series of big-character posters penned by Beijing Red Guards in the summer of 1966 and subsequently emulated by rebel organizations around the country.

Still operating under the thumb of school work teams, these student Red Guards nevertheless made clear their defiance of conventional authority. Titled "Long Live the Revolutionary Rebel Spirit of the Proletariat," their poster series raised the famous slogan of "rebellion" (*zaofan*) that quickly caught fire on campuses across the land. While the Beijing Red Guards are widely credited with this contribution to Cultural Revolution sloganeering,[9] another aspect of their linguistic influence has received less attention. Yet every bit as significant as the introduction of the electrifying new slogan of rebellion was the crude language that appeared in several of the posters: "as for balance and tact, damn it all to hell" (*shenma quanmian celue, gun tama de dan*)!

The imprecation "damn it" (*tama de*) had originated in the spoken vernacular of North China. Prior to the Cultural Revolution, it was rarely found in written works and then only in fictional literature to describe the speech of coarse characters. In the Red Guard posters, by contrast, this vulgar phrase was being used in a formal essay to clinch a political argument. Although both the content and the language of these big-character posters aroused the ire of the work teams, they caught the sympathetic eye of Jiang Qing, who shared them with her husband. In a few days Chairman Mao's verdict was publicized: "Very good big-character posters." Immediately the essays were distributed and imitated by radicals across the country. Not only rebellion, but rudeness, was thereby justified. "Damn it" became a hallmark of Red Guard phraseology – an expletive that served to differentiate these young rebels from their more complacent classmates by demonstrating their utter disdain for traditional linguistic restraint.

Soon every Red Guard poster, whether the content called for it or not, inserted several "damn its" or "damn it to hells". During the highpoint of the Red Guard movement in August 1966, these curses seemed omnipresent. The then popular adage "On Blood Lineage" and the related Red Guard song "Gloomy Ghosts" contained a string of such epithets appended as slogans. As the song goes,

> If one's old man is a hero, his son is a brave fellow.
> If one's old man is a reactionary, his son is a bastard.
> If you're a revolutionary, then stand up.
> If you're not a revolutionary, then damn you to hell.
> Damn, damn, damn, damn you to hell!

The insertion of these colloquial North China swear words had a shocking effect, especially in southern dialects of Chinese.

The phrase "damn it" was the harbinger of a veritable flood of vulgarity that engulfed popular and official publications alike. Expletives like "bastard" (*hundan*), "to hell" (*gundan*), "son of a bitch" (*wang ba dan*), "cuckold kid" (*wangba gaozi*), "go to hell" (*jian gui qu*), and "damnable" (*gaisi*) became commonplace in big-character posters, handbills, and even government directives.[10] Newly coined invectives, e.g., "rotten dog's head" (*zalan goutou*), also made an appearance. What had previously passed as proper language was now regarded as altogether too conformist. Polite phrasing was reviled as "the disgusting etiquette of the bourgeois and feudal classes." The cruder one's language, the closer one felt to the workers, peasants and soldiers. The less refined, the more revolutionary.

The young students did not sever all identification with the "feudal" Chinese literati tradition, however. As an ex-Red Guard remembered, "Following the practice of the ancients who composed couplets to commemorate staying somewhere, Red Guards covered the walls of temples with untidy characters like 'XXX of Class 302, Fudan University Shanghai, visited this place September 20, 1966.'" This habit exercised other Red Guards, as evidenced in one defiant – and of course ironic – wall scribbling: "Damn it all, I oppose writing characters all over these walls!"[11] But Red Guard graffiti was in any event no more than a faint echo of the cultivated tradition of literati travel inscriptions.

Vulgarity permeated the spoken language as well. Firsthand accounts of Red Guard experiences are replete with coarse verbiage. One former Red Guard described a conflict over space on a train: "they began to curse those inside: 'You rotten sons of bitches, sitting in there so cozy, get the hell out right away. . . . Those inside came back strongly. 'If you dare, I'll push your face in'."[12] This sort of gutter language had long been the trademark of Chinese gangsters, but never before had it enjoyed such currency among the educated.

Vilification of the other

The general corruption of language brought with it a whole new vocabulary of abuse toward one's opponents. Terms intended to belittle or dehumanize members of an enemy faction became standard fare in political debate: "tiny minority" (*ji shaoshu*), "handful" (*yi xiaocuo*), "little reptile" (*xiao pachong*), "big pickpocket" (*da pashou*), "big black umbrella" (*da heisan*), "big black hand" (*da heishou*), "cow-devils and snake-spirits" (*niugui sheshen*), "evil wind" (*yao feng*), "out-and-out scoundrel" (*hunzhang touding*). The emotions, motivations and behaviors of one's rivals were characterized as "gall" (*dangan*), "monstrous audacity" (*goudan baotian*), "vain attempts" (*wangtu*), "threats" (*yangyan*), "howls" (*jiaorang*), "clamorings" (*jiaoxiao*), "false pretenses" (*menghun guoguan*), "new counteroffensives" (*xin fanpu*), "launching unbridled attacks" (*dasi gongji*), "inflaming and agitating" (*shanfeng dianhuo*).

Metaphors of vampirism and bestiality were commonplace in the stinging criticisms leveled against so-called "enemies of the people." One former Red Guard recalls the shock he experienced when he came upon a big-character poster portraying his father as sub-human: "He used the *blood he sucked* away to fatten himself up, and what did he give the people? Not artwork, but shit, garbage, poisonous weeds. . . . We now order Liang Shan to confess his crimes, or else we will break his *dog's head*!!!!!"[13] A popular refrain sung by the Red Guards vowed that "armed with Mao Zedong's Thought, we'll wipe out all *pests and vermin*."[14]

The phrase "cow-devils and snake-spirits," rooted in Buddhist demonology, was an especially potent weapon in the battle to demonize one's opponents.[15] As an ex-Red Guard explained, "We forced the teachers to wear caps and collars which stated things like 'I am a monster [snake-spirit]'. . . . While we respected them before, our feelings changed to hatred as soon as they were denounced as 'monsters and ghosts [cow-devils and snake-spirits]'."[16] Another Red Guard, searching for his friend and her grandmother, was informed by an inhabitant of their former village: "People said they were monsters and ghosts. They can't stay in our town."[17] To be deemed "monsters and ghosts" was to be banished from the community.

Women were often likened to the White Bone Demon (*baigu jing*), a nefarious and chameleonic serpent from the Buddhist-inspired novel, *Journey to the West*. A Red Guard remembered the poster attacking his teacher: "Guo Pei is a venomous snake who disguised herself as a beautiful woman. . . . We must break the venomous snake's spine!"[18] Accusations of promiscuity and bestiality were linked with political crimes, as in the common epithets "counterrevolutionary whore" and "counterrevolutionary savage."[19]

Dehumanizing terminology permeated popular and official discourse alike.[20] On 1 June 1966, *People's Daily* published an editorial titled "Sweep out All Cow-Devils and Snake-Spirits." The following spring, the public denunciation of top-Party officials Liu Shaoqi, Deng Tuo and Tao Zhu was punctuated by strident cries of "Down with Liu, Deng and Tao! Down with cow-devils and snake-spirits!"[21] Verbal abuse was accented by material symbolism; victims of struggle were made to don five-meter-high dunce caps decorated with paper cutouts of skeletons, monsters, turtles and oxheads.[22]

Martial influence

While enemies of the people were forced into garb that marked them as the demonic "other," the Red Guards themselves were inclined toward military attire. The heavily peasant and proletarian composition of the army rendered it an alluring exemplar to students seeking to merge with "the masses" in waging class struggle. Military uniforms accented by wide leather belts became standard dress for young "radicals" anxious to claim the mantle of the People's Liberation Army. The attraction was intensified by Mao's slogan, raised on the eve of the Cultural Revolution: "Let the whole nation learn from the PLA."

Vocabulary drawn from the military tradition assumed an important place in the Red Guard lexicon. To be sure, civilian adoption of martial terminology was not born in the Cultural Revolution. The trend can be traced back to the early years of the PRC when large numbers of demobilized soldiers assumed positions as local cadres, taking with them certain military phrases. Accordingly, local assignments became known as "work stations" (*gongzuo gangwei*, especially burdensome posts were designated "frontlines" (*qianxian*), and tackling a problem involved "staging an offensive" (*faqi jingong*). Military phraseology reached new heights with the launching of the Great Leap Forward.[23] But only during the Cultural Revolution, encouraged by the youthful adulation of martial ways, did this sort of language move beyond administrative circles to pervade ordinary speech.

Political struggles were now characterized as "fiercely opening fire" (*menglie kaihuo*), "shooting wars" (*daxiang zhandou*), "staging general offensives" (*faqi zonggong*), "sounding the signal to charge" (*chuixiang jinjun hao*), "standing guard, standing sentry" (*zhangang fangshao*). Targets of condemnation meetings were told to "surrender or be destroyed."[24] At a school pageant in the spring of 1966 to criticize "Three-Family Village" – a group of writers whose works were denounced as "poisonous weeds" – the children, acting the role of workers, peasants and soldiers, "wielded huge cardboard pencils like bayonets, shouting, 'Angrily open fire!'"[25]

The nomenclature for rebel organizations also evidenced military inspiration: "struggle small-groups" (*zhandou xiaozu*), "columns" (*zongdui*), "headquarters" (*zhihui bu*), "general command" (*siling bu*), "allied corps" (*lianhe bingtuan*). Increasingly the country resembled a military barracks, with "Red Guard warriors" (*hongweibing zhanshi*) dressed in military uniforms, organized in martial hierarchies, speaking like soldiers, and even opening fire with real guns and ammunition. By the summer of 1967 the fondness for the military had been superseded by a love of violence itself, resulting in pitched battles against the regular military forces in some parts of the country (e.g., Qinghai, Wuhan, Sichuan). The nation seemed poised at the brink of civil war.

Color coding

The intense struggles of the day afforded little opportunity for compromise or complexity. People were either friends or foes; thoughts were either correct or incorrect. As previous scholars have noted, color coding was a key component of the Manichean imagery underlying the Cultural Revolution. Red, the symbol for revolutionary valor, was contrasted to black, the color of counterrevolutionary evil.[26] Thus "Red Guard" students from "five kinds of red" (*hong wulei*) class backgrounds battled "black elements" (*hei fenzi*) and "five kinds of black" (*hei wulei*). The supreme good, Chairman Mao, was none other than the "red sun" (*hong taiyang*).

As in the French Revolution, street names were changed to fit the new revolutionary symbology.[27] Thus Beijing's "Boulevard of Perpetual Peace" (*Changan jie*) became "East-is-Red Boulevard" (*Dongfang hong jie*).[28] Personal names were also altered, with more than a few youngsters assuming the appellation "inherit red" (*Jihong*).[29] On 16 July 1966 newspapers took the startling step of printing with red ink to commemorate Chairman Mao's swim in the Yangzi River. The occasion marked the start of color battles within the media: "the printing color became an issue of unusual revolutionary sensitivity. Once, when black ink was used when it should have been red, there were demonstrations for days."[30] Enemies were accused of attempting to manipulate colors in sinister fashion. "Waving the red flag to oppose the red flag" was a common characterization of counterrevolutionary activity. Similarly, at a school morality play the counterrevolutionaries were assigned the blasphemous lines "The sun is black" and "Not all flowers are red."[31]

Debating techniques

The strategy of wrapping oneself in revolutionary colors at the same time that one painted the opponent in counterrevolutionary hues was one element in a whole repertoire of debating techniques that marked Cultural Revolution discourse. Yao Wenyuan, the infamous Shanghai essayist, developed a prose style of debate widely imitated by the young Red Guards: "The method was, first, to declare yourself a defender of Marxism-Leninism and Mao Zedong Thought; second, to pose a series of accusatory

228

questions about your target; and third, to expose it as yet another example of counterrevolutionary infiltration of the Party."[32]

Integral to this new style of debate was a brashness that embraced the accusations of one's opponents with gusto, thereby turning the criticism around: "You say the smell of our gunpowder is too strong? Well, what we're after is a *super*-strong smell of gunpowder!" "So you call us rude? Well, just for that we'll *be* rude to you!" Again the phrasing was reminiscent of a type of speech previously associated with gangsters: "You say I hit people? Well, then, I'll just *give* you a thrashing and see what you can do about it!"

This sort of debate style proceeded not by countering competing arguments with the power of logic, but by "out-*macho*ing" one's adversaries – whether real or imagined – with the force of sheer bravado. A supercilious tone infused the big-character posters, delighting youngsters dissatisfied with the status quo and itching to let off some steam. From 1966 to 1968, Red Guard handbills, tabloids and ordinary speech were filled with such bluff and bluster. Imperious terms like "order" (*leling*), "general order" (*tongling*), and "stern warning" (*zhenggao*) imbued rebel utterances with an arrogant aura of assumed authority.

This daredevilish and defiant debate technique was captured by several popular Red Guard phrases: when outwitted "don't surrender, just declare total victory" (*bu touxiang jiu jiao ta miewang*), "rein in only at the brink of the precipice" (*xuanya le ma*), "struggle till they collapse, criticize till they stink" (*doudao pichou*).

Maoist influence

The highhanded manner of dispensing with one's foes was matched by a servile, obsequious demeanor toward the ultimate authority of Chairman Mao. A notable feature of the language of the period was of its adulation of Mao Zedong, exemplified in the widespread emulation of Mao's writings. In addition to the ubiquitous practice of liberally citing from the Chairman's *Quotations* and poems, rebel writers strived to structure their own essays according to Mao's stylistic exemplar. Mao Zedong's "Combat Liberalism" was an especially popular model for adaptation to the analysis of problems internal to the rebel faction, whereas attacks on enemy "capitalist-roaders" or "small reptiles" were typically patterned on Mao's "Letter to Urge the Surrender of Du Luming."

After the January Revolution of 1967, a new method of honoring Chairman Mao became common. Especially visible in so-called "telegrams of respect" (*zhijing dian*) and "loyalty letters" (*xian zhongxin shu*), a flowery literary style replete with terms of adoration and flattery developed. This type of essay, ostensibly addressed to the Chairman himself, demonstrated considerable rhetorical skill in its use of parallelism, matching couplets, and the like. Although utterly devoid of the subtlety and elegance of the best of traditional Chinese poetry, it nevertheless self-consciously emulated the structure of classical verse (*fu*):

> Chairman Mao, oh Chairman Mao,
> Heaven is vast, earth is vast,
> But vaster still is your loving-kindness.
> Rivers run deep, seas run deep,
> But deeper still is your loving-kindness.
>
> Whoever supports you is our friend;
> Whoever opposes you we'll fight to the end.
>
> Heaven may change, earth may change,
> But our red hearts – loyal to you – will never change.
> The earth may move, the mountains may shake,
> But our great red banner raised high to your glorious thought
> Will never waiver.

In 1967, when revolutionary committees were established around the country, the telegrams of respect – composed to commemorate the occasion – were invariably of this adulatory genre. This sort of sycophantic language, arising in right tandem with the explosion in vulgarity, reinforced the "binary oppositions" so characteristic of Cultural Revolution thought and expression.[33]

After the restoration of order in 1969, Mao evidently began to weary of the escalating adoration. With handbills and tabloids banned from circulation, one saw fewer written examples of the ornate language characteristic of the opening years of the Cultural Revolution. In ordinary speech, however, the influence of early Red Guard rhetoric lingered on. Flowery exaggeration joined vulgar curses and militaristic commands as the linguistic legacy of this period.

Working-class language

The fundamental changes in language that can be traced to the Red Guard movement of 1966–68 had implications for other segments of the populace, most notably the workers. Thanks to Red Guard efforts to link their activities to proletarian revolution, the working class was quickly drawn into the vortex of the struggle. The earliest big-character posters put up by workers' rebel factions replicated the point of view of contemporary Red Guard tabloids and handbills. Compared to the writings by students, however, the language adopted in workers' posters was fairly tame. Absent were the shocking shibboleths of Red Guard fame.

At that time most of the printed handbills and political essays issued in the name of workers' rebel factions were in fact penned by Red Guards or pre-Cultural Revolution cadres. The workers' rebels were quite limited in their literary abilities; the public speeches of Wang Hongwen and other top leaders of the Shanghai workers' general headquarters were ghost-written by their secretaries, for example. From the remaining records of their meetings, we see that the impromptu remarks of these rebel worker leaders – like their big-character posters – were notably lacking in the fiery rhetoric of their student mentors. What we find instead is a straightforward, rather lackluster style of expression.

Eventually the public vulgarity pioneered by the Red Guards did make its way into the factory workshop. The uncouth mannerisms of "ruffians" (da lao cu) were celebrated, and a number of heretofore derogatory terms were transformed into compliments. Phrases such as "horns on the head, thorns on the body" (toushang zhangjiao shenshang zhangci) or "shrewish" (pola) – which in the past had indicated impolite behavior – were now used to characterize a proper revolutionary spirit. When recommending workers for admission to the Party or factory cadres for promotion, the designation "shrewish work style" (zuofeng pola) in their dossiers served as a ringing endorsement of a bold and vigorous manner. Chinese workers were no strangers to crude phrases, of course, but the Red Guards' exaltation of vulgarity was an invitation to go public with such language.

After 1968, Chairman Mao – via an essay by Yao Wenyuan – insisted that "the working class must lead in everything." Accordingly, workers' propaganda teams were dispatched to schools and other elements of the "superstructure." Almost overnight, working-class rebels replaced student Red Guards as the most influential "revolutionary" force. Droves of Red Guards were now assigned jobs, mostly down in the countryside. Rather than strut proudly into factories as "young revolutionary marshals" to stir up cultural revolution, these erstwhile mentors were forced to undergo re-education themselves – as pupils of the working class. The era of the Red Guard had ended.

With this changing of the revolutionary vanguard, one might well have expected a commensurate linguistic change. However, a substantial number of former Red Guards were assigned to factory work at this time. Having experienced the heady exhilaration of political activism and revolutionary responsibility, these youngsters were reluctant to withdraw from such engagement. Boasting literary skills well above those of the average worker, more than a few ex-Red Guards became secretaries in their factory propaganda departments. Thus many of the articles published in the media in the name of workers were actually authored by these former student radicals.

During the Criticize Lin Biao–Criticize Confucius campaign of the early 1970s, "workers' small groups for theoretical study" were established around the country. The group leaders were typically workers who had entered their factory before 1966; often they were older workers with lengthy work experience. At the same time, however, the backbones of these groups were virtually all young students sent down to the factory during the Cultural Revolution. Take, for example, the nationally famous workers' theory group at the Number Two Workshop of Shanghai's Number Five Steel Mill. The deputy-director of the group, a middle-school student who entered the factory in 1968, was responsible for composing or rewriting almost all the literary output of that prolific group.

By late 1968, virtually everything published in the press in the name of workers was really written by Red Guards or reporters. But because of the need to honor the principle of the leading role of the proletariat, these articles went to great lengths to adopt a veneer of working-class language. Artificial, stilted adages were invented to serve as the "authentic" voice of labor:

- Be masters of the wharf, not slaves of the tonnage
- In a downpour work as usual, in a light rain work hard, and when there's no rain work your heart out
- For the revolution, no bone is too hard to gnaw through
- A hand that can hold a hammer can also hold a slide rule
- This rule, that regulation – every stipulation is a rope that binds the hands and feet of us workers
- Homemade equipment brings credit to the working class

These unfelicitous aphorisms were widely propagated as "the language of labor." When Shanghai's *Liberation Daily* ran the news headline "Be masters of the wharf, not slaves of the tonnage," copy-cat phrases cropped up in other periodicals: "Be masters of the machine, not slaves of the product," "Be masters of the electrical machine, not slaves of the kilowattage," and the like. Prevalent as such maxims became during the Criticize Lin Biao–Criticize Confucius Campaign, they were never really accepted into ordinary speech.

Conclusion

In contrast to the French Revolution, with its marked distinctions among social classes, China's Cultural Revolution fell linguistically flat. The influential role of the brash young Red Guards from Beijing lent the language of this period a peculiar uniformity. The very efforts of the young radicals to represent the Chinese masses led them to construct a rhetorical style that was alien to literati and popular practice alike.

Part of the explanation for the relative social homogeneity of Cultural Revolution language lies simply in historical timing. While the French Revolution was aimed at a monarchy whose feudal hierarchy remained largely intact, the Cultural Revolution occurred more than half a century after the Chinese imperial system had collapsed. Moreover, thanks to the

New Culture Movement of the 1920s, linguistic distinctions based on class status had already been considerably muted in China.

A second factor in the uniformity of Cultural Revolution language was the authoritarian role of Chairman Mao. As an event inspired and directed by the "Great Helmsman," the movement was severely constrained in its cultural expression. Again the contrast with France is instructive. There the revolution brought an explosion in the publication of new periodicals and the performance of new dramas:

> The crumbling of the French state after 1786 let loose a deluge of words, in print, in conversations, and in political meetings. There had been a few dozen periodicals – hardly any of which carried what we call news – circulating in Paris during the 1780s; more than 500 appeared between 14 July 1789 and 10 August 1792. Something similar happened in theater: in contrast to the handful of new plays produced annually before the Revolution, at least 1,500 new plays, many of them topical, were produced between 1789 and 1799, and more than 750 were staged just in the years 1792–94.[34]

In China, the situation was exactly the reverse. The Cultural Revolution Small Group – which reported directly to Mao – shut down hundreds of journals and placed unprecedented restrictions on the performing arts.[35] Only works deemed politically correct by the central leadership were permitted.

A third, and perhaps most telling, reason for the flatness of cultural expression lies in the changing role of Chinese intellectuals. Classical Confucian theory, institutionalized in an "open" examination system for aspiring literati, had served to elevate intellectuals to a pivotal position as mediators between state and society. With their upward mobility dependent upon performance in government-sponsored examinations, intellectuals in imperial China tended to identify closely with state interests. Charged with shepherding the masses, they nonetheless spoke in the orthodox language of the state.

The abolition of the Confucian examinations in 1905, followed by the toppling of the dynastic system a few years later, loosened the centuries-old grip that had held educated Chinese in the tight embrace of the state. The extraordinary cultural ferment which exploded in the aftermath of the May Fourth Movement of 1919 revealed the power of an intelligentsia freed from the bonds of state servitude. In the first half of the twentieth century, educated Chinese broke with their Confucian forbearers by going to the masses for linguistic inspiration as well as political mobilization.

The Communist revolution was launched by young intellectuals who learned to speak the language of the people so as to mount a united assault against a discredited Republican regime. The process of merging with the masses was by no means easy. Linguistic barriers proved especially formidable to overcome. As a young Communist cadre reported his disillusionment after returning to his home province of Henan to organize the masses in the summer of 1927:

> According to all we had heard, the Henan peasantry was very revolutionary. So when we went to Henan we were prepared to lead the peasants to participate in revolutionary work. Our hopes were very high. However, when we arrived in Henan we saw that conditions were completely different from our expectations. . . . Because the peasants' conservatism was so strong and their feudalist thought so pronounced, we had great difficulty in propaganda work, finding that all the handbills and slogans we had brought with us were inappropriate. We were forced to change our strategy, writing in official government style and affixing seals in order to gain their trust. . . . Further-more, our cadres are too few and lack experience. Most are from South Henan and, because of language difficulties, cannot work effectively in the north.[36]

Tortuous as the process of popular mobilization was, Communist cadres did of course eventually succeed in rendering their cause intelligible to a mass constituency. The outcome of this effort was a powerful new socialist state capable of demanding once again the full allegiance of its educated youths.

The bizarre language of the Cultural Revolution bespoke the altered status of the Chinese intellectual under socialism – rewedded to the state apparatus, but now required to masquerade as part of the ordinary masses.[37] The schizophrenic rhetoric of the Red Guards expressed this ambivalent position. On the one hand, the extravagant praise of "red sun" Chairman Mao reflected the heliotropic pull of the central state. On the other hand, the vulgarity, violence, and vain construction of a phoney "language of labor" represented the forced efforts of young students to present themselves as *bona fide* proletarians.

Superficial similarities to the proletarian culture of the French Revolution – with its occult symbolism of witchcraft, its "burlesque legalism" of mock trials and its vulgar sexual imagery of cuckolding, for example[38] – belie a deeper difference. The class variation so characteristic of political discourse in eighteenth-century France was much less apparent in China's Cultural Revolution. Despite constant lip service to carrying on class struggle, the language of the Red Guards was surprisingly "classless" – a crude attempt by rude youngsters to appropriate the revolutionary culture of the Chinese proletariat.

NOTES

1 On the language of the French Revolution, see for example William Sewell, *Work and Revolution in France: The Language of Labor from the Old Regime to 1848* (Cambridge: Cambridge University Press, 1980); Robert Darnton, *The Literary Underground of the Old Regime* (Cambridge, MA: Harvard University Press, 1982); Robert Darnton and Daniel Roche, eds, *Revolution in Print: The Press in France, 1775–1800* (Berkeley: University of California Press, 1989); John Renwick, ed., *Language and Rhetoric of the Revolution* (Edinburgh: Edinburgh University Press, 1990); Lynn Hunt, *The Family Romance of the French Revolution* (Berkeley: University of California Press, 1992).

2 Perry Link, *Evening Chats in Beijing: Probing China's Predicament* (New York: Norton, 1992), especially chapter four; Michael Schoenhals, *Doing Things with Words in Chinese Politics* (Berkeley: Institute of East Asian Studies, University of California, 1992); and Jeffrey N. Wasserstrom "The First Chinese Red Scare: 'Fanchi' Propaganda and Pro-Red Responses during the Northern Expedition," *Republican China* 11, 1 (1985): 32–51. On the special importance in Chinese politics of the written word, as expressed through the practice of calligraphy, see Richard Curt Kraus, *Brushes with Power: Modern Politics and the Chinese Art of Calligraphy* (Berkeley: University of California Press, 1991).

3 John K. Fairbank, *The Great Chinese Revolution* (New York: Harper and Row, 1986).

4 Lowell Dittmer, *China's Continuous Revolution* (Berkeley: University of California Press, 1987), 90–91. Previous studies of Cultural Revolution language include H.C. Chuang, *The Great Proletarian Revolution – A Terminological Study* (Berkeley: University of California Center for Chinese Studies, 1967); H.C. Chuang, *The Little Red Book and Current Chinese Language* (Berkeley: University of California Center for Chinese Studies, 1968); Lowell Dittmer and Chen Ruoxi, *Ethics and Rhetoric of the Chinese Cultural Revolution* (Berkeley: University of California Center for Chinese Studies, 1981); and Jin Chunming *et al.*, eds, *"Wenge" shiqi guaishi guaiyu* [Strange things and strange words of the "Cultural Revolution" era] (Beijing: Qiushi chubanshe, 1989).

5 See Jeffrey N. Wasserstrom and Elizabeth J. Perry, eds, *Popular Protest and Political Culture in Modern China: Learning from 1989* (Boulder: Westview Press, 1991) as one example of revived interest in Chinese revolutionary political culture.

6 Gabriel A. Almond and Sidney Verba, *The Civic Culture* (Boston: Little, Brown, 1965); Lucian W. Pye, *The Spirit of Chinese Politics* (Cambridge, MA: M.I.T. Press, 1968); Richard Solomon, *Mao's Revolution and Chinese Political Culture* (Berkeley: University of California Press, 1971).

7 Robert Darnton, *The Great Cat Massacre and Other Episodes in French Cultural History* (New York: Basic Books, 1984).

8 For one illuminating study along these lines, see Richard Curt Kraus, *Pianos and Politics in China: Middle-Class Ambitions and the Struggle over Western Music* (New York: Oxford University Press, 1989).

9 On the Red Guards' promotion of the term *zaofan*, see H.C. Chuang, 1967, 13ff.

10 On uses (and pictorial representations) of these and related terms in ordinary folk language as well as in previous and subsequent popular protest movements, see Wolfram Eberhard, *A Dictionary of Chinese Symbols: Hidden Symbols in Chinese Life and Thought* (London and New York: Routledge and Kegan Paul, 1986), 80–83, 268–296; Jeffrey N. Wasserstrom, *Student Protests in Twentieth-Century China: The View from Shanghai* (Stanford: Stanford University Press,

1991), 125, 222–223, 319; and Roxane Witke, *Comrade Chiang Ch'ing* (Boston: Little, Brown, 1977), 335.

11 Gordon A. Bennett and Ronald M. Montaperto, *Red Guard: The Political Biography of Dai Hsiao-ai* (Garden City: Doubleday, 1971), 99.

12 Bennett and Montaperto, 116.

13 Liang Heng and Judith Shapiro, *Son of the Revolution* (New York: Vintage, 1983), 54.

14 Gao Yuan, *Born Red* (Stanford: Stanford University Press, 1987), 86.

15 On the origins of this metaphor, see H.C. Chuang, 1967, 23–24.

16 Bennett and Montaperto, 39.

17 Gao Yuan, 124.

18 Gao Yuan, 68.

19 Gao Yuan, 285.

20 The influence of this derogatory rhetoric outlasted the Cultural Revolution and spread far beyond China's own borders. Thus the Shining Path in Peru, a Maoist guerrilla outfit much enamored of Cultural Revolution exemplars, refers today to its enemies as "reptiles," "serpents," "wimpering revisionists," "animal generals with worm-eaten brains," "beetles," "genocidal hyenas," "man-eating imperialist lackeys" and the like. See James Brooke, "Guerrilla Newspaper in Peru Tries to Dehumanize Enemy," in *The New York Times*, 10 February 1993. We are grateful to Elinor Levine for bringing this to our attention.

21 William Hinton, *Hundred Day War: The Cultural Revolution at Tsinghua University* (New York: Monthly Review Press, 1972), 104.

22 Gao Yuan, 75. Here again we can find precursors in earlier protest movements. For analogies with the May Thirtieth Movement of 1925, see Elizabeth J. Perry, *Shanghai on Strike: The Politics of Chinese Labor* (Stanford: Stanford University Press, 1993), 256; and Wasserstrom, 1991, 223.

23 T.A. Hsia, *Metaphor, Myth, Ritual and the People's Commune* (Berkeley: University of California Center for Chinese Studies, 1961).

24 Bennett and Montaperto, 35.

25 Liang and Shapiro, 41.

26 Dittmer, 1987, 81–82; H.C. Chuang, 1967, 6–10, 17–22.

27 On the French case, see Lynn Hunt, *Politics, Culture and Class in the French Revolution* (Berkeley: University of California Press, 1984), 20–21.

28 Gao Yuan, 85.

29 Gao Hong, 96. Others took on more militaristic names, such as "Liquidate the bourgeoisie" (*Miezi*).

30 Liang and Shapiro, 43.

31 Liang and Shapiro, 41.

32 Gao Yuan, 41.

33 See Dittmer, 1987, 81–90. Although Dittmer does not focus specifically on the use of either obscene or obsequious language, the dichotomy fits well within his pure/defiled distinction.

34 Lynn Hunt, 1984, 19–20.

35 See An-jen Chiang, *Models in China's Policy toward Literature and Art*, University of Washington Ph.D. dissertation (Seattle, 1992).

36 Jiang Yongjing, *Baoluoding yu Wuhan zhengquan* [Borodin and the Wuhan government] (Taipei: Chuanji wensue chubanshe, 1963), 373–74.

37 For a fuller discussion of relations between the state and intellectuals in socialist China, see Timothy Cheek, "From Priests to Professionals: Intellectuals and the State under the CCP," in Wasserstrom and Perry, eds, 124–45.

38 Darnton, 1984, 97.

Part IV

POLITICAL LEGITIMACY
AT THE CENTURY'S END

11

TIANANMEN 1989

Background and consequences

Marie-Claire Bergère

When Chinese students took to the streets in mid-April 1989 and then were joined there by members of other social groups, their protests captured the attention of the world. This was partly due to the drama of events that unfolded at Tiananmen Square (the main hub of protest activity) and on the streets surrounding it (which were the site of giant marches and eventually became the main killing fields of the June 4 massacre). It was also in part the result, though, of the fortuitous presence in Beijing at the time of a disproportionate number of international journalists. These reporters, some of whom sent televised reports around the globe via the then-new technology of satellite feeds, had come to the PRC to cover a promised breakthrough in Sino-Soviet relations: an early May summit meeting between Mikhail Gorbachev and Deng Xiaoping. They ended up devoting much of their reporting, however, to the actions of protesting crowds and the state violence that brought the movement to a tragic end in early June. The intense global scrutiny of the Tiananmen protests – which also received an unprecedented amount of domestic press coverage for events of this sort, some of it quite sympathetic – had a profound impact on international views of China toward the century's end. It also helped ensure that, in the wake of the June 4 massacre and the crackdown that followed, distorted ideas about China's 1989 would proliferate. Since the cameras were all in Beijing, for example, it soon became remembered as a local as opposed to a national event. In fact, there were marches in scores of cities and some of these were enormous (the crowds in certain Shanghai gatherings were estimated at close to half a million) and soldiers did not only kill protesters in the capital (a massacre, albeit much smaller in scale, also occurred in Chengdu). More generally, mythic readings of the meaning of the protests quickly took hold, hindering the development of a nuanced historical understanding of the events. China's 1989 became, in the minds of many, a struggle that could only be viewed through the prism of a set of powerful images (of a lone man stopping tanks, of students rallying around something that looked like the Statue of Liberty) that seemed self-explanatory. These images of China's thwarted "democracy movement" were then overlaid by year's end with visions of the Berlin Wall crumbling.

In the provocative essay that follows, Marie-Claire Bergère argues for the need to disentangle the Chinese story from a larger tale of the unraveling of state-socialist regimes in 1989 and to tease out the factors other than a general desire for democracy that propelled the protesters. She insists on seeing the Tiananmen struggle as a multifaceted one that defied mono-causal analysis, and seeing it as an anti-corruption movement as much as a democracy one. This is something that many scholars now accept readily but at the time she wrote (at the start of the 1990s), it was certainly not the standard popular view of the situation outside of China. She gives no ground to Beijing's "Big Lie" version of 1989 as a year when "thugs" in league with the "West" instigated a series of "counter-revolutionary riots" that the PLA quelled in a restrained fashion. But she argues that scholars need to avoid the trap of allowing "enthusiastic approval" (for the movement's aims) and "simplistic analysis" (of its causes and dynamics) to lead us astray – as it often did as the drama unfolded that year. For her, to understand China's 1989 it is crucial to take into account and give due measure to a wide array of factors, from economic shifts, to splits within the Party leadership, to the relative weakness of civil society institutions in the PRC. And, above all, she insists, attention needs to be paid to placing Tiananmen into the very specific historical and cultural context in which it occurred.

* * *

The Tiananmen movement in the spring of 1989 fascinated Western public opinion; in the same way, the brutal repression of the Chinese students and citizens on 4 June, putting a tragic end to the movement that had roused so many hopes, provoked a cry of outrage. Yet, sympathy and compassion are not always conducive to a real understanding of events. While the French were celebrating the bicentennial of their revolution, many observers yielded to the temptation to analyse the events in Tiananmen by using the standard of Western democratic traditions and the ideology of human rights. But China has its own idiosyncrasies, its own political culture, its own geographic characteristics and its own historical and demographic peculiarities. This is not to say that China cannot aspire to the freedom and democracy that Western societies enjoy. But historians must put emotions aside and be as objective as possible in their analyses. The opportunity for more detached thought offered by the relative indifference towards China of public opinion today, captivated by the downfall of the Communist regimes in Eastern Europe and the changes in the Soviet Union, must not be lost. Otherwise, the events in Tiananmen Square risk being seen merely as a reference point for Western debate on Socialism and post-Socialism, with the consequence that Western-liberal perceptions remain as distant from Chinese reality as European and American perceptions of the Cultural Revolution were during the 1960s and 1970s.

The most important question is about the *nature* of the Tiananmen movement. From a Western perspective, the movement has frequently been perceived as the rejection of Communism by the Chinese people, tired of the failures of the regime and stripped of all faith in Marxist–Leninist ideology. On the other hand, a few experts see it as just another wave of popular protest (previous waves were in 1976, 1978–9, 1985–6), the periodical recurrence of which is facilitated by conflicts within the leadership group, particularly during periods of succession. In their view, the explosion in Beijing in the spring of 1989 coincided with the exacerbation of the political conflict and the struggle among factions for succession to Deng Xiaoping: above all, the struggle between the then General Secretary of the CCP, reformist Zhao Ziyang, and the Prime Minister Li Peng, who had the support of the conservatives and the veterans. Moreover, the spring movement would not have differed from previous protests if it had not been for the exceptional presence of the media, involving the world in the demonstrators' hopes and frustrations.

Avoiding both enthusiastic approval and simplistic analysis, this essay attempts a detached study of the following issues: the importance of popular mobilisation, the ideological orientations given to the movement by students and intellectuals, the strength drawn by the protest movement from the hesitations of, and the divisions within the leadership.

The mobilisation of the urban population

From the beginning of the 1980s, latent student unrest flared a number of times into large demonstrations: in September–November 1985 against the new Japanese economic imperialism and in November–December 1986 in support of the reformist policy of Hu Yaobang. But on those occasions, the urban population did not unite with the students. In May 1989, on the other hand, blue- and white-collar workers, small entrepreneurs and even some members of the police and the army mobilised en masse in Beijing and in a number of other large cities in support of the student demonstrations.[1] Why the change?

Stressing the rapid growth in the Chinese economy (approximately 11–12 percent per annum between 1978 and 1988) and the improvement in the standard of living of most of the urban population, many observers conclude that the crisis was caused by the contrast between the success of economic reform and the lack of political reform. Referring to the instability marking the recent evolution of the newly industrialising countries in Asia, these observers feel that after ten years of economic reform, China is as ready for democracy as Taiwan and South Korea are after four decades of "miraculous" growth. They feel that the Chinese protest movement has the same motivations as the discontent of the new Taiwanese and Korean middle classes: economic growth. But this kind of analysis raises a number of doubts.

After considerable success in the early 1980s, the economic reform undertaken by Deng Xiaoping came up against a series of difficulties in 1984 and 1985, that is, when it was extended to the urban/industrial sector; de facto, the reform generated excessive growth, instability and inflation. In 1988, investments constituted 39 percent of the GNP. Moreover, it should be pointed out that, despite greater autonomy, firms did not operate according to market laws, while the loosening of controls on monetary policy and loans forced local authorities to increase financing. In this way, the pressures exerted on the economy spurred inflation, which rose to over 20 percent in 1987–8. The austerity programme and the new centralisation decided upon in September 1988 did not yield the desired results: they led to stagflation rather than stabilisation. Thus, besides being deprived of the security and guarantees they had enjoyed under central planning, the urban blue- and white-collar workers now also saw the benefits they had received from the economic reform (higher salaries and more bonuses) threatened. Discontent and unrest spread. Each group advanced specific demands that were often divergent from or contradictory to others. Social envy of the nouveau riche was also a factor.

The students appealed to their compatriots to mobilise by demonstrating above all against the corruption and the rapid accumulation of wealth by public officials exploiting their positions for personal gain. In this the students hit the mark: the city dwellers were more concerned about inflation and its consequences than about democracy. The consensus between students and the population was based on the shared indignation at the personal increase in wealth of corrupt party officials. That is why it is argued here that the equation *economic prosperity + political immobility = popular mobilisation* does not apply to the Tiananmen protest movement. Mobilisation was the result of economic instability and of uncertainty about future prospects. In brief, it was the result of the shortcomings of the economic reforms rather than of their success. The main obstacle to the economic reforms was not the lack of political liberalisation, but the way in which the reforms were managed: alternate acceleration and braking. These cycles were more indicative of the inexperience and the infighting among political leaders than of a lack of democracy. Unity of discretion, bureaucratic competence and popular support – indispensable ingredients for any balanced economic growth – are not characteristics peculiar to, and not even always characteristics *tout court* of, democratic regimes. Viewed in this light, the Tiananmen movement seems radically different from the movements that have arisen in the newly industrialised countries of Asia. Tiananmen was not the result of successful modernisation, because modernisation has not yet been achieved in China and may not be for many years. Yet, while being exposed to all the inconveniences of a modernisation process, the people were still far from enjoying its benefits and demanding the transformation of an economic power over which they did not have political control. This does not rule out the fact, however, that the leaders of the movement, both the students and the intellectuals that inspired it, aspired to changing the political system.

The role of the students and the intellectuals

The students who demonstrated in Tiananmen were not merely seeking to improve their own lot, although the corporative difficulties they face (deterioration of campus life, employment uncertainty) were not totally unrelated to their mobilisation.[2] Their slogans and their banners demanded mainly democracy, freedom – of the press and of the judicial system – and the defence of human rights.

These demands sprang from a line of thought developed during the 1980s in the ever more numerous and explicit debates published in newspapers and magazines and in discussions in the so-called "democratic salons" and on university campuses. These debates vitalised the activity of cultural groups which, in the summer of 1986 with the so-called "double 100 flowers movement," reached a level of freedom and intensity close to that of 4 May 1919. The students drew their ideas from the protagonists of these debates: men like physicist Fang Lizhi, writer and journalist Liu Binyan, theorist Yan Yiaqi, reformers Bao Tong and Gao Shan, economist Chen Yizi, novelist Zhang Xianliang and many others.

The transformation of the Chinese political system into a Western-type democracy was not the main subject of these debates (even though some intellectuals, such as Zhang Xianliang, explicitly called for it). Emerging after decades of silence and oppression, many Chinese intellectuals spontaneously returned to the traditional attitude of Confucian scholars, associated for centuries with the dominant ideological and political structures of imperial power. They called for a reform of the CCP that would bring people of quality to power, whom they, as intellectuals, could serve as advisers. Very few of them were actually concerned with the problem of creating new institutions or modifying the structure of the state. According to men like Fang Lizhi or Liu Binyan, all problems, including those of economic modernisation and political reform, could be solved by good leaders and honest administrators.

Thus, the students found inspiration in these ideas. Their aspirations to democracy and freedom were expressed in slogans like "Down with Deng Xiaoping" and "Down with Li Peng," while their hopes were concentrated on the "good" Zhao Ziyang. Instead of trying to channel their opposition into an institutional framework, all hopes were placed in one man. Only at the end of May was a fleeting attempt (which ended in failure) made to turn to the NPC, whose president Wan Li was said to be a reformist. This non-institutionalisation of the conflict proved to be fatal for the movement, in that there were no political alternatives to the intervention of the army. In fact, at the end of May, the army appeared to be the only part of the old state structure still on its feet.

Yet the intellectuals and their student spokesmen were not the only ones responsible for the failure to translate the popular power gained at Tiananmen into political leverage. The persistence of traditional moral and political values was not the only obstacle to the institutionalisation of the opposition; it was also paralysed by the absence of support for the demonstrators from civilian society and autonomous structures. Checked by those in power and rejected by the people, who did not identify with them, the mass organisations (the youth league, the student federations and the trade unions) had no political weight. And the associations created by the students (the Beijing Students' Autonomous Federation, founded on 20 April, the Dialogue Delegation for College Students, founded on 5 May, the Hunger Strikers Delegation established on 13 May, the Federation for students coming from the provinces) and by the intellectuals (the Beijing Association of Intellectuals, headed by Yan Jiaqi) and by the workers (the Capital Workers' Autonomous Federation) remained at an embryonic stage, lacking any real representative capacity.[3] In this sense, the situation in China was quite different from those in countries like Poland or Eastern Germany, where the churches, active despite persecution, provided material support and an organisational framework for the protest movements.

While ideological weakness and the lack of a civil society (that is, an organised social structure with autonomous institutions) may be considered as reasons for the final failure of the movement, how can its extraordinarily wide-ranging initial success be explained? Enthusiasm, patriotism and the courage of the student demonstrators were definitely factors. But perhaps most important of all was the students' extremely skilful and intelligent strategy. Through strict respect of the precepts of non-violence, using the funeral (22 April) of a respected party leader (Hu Yaobang) as a pretext, and the visit of Gorbachev to Beijing (16–17 May) as a political platform, declaring their loyalty to the country and the party, the students managed to avoid open conflict and repression for many weeks. When time started working against them – as of 13 May – they resorted to a hunger strike. Although borrowed from the Western protest repertoire, this new strategy was well suited to the Confucian contest between the demonstrators who were eager to appear as the champions of virtue and truth and the oligarchy which, in the name of the same Confucian political moral, declared itself open to their criticism. In fact, according to traditional concepts, the use of violence reduces the legitimacy of the authorities who are to blame for it. Thus, the hunger strike threatened to throw discredit on the regime by making it responsible for the martyrdom which it had scrupulously tried to avoid up to that time. The hunger strike forced the regime to put an end to hesitations and to set a deadline: that of the physical limit of the strikers.

The political acumen of the young demonstrators and the rigid discipline they observed were indeed so remarkable that they authorise conjecture of expert political help or guidance from members of government and mass organisations or party officials sharing some of the students' ideas and hoping to be able to exploit the popular mobilisation to further their own power. Recognition of the role of these advisers in no way denies the existence of a spontaneous student movement or suggests that the students blindly followed the directives of some figures working behind the scenes. It merely means that the protest movement would not have enjoyed its initial success without the help of numerous powerful allies in the party and state apparatus.

Government divisions and hesitations

The rivalries among the various factions of the CCP, the generation struggle and the political and personal conflicts among the leaders played an important role in the events in Tiananmen. They paralysed the ruling group from day to day, keeping it silent from 16 May to 9 June 1989. The consensus between moderate and radical reformers, upon the support of which Deng Xiaoping had relied for his return to power in 1978, disintegrated in 1985. From that date, the moderate reformers – defined as "conservatives" – continued to express their opposition to the evolution of the reform. In September 1985, at the Party's Conference on Labour, Chen Yun made a solemn appeal for prudence. In autumn 1986, Peng Zhen, then Chairman of the NPC, headed an offensive against the CCP General Secretary, Hu Yaobang, who was finally removed in January 1987. After the victorious counteroffensive of Zhao Ziyang at the Thirteenth Party Congress (October 1987), violent inflationary pressure again swung the internal balance of the leadership group towards conservative Prime Minister Li Peng and central planner Yao Yilin.

Conservatives and reformers did not agree on the extent of economic and political changes. According to the conservatives, the reforms had been carried out too quickly and had gone too far; it was imperative to reestablish the control of the state (that is, of the central government) over the economy. For the reformers, the reforms had not been completed; it was important to push ahead to allow a real market economy to develop. These political divergences were exacerbated by the generational conflict between the veterans, deprived of their power and positions – but not their privileges – and given honorary functions as advisers at the Thirteenth Party Congress, and the fifty- to sixty-year-old party officials, more receptive to technical requirements and the need for change and eager to assert their authority.

Deng Xiaoping tried to manage these contrasts in the leadership group by alternately supporting one faction and then the other. But as the crisis and the conflicts deepened, this oscillatory tactic lost much of its efficacy. And since the old guard seemed unable to choose an heir that was acceptable to both the party and Deng himself, the rivalry became fiercer. Compromises between the factions became more difficult, making the oligarchy appear more undecided, impotent, lacking any strategy for the future and unable to come to an agreement on the present.

While Li Peng and Yao Yilin implemented the "adjustment" policy officially adopted by the party in September 1988, Zhao Ziyang and his allies openly expressed their opinion that it should be abandoned as soon as possible. Li Peng and the conservatives had the support of the veteran advisers in the Central Committee of the CCP. Zhao Ziyang and the reformers sought the support of the intellectuals, the students and public opinion, exactly as Deng Xiaoping had done during a previous "spring" in November–December 1978, in order to get rid of his rival Hua Guofeng (the successor designated by Mao Zedong) and to consolidate his power.

But in 1989, the spread of popular mobilisation and the weakening of the leadership apparatus upset the rules of the game. Internal conflicts in the ruling group could no longer be settled by negotiation. On 19 May, Zhao Ziyang was not able to prevent the declaration of martial law. But at the same time, the conservatives were not able to form a majority to condemn Zhao Ziyang during the Politburo meeting of 23–4 May, a meeting which had been expressly expanded to include representatives from the Central Advisory Commission, i.e. the veterans. So, when the protest movement threatened the very existence of the regime, Deng Xioaping reacted in the same way as his predecessors, Mao Zedong and the imperial dynasties had done. He called in the army.

The recourse to the use of the armed forces started with the declaration of martial law. Initially, however, it failed: the citizens of Beijing physically opposed the entry of troops into the city and some officers hesitated to use force against the people. These divisions in the army between the moderates and the advocates of brutal repression evoked images of civil war and chaos. The urgency of the situation triggered a reaction by the government. There can be no doubt about the fact that the military leaders played an active part in the negotiations that finally concluded in the bloody repression of 4 June and the reunification of the political leadership of the party under Deng Xiaoping and the new General Secretary of the Party, Jiang Zemin.

Tiananmen: a "Chinese" failure

After this brief reconstruction, it is clear that the Liberal–Western interpretation of the Chinese crisis must be discarded. The Tiananmen movement was not an expression of protest by a society anxious for political change, whose aspirations are interpreted by a democratic vanguard. In spite of the diversification and dynamism introduced by the reforms, the Chinese (urban) society was still fragmented and cellular. The convergence of the discontent of various sectors that occurred during the course of the Tiananmen movement was not enough to unify and orient the social drive. In the absence of institutional structures and guiding ideologies, the popular mobilisation did not turn into a political movement: it remained the expression of a generalised feeling of discontent.

The strength and duration of the popular mobilisation was strongly affected by the internal divisions of the government. Its democratic prestige was, to a large extent, conferred on it by foreign observers and media, misled by the vocabulary used by the intellectual vanguard. Actually, the words "freedom" and "democracy" seem to have been used as "fetish words"; the young demonstrators were unable to give them any meaning other than their own immolation. The intellectuals and the reformist party members with whom the students were allied tried above all to use the impulse of the popular protest to reform the party rather than change the regime. But has democracy ever been known to be "good government" by a "good party"? One is tempted to conclude that the immaturity of a society corresponds to the shortcomings of its elites.

But it is obvious that the key to the events in Tiananmen must not be sought in the West, even though the country's opening to foreign technology, capital and influences somehow precipitated the crisis. Evaluation is required of the internal contradictions of the Socialist post-Stalinist regime and, above all, the Chinese political culture – a culture that is still profoundly rooted in Confucianism and that gives priority to the role and the responsibility of the elites and that mediates relations between the government and the people through an almost autonomous bureaucracy. The tragedy of Tiananmen is not so much the substantiation of the failure of a democratic revolution as that of the antiquatedness of a state unable to undertake modernisation, of the backwardness of a fragmented society and of the decomposition of a system stripped of its "heavenly mandate." In fact, the meaning of the word "virtue" underlying the words "freedom" and "democracy" has to be understood, and the persistence of a Confucian moral regulating the reciprocal rights and duties of the governors and the governed in the common interest recognised. It was, in fact, in the name of virtue that the honest critics, the generous students and the indignant population arose. In the same way, the recourse to brutal force was part of a tradition that has always, throughout the centuries, been able to combine moral imperatives with the constraints of power. The conservative reaction under way since June 1989 is presented as a restoration of the virtue (meaning orthodoxy) jeopardised by the disorders in the streets and the dangerous influences of the outside world.

This kind of analysis, which deliberately gives priority to cultural and specific features of the Tiananmen movement that are systematically concealed, should make it possible to see the failure of the Chinese protest as insignificant with respect to the experiences of Socialism and post-Socialism in Eastern Europe. Then again, very recent history has belied the pertinency of the Chinese model in this field. But it does beg another question: what will be the fate of the conservative restoration under way in China since June 1989, given the general downfall of the European and Soviet socialist systems?

After the repression of 4 June, the government regained control of public activity and consolidated its political and ideological power through arrests, purges and propaganda campaigns. Deng Xiaoping, the target of student protests, maintained his pre-eminent role. On 9 November 1989 he resigned from his last official position as Chair of the party's Military Affairs Commission, but most observers feel that, like Empress Cixi, he is still behind the scenes guiding and checking on his appointed successor, the new General Secretary of the CCP, Jiang Zemin. This recovery of power was officially announced as a mere restoration of the status quo. On his first return to public view on 9 June 1989, Deng Xiaoping stated that the "open-door policy" and the reforms would continue. Therefore, the first problem to be examined is whether the centralisation currently under way is still a part of the reform process or whether it constitutes a return to a centrally planned economy and a state-dominated society.

Economic reform or counter-reform?

This question may come as a surprise. At first glance, the violence of the repression suggests that the counter-revolution won and throws doubt on the credibility of the official reform plans. Nevertheless, on an economic plane, this would not be the first time that a reform has been slowed down by a phase of stabilisation and consolidation which does not, however, stop the course of the reform. In 1981–2 and again in 1986–7, measures reintroducing central control helped combat the distortions of an essentially pragmatic policy, the accelerations and slowdowns of which responded to the economic priorities of the moment. It can also be claimed that the current policy of a return to centralisation was not caused by Tiananmen, since it was introduced in the summer–autumn of 1988. Finally, it should be pointed out that it partly corresponds to recommendations made at that time by some foreign experts concerned about the excesses of decentralisation and runaway inflation. In its report on China in autumn 1989, the World Bank gave its cautious and conditional approval of this policy: the report recognised the usefulness in the short term of the new centralisation (in order to re-establish the economic balance), but added that prolonged application would have negative effects.

After the Fifth Plenum of the Thirteenth Central Committee (November 1989) – the resolutions of which were only published on 17 January 1990 – it is difficult to consider the current policy a mere extension of the adjustments undertaken a year earlier. The text of the adopted "Decision"[4] distributed to the main central and provincial officials at the end of the plenum, established the terms of implementation of a clearly conservative political line; the line advocated by Li Peng and Jiang Zemin in October 1989 during the celebrations of the fortieth anniversary of the foundation of the PRC. Distinguishing between "two kinds of reforms and openings," one of which upholds the priorities of Socialism and the other of which paves the way for capitalism and "bourgeois liberalisation," this new line calls for a limitation of the activities of the collective and private sectors, a strengthening of command planning, restoration of the state monopoly for the marketing of essential raw materials (starting with coal) and abolition of the "double" price system by eliminating fluctuating prices and returning to official fixed prices. The managers of public enterprises will once again have to reckon with the authority of the party committee; while foreign trade will be channelled through resuscitated state companies. The new three-year adjustment plan (1989–90), prepared by the state planning commission under the direction of Yao Yilin, goes far beyond the austerity plan adopted in September 1988. In order to acquire the instruments for this new policy, the government has sought to increase its resources by imposing the purchase of treasury bonds on administrations, enterprises and the public, and by reassessing remittals when the contracts for the provincial budgets are reviewed.

Yet, the new policy does not imply abolition of the reform: the decisions on rural decollectivisation and family farming have not been reneged. The collective/private sector in the country and in the cities is still acknowledged, but its activities have been limited by higher taxation, new credit restrictions and the rationing of raw materials and energy supply. Its growth should not exceed 15–20 percent per year (against the 30–40 percent recorded in 1987–8). The autonomy of public enterprise has not been abolished, only strongly restricted. The production quota provided for by the plan has been increased to 80 percent. The decline of production beyond that quota (limited to 20 percent) and new central controls on raw materials and prices have shifted the role of the market into a secondary position. Public enterprises have once again been subjugated to the state, but to a poorer state, ready to cut credit and fire workers. Thus, the return has not been to the pre-reform era prior to 1978, but to an era of limited reform experienced between 1978 and 1984 – the period in which the influence of Chen Yun was felt and in which the large public enterprises in the cities dominated the small business and tertiary sector left open to private and collective activity.[5]

The government's primary economic objective was to curb inflation and bring it below a 10 percent ceiling. In fact, the inflation rate fell in 1989 to around 20 percent. But the austerity policy implemented through a return to central controls seriously limited production. In October 1989, for the first time after many years, China recorded negative industrial growth (–2.1 percent as compared to 10.6 percent in October 1988). The enterprises hardest hit were obviously those in the private and collective sectors, in both the countryside and the cities. But even the public enterprises were obliged to lay off workers (15 to 20 million workers and employees out of a total of 135 million), to lower wages (as of September 1989), to eliminate production prices and increase wage deductions through the acquisition (of up to 10 percent of the salary) of state treasury bonds. Unemployment estimates vary between 4 and 5 percent, with tens of millions of uprooted farmers and workers roaming the countryside and the cities in search of work.[6]

But is there no risk that the high price of economic stabilisation and the authoritarian methods adopted to implement it will kindle the protest movement? It seems unlikely. Left on its own, social pressure seems to be neither strong enough nor, above all, consistent enough to generate a protest movement. In the rural areas, the regime does not have much to fear from the hundreds of millions of farmer families broken up and subjugated to the tyranny of the local party officials charged with administering collective property. It is in the cities that the situation could become explosive. In January 1990, workers demonstrated against worse work conditions in Wuhan, Tianjin and Chongqing. To counter this risk, the regime again embraced the theory of the leading role of the proletariat and revived the alliance which was so strong in the 1950s between the CCP and the workers owning nationalised companies, seen as the worker elite. Obliged by the economic austerity programme to cut back the public sector activity, the government guaranteed laid-off workers 70 percent of their salary (aiming for 100 percent by December 1989). The municipality of Beijing recommended that laid-off workers replace workers under contract, who will simply be sent to the countryside or out onto the streets.

Undoubtedly, the participation of the Beijing workers in the Tiananmen demonstrations came as a shock to political leaders. Had the "noble" working class of the cities not always been a privileged ally of the regime? But the reform and the resulting inflation threatened this privileged status. The counter-reform and above all the austerity programme has hit the workers a second time. As a result, the regime has taken the necessary precautions. They may not be sufficient and there may be new urban protests, but the social discontent will only be forceful enough if it coincides with a crisis of succession or the overturning of the balance of power within the leadership group. Otherwise, it will not, for the reasons mentioned above, be able to provoke significant political changes. It is more likely, that the counter-reform will aggravate the conflict – potentially very dangerous for the regime – between the central power and regional authorities.

State power and regional authorities

The place in which the demonstrations took place – the large square in the centre of the capital, the place of all official ceremonies – gave the Tiananmen demonstration an exceptional symbolic force. Thousands of provincials stormed the trains to join the demonstrators in Beijing. Many cities throughout the country were inspired by the capital to launch their own movements. But not all made the same effort. The reticence of the cities in the south, especially Canton, was particularly evident. It was as if the political pressures originating in the centre – both the protests against central power and the recovery of control by the power structure – ran up against the primary concern shared by all in the south of preserving the wealth attained and not jeopardising the development under way.

The economic separatism of the southern provinces was based on the actions of the local bureaucracy, the main beneficiary of the reforms and the prosperity deriving from them in these regions. In the autumn of 1988, Guangdong refused to implement the slowdown ordered by Beijing and to put a brake on the economic growth which peaked at 33 percent between January and September of that year. The collective and private enterprises to which the government threatened to cut credit resorted to their own reserves and appealed to the participation of the workers and local credit co-operatives. Political and economic interests allied to exert pressure on the central government or to circumvent the directives. In fact, these interests were often interwoven, since the decentralisation of power in the period from 1984 to 1989 mainly benefited local officials. Using various legal and illegal means, these officials financed, exploited and controlled the enterprises, exercising an authority that the Chinese compare to the traditional power of the "mother-in-law." When the regime tried to regain control over this sector, it came up against the opposition of the local patrons, that is, the bureaucrats, more than that of the entrepreneurs or the managers. Thus, the government ran the risk of conflict with its own administration. The new centralisation of the economy decided upon by the government required a parallel centralisation of the bureaucracy to regain control of command.

The recovery of control over the bureaucracy was pursued by means of an ideological campaign. The fight against corruption in the party is a popular subject (the slogans used in Tiananmen prove it) and at the same time constituted an effective way to strike at members that were too independent and often the most enterprising in business. In 1989, 12,500 members were expelled from the party. The purge was especially strong in the southern provinces. The Governor of Hainan, Liang Xiang, was removed in September 1989 and replaced by a bureaucrat from Beijing. The accusations of corruption against Liang Xiang (exorbitant expenses for banquets, private speculation) actually disguised other motivations: he was guilty of having tried to modernise Hainan through its link with Hong Kong, opening it to foreign capital and transforming it into a free port. The province bordering on Guangdong was also a target: the person mainly responsible for foreign trade, Xu Yunian, was removed. The positions of the Guangdong provincial Governor, Ye Xuanping, and the Vice-Governor, Yu Fei, seem uncertain.

Yet, this regional bureaucracy was not without its supporters at the centre. Zhao Ziyang, close to men like Liang Xiang and Yu Fei, was its principal patron. After his downfall, the coastal provinces were not as effectively safeguarded. But the appointment to the Politburo of the former Mayor of Tianjin, Li Ruihuan, and the former Mayor of Shanghai, Jiang Zemin, made the new General Secretary, suggest that regional interests continue to be taken into account in CCP internal debates. Some political scientists have pointed to a "regionalist" faction besides the conservative and reformist ones in the party.

Thus, it is quite likely that the new centralisation policy, reinforced after Tiananmen, will come into more or less open conflict with an important part of the high-ranking regional bureaucracy. The outcome of that conflict is not yet clear. During the agricultural reform of 1950, the central government was forced to intervene brutally, sending ten thousand administrators from the north to quell the autonomy of the Cantonese apparatus. Since then, this autonomy has been frequently reasserted, but never as forcefully as in the 1980s. It should not be forgotten, in this context, that the first attempts at modernisation in China made by the central, authoritarian and reformist government at the beginning of this century, came up against the opposition of the local administrations, supported by the local elites, who wanted to implement their own reform, not one imposed on them by the central government and one that was more in keeping with their own interests. As is known, this conflict led to the downfall of the last imperial dynasty with the revolution of 1911 and the establishment of a regime that was a republic in name only.

The return of the army

The decisive role played by the army in the outcome of the crisis of June 1989 has already been mentioned. Before that date, the last spectacular intervention of the army in Chinese political life dated back to the Cultural Revolution in 1967–8, when Mao Zedong asked the PLA to support him and later to eliminate the Red Guards. At the CCP's Ninth Congress in 1969, Mao designated Field Marshal Lin Biao as his heir. At the time, generals and officers controlled the regional apparatus of the revolutionary committees and held numerous positions in the party leadership. It took fifteen years – from 1970 to 1985, first under Mao and later under Deng Xiaoping – to confine the military to their barracks and to limit their influence. But the appeal to them in May 1989 to suppress the protest movement brought the army back to the centre of the political stage. It is clear that in the case of crisis – whether or not it be linked to Deng's succession – its weight will be decisive.

Its influence is already demonstrated by the increasingly important role played by the Military Affairs Commission in the party, not only in guaranteeing domestic and foreign security but also in managing political life.[7] The dominant figure in the Commission is General Yang Shangkun, the main advocate of the declaration of martial law (19 May 1989) and the subsequent suppression. Although Deng Xiaoping was succeeded in November 1989 by Jiang Zemin as Chair of the Commission and Yang Shangkun had to settle for the position of first Vice-Chairman, the decision-making power seems to rest in the general's hands. This is thanks to a strong network of personal contacts in the army and in the party; within the Commission, Yang Shangkun can rely on the support of his brother-in-law Yang Baibing.

Yang Shangkun and his clan exert a strictly conservative influence; the army is interested in regaining ideological and political control throughout the country. An investigation has been opened into 3,500 officers, suspected of having actively participated in the May–June protest movement. The highest-ranking officer is General Xu Qinxian, commander of the Thirty-eighth Army, who refused to open fire on the demonstrators and is supposedly in prison now.

As in the other socialist regimes of Eastern Europe and the Soviet Union, the power of the military is limited by other institutions, in particular, by the forces of law and order. But the Chinese people's police force, while 500,000 strong and adequately equipped, did not play the role the regime expected of it in May 1989 and rapidly let the situation slip out of control. Today, the body seems weakened with respect to the PLA. Its commander has been replaced by an army general, Zhou Yushu, and after the abolition of martial law (11 January 1990), a certain number of PLA contingents that had been moved to Beijing to enforce martial law have been integrated into the force.

In essence, the PLA has strengthened its role and a conservative tendency has taken the upper hand within it. This tendency is not monolithic, however. There continue to be divisions in the army, as in the party. "Moderates" and "professionals" (the group to which the Minister of Defence, Qin Jiwei, seems to belong) have not been eliminated. And the purges under way, while striking open and active sympathies for the protest movement, do not impede hidden sympathies. In case of crisis, the army has a number of options open to it. This is confirmed by the extreme nervousness of the Chinese leaders, who put the armed forces in Beijing and Shenyang on maximum alert after the downfall of the Romanian dictator Nicolae Ceauşescu (26 November 1989).

Whatever the scenarios for the future, one thing is certain: it will not be easy to reduce the army's role. It is unlikely that the successors to Deng Xioaping, given their minor prestige, will be able to do what Mao and he managed to do after 1970 and after 1978. And it is very probable that the political choices of the army will be decisive. Although a prospect of this kind does not rule out the possibility of a transition to a pluralist political regime, as proven by the East European countries, it does suggest some kind of Bonapartist or authoritarian–reformist solution, if, that is, the regional trends within the military and civilian apparatus do not lead to a return to a regime of warlords!

NOTES

1 For a description of the events of Tiananmen and a more detailed analysis of the economic, social and political evolution in the previous months, see M.C. Bergère, *Histoire de la République populaire de Chine* (History of the PRC) (Paris: Colin, 2nd edition, 1989), Chapter 2.

2 See the analysis by Jacques Andrieu, "La mobilisation des intellectuels et des étudiants" ("The Mobilisation of the Intellectuals and the Students"), *Où va la Chine?* (Whither China?), texts from a colloquium organised at the Senate, 2 February 1990 (Paris: IFRI/INALCO, 1990).

3 See Tony Saich, "The Beijing People's Movement, Spring 1989", *The Australian Journal of Chinese Affairs*, July 1990.

4   A Translation of "Decision on Further Improving the Economic Environment, Straightening out the Economic Order, and Deepening the Reforms (Excerpts)" can be found in *Beijing Review*, Vol. 33, No. 7, 12–18 February 1990.
5   See Yves Chevrier, "Les nouvelles classes urbaines après la repression de Tiananmen" ("The New Urban Classes After the Suppression of Tiananmen"), *Où va la Chine?*
6   See Claude Aubert, "The Agricultural Crisis in China at the end of the 1980s", report presented to the European Conference on "Agriculture and Rural Development in China", Sandbjerg, Denmark, 18–20 November 1990; and by Claude Aubert, "Le poids de la paysannerie" ("The Weight of the Peasantry"), *Où va la Chine?*
7   See Jean-Pierre Cabestan, "Le facteur militaire et ses implications politiques" ("The Military Factor and Its Political Implications"), *Où va la Chine?*

12

THE YEAR OF LIVING ANXIOUSLY

China's 1999

Jeffrey N. Wasserstrom

In the early 1990s, when the Soviet Union collapsed in the wake of 1989's transformation of Eastern and Central Europe, the CCP's days seemed numbered. Yes, observers admitted, there had been no immediate sequel to the Tiananmen upheaval in the PRC at the start of this new decade. But surely something had to give soon – if not a complete undoing of the CCP than at least a radical restructuring of it, a shift in the leadership group (so that Li Peng, for example, who had become vilified as the Butcher of Beijing, was stripped of all power). The Communist Party would, however, defy these predictions throughout the 1990s, making more tenuous with every year it stayed in control of the world's most populous country, the notion that an "End of History" had arrived. Moreover, though the Beijing regime certainly began to do a variety of things quite differently in the years following Tiananmen, in part to try to minimize the chances of having to face a similar outburst, Li Peng and others with June 4 blood on their hands remained in the leadership.

The chapter that follows, which is based in part on my experiences in China in May 1999 (when anti-NATO protests broke out) and rooted in my past work on the history of Chinese popular protest, explores the seemingly surprising longevity of the CCP. It argues that the final year of the twentieth century was one in which the regime faced important new challenges on many fronts, while continuing to ride out an ongoing legitimacy crisis that dated back to 1989, and indeed beyond. It also asks the reader to think of the Beijing regime as ending the twentieth century with a complex mixture of resources still at its disposal but also a range of liabilities – and insists that neither the resources nor the liabilities can be appreciated without a keen sense of history. Since the essay moves between the first and last moments of the century, it seems a fitting one with which to end a book on China's turbulent twentieth century.

* * *

A year ago, two unexpected incidents, one involving an international crisis and the other a domestic one, each associated with protests, sent shock waves through China and provoked surprising responses by the Beijing regime. Taken together, these incidents and the reactions to them made 1999 the most confusing year of the decade for China specialists to figure out. We saw many departures from what seemed to be settled post-1989 patterns. The very unpredictability of the year, however, conformed to a long-term pattern. Years ending with the numeral nine have often been trying ones for Chinese regimes, the fall of the Nationalist Party in 1949 being the most famous case in point. Nineteen ninety-nine was no exception.

As we start the year 2000, the Chinese Communist Party (CCP) shows no sign of following soon in the footsteps of its erstwhile rival, but recent events show that the CCP is still dealing with the legitimacy crisis that both caused and was exacerbated by the demonstrations of 1989. The CCP is in much the same predicament now that it was in at the start of 1990: struggling to reposition itself so as to hold onto power at a time when few Leninist regimes remain on the world scene. In addition, now as a decade ago, it must contend with a populace that is skeptical about the official ideology, doubtful about the moral character of top government leaders, and has recently been reacquainted with a potent repertoire of political street theater. Looking at the surprises of 1999 and how official responses to them diverged from post-1989 patterns can be useful to us as we enter the second decade of the "New World Disorder" and the CCP starts the second decade of its ongoing legitimacy crisis.

I will begin with the two main unexpected incidents of 1999. The first, which occurred on April 25, was a sit-in staged by some ten thousand members of Falun Gong, a spiritual group that extols the virtues of special breathing practices and physical movements that are said to have curative powers, and that incorporates into its creed beliefs derived from a variety of Chinese folk religious traditions. The surprising response to the sect's sit-in came only in July when the CCP announced a ban on Falun Gong gatherings, and then began to arrest members of the group. Accompanying this crackdown was a media campaign, involving everything from political posters to comic books, designed to discredit Li Hongzhi, Falun Gong's China-born but now New York-based leader.

The second important, unexpected event came in early May when NATO missiles destroyed the Chinese Embassy in Belgrade, killing a trio of Chinese journalists. The surprising response in this case came immediately. The regime reversed its nearly decade-long policy of discouraging all forms of student activism and allowed, even encouraged, students to take to the streets to express patriotic outrage. In this case, too, a mass media publicity campaign was launched. Officially sponsored instant histories detailing the horrors of the bombing raid and celebrating the demonstrations by Chinese students were issued. These included everything from photographs of campus wall posters mocking President Clinton to reprints of emotional speeches by CCP leaders decrying NATO's abuse of human rights. Video disks were produced containing television footage of state-sponsored funerals for the three "revolutionary martyrs" of Belgrade and of anti-American rallies outside consular buildings – the latter made to seem less rowdy affairs than the one I witnessed at close range in Beijing on the evening of May 9.

The Falun Gong sit-in and the destruction of the Chinese Embassy are usually discussed separately, which makes sense given the obvious differences between the events, one non-violent, the other part of a war. Unfortunately, the regime's responses to the two are also treated as unrelated. In fact, however, they were part of the same dynamic. And the two publicity campaigns have even more in common.

In each case the CCP leadership took risky moves to minimize a potential threat to its legitimacy. The two publicity campaigns represent parallel efforts to shore up the regime's position by criticizing the ethics and motivations of a particular group (Falun Gong, NATO) and a specific individual (Li Hongzhi, President Clinton). These organizations and individuals were described – in the case of Li and Falun Gong still are being described – as serious threats to the well-being of the Chinese nation. And the negative traits projected onto them are precisely those that, in recent years, have often been projected onto the CCP leadership by its domestic and international critics. In anti-Falun Gong comic books, for example, Li is shown as a charlatan who cares only about maximizing his own power and wealth, not about the welfare of his followers or even his sect's creed. In a typical illustration, he is pictured standing next to a fancy car with big denomination bills – presumably contributed by hoodwinked followers – falling all around him. Similarly, Clinton was presented as someone who paid lip service to human rights but had no qualms about treating his enemies brutally.

These CCP responses suggest that the regime lives in fear of specters that, if allowed to materialize, could end its rule. The decision to use force ten years ago and then mount a propaganda campaign that justified all acts of repression can be seen as responses to the specter of the Polish workers' movement Solidarity. The 1999 decisions to support the anti-NATO demonstrators, to arrest members of Falun Gong, and to carry out intensive publicity campaigns to celebrate the student activists and denigrate Li Hongzhi's followers were all similarly motivated. This time, however, the specters haunting the regime came from China's own past.

This is not to say that the Solidarity specter has lost its power to frighten China's leaders. The efforts made during the anti-NATO protests to limit the involvement of angry workers who wanted to join the students shows that there is still great concern with cross-class alliances linked to mass movements. In 1999 as opposed to 1989, however, the Solidarity specter was not the main one feared by the regime. More panic was inspired by what might best be called the "May 4 specter," named for a 1919 student-led movement that targeted government ministers viewed as corrupt and insufficiently patriotic. And also by the "religious revolt specter" – recalling the many times in China's pre-revolutionary era when a change of dynasties was associated with the rising influence of spiritual sects led by charismatic figures. A concern with the first of these was a key factor in motivating the regime to support the anti-NATO protests, and understanding this helps make sense of the publicity campaign aimed at denigrating Clinton and linking the CCP leadership to patriotic protesters and martyrs. A concern with the second specter, on the other hand, was a key factor behind the CCP decision to move against Falun Gong last July.

Before describing the specters in more detail, let me clarify a point: though my argument is that the CCP's reactions to the anti-NATO protests and the Falun Gong sit-in were surprising, this does not mean they were unprecedented. Nineteen ninety-nine was not the first year in which Chinese Communist Party leaders had encouraged anti-imperialist demonstrations by students. In the 1950s, they called on students to hold "Resist America, Support Korea" marches; in the 1960s, student demonstrators gathered, with Chairman Mao's blessing, to protest against imperialism; and in 1985 some official support was given to campus rallies decrying perceived Japanese slights to China's honor. The crackdown on Falun Gong has even more precedents from earlier periods in the regime's history. There was nothing novel about the CCP mounting an intense publicity campaign to discredit a group it deemed dangerous to stability and to socialism. And this is not the first time that such a war of words and images has been accompanied by mass arrests. The same thing happened during the anti-rightist purges of the 1950s and in the weeks following the June massacres that took place in Beijing and Chengdu in 1989.

What made the responses of the regime to the anti-NATO protests and to Falun Gong surprising, therefore, was not their novelty within the overall sweep of the regime's history, but rather their break with 1990s patterns. Before 1999, the decade had been unusually free of officially sanctioned "campaigns." The key question then is how to explain the recent change of course – and it is here that thinking about specters is most valuable. It provides a link between the responses to protest in 1989 and in 1999.

Faced with massive gatherings on the streets of many cities in May of 1989, one of the first moves the regime made was to impose martial law, hoping that this would stem the tide of revolt as similar moves had in Poland in 1981. When this did not work, the CCP leadership turned to brute force, most notably in Beijing's June 4 massacre, an event that took place, ironically, on the very day that Solidarity was winning the first free Polish elections in decades. It was no accident that workers, who the government feared might soon form more effective alliances with protesting students, were the main victims of state violence in Beijing and also in Chengdu, nor that labor leaders received some of the longest prison terms handed out in the immediate aftermath of the killing.

The regime fought the Solidarity specter throughout the years leading up to 1999. It prohibited all forms of student activism, punished swiftly and harshly anyone who tried to organize a formal opposition organization, and banned autonomous labor unions that brought together workers from more than a single factory or district. And right up to May of 1999, the CCP routinely denied permits to students requesting permission to hold mass political gatherings of any sort. This was done even when the students involved wanted to hold anti-imperialist rallies to protest presumed slights on China's national pride. Thus the regime refused to allow campus rallies to protest Japanese claims to the disputed Diaoyu Islands, fearing that, once gathered together, students might bring up other grievances. This ban on student demonstrations was periodically coupled with moves against dissidents who tried to form political groups, such as the China Democratic Party.

The CCP leadership also took positive steps to defuse the power of the Solidarity specter. Aware of the role that shortages of material goods and a perception of economic backwardness played in bringing down communist regimes in Europe, Beijing put a great deal of energy into achieving (and drawing attention to) high growth rates. And, especially after the dissolution of the Soviet Union in 1991, it highlighted the problems encountered by the former Leninist states in Europe. To counteract any notion that the end of Communist Party rule was an inevitable and good thing for the citizens of the nations involved, the Beijing leadership made much of the political and economic devastation that had come to Russia and Yugoslavia. Publicizing the sufferings and loss of power in the international arena of these countries, and saying little about the smoother transitions taking place in Central Europe, the CCP made a new kind of case for itself. You may have lost faith in our ideology and you may question the morality of our leaders, the regime argued, but the alternative to our rule may well be even worse for you and for China.

The government tried as well to do specific things to alleviate the discontent that triggered the 1989 protests and allow citizens to let off steam. It made an effort to limit its interference in the private lives of ordinary people, and it gave signs that it was willing to tolerate various oppositional or at least nonconformist activities, so long as these did not directly threaten the CCP's main policies or overall political dominance. Small-scale protests by workers or farmers with very specific grievances were allowed, intellectuals were given the freedom to publish literary reviews that veered far from the Party line on cultural affairs, hotlines were set up so that urban residents could voice complaints about local issues, and so on. The watch-word became, as one person put it to me in 1996, "As long as it is not a movement, anything goes."

The turning point quality of 1999 lies in the extent to which this watch-word was overruled. Falun Gong has never been a clearly defined movement, after all, and many of its followers see its main impact in affecting the way they act in private; yet it has been attacked. The anti-NATO protests, on the other hand, certainly constituted a movement of sorts – a student-led one at that – and yet it was endorsed. So, we come back to two basic questions: Why the sudden break last year from the established pattern of treating all forms of student activism as potentially dangerous? And why the rhetorical and physical attacks on Falun Gong – attacks of a sort that, since the crackdown of 1989, had been reserved for groups that explicitly opposed a major CCP policy (such as its stance on Tibet) or openly attacked the regime's authority?

Answering these questions brings us back to the May 4 and religious revolt specters, and the way each haunts the regime. I've named the former for the upheaval of eighty years ago that began when students in Beijing, and soon in other cities too, took to the streets to protest terms of the Treaty of Versailles transferring sovereignty over parts of China formerly under German control to Japan. China as well as Japan had fought on the side of the allies in World War I, so this territory, the students claimed, should rightfully be returned to Chinese rule. Though directed against the nations involved in framing the Treaty of Versailles, Japan in particular, this movement was also from the beginning an attack on the corrupt warlord regime in Beijing that students accused of failing to protect the nation's interest. The students singled out for special criticism the "Three Traitorous Officials," government ministers who, they claimed, showed a consistent willingness to make concessions to Japan in order to line their own pockets and retain their hold on power. The May 4 Movement soon developed into a multi-class alliance, with workers and merchants joining the struggle. It also became, after students were arrested and beaten up by police, a fight for the right of protest itself. Even though the Treaty of Versailles ultimately went into effect unchanged, the protesters achieved many of their central goals. All arrested students were released from jail, and each of the "Three Traitorous Officials" was dismissed from his post.

The May 4 Movement is enshrined in CCP official history as one of the most sacred moments in the long revolution that culminated in the founding of the People's Republic in 1949. One of the main monuments in Tiananmen Square is dedicated to the memory of May 4 activists, and the anniversary of this struggle is celebrated with considerable fanfare each spring. Particular attention is paid to it in years that end with a nine. Throughout early May in these years, official newspapers are filled with editorials and stories extolling the heroism of the students of 1919, as well as calls to contemporary youth to show that they too are committed patriots. But in the new situation of post-1949 China, it is said, the way to do this is not by holding protests but by studying hard to help build socialism. From time to time, however, new generations put a dissenting spin on the official commemorative line. Most famously, in 1989, student activists gathered at Tiananmen Square on the seventieth anniversary of the 1919 struggle to call for a "New May 4 Movement" to challenge the latest group of corrupt officials endangering the nation. The power of the May 4 anniversary is one reason that years ending with nines, like 1999, are anxious ones for Chinese regimes.

In light of this, it is easy to see why the coming of the eightieth anniversary of the 1919 struggle generated a good deal of nervousness. On the one hand, the regime had no choice but to mark the occasion; on the other, it had every reason to want to avoid a replay of 1989. The uneasiness with which the CCP leadership awaited the arrival of this anniversary day – I was in China at the time, invited to Beijing University to take part in a May 4 commemorative conference – was almost tangible. So, too, was the sense of relief when the day passed with only minor incidents, such as the China Democratic Party's proclamation, issued from hiding, that it, not the CCP, had the best claim to continue the May 4 tradition.

The fact that the Chinese Embassy was destroyed just a few days later – when the events of 1919 were still fresh in the minds of CCP leaders and students alike – should be remembered when we try to make sense of what followed. Students were, in part because of the anniversary, primed to do something to demonstrate their patriotism, and this helps account for the speed with which they took to the streets after the news reached China. Members of the regime were, again in part because of the anniversary, thinking about moments in the past when leaders viewed as corrupt, as they know they are by many citizens, fell from power for failing to act decisively to protect the national interest. This helps explain why a quick decision was made to leap ahead of the movement, rather than run the risk of suppressing it – and so give protesters cause to combine anger at NATO with anger at the CCP. It also helps explain why the ensuing publicity drive placed such emphasis on linking leaders of the regime to patriotic symbols and insisting that it was foreign leaders, not Chinese ones, that had no respect for the people of China. In addition, playing on the American president's sex scandal, which was well known in China, both student wall posters and official publications made much of the fact that Clinton was someone who cared only about satisfying his own desires – whether for power or pleasure. One student poster reprinted in an instant history of the protests has Monica Lewinsky suggesting to Bill that it was dangerous to bomb the Chinese Embassy. The President responds that there is nothing to worry about because there are no traces of his DNA on any of the missiles.

If the May 4 specter's power to influence official behavior is the main thing to keep in mind when thinking about the anti-NATO protests, worries relating to the religious revolt specter are the key to making sense of the crackdown on Falun Gong. Throughout China's imperial period, popular sects that made use of religious traditions, including Buddhism and Taoism, were continually being formed. These groups often had charismatic leaders who promised adherents, as Li Hongzhi has promised his, that they would feel better physically and more fulfilled spiritually, if only they agreed to do certain things. Millenarianism was often a feature of these sects, as it is in Falun Gong: the current age is corrupt and will be followed by a purer one; only the faithful will be ideally positioned to take their place in the new cosmic order.

In most periods, these sects were quiescent and the state could take a live-and-let-live attitude toward them. In times of crisis, however, sectarian leaders sometimes put more emphasis on the millenarian side of their beliefs and encouraged their followers to rise up in rebellion to usher in the new epoch. Alternately, the state might fear this possibility and launch a kind of pre-emptive strike against a religious group, declaring it heterodox and illegal, and moving to disband it. Often, these two things would occur in tandem: fear of being suppressed could inspire a sect to become more militant, and moves to militancy could convince officials to take a less laissez-faire attitude toward it. The end result in several famous instances – but by no means in every instance of this cycle of repression and militancy – was the fall of the dynasty at the hands of chiliastic rebels. This result was especially likely if, as in the fourteenth century when the sect leader who founded the Ming Dynasty was gaining power, members of the bureaucratic class threw in their lot with the rebels.

Much about Falun Gong remains mysterious to those outside the group, but there are important parallels between it and some of the popular religious sects that made an impact on political life during the imperial era. There are novelties about the group – the use of Web sites and other new technologies of communication, for example – but it is easy to understand why CCP leaders would see Falun Gong as comparable in many ways to sects that rose up against weakened dynasties. Here, again, the awareness of historical precedents for contemporary protests is not an abstract thing. This is because popular uprisings like the one that brought the Ming Dynasty to power are celebrated as great moments in the nation's past, even though efforts are made to downplay the religious and emphasize the economic bases of imperial-era upheavals. Elizabeth Perry, director of Harvard's Fairbank Center, who was in Shanghai during the first stage of the campaign against Falun Gong, reported that a show celebrating the founder of the Ming Dynasty was even shown on television this last summer in China. According to Perry, a political scientist whose insightful essay on Falun Gong, "Reinventing the Wheel," is slated to appear in the

Harvard China Review, the regime did not explicitly draw attention to the parallels between Li's group and millenarian sects of imperial times. Nonetheless, she claims, many of the people she spoke with in China looked at the campaign to discredit Falun Gong as driven by fear of what I have dubbed the religious revolt specter.

This helps explain why the relative quiescence of the sect has not been interpreted by the CCP leadership to mean that they need not worry about Falun Gong. It also helps explain why there has been such deep concern generated by the discovery that Li's followers include not just a broad cross-section of citizens but even some CCP cadres and officials.

Where does all this leave the CCP in the year 2000? Is it safe until 2009 when another round of tense anniversaries will be marked? In the short run, the 1999 change in strategy seems to have defused the threat of the May 4 specter. It also seems to have managed, for now, to keep the religious revolt specter at bay. And Solidarity is less of a threat than it was in 1989.

In the long run, however, things look very different, and only the most naive CCP leader imagines now that the regime will have a smooth ride to the end of the decade – or even feels confident that the year 2000 will conclude without some new crisis occurring. This is because none of the three specters discussed here have been completely exorcized, and there are ways they could come together. In fact, the greatest danger for the current regime lies in this possibility – that elements of two or three types of movements and sources of discontent will create a hybrid menace to the regime. A combining of forces is especially likely if the high economic growth rates of the last decade do not continue into the new century, if the gap between rich and poor groups and regions continues to grow, and if novel challenges arise in the international arena.

What this means is that the new decade is starting much as the last one did: with nervousness on the part of the regime. The massive layoffs of the past few years – likely to be followed by still larger ones if China enters the World Trade Organization – have created an ever-growing pool of discontented workers. So the Solidarity specter still hovers on the horizon. In addition, though the CCP leadership succeeded in keeping student outrage at NATO from spinning out of control, the change of course regarding campus activism has served to provide a new generation of young people with hands-on training in the mounting of a mass movement. It is very possible, indeed likely, that at some point in the near future another series of student demonstrations will take place, which will not be as easy to control. The regime still has to worry about the May 4 specter. Finally, though Falun Gong shows no signs of emerging as the central focus of a nationwide rebellion, its members have demonstrated a willingness to take great personal risks to resist efforts to disband the sect and destroy Li's credibility.

The familiar cycle of official suppression leading to increased militancy, and vice versa, is playing out once more: the religious revolt specter is still threatening. In sum, the regime is still haunted. It lives on borrowed time.

Index

Printed in the USA/Agawam, MA
August 20, 2010

543699.026